THE CAMBRIDGE EDITION OF THE WORKS OF F. SCOTT FITZGERALD

Fitzgerald in 1940 (photo by Belle O'Hara).

The Love of
THE LAST TYCOON
A Western

* * *

F. SCOTT FITZGERALD

Edited by
MATTHEW J. BRUCCOLI
University of South Carolina

CAMBRIDGE
UNIVERSITY PRESS

123837

Published by the Press Syndicate of the University of Cambridge
The Pitt Building, Trumpington Street, Cambridge CB2 1RP
40 West 20th Street, New York, NY 10011–4211, USA
10 Stamford Road, Oakleigh, Melbourne 3166, Australia

© Cambridge University Press 1993

First published 1993
Reprinted 1994

Printed in the United States of America

Library of Congress Cataloging-in-Publication Data
Fitzgerald, F. Scott (Francis Scott), 1896–1940.
The love of the last tycoon : a western / F. Scott Fitzgerald :
edited by Matthew J. Bruccoli.
   p.   cm.–(The Cambridge edition of the works of F. Scott
Fitzgerald)
"The first authoritative text of the brilliant work in progress"–
prelim. p.
ISBN 0-521-40231-X
   1. Motion picture industry–California–Los Angeles–Fiction.
2. Hollywood (Los Angeles, Calif.)–Fiction.   I. Bruccoli, Matthew
Joseph, 1931–   . II. Title.   III. Series: Fitzgerald, F. Scott
(Francis Scott), 1896–1940. Works. 1991.
PS3511.I9L68   1994
813'.52–dc20
                                                93–8423
                                                    CIP

A catalog record for this book is available from the British Library.

ISBN 0–521–40231–x hardback

CONTENTS

v

ACKNOWLEDGMENTS

My chief debt is to Mary Jo Tate for extraordinary editorial support. When Mrs. Tate was compelled to migrate, Judith S. Baughman heroically took over. I am fortunate to be at the University of South Carolina, where I can do my work: Bert Dillon, Chairman of the Department of English, and Carol McGinnis Kay, Dean of the College of Humanities and Social Sciences, have provided encouragement. Joel Myerson, former chairman of the department and the textual consultant for this volume, has been my friend and disputant for twenty years.

Since the manuscripts for *The Love of the Last Tycoon* and related documents from which this volume was edited are at the Princeton University Library, the editor is deeply obligated to the library and its admirable staff. I owe great debts to William L. Joyce (Associate University Librarian for Rare Books and Special Collections), Don C. Skemer (Curator of Manuscripts), and John Delaney (Leader of the Rare Books and Manuscripts Cataloguing Team). Material relating to Edmund Wilson's work on *The Last Tycoon* was provided by William Cagle, Director of the Lilly Library, Indiana University.

Large debts have accrued to Jeanne Bennett and R. L. Samsell, Los Angeles conscripts. Frances Kroll Ring and Budd Schulberg patiently searched their memories, as did the late Sheilah Graham. Charles Scribner III of Charles Scribner's Sons facilitated the Cambridge Edition of F. Scott Fitzgerald; I am fortunate in his friendship. Additional obligations have been incurred to members of my English 841B seminar on F. Scott Fitzgerald and to Professor William Leary (University of Georgia), Professor Ahmed Nimeiri (University of Khartoum), Professor Douglas Porch (The Citadel), Professor Kiyohiko Tsuboi (Okayama University), Professor John Winberry (University of South Carolina), David G. Chandler (Royal Military Academy, Sandhurst), Kristine Krueger (Academy of Motion Picture Arts and Sciences, National Film Information Service), Samuel Marx, M. E. Olsen (American Airlines), Stephen J. Perrault (Merriam-Webster, Inc.), Dr. John Swan (Bennington College Library), Fred Zentner (Cinema Bookshop, London), and the late Vernon Sternberg (Southern Illinois University Press), who edited and published my 1977 volume *"The Last of the Novelists": F. Scott Fitzgerald and The Last Tycoon*. Dr. Andrew Brown of Cambridge University Press has endeavored to improve my work. Julie Greenblatt of the New York office of Cambridge University Press bestowed her friendship on me while overseeing the editing of this volume. Katharita Lamoza ably supervised the later stages of production.

Fredson Bowers did not vet this volume. At the time of his death in April 1991 we had agreed on an editorial plan and had identified the base-text.

I rely on Arlyn Bruccoli's literary judgment.

My editorial work on this volume is dedicated to Scottie, but it was no fun without her.

M.J.B.
21 August 1992

F. SCOTT FITZGERALD SELECTED CHRONOLOGY: 1927–1941*

JANUARY 1927 Fitzgerald works on "Lipstick" in Hollywood for United Artists; screenplay rejected; meets Irving Thalberg.

NOVEMBER–DECEMBER 1931 Works on *Red-Headed Woman* in Hollywood for M-G-M; screenplay rejected.

OCTOBER 1932 Publishes "Crazy Sunday."

14 SEPTEMBER 1936 Thalberg dies.

JULY 1937 Goes to Hollywood with six-month M-G-M contract at $1,000 per week; lives at The Garden of Allah on Sunset Boulevard, Hollywood.

14 JULY 1937 Meets Sheilah Graham.

JULY–AUGUST 1937 Polishes screenplay of *A Yank at Oxford*.

AUGUST 1937–FEBRUARY 1938 Works with E. E. Paramore on *Three Comrades* for producer Joseph Mankiewicz; Fitzgerald's only screen credit.

DECEMBER 1937–JANUARY 1939 M-G-M contract renewed for one year at $1,250 per week; works on "Infidelity," *Marie Antoinette, The Women,* and *Madame Curie*.

APRIL 1938 Moves to bungalow at Malibu Beach.

1 SEPTEMBER 1938 First mention of "plan for a novel."

OCTOBER 1938 Moves to cottage on "Belly Acres" estate in Encino.

* This chronology is restricted to Fitzgerald's movie work and the composition of *The Love of the Last Tycoon: A Western*.

ix

JANUARY 1939   Termination of M-G-M contract after eighteen months.

JANUARY 1939   Works on *Gone With the Wind* for David O. Selznick.

FEBRUARY 1939   Trip to Dartmouth College with Budd Schulberg to work on *Winter Carnival* for United Artists; fired.

MARCH 1939   Works on "Air Raid" for Paramount.

APRIL 1939   Discusses novel with Maxwell Perkins and Harold Ober; hires Frances Kroll as secretary.

SPRING – SUMMER?   1939   Writes "Last Kiss" and "Director's Special" ("Discard"); both declined by *Collier's*.

MAY 1939   Begins blocking out novel.

JULY 1939   Breaks with Ober.

18 JULY 1939   Offers Kenneth Littauer of *Collier's* serial rights to unwritten novel.

AUGUST – SEPTEMBER 1939   Short jobs for Universal ("Open That Door"), Twentieth Century-Fox (*Everything Happens at Night*), and Goldwyn (*Raffles*).

29 SEPTEMBER 1939   Sends synopsis of novel to Littauer.

NOVEMBER 1939   Sends 6,000 words to Littauer and Perkins; Littauer declines to make advance.

28 NOVEMBER 1939   Breaks off negotiations with *Collier's*; offers serial rights to the *Saturday Evening Post*, which declines.

JANUARY 1940   Publication of "Pat Hobby's Christmas Wish," first of seventeen Hobby stories in *Esquire*.

FEBRUARY 1940   Submits "Dearly Beloved" to *Esquire*; declined.

MARCH – AUGUST 1940   Writes unproduced "Babylon Revisited" ("Cosmopolitan") screenplay for Lester Cowan; intended for Shirley Temple.

MAY 1940   Moves to 1403 North Laurel Avenue, Hollywood.

OCTOBER 1940   Works on *Life Begins at Eight-Thirty* screenplay for Twentieth Century-Fox.

NOVEMBER 1940   Suffers heart attack.

21 DECEMBER 1940   Death of F. Scott Fitzgerald at Sheilah Graham's apartment, 1443 North Hayward Avenue, Hollywood.

MARCH 1941   Edmund Wilson agrees to edit Fitzgerald's work in progress.

27 OCTOBER 1941   Publication of THE LAST TYCOON / AN UNFINISHED NOVEL / BY F. SCOTT FITZGERALD / TOGETHER WITH / THE GREAT GATSBY / AND SELECTED STORIES.

The geography of *The Love of the Last Tycoon* (map by Eleanor Lanahan).

INTRODUCTION

F. Scott Fitzgerald had written the seventeenth episode of the thirty-episode plan for his Hollywood novel when he died on 21 December 1940. The work published in 1941 as *The Last Tycoon* inevitably falls into the sentimental category of "unfinished masterpiece," a designation that hampers proper appraisal of Fitzgerald's achievement. One may grieve that Fitzgerald did not complete his novel, but it is not necessary to make excuses for what he wrote. Fitzgerald's work in progress requires judgment on its merits. That procedure has been impeded because the working drafts have heretofore been published only in the cosmeticized text edited by Edmund Wilson more than fifty years ago. This Cambridge edition allows just reassessment of Fitzgerald's developing novel, "pregnant with latent possibilities of excellence."[1]

The first edition of *The Last Tycoon*, posthumously published by Charles Scribner's Sons, was subtitled *An Unfinished Novel*. Wilson's foreword explains: "The text which is given here is a draft made by the author after considerable rewriting; but it is by no means a finished version. In the margins of almost every one of the episodes, Fitzgerald had written comments—a few of them are included in the notes—which expressed his dissatisfaction with them." And: "This draft of *The Last Tycoon*, then, represents that point in the artist's work where he has assembled and organized his material and acquired a firm grasp of his theme, but has not yet brought it finally into focus."[2]

Wilson's use of "draft" may be inadvertently misleading, indicating a more advanced document than actually exists. There is nothing that can be accurately described as "this draft": there are layers of working drafts for seventeen episodes or sections that Fitzgerald did not assemble into a single draft—or into chapters after Chapter I. Moreover, there are breaks in the continuity of these episodes. Fitzgerald wrote new episodes without attempting to put the existing ones into finished condition. The whole work was still developing through a process of composition by accretion. Indeed, it would have been impossible for him to give final form to some of the first seventeen episodes because he had not resolved the plot details in the thirteen unwritten ones. There is no evidence that he had decided on the ending. The 1941 Wilson edition silently emends—not always correctly—Fitzgerald's words, styles the punctuation, combines episodes into chapters, and moves two scenes. Wilson's text conveys the impression of a more finished work than is represented by the working drafts. It is characteristic of Wilson's editorial policy that no source is provided for the title—allowing the reader to assume that *The Last Tycoon* was Fitzgerald's final choice. Yet Fitzgerald never referred to his novel by title in his correspondence. The only title page that survives with the draft material names the work "STAHR / A Romance."

When Fitzgerald's lover, Sheilah Graham, sent his work in progress to Scribners editor Maxwell Perkins in January 1941 (see p. lxvii), she reported that the working title was "Stahr," and she added that three weeks before he died Fitzgerald had asked her what she thought of "The Love of the Last Tycoon," saying that he would submit it for Perkins's reaction. Graham explained that "he wanted it to sound like a movie title and completely disguise the tragi-heroic content of the book."[3] In her June 1941 response to Wilson's summary of the novel, Fitzgerald's secretary, Frances Kroll, referred to it as "Stahr" three times and mentioned that "Scott satirically considered the alternative title for the book 'The Last of the Tycoons' " (see pp. lv–lvi). In these 1941 letters neither Graham nor Kroll used "The Last Tycoon." There are no extant letters from Wilson to Graham or Kroll bearing on the title; and there is no discussion of the title in the correspondence between Perkins and Wilson. Perkins first referred to the novel as "The Last Tycoon" in an 18 June 1941 letter to Wilson.

The only appearance of "The Last Tycoon" in Fitzgerald's hand is on a page of holograph notes headed *Title* in crayon. All the notes are crossed out except for "The Love of the Last Tycoon / A Western," which has what appears to be a check mark and the designa-

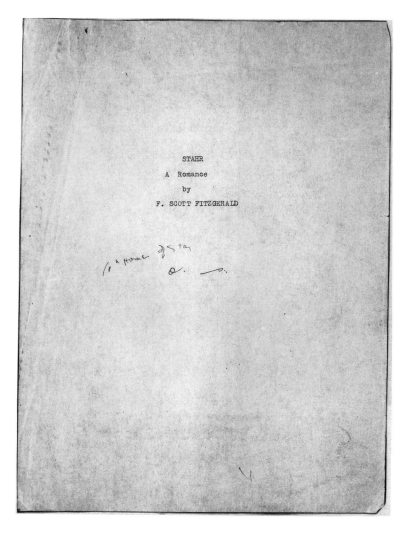

The title page; the note in Frances Kroll's handwriting refers to "The Homes of the Stars," a Pat Hobby story Fitzgerald published in August 1940. There is also a carbon copy of this title page. Princeton University Library.

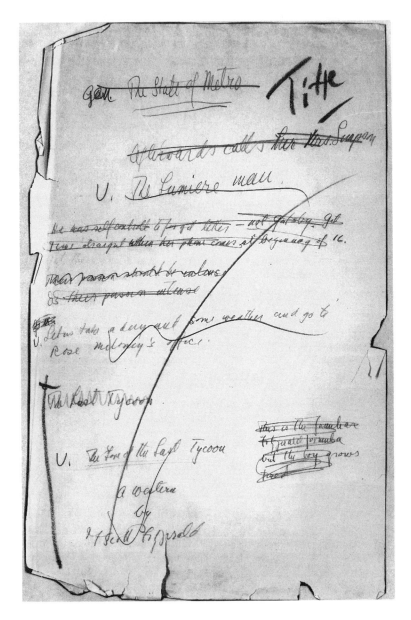

Page from Fitzgerald's working notes. Princeton University Library.

tion "U.", indicating that it was to be recopied for the unclassified section of his notebooks.* This is the only title on the list that Fitzgerald wrote in title-page format, providing the subtitle and the author's name. The deleted comment next to the title reads: "This is the familiar Fitzgerald formula but the boy grows tired." "The Love of the Last Tycoon / A Western" also appears on a page of miscellaneous typed notes headed "UNCLASSIFIED" (see "Selected Fitzgerald Working Notes," p. 197). No good case for the title "The Last Tycoon" can be made on the basis of the surviving Fitzgerald documents. The choice is between "Stahr: A Romance" and "The Love of the Last Tycoon: A Western." The latter is preferable because it is close to the title by which the novel has been known and because it has the Fitzgerald bouquet. Fitzgerald was in fact writing a western—a novel about the last American frontier, where immigrants and sons of immigrants pursued and defined the American dream. It is appropriate that these tycoons made movie westerns: they too were pioneers.

The following account of the gestation and composition of the novel perforce repeats many of the details in *"The Last of the Novelists": F. Scott Fitzgerald and The Last Tycoon.*[4]

I. BACKGROUNDS: IRVING THALBERG, M-G-M, AND FITZGERALD IN HOLLYWOOD

The seed for *The Love of the Last Tycoon: A Western* is preserved in Fitzgerald's undated note on his January 1927 meeting with Irving Thalberg, the "boy wonder" of the movie industry (see "Selected Fitzgerald Working Notes," p. 140):

We sat in the old commissary at Metro and he said, "Scottie, supposing there's got to be a road through a mountain—a railroad and two or three surveyors and people come to you and you believe some of them and some

* Fitzgerald organized his notebooks into twenty-three sections such as "Descriptions of Girls," "Ideas," "Literary," and "Unclassified." See *The Notebooks of F. Scott Fitzgerald,* ed. Bruccoli (New York: Harcourt Brace Jovanovich/Bruccoli Clark, 1978).

of them you don't believe, but all in all, there seem to be half a dozen possible roads through those mountains, each one of which so far as you can determine, is as good as the other. Now suppose you happen to be the top man, there's a point where you don't exercise the faculty of judgment in the ordinary way, but simply the faculty of arbitrary decision. You say, 'Well, I think we will put the road there' and you trace it with your finger and you know in your secret heart and no one else knows, that you have no reason for putting the road there rather than in several other different courses, but you're the only person that knows that you don't know why you're doing it and you've got to stick to that and you've got to pretend that you know and that you did it for specific reasons, even though you're utterly assailed by doubts at times as to the wisdom of your decision because all these other possible decisions keep echoing in your ear. But when you're planning a new enterprise on a grand scale, the people under you mustn't ever know or guess that you're in any doubt because they've all got to have something to look up to and they mustn't ever dream that you're in doubt about any decision. Those things keep occurring."

At that point, some other people came into the commissary and sat down and the first thing I knew there was a group of four and the intimacy of the conversation was broken, but I was very much impressed by the shrewdness of what he said—something more than shrewdness—by the largeness of what he thought and how he reached it at the age of 26, which he was then.

This encounter was written into the novel as Monroe Stahr's lecture on responsibility to the pilot in the first chapter.

Irving Grant Thalberg was born in Brooklyn, New York, in 1899. His parents were of German-Alsatian Jewish stock. He was not a poor boy; his father was a lace importer, and the family was solidly middle class. Thalberg was a "blue baby," born with cyanosis (a congenital heart defect in which the flow of venous blood to the lungs is impeded) and was not expected to have a long life. Rheumatic fever terminated his high-school education in 1916. After a night-school commercial course he was employed by Carl Laemmle in 1918 as a secretary-stenographer in the New York office of Universal Pictures. At twenty he was managing the California studio.

Thalberg was 5 feet 6 inches tall and slim. He was handsome, spoke quietly, and had pleasant manners; but he was a forceful figure who commanded intense loyalty. His success and reputation resulted from his capacity for work, attention to detail, story sense, taste, and perfectionism. He worked closely with writers and respected good writing; nevertheless, he was regarded as insensitive to writers' feelings, and he was responsible for the system of assigning different writers to work simultaneously on the same screenplay.

In 1923 Thalberg joined Louis B. Mayer as Vice-President of the Mayer Company; when Metro-Goldwyn-Mayer was formed by Loew's, Inc., in 1924, Thalberg became Second Vice-President and Supervisor of Production. He was largely responsible for M-G-M's reputation for expensively produced movies, and he insisted on retakes to improve movies that were regarded as completed. The movies he personally produced included *The Merry Widow* (1925), *The Big Parade* (1925), *Ben-Hur* (1926), *Flesh and the Devil* (1927), *The Broadway Melody* (1929), *The Big House* (1930), *Anna Christie* (1930), *Trader Horn* (1931), *The Sin of Madelon Claudet* (1931), *Strange Interlude* (1932), and *Grand Hotel* (1932).

Bad feelings developed between Thalberg and Mayer over the division of the M-G-M profits, as Thalberg insisted that his share be commensurate with his responsibilities. Mayer, who had a powerful ego, felt that he was being disparaged and overshadowed by his protégé. In 1933, while Thalberg was in Europe recuperating from a collapse caused by overwork, Mayer removed him as M-G-M production head, although Thalberg retained his own production unit. Mayer also instituted a pay cut for M-G-M employees, which Thalberg had opposed. The Thalberg unit produced *The Barretts of Wimpole Street* (1934), *China Seas* (1935), *Mutiny on the Bounty* (1935), *A Night at the Opera* (1935), *Romeo and Juliet* (1936), *The Good Earth* (1937), and *Camille* (1937)—the last two released after his death.

Thalberg's stand on the Screen Writers Guild provided a plot element in Fitzgerald's novel. According to his biographer Bob Thomas, Thalberg opposed the leftist Guild and supported the studio-backed Screen Playwrights. Thomas states that Thalberg defeated a Guild strike vote by declaring: "For if you proceed with this strike, *I shall close down the entire plant,* without a single exception."[5] Budd Schulberg, who was a Hollywood insider as the son of Paramount executive B. P. Schulberg and a member of the

(*Top*) Irving Thalberg at Universal Pictures, age 20.

(*Center*) Director King Vidor, Thalberg, and Lillian Gish on the set of *La Boheme* (1926).

(*Left*) Thalberg accepts the Oscar for *Mutiny on the Bounty*, with Clark Gable and Frank Capra.

(*Top*) Buster Keaton, producer Harry Rapf, Irving Thalberg, Nicholas M. Schenck (president of Loew's, Inc.), Mrs. Schenck, Louis B. Mayer, producer Eddie Mannix, producer Hunt Stromberg.

(*Right*) Sheilah Graham and F. Scott Fitzgerald in Tijuana.

(*Bottom*) M-G-M Studio, Culver City, 1932.

Screen Writers Guild Board, endorses Thomas's report: "Not only was Irving strongly opposed to the organization of a Writers Guild, he was in the forefront of the fight to break the Guild."[6] Thalberg married actress Norma Shearer in 1927; they had two children, and the marriage was regarded as solid. His health remained precarious, but he continued to work to exhaustion. Irving Thalberg died of pneumonia in September 1936.

When Fitzgerald met Irving Thalberg in 1927 the novelist was in Hollywood for the first time and working for United Artists—not for Thalberg at M-G-M. His original screenplay, "Lipstick," was rejected. Fitzgerald's second Hollywood trip in 1931 had him working for M-G-M but not directly with Thalberg; again his screenplay—based on Katharine Brush's novel *Red-Headed Woman*—was rejected.[7] During this visit Fitzgerald, inspired by alcohol, made himself conspicuous by performing a humorous song at a party given by the Thalbergs. Fitzgerald's short story "Crazy Sunday" (*American Mercury,* October 1932) provides a version of this debacle, with Thalberg and director King Vidor amalgamated into the character Miles Calman. The last contact between Fitzgerald and Thalberg was a 1934 phone call in which the presumably intoxicated Fitzgerald tried to sell Thalberg movie rights to *Tender Is the Night.*[8] Five days after Thalberg died, Fitzgerald wrote: "Talbert's final collapse is the death of an enemy for me, though I liked the guy enormously. He had an idea that his wife and I were playing around, which was absolute nonsense, but I think even so that he killed the idea of either Hopkins or Frederick Marsh doing 'Tender is the Night.' "[9] A month after Thalberg's death Fitzgerald reported to Perkins: "I have a novel planned, or rather I should say conceived, which fits much better into the circumstances, but neither by this inheritance [from his mother's estate] nor in view of the general financial situation do I see clear to undertake it."[10] This letter does not mention Thalberg, and Fitzgerald did not yet have enough Hollywood experience to write a novel about the movie industry.

In 1937 Fitzgerald, deep in debt following his "crack up," went on the M-G-M payroll at $1,000 per week. He expressed high hopes and ambitions for a new career in a letter to his daughter written en route to California:

I feel a certain excitement. The third Hollywood venture. Two failures behind me though one no fault of mine. The first one was just ten years ago. At that time I had been generally acknowledged for several years as the top American writer both seriously and, as far as prices went, popularly. I had been loafing for six months for the first time in my life and was confidant to the point of conciet. Hollywood made a big fuss over us and the ladies all looked very beautiful to a man of thirty. I honestly believed that with *no effort on my part* I was a sort of magician with words—an odd delusion on my part when I had worked so desperately hard to develop a hard, colorful prose style.

Total result—a great time + no work. I was to be paid only a small amount unless they made my picture—they didn't.

The second time I went was five years ago. Life had gotten in some hard socks and while all was serene on top, with your mother apparently recovered in Montgomery, I was jittery underneath and beginning to drink more than I ought to. Far from approaching it too confidently I was far too humble. I ran afoul of a bastard named de Sano, since a suicide, and let myself be gyped out of command. I wrote the picture + he changed as I wrote. I tried to get at Thalberg but was erroneously warned against it as "bad taste." Result—a bad script. I left with the money, for this was a contract for weekly payments, but disillusioned and disgusted, vowing never to go back, tho they said it wasn't my fault + asked me to stay. I wanted to get east when the contract expired to see how your mother was. This was later interpreted as "running out on them" + held against me.

(The train has left El Paso since I began this letter—hence the writing—Rocky Mountain writing.)

I want to profit by these two experiences—I must be very tactful but keep my hand on the wheel from the start—find out the key man among the bosses + the most malleable among the collaborators—then fight the rest tooth and nail until, in fact or in effect, I'm alone on the picture. That's the only way I can do my best work. Given a break I can make them double this contract in less than two years.[11]

Although M-G-M raised his weekly salary to $1,250, Fitzgerald was let go after eighteen months with a single screen credit, an adaptation of Erich Maria Remarque's *Three Comrades,* on which he was required to collaborate with E. E. Paramore, with whom he feuded. Fitzgerald was angry and dismayed when his work was rewritten by producer Joseph L. Mankiewicz.[12] Although he was subsequently assigned to important M-G-M movies—including "Infidelity" (unproduced), *Marie Antoinette, The Women,* and *Madame Curie*—Fitzgerald's scripts were not used.[13] His free-lance studio assignments in 1939 and 1940 included a disastrous alcoholic trip with Budd Schulberg to Dartmouth College for location work on *Winter Carnival;* he also worked briefly on *Gone With the Wind.*[14]

While Fitzgerald was in California during 1937–40 his wife, Zelda, was being treated for schizophrenia in North Carolina. Shortly after his arrival in July 1937 he met Sheilah Graham; they maintained separate residences, but their relationship endured despite crises caused by his alcoholism. As a syndicated Hollywood columnist she was able to provide him with information about the studios. After Fitzgerald's death Graham wrote books detailing their time together.[15]

Fitzgerald was an unsuccessful screenwriter—partly because he was a difficult collaborator, but mainly because it is impossible to film literary style. Yet he recognized the force of the movies as an alternative to print, stating in 1936:

I saw that the novel, which at my maturity was the strongest and supplest medium for conveying thought and emotion from one human being to another, was becoming subordinated to a mechanical and communal art that, whether in the hands of Hollywood merchants or Russian idealists, was capable of reflecting only the tritest thought, the most obvious emotion. It was an art in which words were subordinated to images, when personality was worn down to the inevitable gear of collaboration. As long past as 1930, I had a hunch that the talkies would make even the best selling novelist as archaic as silent pictures. . . . there was a rankling indignity, that to me became almost an obsession, in seeing the power of the written word subordinated to another power, a more glittering, a grosser power. . . .[16]

Despite Fitzgerald's resentment of the movie industry and his Hollywood failures, his decision to write a novel about a heroic Hollywood figure is not difficult to comprehend. His imagination was stimulated by the saga of Irving Thalberg, which embodied Fitzgerald's defining theme of aspiration.

Fitzgerald's Hollywood novel is usually described as a *roman à clef* (a novel with a key): a work of fiction in which recognizable persons and events are more or less disguised as fictional. The term is imprecise and subject to interpretation because realistic fiction draws upon life. Some writers work closer to life than others; some conceal their sources; some expect their material to be identified by readers. The distinction between lifelike fiction and the *roman à clef* depends upon the key, that is, the extent to which the effect of the work requires reader recognition and whether the writer provides the key to his sources. The *roman à clef* can be read by the uninitiated, but the insider will read it more meaningfully.

Although *The Love of the Last Tycoon: A Western* has elements in common with the *roman à clef,* it does not strictly belong in that category. Fitzgerald's best fiction is transmuted autobiography: Stahr is Fitzgerald's imaginative projection of himself into Thalberg. Stahr, like Fitzgerald, is ill and tired; the dead Minna Davis represents the hopelessly disturbed Zelda Fitzgerald; and Kathleen Moore derives from Sheilah Graham. (Kathleen resembles Minna in the novel; Fitzgerald's friends saw a close resemblance between Sheilah Graham and Zelda Fitzgerald.)

That Fitzgerald had Thalberg in mind as he wrote is indicated in the manuscript where Stahr is addressed as "Irving" (Episode 11). When Fitzgerald was endeavoring to obtain an advance from *Collier's* in 1939 he explained to the magazine's fiction editor, Kenneth Littauer: "Milton Stahr (who is Irving Thalberg—and *this is my great secret. . . .* So much so that he may be recognized—but it will also be recognized that *no single fact is actually true*" (see p. xxxi). He also wired Perkins at the time of the *Collier's* negotiations: ". . . I THINK I CAN WRITE THIS BOOK AS IF IT WAS A BIOGRAPHY BECAUSE I KNOW THE CHARACTER OF THIS MAN."[17] Nevertheless, Stahr is not a direct portrait of Thalberg; the events in the novel do not duplicate his life. The love plot is invented, as is Stahr's relationship with Cecelia Brady, his partner's daughter. The inscription Fitzgerald drafted for the copy of the novel that was to be

Fitzgerald's draft letter to Norma Shearer Thalberg. *A Star Is Born* (Selznick, 1937) was a movie about Hollywood written by Dorothy Parker, Alan Campbell, and Robert Carson. Princeton University Library.

presented to Thalberg's widow explains that he "inspired the best part of the character of Stahr" but that the character is an amalgam. Since Fitzgerald was not a Hollywood insider, his novel drew upon other people's memories. He talked at length with Budd Schulberg about B. P. Schulberg and about Thalberg's working routine. When Budd Schulberg read the work in progress Fitzgerald told him: "I sort of combined you with my daughter Scottie for Cecilia."[18] (Scottie was nineteen in 1940, and Schulberg was twenty-six.) Other characters are loosely based on actual figures. Cecelia's father, Pat Brady—whose rivalry with Stahr reflects the relationship between Thalberg and Louis B. Mayer—combines aspects of Mayer and M-G-M vice-president Eddie Mannix, an Irishman. Certain of Stahr's associates resemble M-G-M personnel Fitzgerald knew. Jaques La Borwits is Fitzgerald's portrayal of Joseph L. Mankiewicz. One of Fitzgerald's notes reads: "La Borwitz. Joe Mank—pictures smell of rotten bananas" (see p. 159). Rienmund may be Fitzgerald's version of producer Hunt Stromberg. These characterizations are obviously satirical, for Fitzgerald resented his hired-hand status at the studio. Schulberg has identified the source for Robinson as Otto Lovering, the second-unit head who went to Dartmouth for *Winter Carnival.*[19] Schulberg also notes that "the Brimmer character is based on an actual communist organizer that Maurice Rapf and I knew in Hollywood. . . . he remembers telling Scott about the ping-pong scene involving his father Harry Rapf, one of the established producers at MGM in the Thalberg era."[20] Other minor characters can be identified: Boxley is based on British novelist Aldous Huxley; Mike Van Dyke on gag writer Robert Hopkins; Johnny Swanson on actor Harry Carey (see p. liv); Popolous on executive Spyros Skouras of Twentieth Century-Fox. Broaca may be based on Frank Borzage, who directed *Three Comrades.*

The Love of the Last Tycoon was not intended to provide data for a guessing game. The possible character sources are interesting to students of movie history but are not necessary for a proper understanding of the novel. Even the Irving Thalberg identification is not essential. Fitzgerald was writing a novel; the Monroe Stahr story combines biographical, autobiographical, and fictional elements.

2. PREPARATION FOR THE NOVEL
AND WRITING

Fitzgerald was concerned about being forgotten as a novelist when he was in California and expressed his desire to write another novel, but he was unable to work on extended fiction while on the M-G-M payroll. In March 1938 he wrote Perkins: "I am filling a notebook with stuff that will be of more immediate interest to you, but please don't mention me ever as having any plans. 'Tender Is the Night' hung over too long, and my next venture will be presented to you without preparation or fanfare."[21] In the fall Fitzgerald informed Beatrice Dance: "I have a grand novel up my sleeve and I'd love to go to France and write it this summer. It would be short like 'Gatsby' but the same in that it will have the transcendental approach, an attempt to show a man's life through some passionately regarded segment of it."[22] If Fitzgerald was referring to a Hollywood novel, he must have been aware that there was no important novel dealing with the movie industry and that he had untouched material. Nathanael West's *The Day of the Locust* was published in May 1939 while Fitzgerald was working on his novel, and he read it in proof; but their techniques and material were so different that there was no overlap.[23]

Fitzgerald began writing his Hollywood novel in 1939 after the termination of his M-G-M contract. Although he had earned some $90,000 in eighteen months, much of it had gone to pay debts, and he had no savings. His wife required expensive treatment in North Carolina, and his daughter was attending Vassar. He informed Perkins in January that he expected to combine free-lance screenwriting jobs with his own writing:

... if periods of three or four months are going to be possible in the next year or so I would much rather do a modern novel. One of those novels that can only be written at the moment and when one is full of the idea—as "Tender" should have been written in its original conception, all laid on the Riviera.[24]

In March he wrote to Scottie:

Sorry you got the impression that I'm quitting the movies—they are always there—I'm doing a two weeks rewrite for Paramount at the moment after finishing a short story. But I'm convinced that maybe they're not going to make me Czar of the Industry right away, as I thought 10 months ago: It's all right, Baby—life has humbled me—Czar or not, we'll survive. I am even willing to compromise for Assistant Czar!

Seriously, I expect to dip in and out of the pictures for the rest of my natural life, but it is not very soul-satisfying: because it is a business of telling stories fit for children and this is only interesting up to a point. It is a pity that the censorship had to come along + do this, but there we are. *Only*—I will never again sign a contract which binds me to tell none other than children's stories for a year and a half!25

In February and again in April 1939 Fitzgerald was hospitalized in New York after binges. During the April trip he discussed his writing plans with Maxwell Perkins and his agent, Harold Ober. Charles Scribner, head of the publishing house, wrote Fitzgerald an encouraging letter:

Max and I have always thought that, apart from squaring you with the world, living where you have should give you a vast source of material that someday you should be able to use. There has been plenty about Hollywood but no one to my knowledge has told anything about it that made the people live, and while their surroundings and the form of life they lead may make them absurdly glamorous or dissolute they must have originally been born like other men and women and fundamentally have the same insides.26

Fitzgerald responded untruthfully to Perkins:

[Scribner] seemed under the full conviction that the novel was about Hollywood and I am in terror that this mis-information may have been disseminated to the literary columns. If I ever gave any such impression it is entirely false: I said that the novel was about some things that had happened to me in the last two years. It is distinctly *not* about Hollywood (and if it were it is the last impression that I would want to get about.)27

The novel was, of course, about Hollywood; but, as his parenthetical words indicate, Fitzgerald was protecting his material and his studio employment.

In April 1939 Fitzgerald hired Frances Kroll as his secretary to work with him at home, being careful to find someone with no studio connections.[28] At the end of May Fitzgerald sent Ober an optimistic status report:

> *First,* I have blocked out my novel completely with a rough sketch of every episode and event and character so that under proper circumstances I could begin writing it tomorrow. It is a short novel about fifty thousand words long and should take me three to four months.
>
> However, for reasons of income tax I feel I should be more secure before I launch into such a venture—but it will divide easily into five thousand word lengths and *Collier's* might take a chance on it where the *Post* would not. They might at least be promised a first look at it when its finished—possibly some time late in the Fall.[29]

In July 1939 Fitzgerald broke with Ober over the agent's refusal to resume the practice of advancing him money against unsold stories; thereafter Fitzgerald tried to act as his own agent in obtaining an advance for serial rights to the unwritten novel. On 18 July Fitzgerald informed Kenneth Littauer that he had blocked out a short novel "on a basis of 2500 word units. The block-out is to be sure that I can take it up or put it down in as much time as is allowed between picture work and short stories." He asked for an advance of $750 from *Collier's* for *"first look at the novel* and at *a specified number of short stories in a certain time."*[30] Littauer declined the proposition.

Fitzgerald sent a synopsis to Littauer, and a copy to Perkins, on 29 September 1939:

> This will be difficult for two reasons. First that there is one fact about my novel, which, if it were known, would be immediately and unscrupulously plagiarized by the George Kaufmans,* etc., of this world. Second, that I live always in deadly fear that I will take the edge off an idea for myself by summarizing or talking about it in advance. But, with these limitations, here goes:

---

* Fitzgerald was convinced that his play *The Vegetable* had provided playwright George S. Kaufman with the idea for *Of Thee I Sing* (1931). Editor.

The novel will be fifty thousand words long. As I will have to write sixty thousand words to make room for cutting I have figured it as a four months job—three months for the writing—one month for revision. The thinking, according to my conscience and the evidence of sixty pages of outline and notes, *has already been done*. I would infinitely rather do it, now that I am well again, than take hack jobs out here.

* * *

The Story occurs during four or five months in the year 1935. It is told by Cecelia, the daughter of a producer named Bradogue in Hollywood. Cecelia is a pretty, modern girl neither good nor bad, tremendously human. Her father is also an important character. A shrewd man, a gentile, and a scoundrel of the lowest variety. A self-made man, he has brought up Cecelia to be a princess, sent her East to college, made of her rather a snob, though, in the course of the story, her character evolves *away from this*. That is, she was twenty when the events that she tells occurred, but she is twenty-five when she tells about the events, and of course many of them appear to her in a different light.

Cecelia is the narrator because I think I know exactly how such a person would react to my story. She is *of* the movies but not *in* them. She probably was born the day "The Birth of a Nation" was previewed and Rudolph Valentino came to her fifth birthday party. So she is, all at once, intelligent, cynical but understanding and kindly toward the people, great or small, who are of Hollywood.

She focuses our attention upon two principal characters—Milton Stahr (who is Irving Thalberg—and *this is my great secret*) and Thalia, the girl he loves. Thalberg has always fascinated me. His peculiar charm, his extraordinary good looks, his bountiful success, the tragic end of his great adventure. The events I have built around him are fiction, but all of them are things which might very well have happened, and I am pretty sure that I saw deep enough into the character of the man so that his reactions are authentically what they would have been in life. So much so that he may be recognized— but it will also be recognized that *no single fact is actually true*. For example, in my story he is unmarried or a widower, leaving out completely any complication with Norma.

In the beginning of the book I want to pour out my whole impression of this man Stahr as he is seen during an airplane trip from New York to the coast—of course, through Cecelia's eyes. She has been hopelessly in love with him for a long time. She is never going to win anything more from him than an affectionate regard, even that tainted by his dislike of her father (parallel the deadly dislike of each other between Thalberg and Louis B. Mayer). Stahr is over-worked and deathly tired, ruling with a radiance that is almost moribund in its phosphorescence. He has been warned that his health is undermined, but being afraid of nothing the warning is unheeded. He has had everything in life except the privilege of giving himself unselfishly to another human being. This he finds on the night of a semi-serious earthquake (like in 1935) a few days after the opening of the story.

It has been a very full day even for Stahr—the bursted water mains, which cover the whole ground space of the lot to the depth of several feet, seems to release something in him. Called over to the outer lot to supervise the salvation of the electrical plant (for like Thalberg, he has a finger in every pie of the vast bakery) he finds two women stranded on the roof of a property farmhouse and goes to their rescue.

Thalia Taylor is a twenty-six year old widow, and my present conception of her should make her the most glamorous and sympathetic of my heroines. Glamorous in a new way because I am in secret agreement with the public in detesting the type of feminine arrogance that has been pushed into prominence in the case of Brenda Frazier,* etc. People simply do not sympathize deeply with those who have had *all* the breaks, and I am going to dower this girl, like Rosalba in Thackeray's "Rose in the Ring" with "a little misfortune". She and the woman with her (to whom she is serving as companion) have come secretly on the lot through the other woman's curiosity. They have been caught there when the catastrophe occurred.

Now we have a love affair between Stahr and Thalia, an immediate, dynamic, unusual, physical love affair—and I will write it so that you can publish it. At the same time I will send you a copy of how it will appear in book form somewhat stronger in tone.

This love affair is the meat of the book—though I am going to treat it, remember, as it comes through to Cecelia. That is to say by making Cecelia at the moment of her telling the story, an intelligent and observant woman, I shall grant myself the privilege, as Conrad did, of letting her imagine the actions of the characters. Thus, I hope to get the verisimilitude of a first person narrative, combined with a Godlike knowledge of all events that happen to my characters.

Two events beside the love affair bulk large in the intermediary chapters. There is a definite plot on the part of Bradogue, Cecelia's father, to get Stahr out of the company. He has even actually and factually considered having him murdered. Bradogue is the monopolist at its worst—Stahr, in

---

* New York celebrity debutante. Editor.

spite of the inevitable conservatism of the self-made man, is a paternalistic employer. Success came to him young, at twenty-three, and left certain idealisms of his youth unscarred. Moreover, he is a worker. Figuratively he takes off his coat and pitches in, while Bradogue is not interested in the making of pictures save as it will benefit his bank account.

The second incident is how young Cecelia herself, in her desperate love for Stahr, throws herself at his head. In her reaction at his indifference she gives herself to a man whom she does not love. This episode is *not* absolutely necessary to the serial. It could be tempered but it might be best to eliminate it altogether.

Back to the main theme, Stahr cannot bring himself to marry Thalia. It simply doesn't seem part of his life. He doesn't realize that she has become necessary to him. Previously his name has been associated with this or that well-known actress or society personality and Thalia is poor, unfortunate, and tagged with a middle class exterior which doesn't fit in with the grandeur Stahr demands of life. When she realizes this she leaves him temporarily, leaves him not because he has no legal intentions toward her but because of the hurt of it, the remainder of a vanity from which she had considered herself free.

Stahr is now plunged directly into the fight to keep control of the company. His health breaks down very suddenly while he is on a trip to New York to see the stockholders. He almost dies in New York and comes back to find that Bradogue has seized upon his absence to take steps which Stahr considers unthinkable. He plunges back into work again to straighten things out.

Now, realizing how much he needs Thalia, things are patched up between them. For a day or two they are ideally happy. They are going to marry, but he must make one more trip East to clinch the victory which he has conciliated in the affairs of the company.

Now occurs the final episode which should give the novel its quality— and its unusualness. Do you remember about 1933 when a transport plane was wrecked on a mountain-side in the Southwest, and a Senator was killed? The thing that struck me about it was that the country people rifled the bodies of the dead.* That is just what happens to this plane which is bearing Stahr from Hollywood. The angle is that of three children who, on

---

* On 6 May 1935 Senator Bronson M. Cutting and four others were killed when a passenger plane crashed at Atlanta, Missouri. Also aboard were members of a Paramount film crew. The local people aided in rescuing the injured; the wreckage was not plundered. See Richard Lowitt, *Bronson M. Cutting* (Albuquerque: University of New Mexico Press, 1992). Editor.

a Sunday picnic, are the first to discover the wreckage. Among those killed in the accident besides Stahr are two other characters we have met. (I have not been able to go into the minor characters in this short summary.) Of the three children, two boys and a girl, who find the bodies, one boy rifled Stahr's possessions; another, the body of a ruined ex-producer; and the girl, those of a moving picture actress. The possessions which the children find, symbolically determine their attitude toward their act of theft. The possessions of the moving picture actress tend the young girl to a selfish possessiveness; those of the unsuccessful producer sway one of the boys toward an irresolute attitude; while the boy who finds Stahr's briefcase is the one who, after a week, saves and redeems all three by going to a local judge and making full confession.

The story swings once more back to Hollywood for its finale. During the story *Thalia has never once been inside a studio.* After Stahr's death as she stands in front of the great plant which he created, she realizes now that she never will. She knows only that he loved her and that he was a great man and that he died for what he believed in.

This is a novel—not even faintly of the propoganda type. Indeed, Thalberg's opinions were entirely different from mine in many respects that I will not go into. I've long chosen him for a hero (this has been in my mind for three years) because he is one of the half-dozen men I have known who were built on the grand scale. That it happens to coincide with a period in which the American Jews are somewhat uncertain in their morale, is for me merely a fortuitous coincidence. The racial angle shall scarcely be touched on at all. Certainly if Ziegfeld* could be made into an epic figure than what about Thalberg who was literally everything that Ziegfeld wasn't?

There's nothing that worries me in the novel, nothing that seems uncertain. Unlike *Tender is the Night* it is not the story of deterioration—it is not depressing and not morbid in spite of the tragic ending. If one book could ever be "like" another I should say it is more "like" *The Great Gatsby* than any other of my books. But I hope it will be entirely different—I hope it will be something new, arouse new emotions perhaps even a new way of looking at certain phenomena. I have set it safely in a period of five years ago to obtain detachment, but now that Europe is tumbling about our ears this also seems to be for the best. It is an escape into a lavish, romantic past that perhaps will not come again into our time. It is certainly a novel I would like to read. Shall I write it?[31]

---

* Florenz Ziegfeld (1869–1932), producer of lavish annual Broadway shows called *The Ziegfeld Follies*. Editor.

A carbon copy of this document has Fitzgerald's note "Orig Sent thru here" after "Shall I write it?" The letter continues:

As I said, I would rather do this for a minimum price than continue this in-and-out business with the moving pictures where the rewards are great, but the satisfaction unsatisfactory and the income tax always mopping one up after the battle.

The minimum I would need to do this with peace of mind would be $15,000., payable $3000. in advance and $3000. on the first of November, the first of December, the first of January and the first of February, on delivery of the last instalment. For this I would guarantee to do no other work, specifically pictures, to make any changes in the manuscript (but not to have them made for me) and to begin to deliver the copy the first of November, that is to give you fifteen thousand words by that date.

Unless these advances are compatible with your economy, Kenneth, the deal would be financially impossible for me under the present line up. Four months of sickness completely stripped me and until your telegram came I had counted on a build up of many months work here before I could *consider* beginning the novel. Once again a telegram would help tremendously, as I am naturally on my toes and [*the rest is missing.*]

Littauer replied on 10 October that he could not make an advance without seeing a "substantial sample of the finished product"—15,000 words. Fitzgerald needed the advance to write the sample. On the 20th he asked Perkins if Scribners would support the writing of the first 10,000 words. Perkins's answer has not been found—Fitzgerald was telephoning and wiring Perkins during the *Collier's* negotiations—but Scribners was unwilling to increase Fitzgerald's outstanding debt to the firm. (Although he had discharged loans from Ober and Perkins and paid his wife's medical bills, Fitzgerald still owed Scribners more than $5,000.) He worked on two short free-lance assignments in September, polishing the scripts for *Everything Happens at Night* (Twentieth Century-Fox) and *Raffles* (Goldwyn).

Fitzgerald established a source of income in fall 1939 by writing the Pat Hobby stories and other short-shorts for editor Arnold Gingrich of *Esquire* at $250 each.[32] He was unable to write salable commercial-length stories after his move to California. Two stories about Hollywood, "Director's Special" and "Last Kiss," were rejected by *Collier's;* but both were posthumously published—the former as "Discard." Fitzgerald stripped "Last Kiss" for use in his novel. Most of the seventeen Hobby stories about a hack movie writer are disappointing.[33] The relationship between the Hobby stories and the novel Fitzgerald was writing at the same time has been misunderstood. There was no literary sharing or reciprocity. Pat Hobby is not a self-portrait. The Hobby stories are mainly travesties. Their function was to earn money to support the writing of the novel. Fitzgerald's Hollywood short stories, with the possible exception of "Crazy Sunday," are undistinguished.

In November Fitzgerald sent a 6,000-word section to both Littauer and Perkins—a draft of the opening of the novel—telling Perkins on the 20th that "the material is definitely 'strong.' . . . I am by no means sure that I will ever be a popular writer again. This much of the book, however, should be as fair a test as any."[34] On 28 November Littauer wired: FIRST SIX THOUSAND PRETTY CRYPTIC THEREFORE DISAPPOINTING. BUT YOU WARNED US THIS MIGHT BE SO. CAN WE DEFER VERDICT UNTIL FURTHER DEVELOPMENT OF THE STORY? IF IT HAS TO BE NOW IT HAS TO BE NO. REGARDS.[35] Fitzgerald responded: NO HARD FEELINGS THERE HAS NEVER BEEN AN EDITOR WITH PANTS ON SINCE LORIMER.[36] The great *Saturday Evening Post* editor George Horace Lorimer was dead; but Fitzgerald asked Perkins to send the sample to the *Post*, which found it too "broad" for them.[37]

Perkins then performed one of the acts that shaped his legend as an editorial saint. Concerned that Fitzgerald's morale would be damaged by Littauer's rejection, Perkins wired on the 29th: A BEAUTIFUL START. STIRRING AND NEW. CAN WIRE YOU TWO HUNDRED FIFTY AND A THOUSAND BY JANUARY.[38] Perkins—who was not wealthy but had come into a small inheritance—was acting in a personal capacity, not on behalf of Scribners. The next day he wrote Fitzgerald: "I thought the book had the magic that you can put into things. The whole transcontinental business, which is so strong and new to people like me, and to most people, was marvellously suggested, and interest and curiosity about Stahr was aroused, and sympathy with the narratress. It was all admirable, or else I am no judge any more."[39]

The day after Littauer's wire, Fitzgerald wired Perkins to show the synopsis to agent Leland Hayward, who handled theatre and movie properties, in the hope that a studio would make an advance in return for movie rights.[40] This idea represented a complete reversal of Fitzgerald's earlier insistence on keeping his novel a secret from the studios. Hayward responded that he could not place the novel until it was written. Thereafter Fitzgerald made no further attempts to secure advances for his novel. On 7 December 1939 Fitzgerald sent Perkins "a little more, introducing the character of the heroine,"[41] but did not discuss his work in progress with the editor.

Thirty-five years later Kroll recalled that Fitzgerald was unable to resume steady work on his novel until May or June 1940:

Scott made so many starts before he got into working on the book full time, that he necessarily made changes with each new start. In Encino, he worked mostly on notes interrupted by turning out the Pat Hobby stories for bucks. When he moved to Laurel,* he began to work on LT again. This time, the interruption was the Babylon Revisited screenplay. He didn't begin writing the book in a continuous stream until after the screenplay was done.[42]

From March to early August Fitzgerald wrote the unproduced screenplay for his story "Babylon Revisited," which earned him about $6,000; but he was still financially unable to devote full time to the novel. In September Perkins expressed his pleasure at John O'Hara's report that "you had actually written about 25,000 or more words, and that they were extraordinarily expressive words."[43]

Fitzgerald's progress on the novel in the fall of 1940 is documented in weekly letters to his wife:

11 October: I expect to be back on my novel any day and this time to finish a two months' job.

19 October: I'm trying desparately to finish my novel by the middle of December and it's a little like working on "Tender is the Night" at the

---

* 1403 North Laurel Avenue in Hollywood Estates.

end—I think of nothing else. . . . My room is covered with charts like it used to be for "Tender is the Night" telling the different movements of the characters and their histories.

23 October: I am deep in the novel, living in it, and it makes me happy. It is a *constructed* novel like *Gatsby*, with passages of poetic prose when it fits the action, but no ruminations or sideshows like *Tender*. Everything must contribute to the dramatic movement. . . . Two thousand words today and all good.

2 November: The novel is hard as pulling teeth but that is because it is in its early character-planting phase. I feel people so less intently than I did once that this is harder. It means welding together hundreds of stray impressions and incidents to form the fabric of entire personalities.*

13 December: The novel is about three-quarters through and I think I can go on till January 12 without doing any stories or going back to the studio. I couldn't go back to the studio anyhow in my present condition as I have to spend most of the time in bed where I write on a wooden desk. . . .⁴⁴

That day he also wrote Perkins: "The novel progresses—in fact progresses fast. I'm not going to stop now till I finish a first draft which will be some time after the 15th of January. . . . Meanwhile will you send me back the chapters I sent you as they are all invalid now, must be completely rewritten etc. The essential idea is still the same and it is still, as far as I can hope, a secret."⁴⁵

F. Scott Fitzgerald died of a heart attack on 21 December 1940. He had written 44,000 words for the latest working drafts of seventeen episodes in his novel.

3. THE OUTLINES AND THE DRAFTS

Fitzgerald's outline-plan for the novel survives in five documents. All are typescripts: the second through fourth are revised in Fitzgerald's hand, and the third through fifth are each retyped from the preceding outline. None is dated, but the order can be readily estab-

---

* The reference to "early character-planting phase" is puzzling because Fitzgerald was well into the novel by this time. Editor.

lished from the structural revisions and character name changes. The earliest outline is headed "(version Y)"—probably to indicate that he regarded it as penultimate, not that it was Fitzgerald's twenty-fifth outline. It organizes the novel into ten chapters with a total of twenty-three episodes. The plot establishes two interconnected stories—Stahr's love for Thalia (Kathleen) and his struggle with Bradogue (Brady) for control of the studio. The material about Robinson and the Dartmouth College Winter Carnival (VIII A) was dropped in subsequent outlines. In every stage Fitzgerald projected a *Gatsby*-length novel of some 50,000 words.

The second outline has eight chapters and thirty-one episodes. Robinson's role is reduced; and Smith, who is Thalia's husband or lover, is introduced in episode twenty-five. "S.G." indicates material based on Sheilah Graham or provided by her. This outline establishes the three-column format: column two designates the five-act structure and estimated word counts; column three has notes on the plot.

The third outline is an elaboration of the second. The structure still calls for eight chapters and thirty-one episodes, and Fitzgerald inserted dates indicating the pacing of the action from 28 June to 30 September–October.

The fourth outline establishes the nine-chapter and thirty-episode structure. Old Episode 7 is deleted—an encounter between Stahr and Thalia immediately following the flood. Episodes 14–21 are reordered—canceling Episode 18; and a new Episode 20 is inserted. This outline transposes the second and third columns.

The fifth outline is a clean retyping. An inaccurate transcription of this document was printed in Wilson's *The Last Tycoon* edition; among other changes it altered the dates for Episodes 17–18 and 20–21 and deleted references to "S.G."—an obligatory omission at that time.

Although he did not note this in the outlines, Fitzgerald considered opening the novel with a scene that would have framed the narrative. Cecelia, who is dying of tuberculosis, tells her story to a fellow-patient who retells it to the reader—thereby introducing a double perspective (see Appendix 1: The Sanitarium Frame). Since this material is not noted in the outlines, it is impossible to place it

CHAPTERS   (version Y)

I. The airplane trip; and Cecelia decides to tell her   7500
    story
    A. Introduction
    B. In some stop--Schwartz and Rogers
    C. With Stahr in Front

II. A. Stahr meeting Thalia   2500
    B. Stahr meeting Rogers--Rogers conversation with
                                                    Stahr   2500

III Thalia's response to Stahr   2500

IV Thalia and part of her story   2500

V   How Stahr worked out a picture   5000
    A. Story conference
    B. Railroad episode and idealism about making
                                   non-profit picture
    C. Stahr's Visit to Sets

VI A. Cecelia's seduction and her love for Stahr)
    B. A good part of Stahr's story   )   7500
    C. Cecelia takes her father off guard   )

VII Stahr and Thalia alone--Stahr's house   5000

VIII A. Robinson, the Cutter & Dartmouth   2500
     B. Stahr sick in East hears.
     C. On Coast. The meeting of writers, etc.   2500
     D. Firing of secretaries, technicians, etc.   2500

IX. A. Stahr's return and anger
    B. Bradogue Plot
    C. Stahr's departure to include big scene for
                                           Thalia   2500

X   A. The Fall of the Plane   5000
    B. Epilogue in Hollywood   2500
                                                                  ───────────
                                                                      52,500

First outline.

Episodes		Act I ("The Plane")	Act II (The Circus)	Act III (The Underworld)	Act IV (The Murderers)	Act V (End)	
4. 1. The Plane		6,000					Chapter Ⓐ Introduce Cecelia, Stahr, Wylie, Schwartz Jr.
2. Nashville							
3. Up forward							Chapter Ⓑ is good & quick but P. story's point up. P's airoveryday ad ten.
B. 4. Hand Out - Power - School theory	6000		19,000				Chapter Ⓒ Introduce Prysd & Thalia, Bodmann + recoinment
5. The Earthquake							
6. The Back lot							Chapter Ⓓ Introduces Brady
7. Afterwards (No do with Thalia)	6000						
C. 8. Stahr's work and health. From something she wrote							
9. Sleeps at studio. The Camera man.							
10. Taking the guest around - the story.							
11. ... conference							
12. Idealism about ham- part pictureline							
13. Visit to Sets/Cuckoo							
14. Second Meeting that night Small	7000						
D. 15. Football game. Cells and Wylie.	6000						
16. Malibu seduction. DEAD MIDDLE							
E. 17. Cecelia breaks in on father. Telling of Stahr			11,000				
18. Cecelia and Stahr - drove that end friend with Wylie							
19. The Commerband - market							
20. Stahr goes with Cecelia - Trocadero & Point	6000						
21. Cecelia and Thalia meet							
F. 22. The Storm breaks. Cecelia, Guild, Dame							
23. Throws over Cecelia. Stops. Old (Starmaker) 600 Cuckoo				2300			
24. Last fling with Thalia.							
G. 25. Paddock							
26. Robinson Smith (Kentucken + Cecelia (Society)							
27. Pilot							
28. ... plan and execution							
29. Thalia at airport. S.G. Hoverer					5500		
H. 30. The Plane falls Thalia (Air picture in Kilnmaker							
31. ... Outside the studio. S.G.							
32. Harry Corry Johnny Swanson funeral	5500				5500		
33. Stahr hears plane. Camera man. O.K.							
34. Stops in at Glen & Cody.							
35. ... Aldo							
36. Cecelia and Stahr.						59,000	

Second outline.

xli

Three — the Second column (its acts) should be the 3rd ... mild copy ... will show of three?

Episodes		
	June 28ᵗʰ	(The Plane) 6,000 June
A 1. The Plane		Stahr
2. Nashville		
3. Un Forward Duffont. 6000		
B 4. Johnny Swanson—Baird—Power— S.A.—R. Schwartze leaving July 28ᵗʰ	Act I July—early August 19,000	Chapter (A). Introduce Cecelia, Stahr, White, Schwartze.
5. The Earthquake	(The Circus)	Chapter (B) Introduces Baird, Thalia, Robinson and secretaries.
6. The Back lot		Chapter (C) is equal to guest
7. Afterwards (To do with Thalia) 6000		list and Gatsby's party. Throw
C 8. Stahr's work and health. From something she wrote July 29ᵗʰ	The Movement forward Italia	everything into this with selection... Chapter (D) Introduces Smith.
9. Sleeps at studio. The Camera man.		
10. Taking the guest around—the story conference/...		
11. Commissary and Idealism about now. profit pictures. Phone call.		
12. Visit to Sets. 75.00		
13. Second Meeting that night. August 6ᵗʰ		These episodes. Atmosphere is... most important that first half of the time for etc
D 14a. Cecelia and Stahr.		
14. Football game. Cecelia and Wylie... 5500.		
15. Malibu seduction. Try to get on lot. DS-D MIDDLE Aug 10ᵗʰ	Aug—early Sept 11,800 Act III (The Underworld)	Chapter (E) Run then go to the women of introduces Smith (or Ce
Jack arrives.		
E 16. Cecelia breaks in on Father. Aug 10ᵗʰ		

The Struggle

17. Baird and Stahr--double blackmail. Qn reel with Wylie.

16.14 The Gumeround - market - Brush (Stahr/Mala

19.18 Stahr goes with Cecelia - Trocadero   aug 26*
or Bowl.

20.19 Secolia and Thalia mood + Fly.   6000

F 21 20 The Storm breaks at Screen Guild. Danco   Oct 26th
— Sept 14th

22.21 Sick in Washington. To quit?
21a Stay ...
23. Throws over Cecelia. Stops making pictures.
Lies low after Out
wave at Encino.

24. Last fling with Thalia. Old stars in heat   5500

G 25. Baird gets Smith. Fleishacker and Cecelia.   5500
(S.G. & K)

26. Stahr hears plan. Camera man. O.K.

27. Stops it--very sick. (Cecelia to college;

28. Resolve problem. Thalia at airport V.s.g.*   8000

H 29. The Plane falls. Portests of the future in   Sept
Fleishacker.   — Oct

30. Outside the studio. S.G.

31. Johnny Swanson at funeral   5500

Act IV (The Murderers)	Defeat	8000
Act V (End)	Silence	5500
		50,000

Chapter (F) The Storm
(all on Stahr, Queen of
best all time, culminating
in 24

Chapter (G) The ... will and
the plot.

Chapter (H) Stahr's death

(m) Walla for two people — for V.S.T. act 17 and for E.W. a 45 — it must
please them both.

Third outline.

Episodes

A 1. The plane   June 23
    2. Nashville
    3. Up Forward. Different 6000

B 4. Johnny Swanson--Still July 28th
    Schenck leaving
    5. The Earthquake
    6. The Back lot 3000
             6000

C 7. Stahr's work and health. From July 29th
         something she wrote (The Camera man).
    9. Teaching the guest around--the story
      Second conference--first half afterwards.
  10. Commisary and idealism about non-
      profit pictures. Phone call 500

D 11. Visit to see.
  12. Second Meeting that night.

E 13. Cecelia and Stahr and Ball August 6th
  14. Football game Cecelia and Wylie
      and Maude.
    Malibu seduction. Try to get on lot. 6000
                August 10th

F The Quennyfund - market.
              August 20th

(Surtaper)

Chapter (A) Introduce Cecelia, Stahr, White, Schwartz.

Chapter (B) Introduces Cecelia, Thalia, Robinson and secretaries. Atmosphere of night-sustain.

Chapters (C) Dan is equal to guest list and Gatsby's party. Throw everything into this, with selection. It must have a plot, though, leading to 13.

Chapter (E) Three episodes. Atmosphere in 15 most important. Hint of Waste Land of the house too late.

Chapter (F) This belongs to the women. It introduces Smith (for the first time?)

Act I   June 6,000
(The Plane)
STAHR

Act II   July--early August
(The Circus)
The Mystery of... Thalia

STAHR AND KATHLEEN

Act III Aug--early Sept.

(The Underworld)

THE...

19. The four meet, like Hopf & Lefty [General Ideas] $000

17. The ... breaks ...
    August 28th.
    Sept. 14th.

20. Wylie with coffee

21. Sick in Washington. To quit?

22. Story conference, second half--rushes

22. [Ruddy] and Stahr--double blackmail.
    Quarrel with Wylie

23. Throws over Cecilia who tells her father.
    Stops making pictures. Wies
    low after Cut.

24. Last fling with [Kathleen]. Old stars in heat
    wave at Encino. $6500

26. [Buddy] gets to Smith, Fleishacker and
    Cecilia. Sept. 15--
    Sept. 30th.

26. Stahr hears plan. Camera man O.K. STOPS

27. Resolve problem. KATHLEEN at airport. Off
    to college; ... at
    airport. $7000

28. The Plane falls. Foretasts of the future
    in Fleishacker Sept 30th
    --Oct.

29. Outside the studio. $45.

30. Johnny Swanson at funeral $4500

Chapter B. The blows
fall on Stahr. Sense of
heat all through, culmin-
ating in 26.

Chapter H. The suit
and the price.

Chapter H. Stahr's
death.

Act IV September
(The Murderers)

DEFEAT $7000

Act V October $3500

(The End)

EPILOGUE

$51,000

WRITTEN FOR THE PEOPLE ... FOR SP ... AT IV AND FOR EN AT 45 - IT WOES. PARKER THEM 30TH.

Fourth outline.

xlv

Episodes		

A 1. The plane   June 28
  2. Nashville
  3. Up /orward. Different   6000
	Chapter (A) Introduce Cecelia, Stahr, White, Schwartze.	Act I June
		(THE PLANT) 6000
		
		STAHR

B 4. Johnny Swanson--Marcus leaving
    --Brady   July 28th.
  5. The Earthquake
  6. The Back lot   3000
	Chapter (B) Introduces Brady, Kathleen, Robinson and secretaries. Atmosphere of night-sustain	Act II
		(THE CIRCUS)
		July-early August
		21,000

C 7. The Camera man. July 29
  Stahr's work and health. From something she wrote
  First Conference
  Second conference and afterwards.
  8.
  9. Commisary and Idealism about non-
 10. profit pictures. Rushes Phone call, etc.   5000
	Chapters (C) & (D) are equal to guest list and Gatsby's party. Throw everything into this, with selection. They must have a plot, though, leading to 13	STAHR AND KATHLEEN

D 11. Visit to rushes. 12. Second Meeting that night. Wrong girl--glimpse 2500		

E 13. Cecelia and Stahr and Ball - Aug. 6th
    Football game. Cecelia and
    Wylie and Maude.
 14. Malibu seduction. Try to get on lot.
    DEAD MIDDLE
 15. Cecelia and father
 16. Phone call & Wedding.   6000
	Chapter (E) Three episodes Atmosphere in 15 most important. Hint of Waste Land of the house too late.	

F 17. The Dawn breaks with Brimmer
 18. The Cumberbund - market--
    (The theatre with Benchley)
     August 10th
 19. The four meet, like Hop and Lefty.
    Renewal. Palomar
 20. Wylie White in Office
    August 28th-Sept. 14th.
	Chapter (F) This belongs to the women. It introduced Smith (for the 1st time?)	Act III Aug-early
		Sept.
		(The Underworld)
		11,500
		THE STRUGGLE

O 21. Sick in Washington. To quit?
22. Brady and Stahr--double blackmail.
23. Quarrel with Wylie.
    Throws over Cecelia who tells her
    father. Stops making pictures.
    A story conference--rushes and
    sets. Lies low after Cut.
24. Last fling with Kathleen. Old
    stars in heat wave at Encino.
                                6500

H 25. Brady gets to Smith. Fleishacker
    and Cecelia. (S.G.&K.)
                Sept. 15-30th.
26. Stahr hears plan. Camera man O.K.
    Stops it--very sick.
27. Resolve problem. Thalia at airport.
    Cecelia to college; Thalia at
    airport. S.G.   7000

I 28. The Plane falls. Fortaste of the
    future in Fleishacker
                Sept 30th-Oct.
29. Outside the studio. S.G.
30. Johnny Swanson at funeral
                                4500

WRITTEN FOR TWO PEOPLE - FOR SF AT 17 AND FOR EW AT 45 - IT MUST PLEASE THEM BOTH

Chapter (G). The blows
fall on Stahr. Sense of
heat all through, culminating in 25.

Chapter (H). The suit and
the price.

Chapter (I) Stahr's death.

Act IV September
        (The Murderers)
DEFEAT 7000

Act V October
       (The End) 4500

EPILOGUE

$1,000

Latest outline.

in the process of composition; but Fitzgerald was sufficiently serious about the idea to have prepared seven drafts. Graham informed Wilson that Fitzgerald considered salvaging the sanitarium material for the conclusion of the novel.[46]

The novel developed by a process of accretion, expansion, and reduction. Frances Kroll recalls:

> Fitzgerald's work patterns on TYCOON started with notes; then the sorting of notes into chapters; then brief biographies of the characters; then chapter outlines and finally roughly written chapters.
>
> He wrote everything out in longhand. He used the morning and some early noon hours for work. He was not much of a sleeper, so during these fitful times, he made notes which would be on my table when I came to work.
>
> He never dictated the novel, but did considerable revision from typescripts. He also switched chapter notes if they didn't work out in the designated chapters and assigned them to other chapters of the book.
>
> That was basically the pattern without going into too much detail. Of course, all of this was not a continuous process. Work on the chapter notes and outlines was interrupted many times before they were completed and before the actual writing began.[47]

Fitzgerald's holograph pages—up to twelve per writing stint for this novel—were turned over to Kroll for typing. The ribbon typescripts and carbon copies were then pencil-revised by Fitzgerald and retyped by Kroll as necessary. The lengths of the draft episodes vary considerably, indicating that Fitzgerald was not constrained by the projected word counts in the outline. The novel evolved and grew as he wrote. For the first seventeen episodes there are 115 extant manuscript, ribbon-copy, and carbon-copy drafts. The description of these drafts provides a sense of Fitzgerald's working method as he stopped trying to write whole chapters after the first chapter and shifted to writing episodes intended to be combined into chapters during a later stage of revision (see "Inventory of Drafts"). Even for Chapter 1 there is no complete manuscript draft; this chapter developed through layers of revised typescript.

Fitzgerald followed his outline closely—except for Episodes 9 and 10, which survive in rejected and rewritten versions. He encountered difficulties with his plan to utilize Prince Agge, the visiting Dane, as a perambulating witness to Stahr's working day; Agge's role was reduced.

Rejected Episode 9
(Typescript revised by Fitzgerald)

Fitzgerald noted at the top of the first page: "Out / Double talk doesn't jell. Name Lee Spurgeon." Gag-writer Mike Van Dyke confuses Agge with double talk. Stahr, Van Dyke, and Agge go to script conference with writers Mr. and Mrs. Marquand in supervisor Spurgeon's office; Van Dyke ridicules Spurgeon (compare Episode 9, pp. 37–44).

Rejected Episode 10
(Typescript revised by Fitzgerald)

Fitzgerald noted at the top of the first page: "Sidney Franklin's dance.* Another suggestion is a real story to be shown developing later." Stahr asks secretary Miss Doolan about cameraman Pedro Garcia's (Pete Zavras's) eye trouble, but there is no previous reference to the problem. Agge is present at the second script conference in Stahr's office with director Broaca and Wylie White. This draft is the source for the confused phone message from Marcus that Wilson interpolated into his edition before the luncheon meeting in rewritten Episode 10. Gag-writer Pops Carlson demonstrates slapstick routine for Agge; this material was salvaged for the encounter between Mike Van Dyke and George Boxley in Episode 8 (compare Episodes 8 and 10, pp. 33–34, 46).

Agge first appears in rewritten Episode 10 as a guest at the executives' commissary meeting: "My father—I will call him Mr. Brady as Prince Agge did when he told me of this luncheon . . ." (p. 46).

---

* Sidney Franklin (1893–1972); M-G-M producer-director associated with Thalberg. Editor.

But details in rewritten Episode 10 refer to material canceled in preceding episodes: There is no preparation for Stahr's question about the cameraman's eyesight (p. 47), for that information had been deleted in Episode 7; and Popolous's speech is compared to Mike Van Dyke's double talk (p. 46), which is in rejected Episode 9. These inconsistencies establish that Fitzgerald intended further revision of the rewritten Episodes 9 and 10.

The luncheon meeting in rewritten Episode 10 is followed by a four-page revised typescript insert headed "For Episode 10" (changed to "11") in which Stahr—unaccompanied by Agge—goes to director Red Ridingwood's set and fires him. It is not certain where Fitzgerald wanted to position this scene. Wilson placed it after rewritten Episode 10, as does the Cambridge edition. The penultimate outline has Episode 12 "Visit to Sets," which Fitzgerald altered to Episode 11 "Visit to rushes." Revised typescript Episode 11 is the account of Stahr's viewing the rushes in the projection room. At the end of Episode 11 Agge comes to Stahr's office to "thank him for his afternoon on the sets" and Stahr makes his statement that "I'm the unity" (p. 58). Cecelia resumes her narration at the end of Episode 12 and repeats her citation of Agge: "Prince Agge is my authority for the luncheon in the commissary" (p. 67).

The structural problems in Episodes 9 and 10 bear on the point-of-view inconsistencies resulting from Fitzgerald's use of a narrator: a *character in the fiction* who relates the story as a participant or observer. A disembodied authorial voice is not a narrator. Fitzgerald's September 1939 synopsis for Littauer (p. xxxii) explains that in using Cecelia as the narrator "I shall grant myself the privilege, as Conrad did, of letting her imagine the actions of the characters. Thus, I hope to get the verisimilitude of a first person narrative, combined with a Godlike knowledge of all events that happen to my characters." This narrative rationale represents a development from *The Great Gatsby*—also influenced by Joseph Conrad—for Cecelia was to be permitted greater flexibility than Nick Carraway, who witnesses or provides a source for every scene except Gatsby's murder. At the beginning of her account of Stahr at the studio, Cecelia explains: "It is drawn partly from a paper I wrote in college

An early schedule for Stahr's working day; the circled numbers correspond to episodes on the fourth outline. Prince Agge is not mentioned.

on 'A Producer's Day' and partly from my imagination. More often I have blocked in the ordinary events myself, while the stranger ones are true" (see p. 28). She functions inconsistently as a narrator in the drafts. At points she stipulates sources for scenes she did not witness ("Wylie White told me a lot," p. 67); but much of her narrative relates events that she could not have observed—notably the love scenes between Stahr and Kathleen. Cecelia's statement at the opening of Episode 17—"I knew nothing about this"— provides a transition; but it puzzles the attentive reader who wonders about her source. Fitzgerald found it necessary to remind the reader—or himself—when the point of view shifted, as in two sentences that have been cited by critics: "This is Cecelia taking up the narrative in person" (p. 77) and "This is Cecelia taking up the story" (p. 99). These signals also serve as reminders that the latest drafts are works in progress. Fitzgerald had not solved the problems of employing Cecelia as an eyewitness narrator who invents what she cannot observe.

Fitzgerald's notes indicate his uncertainty about the point of view, for he mentions that Cecelia tells the story to "our listener, our recorder, our reader" and to "the recorder or reader." The term "recorder" may indicate that in the planning stage Fitzgerald intended to convey the layered narrative effect of Cecelia's speaking through a recorder who assembles the material for the reader—as in the sanitarium frame. In planning the plane crash Fitzgerald noted: "Here I can make the best transition by an opening paragraph in which I tell the reader that Cecelia's story ends here and that what is now told was a situation discovered by the writer himself and pieced together from what he learned in a small town in Oklahoma, from a municipal judge" (see p. lxii). This reference to "the writer himself" possibly indicates the sanitarium patient who reports Cecelia's story in the discarded frame—not Fitzgerald.

Fitzgerald's authorial voice was an identifying quality of his prose. However, in the drafts of *The Love of the Last Tycoon* there are two voices that are not adequately differentiated: Cecelia and an omniscient author. Perkins recognized the problem in the work in progress but believed that "Scott would have found some way to obviate this difficulty" (see p. lxx). One of Fitzgerald's working notes indicates that he expected to retain the point-of-view inconsistencies but mollify their effect by means of style: "Cecelia does not tell the story though I write it as if she does whenever I can get the effect of looking out" (see p. 153).

By the end of the draft episodes Fitzgerald had completed the first phase of the love plot with Kathleen's marriage in Episode 16. In Episode 17 he had started developing Stahr's struggle to retain control of the studio in his encounter with Brimmer: Stahr is opposed by both capital and labor. The rest of the novel would link the love and tycoon plots, as the renewal of Stahr's affair with Kathleen provides Brady with a weapon.

4. THE UNWRITTEN EPISODES: 18–30

Evidence bearing on Fitzgerald's ideas about the unwritten episodes is provided by memos that Sheilah Graham and Frances Kroll prepared for Edmund Wilson.

Graham to Wilson, 6 March 1941:

If Scribner's publish the unfinished manuscript, it should be trimmed a little, don't you think? There are some parts—particularly parts in the Producer's Day that Scott was going to cut down. The manuscript is 37,000 words now, of which Scott would have cut about 6 or 7,000 words. As I wrote to Max Perkins, I could perhaps help on this in pointing out just where he had planned the cuts. Or is it better for someone who doesn't know Hollywood at all—someone who would only know what was interesting from an outsider's point of view to do that.

This is how it was going to end:

Brady was out to ruin Stahr in the same way that at one time, and perhaps all the time, L. B. Mayer was out to wrest control of Metro from and/or to ruin Irving Thalberg. Stahr was almost kicked out and decided to remove Brady. He resorted to Brady's own gangster methods—he was going to have him murdered.

On a 'plane flying back to Hollywood Stahr decides not to go through with the murder, which has already been planned and which other people are doing for him—if he did, he would be as bad as the Brady crowd. So at the next airplane stop he plans a cancellation of orders. I imagine the murder was to take place within a few hours. Before the next stop, however, the 'plane crashes, and Stahr is killed. Which left the murder to go through.

I think the final scene of all was to have been Stahr's funeral. And Scott was going to use an actual incident that happened at Thalberg's funeral. Harry Carey, a well-known actor in the old silents and popular in the early talkies, had been unable to get a job in pictures for several years before Thalberg died. He did not know Thalberg and was surprised to receive an invitation to act as pallbearer at his funeral. It was considered a great honor and only the most important and most intimate of Thalberg's friends (all of them important) were asked to be pallbearers. Harry Carey—slightly dazed, accepted and big-shots at the funeral were amazed when they saw Carey, presuming he had an inside track of some sort with Thalberg, and as a direct result he was deluged with picture offers and has been working ever since. The invitation was a mistake. It was meant for someone else, whom Scott told me about but whose name I have forgotten.*

Scott was going to have at the funeral all the Hollywood hypocrites assembled in full force. I had told him of the Marx Brothers sobbing their eyes out on the day Thalberg died—always making sure they were within crying distance of the 'right' people. Scott was going to have Stahr's spirit say, "Trash!"

The English girl was to remain an outsider in Hollywood—I think one of Scott's notes has that she would never get inside a studio (although that is where Stahr first saw her on that idol floating down with the flood). Cecelia, the narrator, is writing her story in a sanitarium for T.B.'s, and this, of course, would be revealed at the end.

At the point where Scott left off things were to go badly for Stahr in business and love. Many things, although in the plan, would have been changed in the same way that he deviated within the structure of the plot on what he had already written and the plan. In the plan he had the American man the English girl married, a technician or something in the studio. But I think he was going to change that—make him more powerful, put him in the position of damaging Stahr.

---

* One of Fitzgerald's notes reads: "Harry Cary gets Cary Wilson's invite. A new career." Both Harry Carey and writer Carey Wilson were pallbearers at Thalberg's funeral. The widely reported anecdote about the mistake is disputed in Thomas's *Thalberg*. Editor.

I am coming to New York again for a week at the beginning of May. Perhaps by that time something will have been decided about the manuscript. If some or all of it is published, Scott's dying won't be quite so awful. He worked hard and desperately and hopefully on the book, and it would be terribly sad if it were lost.[48]

Graham and Kroll read the draft of Wilson's synopsis that was published in *The Last Tycoon.* Both responded on 11 June 1941.

Frances Kroll:

I've read and reread your synopsis. I think you've developed a wonderfully clear plot line, considering the mass of notes you had to wade through. However, I do hope you will not consider me audacious if I make a criticism. Believe me, I only venture to do this because STAHR so completely filled those last months. I feel that after reading the book, to plunge into several pages of outline will not carry through to the end any emotional contact with STAHR. Of course, I realize that the purpose of the synopsis is to give the reader an idea of the way the novel might have continued, but I strongly felt the need of a little padding of Stahr even in a synopsis. The story of Hollywood is not as important as the conception of Stahr, the man.

Although Scott definitely told me he did not want to make Stahr a hero in the conventional sense of the word and did not want to justify Stahr's manner of thinking, he did want to present it thoroughly and show the cause of Stahr's reactions. Stahr truly believed that because he quickly climbed the ladder from office boy to executive that all other people had the same chance for success—that the day of individual success was still flourishing. I believe that is why Scott satirically considered the alternative title for the book "The Last of the Tycoons." Despite Stahr's genius and artistry he did not "come along" politically.

He believed in infinite loyalty—if you gave people a chance they should play along with you no matter what opposition they might have to your tactics. That was why he quarreled with Wylie White, whom he had repeatedly given a chance despite White's pranks and drunken habits and who turned after the pay cut even though Stahr had not instigated this cut.

I think, too, it should be emphasized how badly Stahr felt about the pay cut. Brady took advantage of Stahr's absence from the studio to call a meeting of the writers. With a tearful speech he told them that he and other executives would take a cut if the writers consented to take one. If they did, it would not be necessary to reduce the salaries of the stenographers and other low salaried employees. The writers agreed to take the cut and Brady about-faced and slashed the stenographers' salary to a new low anyhow. These are tactics which Stahr's sense of fair play would never have allowed. You mention something about Stahr's change in status as a producer. Unless this is specified in the notes, I don't think this is so. From what I remember of our discussions, Stahr, inherently the artist, was to make one artistic flop—the kind of picture that would not be a movie "box office hit" but one that would be an artistic achievement. It was to be a picture in good taste and perhaps filled with all the ideas Stahr, the artist has always wanted to see realized on the screen, but which Stahr, the Hollywood producer could not very well make because such a film would not be money-making. It was to be a picture he knew from the start would "lose a couple of million" but which he nevertheless makes to satisfy himself despite opposition from other studio financial heads. (This, I believe, was to be the picture followed in the other "day at the studio).

Forgive me for running on like this, but I truly think a few colorful background facts will make STAHR more memorable even though so much of the novel has to peter out in synopsis form.

If my suggestion has no merit, please just forget it, and if you think it might help, I know your expert critical hand will simmer this letter down to a few sentences rightly inserted.

Many thanks for letting me see the synopsis and if I can be of further help do let me know. With very best wishes.

P.S. I believe Kathleen and Cecelia were to have a scene, a rather friendly one, after Stahr's death, although just how or where I do not know. Is it specified anywhere?

About the ending—the airplane sequence was not definitely set as an epilogue, but was as probable as any other. I believe it was in the original outline of the novel submitted to Mr. Perkins. Are you going to use it at all?[49]

Sheilah Graham:

Max Perkins sent your notes on how the story ends.

Mark # 1. What about the name Smith? That's Kathleen's name—isn't it?* And it is also the name of her future husband—W. Bronson Smith. At first, as you know by the notes, Kathleen was to have been a married woman when she met Stahr. Now she is unmarried when they meet, but still called Smith. Is it confusing to have Kathleen have the same surname as the man she is going to marry? Or doesn't it matter? It probably doesn't.

Mark # 2. You say, "A wage cut threatened at *Universal*." This is the name of a studio in Hollywood, and Scott was anxious to avoid the impression of any particular studio as the place of his story. I don't remember his using the word "Universal" in his story. It might be better in your notes to say "Stahr's Studio" or something like that.

Mark # 3. Was it clear that Stahr and Brady were trying to *blackmail* each other? I thought the purpose of wire-tapping was for each to get the goods on the other and that Brady would use it to kick Stahr out of the studio. But Stahr would only use his information to retain his command of studio production. Or is that blackmail anyway?

Mark # 4. Did Brady decide to bump Stahr off? Is that in the notes? I didn't know that. I thought Scott had just meant that Brady was a killer when he decided that Stahr should consider using Brady's own weapon—murder—to get his way. On the separate page—which I found a few days ago, there is reference to Brady's past "the affair of the girl's husband murdered." This, I imagine, refers to the philandering of Brady with a woman whose husband he had murdered. Does it sound confused and too melodramatic that Brady should decide to murder Stahr, then Stahr decide to murder Brady—unless, of course, you have notes to this effect—and you indicate this on page 171. through Pete Zavras? Stahr, of course, was going to have Brady murdered, until he decided in the plane against using Brady's own despicable methods and was going to stop it but the plane crashes.

Mark # 5. I can't quite remember this, but I thought Cecilia went to see her father in his office to try to get a job for that broken-down actress who knew Kathleen—not for Johnny Swanson—or did she try for both?

And finally Scott did not altogether have that feeling of hopelessness about the movies as an instrument for reflecting American life and ideals. True, Stahr and Thalberg died—Thalberg because of over-working and straining against enormous odds—and Fleishacker is sort of left in control. But I know for a fact that Scott felt that the day would come when another great figure—another Thalberg or Griffith—would succeed in again doing something fine with the movie medium. Scott, himself, wanted to be a movie director because of what he thought could be done.[50]

* Kathleen's last name is Moore. Her friend is named Edna Smith. Editor.

The Love of the Last Tycoon: A Western involved a process of discovery through composition. Kroll has explained that the outline was not final; it was a guide for Fitzgerald so that he could interrupt work on the novel for screenwriting assignments.[51] He expected to reconcile the plot inconsistencies in the course of drafting the unwritten episodes. It is therefore uncertain how Episodes 18–30 would have developed. Kroll believes that Fitzgerald had not decided about the conclusion when he died. The synopsis that Fitzgerald sent Littauer in September 1939 describes Stahr's death in a plane crash and the looting of the wreckage, followed by the "finale" in Hollywood. There is no mention of Stahr's funeral at this early stage.

The decisions about the content of the thirteen unwritten episodes would have been influenced by length or proportion considerations. Fitzgerald had projected a short, *Gatsby*-length novel of about 50,000 words; but Episodes 1–17 required about 44,000 words in draft. Assuming that he wanted to retain most of the material in 1–17, it would have been necessary for him either to omit some of the unwritten episodes or to expand the novel to a length of 70,000 words or more.

A week before his death Fitzgerald prepared a schedule for writing Episodes 17–30 in a month, to complete the novel in an additional 28,000 words:

New Schedule from Dec. 14–Jan. 11th inc.
(Have done 36,000 words)
Conception one day
Plan   "   "
Write four days at 1750 a day
Notes, letters + rest one day.

This should finish me up at 7000 words a week. (The assumption is that the episodes average 1750—they must be made to do so. In the planning try to divide the work into seven thousand word units, roughly:
The storm breaks to the Meeting of Four
Wylie White to Lieing low
Last Fling to the Airport
The Plane to the Funeral (short one)

These four "units" combine and perhaps condense the unwritten episodes of the chapters designated F–I (Episodes 17–30) in the latest outline. Some of the material to be covered in the unwritten episodes can be identified from Fitzgerald's notes. The following commentary on Episodes 18–30 is keyed to the first column of Fitzgerald's latest outline (see pp. xlvi–xlvii).

18. The Cummerbund-market— / (The theatre with Benchley) / August 10th

Fitzgerald was amused by Graham's report that she had rejected a suitor because he wore a red cummerbund; but the application of the anecdote to this episode remains a mystery.[52] The writer and movie actor Robert Benchley was Fitzgerald's friend.

19. The four meet, like Hop and Lefty. / Renewal. Palomar

Hop was the husband of Beatrice Dance, with whom Fitzgerald had been romantically involved in North Carolina in 1936. Lefty was Lefty Flynn, a former football star and cowboy actor married to Norah Langhorne; Fitzgerald and the Flynns were friends in North Carolina. "Renewal" probably refers to the resumption of Stahr's affair with Kathleen. The Palomar Ballroom was in Los Angeles.

20. Wylie White in Office / August 28th–Sept. 14th.

This episode was probably going to cover an argument between Stahr and White about Stahr's opposition to the Writers Guild— perhaps a revision of material cut from an early draft of the second chapter (see Episode 22 below).

G. 21. Sick in Washington. To quit?

Fitzgerald's notes for the opening of the seventh chapter indicate that Stahr was to make a trip to Washington, but the purpose of the trip is not provided (see Fitzgerald's working note on p. 180).

22. Brady and Stahr—double blackmail. / Quarrel with Wylie.

Brady was probably going to attempt to force Stahr out of the studio by threatening to reveal Stahr's affair with Kathleen, and Stahr would retaliate by using information about Brady's complicity in the murder of his mistress's husband (see p. lvii). The note on a case involving a 1917 roadhouse raid in which comedian Fatty Arbuckle and several movie executives were charged with indecent behavior indicates that Fitzgerald also considered adapting this material as the basis for Stahr's counter-blackmail against Brady. This note (see pp. 139 and 194) suggests that Schwartze was to have been Stahr's source, and Graham's 11 January 1941 memo to Perkins explains that Fitzgerald was undecided about Schwartze's role (see p. lxix). The Wylie White quarrel may refer to his argument with Stahr about the Guild (Episode 20) or possibly to a quarrel between White and Cecelia.

23. Throws over Cecelia who tells her / father. Stops making pictures. / A
    story conference—rushes and / sets. Lies low after Cut.

Stahr breaks off with Cecelia, and she apparently tells Brady something that he can use against Stahr. After Brady institutes the salary cut that Stahr has opposed, Stahr stops working. Here Fitzgerald planned to show how the studio operated without Stahr—in contrast to the account of his day in Episodes 7–11.

24. Last fling with Kathleen. Old / stars in heat wave at Encino.

Graham suggested that this episode was to be partly based on the heat wave at the time Fitzgerald was living at "Belly Acres" in Encino.[53]

H 25. Brady gets to Smith. Fleishacker / and Cecelia. (S.G.& K) / Sept.
      15–30th

For the opening of the eighth chapter Brady was to persuade Kathleen's husband, Smith, to act against Stahr. Apparently Cecelia becomes involved with Mort Flieshacker, the company lawyer who opposes Stahr. The parenthesis indicates that Fitzgerald planned to base Kathleen's behavior in this episode on Graham.

26. Stahr hears plan. Camera man O.K. / Stops it—very sick.

Pete Zavras, the cameraman who is indebted to Stahr (see Episode 7), was to assist him in counteracting the Brady–Smith plot. On p. 61 Zavras tells Stahr, "If you want anybody's throat cut anytime day or night . . . my number is in the book." Fitzgerald's notes indicate that at one stage he had planned a double-murder plot: Brady and Stahr arrange to have each other killed, and Stahr flies east to establish an alibi. Stahr's health is deteriorating. The notes on p. 145 also suggest that—probably in the early planning stage—Fitzgerald considered giving Robinson, the studio troubleshooter who was introduced in the flood scene, a key role in the murder plot because he is in love with Kathleen. Since Robinson's character is not developed in the written episodes, it appears that Fitzgerald had reconsidered Robinson's role. Graham recalled telling Wilson that Fitzgerald "might eliminate Robinson altogether."[54] Fitzgerald's plans for the murder material are not clear. The latest outline describes the subject of Chapter H as "(The Murderers)"; but the plot was still evolving.

27. Resolve problem. Thalia at airport. / Cecelia to college; Thalia at / airport. S.G.

It cannot be determined which problem was to be resolved in this episode. At 7,000 words the eighth chapter would have been the longest in the novel, and the outline calls for considerable plot action. (The events in outline Chapter H occur between 15 and 30 September, but that is rather late for Cecelia to be returning to college.)

I 28. The Plane falls. Fortaste of the / future in Flieshacker / Sept 30th–Oct.

Fitzgerald was undecided about having the plane wreckage looted by the children in the last chapter. This action was described in the synopsis sent to Littauer, but it is not stipulated in the outline. Fitzgerald explicated the thematic function of the looting material in a working note:

It is important that I begin this chapter with a delicate transition because I am not going to describe the Fall of the Plane but simply give a last picture of Stahr as the plane takes off and describe very briefly in the airport the people who are on board. The plane, therefore, has left for New York and when the reader turns to Chapter X, I must be sure that he isn't confused by the sudden change in scene and situation. Here I can make the best transition by an opening paragraph in which I tell the reader that Cecelia's story ends here and that what is now told was a situation discovered by the writer himself and pieced together from what he learned in a small town in Oklahoma, from a municipal judge. That the incidents occurred one month after the plane fell and plunged Stahr and all its occupants into a white darkness. Tell how the snow hid the wreck and that inspite of searching parties that the plane was considered lost and that will resume the narrative—that a curtain first went up during an early thaw the following March. (I have to go over all the chapters and get the time element to shape up so that Stahr's second trip to New York, the one on which he is killed, takes place when the first snow has fallen on the Rockies.* I want this plane to be like that plane that was lost for fully two months before they found the plane and the survivors). Consider carefully whether if possible by some technical trick, it might not be advisable to conceal from the reader that the plane fell until the moment when the children find it. The problem is that the reader must not turn to Chapter X and be confused, but on the other hand, the dramatic effect, even if the reader felt lost for a few minutes, might be more effective if he did not find at the beginning of the chapter that the plane fell. In fact, almost certainly that is the way to handle it and I must find a method of handling it in that fashion. There must be an intervening paragraph to begin Chapter X which will reassure the reader that he is following the same story, but it can be evasive and confine itself to leading the reader astray thinking that the paragraph is merely to explain that Cecelia is not telling this next part of the story without telling the reader that the plane ran into a mountain top and disappeared from human knowledge for several months.

When I have given the reader some sense of the transition and prepared him for a change in scene and situation, break the narrative with a space or so and begin the following story. That a group of children are starting off

---

* The Rocky Mountains are not in Oklahoma. Fitzgerald's reference below to "that particular atmosphere of Oklahoma when the long winter breaks" suggests that he had another locale in mind. Editor.

on a hike. That there is an early spring thaw in this mountain state. Pick out of the group of children three who we will call Jim, Frances and Dan. That atmosphere is that particular atmosphere of Oklahoma when the long winter breaks. The atmosphere must be an all cold climate where the winter breaks very suddenly with almost a violence—the snow seems to part as if very unwillingly in great convulsive movements like the break-up of an ice flow. There's a bright sun. The three children get separated from the teacher or scoutmaster or whoever is in charge of the expedition and the girl, Frances, comes upon a part of the engine and fly-wheel of a broken airplane. She has no idea what it is. She is rather puzzled by it and at the moment is engaged rather in a flirtation with both Jim and Dan. However, she is an intelligent child of 13 or 14 and while she doesn't identify it as part of an airplane she knows it is an odd piece of machinery to be found in the mountains. First she thinks it is the remains of some particular mining machinery. She calls Dan and then Jim and they forget whatever small juvenile intrigue they were embarking on in their discovery of other debris from the fall of the plane. Their first general instinct is to call the other members of the party because Jim who is the smartest of the children (both the boys ages about 15) recognizes that it is a fallen plane—though he doesn't connect it with the plane that disappeared the previous November) when Frances comes upon a purse and an open traveling case which belonged to the Lola Lane* actress. It contains the things that to her present undreamt of luxuries. In it there's a jewel box. It has been unharmed—it has fallen through the branches of a tree. There are flasks of perfume that would never appear in the town where she lives, perhaps a negligee or anything I can think of that an actress might be carrying which was absolutely the last word in film elegance. She is utterly fascinated.

Simultaneously Jim has found Stahr's briefcase. A briefcase is what he has always wanted and Stahr's briefcase is an excellent piece of leather and some other traveling appurtenances of Stahr's. Things that are notably possessions of wealthy men. I have no special ideas at present, but think what a very wealthy, well-equipped man might be liable to have with him on such an expedition and then Dan makes the suggestion of "Why do we have to tell about this? We can all come up here later and there is probably a lot more of this stuff here and there's probably money and everything." These people are dead—they will never need it again, then we can say about the plane or let other people find it. Nobody will know we have been up here."

* Lola Lane (1909–81) had leading roles in the movies during the Thirties. Editor.

Dan bears, in some form of speech, a faint resemblance to Bradogue. This must be subtly done and not look too much like a parable or moral lesson, still the impression must be conveyed, but be careful to convey it once and rub it in. If the reader misses it, let it go—don't repeat. Show Frances as malleable and amoral in the situation, but show a definite doubt on Jim's part, even from the first, as to whether this is fair dealing even towards the dead. Close this episode with the children rejoining the party.

Several weeks later the children have now made several trips to the mountain and have rifled the place of everything that is of any value. Dan is especially proud of his find which includes some rather disreputable possessions of Ronciman.* Frances is worried and definitely afraid and tending to side with Jim who is now in an absolutely wretched mood about the whole affair. He knows that searching parties have been on a neighboring mountain—that the plane has been traced and that with the full flowering of spring the secret will come out and that each trip up, he feels that the danger is more and more. However, let that be Frances' feeling because Jim has, by this time, read the contents of Stahr's briefcase and late at night, taking it from the woodshed where he has concealed it has gotten an admiration for the man. Naturally, by the time of this episode all three children are aware of what plane it was and who was in it and whose possessions they have.

One day also they have found the bodies, though I do not want to go into this scene in any gruesome manner, of the six or seven victims still half concealed by the snow. In any case, something in one of Stahr's letters that Jim reads late at night decides him to go to Judge——and tell the whole story which he does against the threats of Dan who is bigger than he is and could lick him physically. We leave the children there with the idea that they are in good hands, that they are not going to be punished, that having made full restoration and the fact that, after all they could plead in court that they did not know anything more about the situation than "finder's keeper's". There will be no punishment of any kind for any of the three children. Give the impression that Jim is all right—that Frances is faintly corrupted and may possibly go off in a year or so in search of adventure and may turn into anything from a gold digger to a prostitute and that Dan has been completely corrupted and will spend the rest of his life looking for a chance to get something for nothing.

I cannot be too careful not to rub this in or give it the substance or feeling of a moral tale. I should very pointedly that that Jim is all right and end

---

* One of the passengers, a shady movie producer. Editor.

perhaps with Frances and let the readers hope that Frances is going to be all right and then take that hope away by showing the last glimpse of Frances with that lingering conviction that luxury is over the next valley, therefore giving a bitter and acrid finish to the incident to take away any possible sentimental and moral stuff that may have crept into it. Certainly end the incident with Frances.

The name *Bradogue* and references to Chapter X confirm that this was an early memo-note.

29. Outside the studio. S.G.

Fitzgerald planned to leave the reader with a final view of Kathleen outside the studio, developing the irony that except for their first meeting, she has never seen the great organization Stahr built. There is an early note for this episode:

The epilogue can model itself quite fairly on the last part of Gatsby. We go back to Cecelia as a narrator and have her tell it with the emphasis on herself so that what she reveals about what happened to her father, to the company, to Thalia seems to be revealed as if she was now a little weary of the story, and told all she knew about it and was returning to her own affairs. In it she might discuss whom she married and try to find an equivalent of that nice point in Gatsby where the narrator erases the dirty word that the boy has scrawled in chalk against the doorstep. I think it might be touching if she met Thalia in this episode and was going to take her through the studio and found that she couldn't do it because she was called East so that the reader knows that Thalia won't ever see the studios and I think that I'll leave Thalia's life in the air, her character unimpaired, deepened without quite the pettiness in the end of Gatsby—Thalia all in all being a fuller and richer person than she had been six months before—released from her particular material bondage to Kiki* and perhaps with a little hope embarked on some enterprise that seems to promise a future for her or with the idea that she might marry Robinson, the cutter or even a paragraph which implied that now Thalia was more attractive than she had ever been and that there was no doubt that she was going to be all right. To that extent to reassure the reader and not leave a bitter taste in the reader's mouth about Thalia.

* Kiki was the widow of Kathleen's lover in an early version of the plot. Editor.

And I think I'll do my own method of ending probably on a high note about Stahr but that will solve itself in the writing. And as toward the end I'll tend to go into a certain cadence prose.[55]

30. Johnny Swanson at funeral

The account of Stahr's funeral was to develop a final Hollywood irony: Johnny Swanson, the has-been cowboy actor mentioned by Cecelia on p. 21, is mistakenly asked to be a pallbearer; consequently, his career is revived (see Graham's memo to Wilson, p. liv). Monroe Stahr is a star-maker even in his coffin.

There are structural problems resulting from what were in effect two endings. If, for example, the bodies were not found for months, when does Stahr's funeral take place? The most serious unresolved story element is the effect on Cecelia of the events she relates. Fitzgerald had originally planned to have her ruined by her complicity in the betrayal of Stahr; see the canceled description of the terminally ill Cecelia telling her story in a tuberculosis sanitarium ("Appendix 1: The Sanitarium Frame"). However, the latest outline sends Cecelia back to college in Episode 27, after which she is not mentioned again.

Given Fitzgerald's custom of constructing a work of fiction in the process of writing and his habit of finishing a novel through layers of revision or rewriting, it is naive to think that the unwritten episodes—particularly those for the last chapter—were fixed in his mind. Moreover, Fitzgerald was trying to complete a working draft by January 1941 before his money ran out. This draft would have presumably attracted the advance he needed to progress from working drafts to setting copy.

5. PUBLICATION AND RECEPTION

Maxwell Perkins's decision to salvage the work in progress on *The Love of the Last Tycoon: A Western* involved personal as well as literary considerations. The projected publication was intended as a memorial to Fitzgerald and a means of earning money for his estate.

(Fitzgerald's life insurance was worth less than $35,000, and his last Scribners royalty check in 1940 was for $13.13.)

Before either of them had read the material, Edmund Wilson wrote to Perkins on 2 January 1941: "I saw Sheila Graham the other day and am going to see her again. I think that it will probably turn out that you ought to get out a volume containing the unfinished novel, some letters and perhaps selections from note-books and other things."[56] Although Wilson had no formal connection with Scribners, he had been Fitzgerald's friend since their Princeton days, and he was an influential literary critic and social commentator.

Graham dispatched the work in progress to Perkins with her cover letter on 11 January 1941:

I have today sent air mail and registered a copy of Scott's unfinished novel. It is hard to know where to begin talking about it. There are masses and masses of notes, which you will probably want to see as well; but Scott's secretary has all these, and she only has one copy of them. When and if you want to see them, I will have her make copies if you think it necessary.

I don't know whether you knew that the hero of Scott's book was suggested strongly by Irving Thalberg, who died in the summer of 1936. And I am enclosing a copy of a letter which Scott had penciled with the probable intention of writing it to his wife, Norma Shearer, when he had completed the novel. We also found a fragment addressed to himself, which is so very sad.* I thought you would like to see it now.

With the book you will find a large sheet of paper on which, right at the beginning, he wrote down his plan for the book. He had changed some of it, of course, but not basically. As you see at the bottom, he was writing the book for two people—for Seventeen as symbolized by Scottie, and for Edmund Wilson at forty-five. His idea was to interest both generations.

I don't know whether Scott had discussed titles with you. At first for quite a while, he was going to call it STAHR—which is the name of the book's hero. But about three weeks before he died, he said to me, with a grin—"What do you think of this title?—THE LOVE OF THE LAST TYCOON." My first reaction was "I'm not sure." And he wasn't sure either. But he was going to sit on it, and then submit it to you and see what you thought. In his papers he had written it down as follows:

---

* Unidentified. Editor.

THE LOVE OF THE LAST TYCOON

A Western

By F. Scott Fitzgerald

The title has grown on me quite a bit. He wanted it to sound like a movie title and completely disguise the tragi-heroic content of the book.

When you have finished reading it and you want to know how it was going to end, I will get together again with his secretary, and we can put together his latest ideas for the rest of the book. I am aching to know what you think of it. As you know, he would not let me read it—until he had polished the first draft. But he read from day to day the words he had written, and it seemed pretty good then; but not nearly as good as I found it when I actually did read it, which I have just done. *Don't forget this was the first draft.*

Here are some odd notes that you might want to know. In the early part of the book he mentions 'Cecelia' as having gone to Smith College. Later he changed it to Bennington, and it was the latter that he wanted.

The time of the book's action was most important to Scott. I don't know whether this appears in his notes, but he wanted it to be as of five years ago. He places the period with the songs of 1934–5 and by the mention of a few people who were alive or prominent at that time. When I asked him why he had put the novel back a little in the past, he said it would have been quite a different story if he had written of Hollywood today—and that with the death of Thalberg, the last of the Princes had departed. There weren't many others, but I think he regarded D. W. Griffith as one.

You will find he mentions the near-future death of 'Stahr' in two places. He was going to eliminate one of the references when he had completed the first draft. He wanted it to be where it would have most shock effect.

In Episode # 8, page 5.—he substituted the name 'Brady' for 'Bradogue.' And when I told him that I thought Bradogue was a much better name, suggesting something rather harsh and ruthless, he said that was why he changed it. As he went on writing the novel, he apparently decided that Bradogue should not be quite the horror he had intended him to be at the beginning.

The longest episode in the book deals with Stahr's Day. He was not altogether satisfied with what he had done on this, and was going to work it over and possibly cut and change it a great deal.

In Episode #8 and #9—there is a repetition of his description of 'Rose Meloney.' He intended cutting it out from Episode #9.

He was far from satisfied with all of Episode #11, and was going to work quite a bit on that too.

In Episode 16—First Part—Page 3, he wanted the word turkey spelt 'tuhkey'—as it is typed.

About 'Schwartze' in the first episode of the book. Scott told me he would either have to cut him out completely or find some way of bringing him into the rest of the book. . . . On page 19 in the first part, where he describes 'Stahr' as being the head of his gang when he was a boy, a similar idea appears in Budd Schulberg's book,* which is coming out in a couple of months, and Scott was going to eliminate this.

There may be quite a few errors on the movie production stuff, but he was going to check all this very thoroughly before sending the book to you.

And that is all. Except here's a copy of the plan he had for Stahr's Day.†

P. S. I have initialed the few pencil marks I have done on the copy. Everything else is in Scott's handwriting—with the exception of the word 'English' for British. I was his technical adviser on the English stuff and would have told him to make that change.[57]

On 28 January Perkins informed Wilson:

Now as to Scott's novel, it would break your heart to read it and see what beautiful and illuminating things there are in it—Scott's old magical sentences and scenes—and realize that it is so unfinished. I am still puzzling over it though, for there are ways in which the great part of it could actually be published if it would be fair to Scott. It would require some rearrangement, and it would not be well proportioned, and would chiefly tell a secondary story, a love episode in the life of the hero. It might be fair to do this perhaps if what had been done were explained.– And it might be fairer to do it if it were done at all in a collection which would include "The Great Gatsby" etc. I am still thinking about it, but I would be glad to show you the manuscript any time you want. It is a revelation too of Hollywood ways of life and work such as I have never seen. I'll write you more about it later. Notes by Scott showed that even some of the most finished parts, especially the first chapter, which is very fine indeed, were not the way he wanted them, and I don't know whether we ought to do anything with it at all.

---

* *What Makes Sammy Run?* Editor.
† Probably the schedule facsimiled on p. li. Editor.

Perkins's uncertainty about the proper presentation of the work in progress prompted him to consider having another writer complete the novel. John O'Hara and Budd Schulberg were tentatively approached to undertake a collaboration; both declined because they felt that it was impossible.[58] Perkins seems to have considered seeking Hemingway's help—a notion that Zelda Fitzgerald, who had not read the drafts, opposed: "May I suggest that rather than bringing into play another forceful talent of other inspiration it might be felicitous to enlist a pen such as that of Gilbert Seldes. . . ." This letter includes her explication of Fitzgerald's attitude toward the hero: "The book was a story of Irving Thalberg, as Scott may have told you. Those minds which so nearly control the direction of public sentiment engaged Scott deeply. He wanted to render tangible the indominatable constancy of purpose and the driving necessity to achievement and the capacity for judicious and dextrous juggling of majesterous forces that distinguished such men from others."[59] Perkins wrote to her on 29 January explaining his uncertainty about publishing the work in progress:

I am very much puzzled about Scott's book. It was about two-thirds finished, but those two-thirds were not in a final draft. It has a magnificent first chapter, but even that did not suit Scott, as he indicated by a note in which he told himself to rewrite it to the proper mood. As in "The Great Gatsby", there is a narrator who is also a very important character in the plot,– but as the manuscript stands, a good deal of it seems to be told directly, and not as seen or heard by his "heroine" Celia. Scott would have found some way to obviate this difficulty. The whole narrative is illuminated with those magical sentences and phrases and paragraphs that only Scott could write. Many brilliant things are said in it, revealing ones. And about this new and strange kind of life of movie people, transcontinental flights, and all that. About writers too. And Stahr, the protagonist, comes out of it very remarkably a person.

But the book is not finished, and what is complete is not the way Scott would have wanted it to be in the end. I don't think anybody ought to attempt to write an ending, or even could do it. I do intend to consult Gilbert Seldes and Bunny Wilson about it. . . . I have been turning the whole thing over in my mind, and rather lean to the idea of making some selection from Scott's stories to include "The Great Gatsby". If this were done, with an introduction perhaps by Bunny Wilson, and his very best stories were included, we might find some editorial machinery for explaining this last manuscript, and adding it or some large part of it. The first chapter could easily stand alone with a slight explanation. But it is all a puzzle to me at present, and I'll write you as soon as we can formulate a real plan.[60]

On 16 February, after reading the work in progress, Wilson wrote Perkins proposing a volume that would include the Hollywood novel, *The Great Gatsby,* "The Crack-Up," possibly Fitzgerald's notebooks and his letters to his daughter, and the memorial articles that were appearing in the *New Republic.* This plan combines the 1941 *The Last Tycoon* volume and Wilson's *Crack-Up* collection published by New Directions in 1945. Wilson advised that the work in progress should be printed

... just as it is, except for the few changes he has indicated. There should be a note explaining what he meant to do with the story – which I can't make out from his plan. But Shiela Grahame must know. I will edit the MS [i.e., typescripts] myself, if you want me to. There are spots where it ought to be compared with the written copy [holograph drafts]. The plan probably ought to be reproduced, too: it shows how carefully he was working it out, and it gives a good idea of the kind of effects he was aiming at.

Perkins wrote in the margin of Wilson's letter: "The living artist rather than the dead man."

Perkins responded on 24 February 1941 indicating his resistance to Wilson's proposal, which Perkins felt would present the wrong impression of Fitzgerald:

What I myself would greatly hope about Scott would be, in the first place, to put before the public writings by him which would demonstrate irresistably that he was far more important, far more the distinguished and significant writer, than the public thinks him to be;– that he vastly transcended the Jazz Age kind of writing with which they associate him.

Perkins also wanted to avoid a grab-bag volume. On 4 March he reported to the executor of Fitzgerald's estate, Judge John Biggs, Jr.:

It is a tragedy it is unfinished. It was a clear step forward. I don't say that it was better in actual writing itself, or even that it would have been, than "The Great Gatsby". But it has the same old magic that Scott got into a sentence, or a paragraph, or a phrase. It has a kind of wisdom in it, and nobody ever penetrated beneath the surface of the movie world to any such degree. It was to have been a very remarkable book. There are 56,000 words. If they were published alone, it would only be read as a curiosity, and for its literary interest, because people won't read an unfinished book. But it ought somehow to be published for the sake of Scott's name. My idea was to publish "The Great Gatsby", five or six of the best stories, and then this unfinished book in one volume. But Bunny Wilson, whom Scott so deeply trusted, wants to make a sort of miscellaneous book with those terrible cracked plate pieces from "Esquire" (I am sure Scott would not want them in a book) and perhaps some things from the letters. People won't buy a miscellaneous book like that anyhow, and apart even from the money question, from the question of reputation, we want whatever is published to be as widely read as we can make it be. I don't think Bunny takes a practical view of the matter. Then he is reluctant to write an introduction to the book—though he would write a fine one to the unfinished book as it appeared in a collection. He thinks Dos Passos ought to do it. I wish Bunny would do it because, as he said and would say, each book Scott wrote, including this last one, showed marked progress.[61]

The matter was apparently settled in a late March meeting between Perkins and Wilson, but no written stipulation of Wilson's editorial duties has been located. By April Graham had arranged to visit Wilson on Cape Cod "to go over the manuscript with him to help to arrange it for publication."[62]

Although he informed Perkins at the inception of the project that "there are spots where it [Fitzgerald's revised typescripts] ought to be compared with the written copy," Wilson's editorial procedures are unknown.[63] The Wilson/Perkins correspondence does not discuss editorial problems. Wilson assembled a 182-page typescript from the first seventeen episodes, editing in pencil on Fitzgerald's revised ribbon copies. In addition to styling the punctuation, correcting spelling, and altering names (Pedro Garcia *to* Pete Zavras), Wilson replaced words; but he did not rewrite sentences. Fitzgerald had not designated chapters on the typescripts after the first chapter (Episodes 1–3); Wilson combined Episodes 4–17 into chapters according to the outline. He inserted a discarded Fitzgerald scene to bridge Episodes 9 and 10 and placed Stahr's visit to director Red Ridingwood's set after Episode 10 (see pp. xlix above). Wilson's emendations were not identified in the 1941 edition or any subsequent edition (see "Wilson's Alterations in the Latest Typescripts").

On 24 May 1941 Wilson sent Perkins his foreword, his "synopsis of the unfinished part of the story," and "Scott's outline." In this letter Wilson also asked Perkins for "the whole typed MS," which he wanted to "go through." It is not clear what he meant by "the whole typed MS," but Wilson was almost certainly asking for his edited text, which had been professionally retyped to provide printer's copy—introducing the typist's alterations. Wilson acknowledged receipt of the retyped work on 9 June but again asked for the "whole of the MS" for checking. He corrected and further emended the new typescript (see "Variants in the Scribners Setting Copy and the First Printing").

Wilson sent his rewritten synopsis on 19 June and declined Perkins's proposal that he receive title-page credit as editor: "my name at the end of the foreword will indicate my part in the matter." The first galleys were ready on 21 July, and they generated a four-way discussion among Perkins, Wilson, Biggs, and Ober about possible libel problems. Biggs was troubled by the use of real names in the novel and notes, although Wilson had assured him on 5 May 1941 that there were no problems: "In regard to his introducing the names of real people into his Hollywood novel, I haven't come across anything that seems libelous. Real names have been kept carefully out of the main action, + those that are used merely serve to give the reader his bearings. They are used in just the same way that real names would be used in any novel about a special field."[64] Perkins told Biggs that Ober would read the proofs for possibly libelous matters: "though in fact I doubt if there are any."[65] Ober recommended changing the name of the character Rose Meloney because it belonged to a real person, and he warned that readers would think that the writer named Marquand referred to John P. Marquand. "Rose" was revised to "Jane," and "Marquand" became "Tarleton" in the first printing. Ober also queried retaining real names in Fitzgerald's notes and was concerned that "One of the —— Brothers" would be taken as a reference to the Warner Brothers; the long dash was replaced with "X."[66]

Wilson wrote on 8 September 1941 that "I am just today getting off the last proofs of Scott Fitzgerald's unfinished novel. . . ."[67] Since there are no surviving galleys, marked or unmarked, it is impossible to differentiate Wilson's proof alterations from those of the Scribners proofreaders. The first printing of the book introduced some seventy substantive departures from the retyped Scribners setting copy.

Wilson had undertaken to edit the volume as an act of friendship; on 13 June 1941 he advised Perkins that Scribners ought to credit $500 to Fitzgerald's account in lieu of an editorial fee "so that the family will get the benefit of it." Perkins replied on the 18th that the question of an editorial payment must take into account Fitzgerald's remaining debt to the Scribners firm. Perkins also indicated that he was omitting the Pat Hobby stories from the *Tycoon* volume—a decision Wilson protested. On 11 August Wilson informed John Biggs that "I don't see that what Scribner's does in relation to Scott's estate has anything to do with my connection with the editing of the book—which is a transaction between Scribner's and me."[68] Two days later Perkins explained to Biggs that Wilson's insistence on a $500 payment to the estate was "utterly unreasonable" because the book contract provided a generous 15 percent royalty to the Fitzgerald Estate, "and there is doubt if this book will sell the several thousand copies necessary to cover our expenses. . . . the circumstances are not favorable to it in many ways."[69] Perkins had assumed that Wilson was donating his work; otherwise the contract would have stipulated that the editorial fee was to be deducted from royalties.* There is no further mention of this fee in the extant correspondence, and the outcome is unknown. Perkins was acting for Scribners in this business matter. Privately he

---

*   The contract dated 9 June 1941, between John Biggs, Jr., and Charles Scribner's Sons, is signed by Biggs and Perkins. Wilson is not mentioned. Editor.

was generous to Fitzgerald's family, joining with Harold Ober and Gerald Murphy to pay the Vassar College tuition for Fitzgerald's daughter.

THE LAST TYCOON / AN UNFINISHED NOVEL / *BY* / F. SCOTT FITZGERALD / TOGETHER WITH / *THE GREAT GATSBY* / AND SELECTED STORIES was published by Charles Scribner's Sons on 27 October 1941 at $2.75. The stories were "May Day," "The Diamond as Big as the Ritz," "The Rich Boy," "Absolution," and "Crazy Sunday." The volume included Wilson's 1,000-word foreword, his 2,200-word "synopsis of the rest of the story," and thirty pages of edited selections from Fitzgerald's notes. The size of the first printing is unknown, but it was probably only 3,000 copies. A second printing was required within two months. (The Scribner Press records show that a total of 5,108 copies were bound during October–December 1941.) The abridgment of *The Last Tycoon* in the January 1942 issue of *Omnibook* magazine may indicate the extent of interest it generated. Wartime paper restrictions probably discouraged reprinting the book, and a third printing was not ordered until 1945—a year of Fitzgerald republication activity. The 1941 omnibus volume (*The Last Tycoon, The Great Gatsby,* and the stories) was reprinted by Scribners in 1947 and 1948; but the 1951 sixth printing omitted the stories. The first separate Scribners printing of *The Last Tycoon* came in 1958. The first English edition, which was the first separate publication of *The Last Tycoon,* was published by Grey Walls Press in 1949 and reprinted the same year; the size of these printings is unknown.

The 1941 reviewers of *The Last Tycoon* utilized the occasion to assess Fitzgerald's career. Most were generous to the author, endorsing Wilson's assertion in the foreword that it is "Fitzgerald's most mature piece of work" as well as "far and away the best novel we have had about Hollywood." Even the party-line *New Masses* was respectful. J. Donald Adams's laudatory front-page *New York Times Book Review* article concluded with this cautious prediction: "And I think he will be remembered in his generation."[70] John Chamberlain's little-noted *Harper's* review placed Fitzgerald in the mainstream of American social fiction: "Extravagant as Wilson is in his claims for *The Last Tycoon,* he still doesn't give Fitzgerald the right kind of credit for the creation of Stahr. This man is not only a movie man: he is the talented American business executive in any sphere. . . . almost alone among his contemporaries, Fitzgerald was curious about the main drives of American society." After examining Stahr as an American hero and citing Fitzgerald's grasp of American business civilization, Chamberlain concluded on a high note of admiration: "If only he had lived, if only his constitution had served him better, what fiction he might have done! As it is, he was the best of the lot— and I, for one, can't understand why more useful sermons haven't been preached over his grave."[71]

Despite Perkins's uncertainty about publishing the selected working notes, none of the located reviews complained about their inclusion. Poet Winfield Townley Scott praised Fitzgerald's notes in his *Providence Sunday Journal* review: ". . . here is, if not a complete course in the construction of a novel, a revelation of an artist at work—examples and illustrations so much more relevant than any conventional 'course on the novel' that any conscientious writer will find them valuable and instructive."[72] Only three of the located periodical reviews mentioned the Irving Thalberg connection; *Newsweek* stated that the novel "is more than just another Hollywood romance-with-a-key. . . . Monroe Stahr is a real creation, a fully realized character in its own right."[73]

Two responses from other writers influenced the reputation of *The Last Tycoon* and may have catalyzed the Fitzgerald revival. The most emphatic of the initial reviews was Stephen Vincent Benét's in the *Saturday Review of Literature:* "Had Fitzgerald been permitted to finish the book, I think there is no doubt that it would have added a major character and a major novel to American fiction. As it is, 'The Last Tycoon' is a great deal more than a fragment. It shows the full powers of its author, at their height and at their best." Benét closed with his celebrated appraisal of the entire volume: "You can take off your hats now, gentlemen, and I think perhaps you had better. This is not a legend, this is a reputation— and, seen in perspective, it may well be one of the most secure reputations of our time."[74]

A tardy 1942 review by James Thurber in the *New Republic*

stated that Fitzgerald was the only writer who could have written convincingly and satisfyingly about Hollywood. Thurber noted that "no book published here in a long time has created more discussion and argument among writers and lovers of writing than 'The Last Tycoon.' "[75] These arguments must have been conducted orally, for there is no printed evidence of such controversy. Thurber and Benét were not particular friends of Fitzgerald and were not expressing personal loss.

A third influential writer's response was by a friend—though not a close one. John Dos Passos's 1945 *Crack-Up* essay on Fitzgerald expressed high admiration for *The Last Tycoon* as a marker in American literature:

Even as it stands I have an idea that it will turn out to be one of those literary fragments that from time to time appear in the stream of culture and profoundly influence the course of future events. His unique achievement, in these beginnings of a great novel, is that here for the first time he has managed to establish that unshakable moral attitude towards the world we live in and towards its temporary standards that is the basic essential of any powerful work of the imagination. A firmly anchored ethical standard is something that American writing has been struggling towards for half a century.

Serious writers have always understood the force—not just the dazzle—of Fitzgerald's style. Dos Passos concluded: "Even in their unfinished state these fragments, I believe, are of sufficient dimensions to raise the level of American fiction to follow in some such way as Marlowe's blank verse line raised the whole level of Elizabethan verse."[76]

6. EDITORIAL PRINCIPLES AND PROCEDURES

There are at least five editorial options for an edition of a work in progress:

1. Publish a photo-facsimile of all the documents or of one stage of the unfinished work—usually the latest revised draft.*

2. Publish an unemended clear-text transcription of the latest draft. Such an edition is loosely referred to as "unedited"; but transcribing any manuscript or typescript, even a so-called clean copy, requires editorial decisions.

3. Publish a genetic transcription of the latest draft, indicating authorial additions and deletions by means of typographical symbols. However, typesetting with in-text apparatus cannot accurately reproduce the evolutionary characteristics of a revised document.

4. Publish a "reader's edition" or a "popular edition" that prints a silently emended clear text of the latest draft. This general-reader option, which was elected by Edmund Wilson, presents two connected problems: (a) the temptation for the editor to improve the draft for the sake of continuity; and (b) the reader's inability to identify editorial intervention in the absence of textual apparatus.

5. Publish a critical edition: an emended clear text with full apparatus. The Cambridge edition of *The Love of the Last Tycoon: A Western* is a critical edition.

A critical edition does not reproduce a single stage of the text of the work; it establishes a text incorporating authoritative readings from all relevant documents, with necessary editorial emendations. The decision that determines the character of every critical edition is the selection of the form of the work—in manuscript, typescript, or print—which provides the basis for the edition. This form of the work on which the editor performs the tasks of correction and emendation has been traditionally designated as the *copy-text*.

The classic formulation of editorial method for critical editions, Sir Walter Greg's "The Rationale of Copy-Text," identified the extant text of the work closest to the author's process of composition as the copy-text; normally it preserves more of the author's intentions than any other surviving text.[77] Greg held that the copy-

---

* See *F. Scott Fitzgerald Manuscripts V: The Last Tycoon,* 3 vols. (New York & London: Garland, 1990).

text is the best source for authorial punctuation and spelling, which he designated the *accidentals* of the text.* But the words themselves—the *substantives*—in the copy-text are subject to emendation from subsequent authoritative texts. The Gregian rationale as developed by Fredson Bowers has been successfully applied to a range of works from the seventeenth century to the twentieth century.

Greg's experience was limited to English Renaissance literature, for which there is a paucity of manuscripts and proof sheets. The copy-text for works of that period is almost inevitably a printed text. But for Fitzgerald there is an abundance of evidence bearing on the evolution of his texts: holograph drafts, revised or rewritten typescripts, revised or rewritten proofs, editorial correspondence, and postpublication correction or revision. As a practical matter, the apparatus required by the application of the copy-text editorial procedure for certain Fitzgerald works is cumbersome because of the layers of revision and rewriting. Accordingly, as the textual consultant for the Cambridge edition of Fitzgerald, Bowers recommended that these works be edited from what he designated *base-text:* the stage of composition or publication with Fitzgerald's latest decisions. The base-text may also preserve authorial lapses, secretarial or compositorial errors, and house styling; therefore the editor will be required to identify these cruces and emend them. (The Cambridge edition of *The Great Gatsby,* in which Bowers participated, utilized the base-text procedure.) Whether the copy-text or the base-text method is utilized by an editor, the same critical text will be established; however, the apparatus for each edition will differ. Neither copy-text nor base-text provides a mechanical editorial method. As Greg warned in his essay, "An editor who declines or is unable to exercise his judgement and falls back on some arbitrary canon, such as the authority of the copy-text, is in fact abdicating his editorial function."

Depending on the circumstances of composition and production, the documents selected for the copy-text method and for the base-

---

* The term *accidentals* is misleading: textual accidentals are not unintentional. It is perilous to change technical terminology, but a replacement word is needed. Perhaps *stylers* would serve.

text method may well be the same. (Fitzgerald headed the first thirteen segments as "episodes"; he designated the next two segments as "sections" 14 and 15; then he resumed the "episode" heading. For convenience this discussion refers to the seventeen written "episodes" because there is no discernible distinction between Fitzgerald's use of "episode" and "section." Seventeen episodes require seventeen copy-texts or base-texts.) The base-texts for this edition of *The Love of the Last Tycoon* consist of the latest secretarial typescripts for the first seventeen episodes as revised by Fitzgerald in holograph. This choice of base-texts combines the strongest authority with editorial convenience. An editor must select as copy-texts for the episodes either the manuscripts or the revised typescripts. If the manuscripts were utilized as copy-text, an elaborate apparatus would be required to trace the layers of revision from the manuscripts to the revised typescripts. Most editors would agree that the form of this work in progress to be edited is the authorially revised typescripts—whether they are designated copy-texts or base-texts.

A "definitive edition" is conventionally described as one that publishes the author's "final intentions" or "full intentions" with the requisite evidence for the determination of authorial intentions. "Definitive edition" has become worn out from promiscuous usage during the past thirty years; moreover, the term obscures the recognition that different editors may establish somewhat different, but nonetheless equally definitive, editions. Argument about the nature of authorial intention has become a substitute for editing. The Cambridge edition endeavors to establish the works as Fitzgerald expected them to be published. The notion of expectation involves the circumstances of composition, production, and publication—including Fitzgerald's working relationship with Maxwell Perkins and the house of Scribner. Fitzgerald expected editorial help with factual and mechanical details; but his corrected proofs for *The Great Gatsby* and *Tender Is the Night* and his editorial correspondence demonstrate that he did not abdicate responsibility for his texts. That Fitzgerald read his book galleys carefully and that he resisted schoolmarmish interference is demonstrated by his 8 December 1934 letter to Perkins protesting intrusive editing of *Taps at Reveille*: ". . . this proof reader calmly suggests that I correct certain mistakes of construction in the character's dialogue. My God, he must be the kind who would re-write Ring Lardner, correcting his grammar, or fix up the speeches of Penrod to sound like Little Lord Fauntleroy. . . . His second brilliant stroke of Victorian genius was to query all the split infinitives. If, on a fourth version, I choose to let them stand I am old enough to know what I am doing."[78]

It is particularly perilous for an editor to establish Fitzgerald's punctuation preferences in *The Love of the Last Tycoon* since he had not received the editorial aid to which he was accustomed. Those manuscript punctuations that are matters of deliberate expression should be retained; those that are uselessly distracting should be corrected. A Fitzgerald editor's task is to differentiate preference from inadvertence.

Although Fitzgerald's handwriting is generally clear, there are many points in the manuscripts that require editorial judgment or best guesses. Commas and periods are often undifferentiable; word division may not be certain; capital and lower-case letters may look the same; and it is not always clear what has been deleted. Frances Kroll was a careful and nonintrusive transcriber of the manuscripts; but she made necessary improvements, such as correcting spelling, omitting repeated words, inserting articles, or restoring necessary words that Fitzgerald inadvertently deleted. Thus in the manuscript corresponding to 98.29 Kroll correctly retained "Stahr's first" and deleted the repeated "thought." Her typing also introduced punctuation alterations, both necessary and unintended. When there is variation between manuscript and Kroll's typescript that seems to result from misreading or mistyping, the Cambridge text restores the manuscript reading unless there is evidence that Fitzgerald approved the alteration or intervened on her typescript. There are points where the Cambridge edition restores manuscript readings, even though Fitzgerald did not alter the typescript, because it is evident that he failed to notice the variant: for example, 111.34 confidently] MS; confidentially TS.

Since Wilson edited on Fitzgerald's revised typescripts—there are Wilson emendations written over Fitzgerald's holograph revisions—a crucial editorial responsibility was to identify the layers of

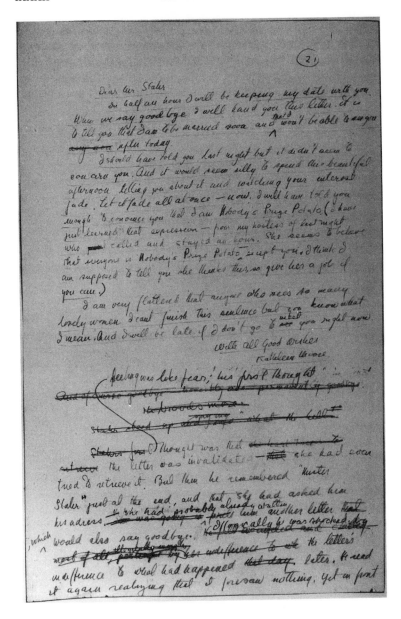

Kroll typed as "Stahr's first feeling was like fear; his first thought was . . .."
Wilson emended "first thought" to "second thought".

alteration (see "Wilson's Alterations on the Latest Typescripts").
Wilson's minuscule hand can be reliably differentiated from Fitzgerald's hand—except for punctuation marks—but it is sometimes
difficult to be sure about the typed punctuation under Wilson's
pencil alterations. In Episodes 4–17 the ribbon typescript readings
and Fitzgerald's revisions have been verified against the carbon
copies. Kroll carefully transferred Fitzgerald's holograph revisions
from the ribbon typescripts to the carbon copies; but she made no
independent alterations. Kroll's handwriting can be differentiated
from Fitzgerald's: e.g., in words with a terminal *e* she wrote ℒ ,
but he wrote ℒ . Since there are no surviving carbon copies of
Fitzgerald's latest revision of Chapter I, Episodes 1–3 were checked
against the penultimate carbon copies from which they were retyped (see "Inventory of Drafts").

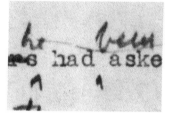 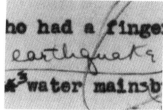

Samples of Fitzgerald's hand (left) and Kroll's hand (right).

After the base-text episodes were, in effect, de-Wilsonized, the
next major procedure was to collate the typescripts for Episodes 4–
17 against Fitzgerald's manuscript drafts to check the accuracy of
Kroll's transcription—which proved to be high—and to verify Fitzgerald's punctuation preferences.

The base-texts were collated against the retyped Scribners setting
copy and against the first printing of the book to identify late editorial interventions and typing or typesetting errors (see "Variants in
the Scribners Setting Copy and the First Printing"). The post–base-
texts variants have no authority; they are reported because the 1941
book was the only printed text for fifty years and has provided the
basis for study of the unfinished novel. All subsequent editions and

reprintings derived from the first edition, and its typographical errors have become enshrined in the text.

The purposes for editorial emendation in the Cambridge critical edition of *The Love of the Last Tycoon: A Western* are to correct positive faults (such as simple misprints or mistranscriptions of Fitzgerald's manuscripts), to correct factual errors, to clarify ambiguous or misleading punctuation without forcing uniformity of texture on Fitzgerald's expression, and to resolve nonfunctional inconsistencies (such as names of characters). The categories of silent emendation—treating such matters as typography, capitalization, and obvious spelling errors—in this edition are described in the headnote to "Editorial Emendations in the Base-Texts."

The decision not to emend is an editorial act. Obviously a critical edition presents the reader with many more silent acceptances of the base-text than with stipulated editorial emendations. *Quod dubitas non disputandum* is a sound warning. Nonetheless, authors require the editorial attention necessitated by the nature of their art and by the conditions under which each work was written and published. It is not sacrilege to emend the correctable errors of detail in a masterpiece. Factual errors undermine the attentive reader's confidence in the author and in the work. Within the limitations of his knowledge and research skills, the editor of a critical edition is responsible for every verifiable detail.[79] This doctrine applies to editing Fitzgerald—for whose intentions and requirements there is abundant evidence, some of it contradictory. He was a social realist who wanted to get details right but got them wrong. He was a delicate stylist who expected routine editorial styling of his punctuation. He used words deliberately but spelled by ear. He was a painstaking reviser and polisher of his prose who has acquired a reputation as a careless writer. He relied on the editorial assistance of Perkins, who was an indifferent copy editor.[80]

Fitzgerald was concerned about the effects of factual blunders in his published work and tried to remedy them. At the time he was planning *The Love of the Last Tycoon,* he attempted to persuade Perkins to publish an omnibus volume of his work to include "my proposed glossary of absurdities and inaccuracies in *This Side of Paradise.*"[81]

The policy for introducing factual corrections in the base-texts of *The Love of the Last Tycoon* is to emend nonfunctional errors—those not affecting meaning or action—that can be corrected by simple substitution. For example, the designation of Siva as a goddess has been corrected; the references to "Diocenes," "Esculpias," and "Minanorus" have been corrected; titles of movies and names of performers have been corrected.

Factual errors that have not been corrected because Fitzgerald's intention is uncertain or because correction would require editorial revision are identified in the Textual or Explanatory Notes. The reference to "sub-microscopic protozoa" has been retained, although the correct term would be *microbes* or *viruses,* because of the possibility—albeit remote—that this error was meant to characterize Cecelia. The placement of the Idaho Sawtooth mountains in the Southwest has not been emended because it is unclear what Fitzgerald wanted. Story inconsistencies have been allowed to stand because corrections would involve rewriting: thus, at p. 30 Stahr asks, " 'Did Robby phone in?' "—but Robby had left a message for Stahr on p. 29.

Factual errors that are integral to the work are discussed in the Textual or Explanatory Notes but not emended. Fitzgerald commits the blunder of having Kathleen marry in violation of the statutory California waiting period; this functional error is essential to the plot and must be retained. Factual errors can also be categorized as *internal errors* (referring to the world within the work of fiction—for example, when Stahr addresses the wrong character at 54.29) or *external errors* (referring to the outside or real world that provides the setting for the fictional events). Fitzgerald's invented characters inhabit a real time and a real place. Stahr's fictional studio is located in the actual Los Angeles County.

Treatment of factual errors or inconsistencies in Fitzgerald's work in progress should take his editorial expectations into consideration. When he delivered a completed novel to Scribners, the house editing queried errors or inconsistencies and suggested corrections. Accordingly, this Cambridge critical edition attempts to identify the cruces that Scribners would have or should have called to Fitzgerald's attention. The names of characters, which are spelled inconsistently in the base-texts, have been regularized on the evidence of the majority usage in the manuscripts.

Cecelia. Fitzgerald's consistent spelling has been retained, although *Cecilia* is the usual form. Wilson's emendation to *Cecilia* is unnecessary.

Pat Brady. There is one appearance in revised typescript of the given name *Bill* and one of *Billy* for Brady—who was originally named *Bill Bradogue*—but *Pat* was clearly Fitzgerald's final choice. Graham wrote Mary McCarthy, at that time married to Edmund Wilson: "I have just remembered why Scott changed the name of BRADOGUE to BRADY. He disliked the first as a name for Cecilia—he wanted something less harsh for the teller of the story."[82]

Jaques La Borwits. Fitzgerald's spelling *Jaques* is unlikely but possible; cf. Jaques in *As You Like It.* *La Borwits* is Fitzgerald's clear preference, but Wilson emended to *Jacques La Borwitz.*

Pete Zavras. The name of this Greek camera man is consistently *Pedro Garcia* in MS and RTS. Frances Kroll's recollection that Fitzgerald used *Pedro Garcia* as a joke, intending to emend it,[83] is supported by a Fitzgerald note: "Change Garcia to a Greek." Wilson renamed the character *Pete Zavras,* which has been retained in this edition because it has become established during fifty years and because a Greek character named *Pedro Garcia* is risible.

Rienmund. This spelling is Fitzgerald's preference and has been retained. Wilson emended to *Reinmund.* (He also emended *Wolfshiem* to *Wolfsheim* in the text of *The Great Gatsby* included with *The Last Tycoon.*)[84]

Flieshacker. Fitzgerald's majority spelling has been accepted. Wilson emended to *Fleishacker,* possibly for the sake of the German–Yiddish pun on flesh cutter or butcher.

Schwartze. Fitzgerald's majority MS and consistent RTS spelling with the final *e* has been retained. Wilson emended to *Schwartz*.

Popolous. Fitzgerald's consistent spelling has been retained. Wilson emended to *Popolos* because *-ous* is an incorrect ending for a Greek surname.

A critical edition retains or restores the acceptable characteristics of the author's habitual expression in preference to wholesale acceptance of the house styling imposed on the work. Fitzgerald's holograph punctuation indicates the rhythms he heard as he wrote; it is inherently as much a part of his total style as the arrangements of words into phrases and sentences. Kroll recalls: "Now and again he would ask me to read a page he had written out loud so he could listen to it for cadence. How it sounded was as important as the sight of the words on paper, as if a blind person had to hear it and a deaf one to read it."[85]

Fitzgerald did not punctuate according to the rules—preferring a light rhetorical style to a heavy syntactical system. Although he accepted editorial repunctuation of dialogue and other mechanical matters,[86] he would restore his own punctuation or nonpunctuation in house-styled proof where required for the sake of sentence rhythm. In the absence of Fitzgerald's setting copy and corrected proofs for *The Love of the Last Tycoon*, the editor is compelled to balance the authority of the underpunctuation in the manuscripts against the Scribners house styling that Fitzgerald accepted in his previous books. A troublesome manuscript idiosyncrasy is Fitzgerald's frequent omission of question marks in interrogative sentences—even in sentences accompanied by "asked." In some instances it is impossible to be certain whether the question mark was inadvertently omitted in the heat of composition or whether it was deliberately omitted because he did not hear the sentence as interrogative.[87] The question mark has been supplied in this edition when the sentence is clearly a question.

Study of the manuscripts for *The Great Gatsby* and *The Love of the Last Tycoon: A Western* confirms that Fitzgerald's punctuation habits did not change during the last fifteen years of his life.

Fitzgerald rationed commas:

a. he usually omitted a comma between two adjectives;

b. he customarily omitted a comma before the conjunction connecting two independent clauses;

c. he almost invariably omitted a comma before *and* or *or* in three-element combinations;

d. he habitually omitted a comma after a short introductory phrase;

e. he used a comma before the name of the character in direct address more often than not, but no system is evident;

f. he inconsistently omitted the first or the second of paired commas with parenthetical phrases.

The Cambridge edition follows Fitzgerald's preferences in Categories *a–e;* in Category *f* the missing comma is supplied when one of the commas is present in manuscript.

Fitzgerald rarely used colons and semicolons, preferring to link or separate sentence units with dashes—a mark he relied on to control the rhythm of his prose.

Fitzgerald resisted hyphens in compound adjectives and in word division. For example, in the manuscripts for *The Love of the Last Tycoon* he omitted the hyphen in "half" compounds ("half past two") except for the two appearances of "half-light." When manuscript hyphenation and word division are inconsistent (drug store, drugstore, drug-store), the majority usage has been accepted. If there is no manuscript preference, reference books that might have been in use at Scribners have been consulted: *A Manual of Style,* 10th edition (Chicago: University of Chicago Press, 1937) and *Webster's New International Dictionary of the English Language* (Springfield, Mass.: Merriam, 1922).*

Fitzgerald eschewed italicizing printed titles, for which he preferred quotation marks; he reserved italic type for emphasis.

The ability to determine Fitzgerald's manuscript punctuation preferences does not justify a policy of blanket restoration. The present

---

* The unpublished concordance to *The Love of the Last Tycoon,* prepared by Mary Jo Tate, facilitated identification of Fitzgerald's habits.

edition endeavors to preserve the characteristics of Fitzgerald's style on a case-by-case basis. His manuscript practice has been emended in two categories: (1) distracting punctuation (see comments on split speech below); and (2) departures from the conventions of typography and printing—such as the placement of punctuation with quotation marks. But Fitzgerald's idiosyncratic manuscript punctuation has been retained when it seems to be functional—for instance, the occasional comma/dash combinations. (An omission of a comma in these paired combinations may be attributed to the heat of composition, but it has not been supplied.)

In general, regularization* has preserved Fitzgerald's manuscript characteristics that were compatible with the usage of his time, even though not strictly conforming to the rules—as with his omitted commas and hyphens. In certain cases, however, Fitzgerald's inconsistent pointing has been retained when there is no necessity for emending it. For a textual editor to enforce uniformity on the accidentals would be to substitute another outside styling for the publisher's house styling. Incorrect or distracting manuscript pointing has been normalized when it cannot be defended as intentional or functional—for example, Fitzgerald's omission of apostrophes in the act of writing. His eccentric punctuation of split speech has been emended here as it has been in the Cambridge *Great Gatsby* because it serves no discernible purpose for style or sense. Thus manuscript and typescript corresponding to 9.22–23 read: "Skip it," said Wylie, "We ought to've brought the stewardess along for you." The Cambridge edition emends this and similar cruces to: "Skip it," said Wylie. "We. . . ."

In the draft statement of editorial principles for *The Cambridge Edition of the Works of F. Scott Fitzgerald,* Fredson Bowers wrote:

. . . a critical, or eclectic, text is demanded by the special circumstances of Fitzgerald's methods of composition, his extensive revision in proof, and

---

* Fredson Bowers, "Regularization and Normalization in Modern Critical Texts," *Studies in Bibliography,* 42 (1989), 79–102. *Regularization:* "the bringing of inconsistent elements in a text into conformity by adjustment of variants to some one regular form already present and assumed to be authorial." *Normalization:* "emendation not from documentary evidence bearing on the text such as is used for regularization but instead from the imposition of an external standard without specific precedent in the text or its associated documents."

his reliance on the publisher to set right his misspellings and other technical faults in writing, a trust that was too often misplaced. To object that such an edited text represents a version that never existed in documentary form is naive, for the whole purpose of the scholarly reconstruction of a text, in addition to its extension to a complete edition with full apparatus of its various preserved documentary forms, is to provide a reading text purged of its errors and in some respects of its incompletely realized authorial intentions insofar as these may be recovered.

This doctrine applies to Fitzgerald's works published during his lifetime, but it also bears on *The Love of the Last Tycoon: A Western.* For any work, the scholar-editor's first responsibility is to determine what the author wrote, to the extent possible from surviving documents. Next the editor determines that author's intentions and expectations from these documents and from evidence of the author's composition practices in other works. Then the editor fulfills these intentions and expectations on a word-by-word, punctuation-by-punctuation basis without transgressing the boundaries of necessary correction and proper emendation. Certainly, "necessary" and "proper" are subject to individual editorial judgment; moreover, the requirements of scholarly editing must vary from author to author and from work to work. There are writers whose responsibility for their work ends with submission of typescript to publisher. F. Scott Fitzgerald was not one of them. Whether editing an ostensibly completed Fitzgerald work or this work in progress, the preparation of a critical edition requires obedience to the same protocols. In certain ways, everything F. Scott Fitzgerald wrote was work in progress.

NOTES

1   Samuel Johnson, "Milton," *Lives of the English Poets,* ed. George Birkbeck Hill (Oxford: Clarendon Press, 1905), vol. I, p. 124.

2   New York: Scribners, 1941; p. ix.

3   Thirty-five years after Fitzgerald's death Graham recalled that *The Last Tycoon* "was a temporary title, but he might have used it for the final. Or *STAHR* or *THE LOVE OF THE LAST TYCOON: A WESTERN.* He really wasn't sure. It's my belief that *THE LAST TYCOON* would

be the title—It has the same sort of rhythm as THE GREAT GATSBY. THE L.T. was SCOTT'S, NOT EDMUND WILSON'S" (to Bruccoli, 25 August 1975). Kroll's memory in 1975 was that 'The book was as far from finished as the title was from being final—He fooled with all of them—He was amused by The Love of "The Last Tycoon; A Western", but I don't know that he would have gone with it—I think "Stahr" was a working title—' (to Bruccoli, 18 August 1975).

4   Bruccoli's *"The Last of the Novelists": F. Scott Fitzgerald and The Last Tycoon* (Carbondale & Edwardsville: Southern Illinois University Press, 1977) reconstructs the writing of the novel. The unpublished "Apparatus for a Definitive Edition: F. Scott Fitzgerald's *The Last Tycoon*" (1976), prepared by Bruccoli for library deposit, is superseded by this Cambridge edition.

5   *Thalberg* (Garden City, N.Y.: Doubleday, 1969), pp. 267–8. Thomas provides no source or date.

6   To Bruccoli, 27 February 1991. But Samuel Marx, who was M-G-M story editor at the time, claims that Thalberg "assumed a neutral position" (to Bruccoli, 26 October 1975); see Marx, *Mayer and Thalberg: The Make-Believe Saints* (New York: Random House, 1975). Thomas and Schulberg are supported by Nancy Lynn Schwartz's *The Hollywood Writers' Wars* (New York: Knopf, 1982).

7   Samuel Marx, *A Gaudy Spree* (New York & Toronto: Franklin Watts, 1987), pp. 63–6.

8   Marx, *Mayer and Thalberg*, p. 222.

9   To C. O. Kalman, 19 September 1936; *The Correspondence of F. Scott Fitzgerald*, ed. Bruccoli and Margaret M. Duggan (New York: Random House, 1980), pp. 451–2 (subsequently noted as *Correspondence*). The misspelling of Thalberg's name was a typist's error. Neither Miriam Hopkins nor Fredric March was under contract to M-G-M at this time; Fitzgerald's suspicion about Thalberg's interference in the sale of *Tender* to M-G-M is unsupported.

10   16 October 1936; Charles Scribner's Sons Archives, Princeton University Library.

11   Undated. *The Letters of F. Scott Fitzgerald*, ed. Andrew Turnbull (New York: Scribners, 1963), pp. 16–17.

12   "Afterword," *F. Scott Fitzgerald's Screenplay for Three Comrades*, ed. Bruccoli (Carbondale & Edwardsville: Southern Illinois University Press, 1978).

13   The "Infidelity" screenplay was published in *Esquire*, 80 (December 1973).

14   Aaron Latham's *Crazy Sundays: F. Scott Fitzgerald in Hollywood* (New York: Viking, 1971) is not entirely reliable.

15   *Beloved Infidel*, with Gerold Frank (New York: Holt, Rinehart &

Winston, 1958); *College of One* (New York: Viking, 1967); and *The Real F. Scott Fitzgerald: Thirty-Five Years Later* (New York: Grosset & Dunlap, 1976).

16   "Pasting It Together," *Esquire*, 5 (March 1936), 35, 182–3. Collected in *The Crack-Up* (New York: New Directions, 1945).

17   *Correspondence*, p. 551.

18   Budd Schulberg, *The Four Seasons of Success* (Garden City, N.Y.: Doubleday, 1972), p. 134. Schulberg wrote a *roman à clef* about his Dartmouth excursion with Fitzgerald: *The Disenchanted* (New York: Random House, 1951). Fitzgerald made use of "Metro-Goldwyn-Mayer," *Fortune*, 6 (December 1932), 50–5, 58, 63–4, 114, 116, 118, 120, 122; collected in *The American Film Industry*, ed. Tino Balio (Madison: University of Wisconsin Press, 1976).

19   *The Four Seasons of Success*, pp. 115–16.

20   To Bruccoli, 11 September 1975.

21   4 March 1938; Charles Scribner's Sons Archives, Princeton University Library.

22   To Beatrice Dance, 11 October 1938; *Correspondence*, pp. 516–17. Perkins's 1 September letter to Fitzgerald mentions that he heard from Harold Ober that "you had a plan for a novel"; *Dear Scott/ Dear Max: The Fitzgerald-Perkins Correspondence*, ed. John Kuehl & Jackson R. Bryer (New York: Scribners, 1971), p. 247.

23   Fitzgerald's reaction to *The Day of the Locust* identifies the nightmarish qualities of the novel: "The book, though it puts Gorki's 'The Lower Depths' in the class with 'The Tale of Benjamin Bunny,' certainly has scenes of extraordinary power—if that phrase is still in use. Especially I was impressed by the pathological crowd at the premiere, the character and handling of the aspirant actress and the uncanny almost medieval feeling of some of his Hollywood background set off by those vividly drawn grotesques." This statement was printed on the dust jackets for *The Day of the Locust*. Schulberg's *What Makes Sammy Run?* was published in spring 1941—after Fitzgerald's death—but Fitzgerald had read it; his letter of endorsement printed on the dust jacket is dated 13 December 1940.

24   4 January 1939; *Dear Scott/Dear Max*, p. 253–4.

25   Undated transcription by Scottie Fitzgerald. *Letters*, p. 48.

26   16 May 1939; *Correspondence*, pp. 529–30.

27   22 May 1939; *Dear Scott/Dear Max*, pp. 256–7.

28   Frances Kroll Ring's memoir, *Against the Current: As I Remember F. Scott Fitzgerald* (San Francisco: Ellis/Creative Arts, 1985), provides a trustworthy record of his working habits.

29   *As Ever, Scott Fitz—: Letters Between F. Scott Fitzgerald and His Literary Agent Harold Ober 1919–1940*, ed. Bruccoli and Jennifer

M. Atkinson (Philadelphia & New York: Lippincott, 1972), pp. 388–90.

30 The full letter is published in *"The Last of the Novelists,"* pp. 23–5.

31 Princeton University Library.

32 A short-short is a story of 1,500–2,000 words instead of the usual magazine length of 5,000 words.

33 The Hollywood stories are "Magnetism" (1928), "Crazy Sunday" (1932), "Discard" (posthumously published, 1948), "Last Kiss" (posthumously published, 1949), and the Pat Hobby series published 1940–1: "Pat Hobby's Christmas Wish," "A Man in the Way," " 'Boil Some Water—Lots of It,' " "Teamed With Genius," "Pat Hobby and Orson Welles," "Pat Hobby's Secret," "Pat Hobby, Putative Father," "The Homes of the Stars," "Pat Hobby Does His Bit," "Pat Hobby's Preview," "No Harm Trying," "A Patriotic Short," "On the Trail of Pat Hobby," "Fun in an Artist's Studio," "Two Old-Timers," "Mightier Than the Sword," "Pat Hobby's College Days."

34 *Letters,* pp. 285–6.

35 New York Public Library.

36 New York Public Library.

37 Joseph Bryan III to Bruccoli, 9 September 1975.

38 Charles Scribner's Sons Archives, Princeton University Library.

39 *Dear Scott/Dear Max,* p. 259.

40 Charles Scribner's Sons Archives, Princeton University Library.

41 Charles Scribner's Sons Archives, Princeton University Library.

42 To Bruccoli, 22 April 1975.

43 *Dear Scott/Dear Max,* pp. 265–6. For O'Hara's account of reading the work in progress, see *"An Artist Is His Own Fault,"* ed. Bruccoli (Carbondale & Edwardsville: Southern Illinois University Press, 1977), p. 137. Fitzgerald's *Babylon Revisited* screenplay has been published (New York: Carroll & Graf, 1993).

44 *Letters,* pp. 126–32.

45 *Dear Scott/Dear Max,* p. 268.

46 6 March 1941; Yale University Library.

47 To Bruccoli, 20 February 1980.

48 Yale University Library.

49 Yale University Library.

50 Yale University Library.

51 Taped telephone conversation with Bruccoli, 8 November 1990.

52 Graham, *The Real F. Scott Fitzgerald,* p. 183.

53 Graham and Bruccoli conversation.

54 Graham to Bruccoli, 8 May 1975.

55 Princeton University Library.

56 Charles Scribner's Sons Archives, Princeton University Library. All

Perkins/Wilson correspondence is at the Princeton University Library unless otherwise noted.

57   Charles Scribner's Sons Archives, Princeton University Library.

58   The testimony is unclear. Schulberg reports: "It was all pretty tentative. As I mentioned before, I thought the suggestion came from Scribner's—quite sure it did. . . . I know that John and I tossed the idea back and forth for a week or so. I believe he suggested—*if* we did it, a very big IF—that we first talk out the final chapters, and that then I should try a first draft, since I was closer to the material, which we would then go over. But the more we discussed this, the clearer it seemed to us that we were in a No-win situation; whatever we wrote, it would seem to Fitzgerald-fans not to measure up to . . . the rest of the ms. We also considered a second approach—in which we by-line the concluding chapters and write them openly as our own. But in the end sanity or reality prevailed and we decided not to tamper with the unfinished work" (to Bruccoli, 6 August 1980). But Graham insisted that "BUDD SCHULBERG WAS *NOT* ASKED TO FINISH *THE LAST TYCOON*. HE *OFFERED* TO DO IT AND EDMUND WILSON INDIGNANTLY REFUSED" (to Bruccoli, 4 November 1976). There is no Wilson or Perkins correspondence bearing on this matter.

59   27 January 1941; Charles Scribner's Sons Archives, Princeton University Library. Gilbert Seldes was a critic and editor.

60   Charles Scribner's Sons Archives, Princeton University Library. When Zelda Fitzgerald read the published work, she wrote: "I confess that I don't like the heroine, she seems the sort of person who knows too well how to capitalize on the unwelcome advances of the ice-man and she smells a little of the rubber shields in her dress. However, I see how Stahr might have found her redolent of the intimacies of forgotten homely glamours, and his imagination has endowed her with the magical properties of his early authorities" (to Margaret Turnbull, 13 November 1941); Nancy Milford, *Zelda* (New York: Harper & Row, 1970), p. 353. There is no evidence that Zelda Fitzgerald had been informed about Sheilah Graham, but she must have understood that Fitzgerald had a woman companion in Hollywood.

61   Charles Scribner's Sons Archives, Princeton University Library.

62   Sheilah Graham to John Biggs, 21 April 1941. Princeton University Library.

63   On 22 May Graham wrote Wilson replying to six queries about details in the drafts. Her most interesting note is: "About your theory that KATHLEEN'S husband, SMITH, was perhaps forced from the studio and that is why she did not get inside—I asked someone who has been here for fifteen years on and off, and he said the technician's union was formed so long ago that he didn't remember whether they

had been fired or black-listed at the time. In any case, this would cancel his getting fired at the period of the book, which is about five or six years ago. Thinking it over, it seems more likely that KATH-LEEN left SMITH voluntarily, or was kicked out when he discovered her association with STAHR, or that after she had married SMITH she realized how much she loved STAHR and left her husband. This makes her remaining a stranger to the studios at the end feasible" (Yale University Library).

64 Princeton University Library.

65 9 July 1941. Charles Scribner's Sons Archives, Princeton University Library.

66 Ober to Perkins, 13 August 1941; Perkins to Biggs, 13 and 14 August and 19 September 1941. Charles Scribner's Sons Archives, Princeton University Library. No Hollywood figure named Rose Meloney has been identified.

67 To Christian Gauss, *Letters on Literature and Politics,* ed. Elena Wilson (New York: Farrar, Straus & Giroux, 1977), pp. 343–4.

68 *Letters on Literature and Politics,* pp. 341–2.

69 Charles Scribner's Sons Archives, Princeton University Library.

70 9 November 1941.

71 "The New Books," *Harper's,* 184 (December 1941), 112–13.

72 2 November 1941, VI, 6.

73 "Unfinished Life," *Newsweek,* 18 (27 October 1941), 58–9. For reprints of the important reviews see *F. Scott Fitzgerald: The Critical Reception,* ed. Jackson R. Bryer (New York: Franklin, 1978), pp. 355–83.

74 "Fitzgerald's Unfinished Symphony," *Saturday Review of Literature,* 24 (6 December 1941), 10.

75 "Taps at Assembly," *New Republic,* 106 (9 February 1942), 211–12.

76 "A Note on Fitzgerald," *The Crack-Up,* ed. Edmund Wilson (New York: New Directions, 1945), pp. 339, 343. Dos Passos augmented his 1941 *New Republic* tribute to Fitzgerald for *The Crack-Up,* inserting material about *The Last Tycoon.*

77 "The Rationale of Copy-Text," *Studies in Bibliography,* 3 (1950–1), 19–36; reprinted in *The Collected Papers of Sir Walter Greg,* ed. J. C. Maxwell (Oxford: Clarendon Press, 1966).

78 *Dear Scott/Dear Max,* p. 216.

79 See pp. xliv–xlix in *The Great Gatsby* for a discussion of general emendation policy in the Cambridge edition of Fitzgerald. For a rationale of emendation in realistic fiction, see Bruccoli, "Getting It Right: The Publishing Process and the Correction of Factual Errors—With Reference to *The Great Gatsby," The Library Chronicle of the University of Texas at Austin,* 21, nos. 3/4 (1991), 41–60. See also Fred-

son Bowers, "Notes on the Theory and Practice in Editing Texts," *The Book Encompassed: Studies in Twentieth-Century Bibliography,* ed. Peter Davidson (Cambridge: Cambridge University Press, 1992), p. 249: "The kinds of errors he [Fitzgerald] made, and his firm intention to correct them when they were pointed out to him may well encourage an editor to assist." There are readers and critics who are not merely indifferent to factual accuracy in literature, but who are incredulous that others value it; well-edited texts are wasted on them.

80   Charles Scribner, Jr., the former head of the house, has stated that "Perkins was totally useless when it came to copyediting or correcting a text. Such details meant very little to him" (*In the Company of Writers: A Life in Publishing* [New York: Scribners, 1991], p. 44).

81   *Dear Scott/Dear Max,* pp. 250–1.

82   N.d. (c. June 1941), Princeton University Library.

83   Frances Kroll Ring's taped telephone conversation with Bruccoli, 8 November 1990.

84   See Bruccoli, "The Perkins/Wilson Correspondence About Publication of *The Last Tycoon," Fitzgerald/Hemingway Annual 1978,* pp. 63–6.

85   *Against the Current,* pp. 42–3.

86   The style manual in use at Scribners has not been identified.

87   Kroll does not remember whether Fitzgerald had a policy on question marks; to Bruccoli, 20 July 1992.

The Love of
THE LAST
TYCOON

A Western

BY

F. SCOTT FITZGERALD

CHAPTER I

Though I haven't ever been on the screen I was brought up in pictures. Rudolph Valentino came to my fifth birthday party—or so I was told. I put this down only to indicate that even before the age of reason I was in a position to watch the wheels go round.

I was going to write my memoirs once, "The Producer's Daughter," but at eighteen you never quite get around to anything like that. It's just as well—it would have been as flat as an old column of Lolly Parsons'. My father was in the picture business as another man might be in cotton or steel, and I took it tranquilly. At the worst I accepted Hollywood with the resignation of a ghost assigned to a haunted house. I knew what you were supposed to think about it but I was obstinately unhorrified.

This is easy to say, but harder to make people understand. When I was at Bennington some of the English teachers who pretended an indifference to Hollywood or its products really *hated* it. Hated it way down deep as a threat to their existence. Even before that, when I was in a convent, a sweet little nun asked me to get her a script of a screen play so she could "teach her class about movie writing" as she had taught them about the essay and the short story. I got the script for her and I suppose she puzzled over it and puzzled over it but it was never mentioned in class and she gave it back to me with an air of offended surprise and not a single comment. That's what I half expect to happen to this story.

You can take Hollywood for granted like I did, or you can dismiss it with the contempt we reserve for what we don't understand. It can be understood too, but only dimly and in flashes. Not half a dozen men have ever been able to keep the whole equation of pictures in their heads. And perhaps the closest a woman can come to the set-up is to try and understand one of those men.

The world from an airplane I knew. Father always had us travel back and forth that way from school and college. After my sister died when I was a junior, I travelled to and fro alone and the journey always made me think of her, made me somewhat solemn and subdued. Sometimes there were picture people I knew on board the plane, and occasionally there was an attractive college boy—but not often during the Depression. I seldom really fell asleep during the trip, what with thoughts of Eleanor and the sense of that sharp rip between coast and coast—at least not till we had left those lonely little airports in Tennessee.

This trip was so rough that the passengers divided early into those who turned in right away and those who didn't want to turn in at all. There were two of these latter right across from me and I was pretty sure from their fragmentary conversation that they were from Hollywood—one of them because he looked like it, a middle-aged Jew who alternately talked with nervous excitement or else crouched as if ready to spring, in a harrowing silence; the other a pale, plain, stocky man of thirty, whom I was sure I had seen before. He had been to the house or something. But it might have been when I was a little girl, and so I wasn't offended that he didn't recognize me.

The stewardess—she was tall, handsome and flashing dark, a type that they seemed to run to—asked me if she could make up my berth.

"—and, dear, do you want an aspirin?" She perched on the side of the seat and rocked precariously to and fro with the June hurricane, "—or a Nembutal?"

"No."

"I've been so busy with everyone else that I've had no time to ask you." She sat down beside me and buckled us both in. "Do you want some gum?"

This reminded me to get rid of the piece that had been boring me for hours. I wrapped it in a piece of magazine and put it into the automatic ash-holder.

"I can always tell people are nice—" the stewardess said approvingly "—if they wrap their gum in paper before they put it in there."

We sat for a while in the half-light of the swaying car. It was vaguely like a swanky restaurant at that twilight time between meals. We were all lingering—and not quite on purpose. Even the stewardess, I think, had to keep reminding herself why she was there.

She and I talked about a young actress I knew, whom she had flown west with two years before. It was in the very lowest time of the Depression and the young actress kept staring out the window in such an intent way that the stewardess was afraid she was contemplating a leap. It appeared though that she was not afraid of poverty, but only of revolution.

"I know what Mother and *I* are going to do," she confided to the stewardess. "We're coming out to the Yellowstone and we're just going to live simply till it all blows over. Then we'll come back. They don't kill artists—you know?"

The proposition pleased me. It conjured up a pretty picture of the actress and her mother being fed by kind Tory bears who brought them honey, and by gentle fawns who fetched extra milk from the does and then lingered near to make pillows for their heads at night. In turn I told the stewardess about the lawyer and the director who told their plans to Father one night in those brave days. If the bonus army conquered Washington the lawyer had a boat hidden in the Sacramento River, and he was going to row upstream for a few months and then come back "because they always needed lawyers after a revolution to straighten out the legal side."

The director had tended more toward defeatism. He had an old suit, shirt and shoes in waiting—he never did say whether they were his own or whether he got them from the prop department— and he was going to Disappear into the Crowd. I remember Father saying: "But they'll look at your hands! They'll know you haven't done manual work for years. And they'll ask for your union card." And I remember how the director's face fell, and how gloomy he was while he ate his dessert, and how funny and puny they sounded to me.

"Is your father an actor, Miss Brady?" asked the stewardess. "I've certainly heard the name."

At the name Brady both the men across the aisle looked up. Sidewise—that Hollywood look, that always seems thrown over one shoulder. Then the young, pale, stocky man unbuttoned his safety strap and stood in the aisle beside us.

"Are you Cecelia *Bra*dy?" he demanded accusingly, as if I'd been holding out on him. "I *thought* I recognized you. I'm Wylie White."

He could have omitted this—for at the same moment a new voice said, "Watch your step, Wylie!" and another man brushed by him in the aisle and went forward in the direction of the cockpit. Wylie White started, and a little too late called after him defiantly.

"I only take orders from the pilot."

I recognized the kind of pleasantry that goes on between the powers in Hollywood and their satellites.

The stewardess reproved him:

"Not so loud, please—some of the passengers are asleep."

I saw now that the other man across the aisle, the middle-aged Jew, was on his feet also, staring, with shameless economic lechery, after the man who had just gone by. Or rather at the back of the man, who gestured sideways with his hand in a sort of farewell, as he went out of my sight.

I asked the stewardess: "Is he the as*si*stant pilot?"

She was unbuckling our belt, about to abandon me to Wylie White.

"No. That's Mr. Smith. He has the private compartment, the 'bridal suite'—only he has it alone. The assistant pilot is always in uniform." She stood up. "I want to find out if we're going to be grounded in Nashville."

Wylie White was aghast.

"Why?"

"It's a storm coming up the Mississippi Valley."

"Does that mean we'll have to stay here all *night*?"

"If this keeps up!"

A sudden dip indicated that it would. It tipped Wylie White into the seat opposite me, shunted the stewardess precipitately down in the direction of the cockpit, and plunked the Jewish man into a sitting position. After the studied, unruffled exclamations of distaste that befitted the air-minded, we settled down. There was an introduction.

"Miss Brady—Mr. Schwartze," said Wylie White. "He's a great friend of your father's too."

Mr. Schwartze nodded so vehemently that I could almost hear him saying, "It's true. As God is my judge, it's true!"

He might have said this right out loud at one time in his life—but he was obviously a man to whom something had happened. Meeting him was like encountering a friend who has been in a fist fight or collision, and got flattened. You stare at your friend and say: "What happened to you?" And he answers something unintelligible through broken teeth and swollen lips. He can't even tell you about it.

Mr. Schwartze was physically unmarked; the exaggerated Persian nose and oblique eye-shadow were as congenital as the tip-tilted Irish redness around my father's nostrils.

"Nashville!" cried Wylie White. "That means we go to a hotel. We don't get to the coast till tomorrow night—if then. My God! I was born in Nashville."

"I should think you'd like to see it again."

"Never—I've kept away for fifteen years. I hope I'll *never* see it again."

But he would—for the plane was unmistakably going down, down, down, like Alice in the rabbit hole. Cupping my hand against the window I saw the blur of the city far away on the left. The green sign "Fasten your belts—No smoking" had been on since we first rode into the storm.

"Did you hear what she said?" said Mr. Schwartze from one of his fiery silences across the aisle.

"Hear what?" asked Wylie.

"Hear what he's calling himself," said Schwartze. "Mr. *Smith*!"

"Why not?" asked Wylie.

"Oh nothing," said Schwartze quickly. "I just thought it was funny, Smith." I never heard a laugh with less mirth in it: "Smith!"

I suppose there has been nothing like the airports since the days of the stage-stops—nothing quite as lonely, as somber-silent. The old red-brick depots were built right into the towns they marked —people didn't get off at those isolated stations unless they lived there. But airports lead you way back in history like oases, like the stops on the great trade routes. The sight of air travellers strolling in ones and twos into midnight airports will draw a small crowd any night up to two. The young people look at the planes, the older ones look at the passengers with a watchful incredulity. In the big trans-continental planes we were the coastal rich, who casually alighted from our cloud in mid-America. High adventure might be among us, disguised as a movie star. But mostly it wasn't. And I always wished fervently that we looked more interesting than we did—just as I often have at premieres, when the fans look at you with scornful reproach because you're not a star.

On the ground Wylie and I were suddenly friends, because he held out his arm to steady me when I got out of the plane. From then on, he made a dead set for me—and I didn't mind. From the moment we walked into the airport it had become plain that if we were stranded here we were stranded here together. (It wasn't like the time I lost my boy—the time my boy played the piano with that girl Reina in a little New England farm house near Bennington, and I realized at last I wasn't wanted. Guy Lombardo was on the air playing "Top Hat" and "Cheek to Cheek" and she taught him the melodies. The keys falling like leaves and her hand splayed over his as she showed him a black chord. I was a freshman then.)

When we went into the airport Mr. Schwartze was along with us too but he seemed in a sort of dream. All the time we were trying to get accurate information at the desk he kept staring at the door that led out to the landing field, as if he were afraid the plane would leave without him. Then I excused myself for a few minutes and something happened that I didn't see but when I came back he and White were standing close together, White talking and Schwartze looking twice as much as if a great truck had just backed up over him. He didn't stare at the door to the landing field anymore. I heard the end of Wylie White's remark. . . .

"—I told you to shut up. It serves you right."

"I only said—"

He broke off as I came up and asked if there was any news. It was then half past two in the morning.

"A little," said Wylie White. "They don't think we'll be able to start for three hours anyhow, so some of the softies are going to a hotel. But I'd like to take you out to The Hermitage, Home of Andrew Jackson."

"How could we see it in the dark?" demanded Schwartze.

"Hell, it'll be sunrise in two hours."

"You two go," said Schwartze.

"All right—you take the bus to the hotel. It's still waiting—*he's* in there." Wylie's voice had a taunt in it. "Maybe it'd be a good thing."

"No, I'll go along with you," said Schwartze hastily.

We took a taxi in the sudden country dark outside, and he seemed to cheer up. He patted my kneecap encouragingly.

"I should go along," he said. "I should be chaperone. Once upon a time when I was in the big money, I had a daughter—a beautiful daughter."

He spoke as if she had been sold to creditors as a tangible asset.

"You'll have another," Wylie assured him. "You'll get it all back. Another turn of the wheel and you'll be where Cecelia's papa is, won't he, Cecelia?"

"Where is this Hermitage?" asked Schwartze presently. "Far away at the end of nowhere? Will we miss the plane?"

"Skip it," said Wylie. "We ought to've brought the stewardess along for you. Didn't you admire the stewardess? *I* thought she was pretty cute."

We drove for a long time over a bright level countryside, just a road and a tree and a shack and a tree, and then suddenly along a winding twist of woodland. I could feel even in the darkness that the trees of the woodland were green—that it was all different from the dusty olive-tint of California. Somewhere we passed a Negro driving three cows ahead of him, and they mooed as he scatted them to the side of the road. They were real cows, with warm fresh, silky flanks and the Negro grew gradually real out of the darkness with his big brown eyes staring at us close to the car, as Wylie gave him a quarter. He said "*Thank* you—thank you" and stood there and the cows mooed again into the night as we drove off.

I thought of the first sheep I ever remember seeing—hundreds of

them, and how our car drove suddenly into them on the back lot of
the old Laemmle studio. They were unhappy about being in pictures
but the men in the car with us kept saying:

"Swell?"

"Is that what you wanted, Dick?"

"Isn't that swell?" And the man named Dick kept standing up in
the car as if he were Cortez or Balboa, looking over that grey fleecy
undulation. If I ever knew what picture they were in I have long
forgotten.

We had driven an hour. We crossed a brook over an old rattly
iron bridge laid with planks. Now there were roosters crowing and
blue-green shadows stirring every time we passed a farm house.

"I told you it'd be morning soon," said Wylie. "I was born near
here—the son of impoverished southern paupers. The family mansion is now used as an outhouse. We had four servants—my father,
my mother and my two sisters. I refused to join the guild, and so I
went to Memphis, to start my career, which has now reached a dead
end." He put his arm around me. "Cecelia, will you marry me, so I
can share the Brady fortune?"

He was disarming enough so I let my head lie on his shoulder.

"What do you do, Celia? Go to school?"

"I go to Bennington. I'm a junior."

"Oh, I beg your pardon. I should have known but I never had the
advantage of college training. But a *junior*—why I read in 'Esquire'
that juniors have nothing to learn, Cecelia."

"Why do people think that college girls—"

"Don't apologize—knowledge is power."

"You'd know from the way you talk that we were on our way to
Hollywood," I said. "It's always years and years behind the time."

He pretended to be shocked.

"You mean girls in the East have no private lives?"

"That's the point. They *have* got private lives. You're bothering
me, let go."

"I can't. It might wake Schwartze, and I think this is the first sleep
he's had for weeks. Listen, Cecelia, I once had an affair with the
wife of a producer. A very short affair. When it was over she said to
me in no uncertain terms, she said: 'Don't you ever tell about this or

I'll have you thrown out of Hollywood. My husband's a much more important man than you.' "

I liked him again now, and presently the taxi turned down a long lane fragrant with honeysuckle and narcissus and stopped beside the great grey hulk of the Andrew Jackson house. The driver turned around to tell us something about it but Wylie shushed him, pointing at Schwartze, and we tiptoed out of the car.

"You can't get into the Mansion now," the taxi man told us politely.

Wylie and I went and sat against the wide pillars of the steps.

"What about Mr. Schwartze?" I asked. "Who is he?"

"To hell with Schwartze. He was the head of some combine once—First National? Paramount? United Artists? Now he's down and out. But he'll be back. You can't flunk out of pictures unless you're a dope or a drunk."

"You don't like Hollywood," I suggested.

"Yes I do. Sure I do. Say! This isn't anything to talk about on the steps of Andrew Jackson's house—at dawn."

"I *like* Hollywood," I persisted.

"It's all right. It's a mining town in lotus land. Who said that? I did. It's a good place for toughies but I went there from Savannah, Georgia. I went to a garden party the first day. My host shook hands and left me. It was all there—that swimming pool, green moss at two dollars an inch, beautiful felines having drinks and fun—

"—And nobody spoke to me. Not a soul. I spoke to half a dozen people but they didn't answer. That continued for an hour, two hours—then I got up from where I was sitting and ran out at a dog trot like a crazy man. I didn't feel I had any rightful identity until I got back to the hotel and the clerk handed me a letter addressed to me in my name."

Naturally I hadn't ever had such an experience, but looking back on parties I'd been to, I realized that such things could happen. We don't go for strangers in Hollywood unless they wear a sign saying that their axe has been thoroughly ground elsewhere, and that in any case it's not going to fall on our necks—in other words unless they're a celebrity. And they'd better look out even then.

"You should have risen above it," I said smugly. "It's not a slam at *you* when people are rude—it's a slam at the people they've met before."

"Such a pretty girl—to say such wise things."

There was an eager to-do in the eastern sky, and Wylie could see me plain—thin with good features and lots of style, and the kicking fetus of a mind. I wonder what I looked like in that dawn, five years ago. A little rumpled and pale, I suppose, but at that age, when one has the young illusion that most adventures are good, I needed only a bath and a change to go on for hours.

Wylie stared at me with really flattering appreciation—and then suddenly we were not alone. Mr. Schwartze wandered apologetically into the pretty scene.

"I fell upon a large metal handle," he said, touching the corner of his eye.

Wylie jumped up.

"Just in time, Mr. Schwartze," he said. "The tour is just starting. Home of Old Hickory—America's tenth president. The victor of New Orleans, opponent of the National Bank, and inventor of the Spoils System."

Schwartze looked toward me as toward a jury.

"There's a writer for you," he said. "Knows everything and at the same time he knows nothing."

"What's that?" said Wylie, indignant.

It was my first inkling that he was a writer. And while I like writers—because if you ask a writer anything you usually get an answer—still it belittled him in my eyes. Writers aren't people exactly. Or, if they're any good, they're a whole *lot* of people trying so hard to be one person. It's like actors, who try so pathetically not to look in mirrors. Who lean *back*ward trying—only to see their faces in the reflecting chandeliers.

"Ain't writers like that, Celia?" demanded Schwartze. "I have no words for them. I only know it's true."

Wylie looked at him with slowly gathering indignation. "I've heard that before," he said. "Look, Mannie, I'm a more practical man than you any day! I've sat in an office and listened to some mystic stalk up and down for hours spouting tripe that'd land him on a nut-farm anywhere outside of California—and then at the end tell me how *prac*tical he was, and *I* was a dreamer—and would I kindly go away and made sense out of what he'd said."

Mr. Schwartze's face fell into its more disintegrated alignments. One eye looked upward through the tall elms: He raised his hand and bit without interest at the cuticle on his second finger. There was a bird flying about the chimney of the house and his glance followed it. It perched on the chimney pot like a raven and Mr. Schwartze's eyes remained fixed upon it as he said: "We can't get in. And it's time for you two to go back to the plane."

It was still not quite dawn. The Hermitage looked like a nice big white box, but a little lonely, and vacated still, after a hundred years. We walked back to the car—only after we had gotten in, and Mr. Schwartze had surprisingly shut the taxi door on us, did we realize he didn't intend to come along.

"I'm not going to the Coast—I decided that when I woke up. So I'll stay here, and afterwards the driver could come back for me."

"Going back East?" said Wylie with surprise. "Just because—"

"I have decided," said Schwartze, faintly smiling. "Once I used to be a regular man of decision—you'd be surprised." He felt in his pocket, as the taxi driver warmed up the engine. "Will you give this note to Mr. Smith?"

"Shall I come in two hours?" the driver asked Schwartze.

"Yes . . . sure. I shall be glad to entertain myself looking around."

I kept thinking of him all the way back to the airport—trying to fit him into that early hour and into that landscape. He had come a long way from some ghetto to present himself at that raw shrine. Mannie Schwartze and Andrew Jackson—it was hard to say them in the same sentence. It was doubtful if he knew who Andrew Jackson was as he wandered around, but perhaps he figured that if people had preserved his house Andrew Jackson must have been someone who was large and merciful, able to understand. At both ends of life man needed nourishment—a breast—a shrine. Something to lay himself beside when no one wanted him further, and shoot a bullet into his head.

Of course we did not know this for twenty hours. When we got to the airport we told the purser that Mr. Schwartze was not continuing, and then forgot about him. The storm had wandered away into eastern Tennessee and broken against the mountains, and we were taking off in less than an hour. Sleepy-eyed travellers appeared from the hotel and I dozed a few minutes on one of those iron maidens they use for couches. Slowly the idea of a perilous journey was recreated out of the debris of our failure: a new stewardess, tall, handsome, flashing dark, exactly like the other except she wore seersucker instead of Frenchy red-and-blue, went briskly past us with a suitcase. Wylie sat beside me as we waited.

"Did you give the note to Mr. Smith?" I asked, half asleep.

"Yeah."

"Who is Mr. Smith? I suspect he spoiled Mr. Schwartze's trip."

"It was Schwartze's fault."

"I'm prejudiced against steam-rollers," I said. "My father tries to be a steam-roller around the house, and I tell him to save it for the studio."

I wondered if I was being fair; words are the palest counters at that time in the morning. "Still, he steam-rollered me into Bennington and I've always been grateful for that."

"There would be quite a crash—" Wylie said, "—if steam-roller Brady met steam-roller Smith."

"Is Mr. Smith a competitor of Father's?"

"Not exactly. I should say no. But if he was a competitor I know where my money would be."

"On Father?"

"I'm afraid not."

It was too early in the morning for family patriotism. The pilot was at the desk with the purser and he shook his head as they regarded a prospective passenger who had put two nickels in the electric phonograph and lay alcoholically on a bench fighting off sleep. The first song he had chosen, "Lost," thundered through the room, followed, after a slight interval, by his other choice, "Gone," which was equally dogmatic and final. The pilot shook his head emphatically and walked over to the passenger.

"Afraid we're not going to be able to carry you this time, old man."

"Wha?"

The drunk sat up, awful looking, yet discernibly attractive, and I was sorry for him in spite of his passionately ill-chosen music.

"Go back to the hotel and get some sleep. There'll be another plane tonight."

"Only going up in ee *air*."

"Not this time, old man."

In his disappointment the drunk fell off the bench—and above the phonograph, a loudspeaker summoned us respectable people outside. In the corridor of the plane I ran into Monroe Stahr and fell all over him, or wanted to. There was a man any girl would go for, with or without encouragement. I was emphatically with*out* it, but he liked me and sat down opposite till the plane took off.

"Let's all ask for our money back," he suggested. His dark eyes took me in, and I wondered what they would look like if he fell in love. They were kind, aloof and, though they often reasoned with you gently, somewhat superior. It was no fault of theirs if they saw so much. He darted in and out of the role of "one of the boys" with dexterity—but on the whole I should say he wasn't one of them. But he knew how to shut up, how to draw into the background, how to listen. From where he stood (and though he was not a tall man it always seemed high up) he watched the multitudinous practicalities of his world like a proud young shepherd, to whom night and day had never mattered. He was born sleepless without a talent for rest or the desire for it.

We sat in unembarrassed silence—I had known him since he became Father's partner a dozen years ago, when I was seven and Stahr was twenty-two. Wylie was across the aisle and I didn't know whether or not to introduce them, but Stahr kept turning his ring so abstractedly that he made me feel young and invisible, and I didn't dare. I never dared look quite away from him or quite *at* him, unless I had something important to say—and I knew he affected many other people in the same manner.

"I'll *give* you this ring, Cecelia."

"I beg your pardon. I didn't realize that I was—"

"I've got half a dozen like it."

He handed it to me, a gold nugget with the letter S in bold relief. I had been thinking how oddly its bulk contrasted with his fingers, which were delicate and slender like the rest of his body, and like his slender face with the arched eyebrows and the dark curly hair. He looked spiritual at times but he was a fighter—somebody out of his past knew him when he was one of a gang of kids in the Bronx, and gave me a description of how he walked always at the head of his gang, this rather frail boy, occasionally throwing a command backward out of the corner of his mouth.

Stahr folded my hand over the ring, stood up and addressed Wylie.

"Come up to the bridal suite," he said. "See you later, Cecelia."

Before they went out of hearing I heard Wylie's question, "Did you open Schwartze's note?" And Stahr:

"Not yet."

I must be slow, for only then did I realize that Stahr was Mr. Smith.

Afterwards Wylie told me what was in the note. Written by the headlights of the taxi it was almost illegible.

Dear Monro, You are the best of them all I have always admired your mentality so when you turn against me I know it's no use! I must be no good and am not going to continue the journey let me warn you once again look out! I know.

Your friend
MANNIE

Stahr read it twice, and raised his hand to the morning stubble on his chin.

"He's a nervous wreck," he said. "There's nothing to be done, absolutely nothing. I'm sorry I was short with him—but I don't like a man to approach me telling me it's for *my* sake."

"Maybe it was," said Wylie.

"It's poor technique."

"I'd fall for it," said Wylie. "I'm vain as a woman. If anybody pretends to be interested in me I'll ask for more. I like advice."

Stahr shook his head distastefully. Wylie kept on ribbing him—he was one of those to whom this privilege was permitted.

"You fall for some kinds of flattery," he said. "This 'little Napoleon stuff.' "

"It makes me sick," said Stahr, "but it's not as bad as some man trying to help you."

"If you don't like advice why do you pay *me*?"

"That's a question of merchandise," said Stahr. "I'm a merchant. I want to buy what's in your mind."

"You're no merchant," said Wylie. "I knew a lot of them when I was a publicity man and I agree with Charles Francis Adams."

"What did he say?"

"He knew them all—Gould, Vanderbilt, Carnegie, Astor—and he said there wasn't one he'd care to meet again in the hereafter. Well—they haven't improved since then, and that's why I say you're no merchant."

"Adams was probably a sour belly," said Stahr. "He wanted to be head man himself but he didn't have the judgement or else the character."

"He had brains," said Wylie rather tartly.

"It takes more than brains. You writers and artists poop out and get all mixed up and somebody has to come in and straighten you out." He shrugged his shoulders. "You seem to take things so personally, hating people and worshipping them—always thinking people are so important—especially yourselves. You just ask to be kicked around. I like people and I like them to like me but I wear my heart where God put it—on the inside."

He broke off.

"What did I say to Schwartze in the airport? Do you remember —exactly?"

"You said 'Whatever you're after, the answer is No.' "

Stahr was silent.

"He was sunk," said Wylie, "but I laughed him out of it. We took Pat Brady's daughter for a ride."

Stahr rang for the stewardess.

"That pilot," he said. "Would he mind if I sat up in front with him awhile?"

"That's against the rules, Mr. Smith."

"Ask him to step in here a minute when he's free."

Stahr sat up front all afternoon. While we slid off the endless desert and over the table-lands, dyed with many colors like the white sands we dyed with colors when I was a child. Then in the late afternoon, the peaks themselves—the Mountains of the Frozen Saw—slid under our propellers and we were close to home.

When I wasn't dozing I was thinking that I wanted to marry Stahr, that I wanted to make him love me. Oh, the conceit! What on earth did I have to offer? But I didn't think like that then. I had the pride of young women, which draws its strength from such sublime thoughts as "I'm as good as *she* is." For my purposes I was just as beautiful as the great beauties who must have inevitably thrown themselves at his head. My little spurt of intellectual interest was of course making me fit to be a brilliant ornament of any salon.

I know now it was absurd. Though Stahr's education was founded on nothing more than a night-school course in stenography, he had a long time ago run ahead through trackless wastes of perception into fields where very few men were able to follow him. But in my reckless conceit I matched my grey eyes against his brown ones for guile, my young golf-and-tennis heart-beats against his, which must be slowing a little after years of over-work. And I planned and I contrived and I plotted—any woman can tell you—but it never came to anything, as you will see. I still like to think that if he'd been a poor boy and nearer my age I could have managed it, but of course the real truth was that I had nothing to offer that he didn't have; some of my more romantic ideas actually stemmed from pictures—"42nd Street," for example, had a great influence on me. It's more than possible that some of the pictures which Stahr himself conceived had shaped me into what I was.

So it was rather hopeless. Emotionally, at least, people can't live by taking in each other's washing.

But at that time it was different: Father might help, the stewardess might help. She might go up in the cockpit and say to Stahr: "If I ever saw love it's in that girl's eyes."

The pilot might help: "Man are you blind? Why don't you go back there?"

Wylie White might help—instead of standing in the aisle looking at me doubtfully, wondering whether I was awake or asleep.

"Sit down," I said. "What's new, where are we?"

"Up in the air."

"Oh, so that's it. Sit down." I tried to show a cheerful interest. "What are you writing?"

"Heaven help me, I am writing about a Boy Scout—*The* Boy Scout."

"Is it Stahr's idea?"

"I don't know—he told me to look into it. He may have ten writers working ahead of me or behind me, a system which he so thoughtfully invented. So you're in love with him?"

"I should say not," I said indignantly. "I've known him all my life."

"Desperate, eh? Well, I'll arrange it if you'll use all your influence to advance me. I want a unit of my own."

I closed my eyes again and drifted off. When I woke up the stewardess was putting a blanket over me.

"Almost there," she said.

Out the window I could see by the sunset that we were in a greener land.

"I just heard something funny," she volunteered. "Up in the cockpit—that Mr. Smith—or Mr. Stahr—I never remember seeing his name."

"It's never on any pictures," I said.

"Oh. Well, he's been asking the pilots a lot about flying—I mean he's interested? You *know*?"

"I know."

"I mean one of them told me he bet he could teach Mr. Stahr solo flying in ten minutes. He has such a fine mentality, that's what he said."

I was getting impatient.

"Well, what was so funny?"

"Well, finally one of the pilots asked Mr. Smith if he liked his business and Mr. Smith said, 'Sure. Sure I like it. It's nice being the only sound nut in a hatful of cracked ones.' "

The stewardess doubled up with laughter—and I could have spit at her.

"I mean calling all those people a hatful of nuts. I mean *cracked* nuts." Her laughter stopped with unexpected suddenness and her face was grave as she stood up. "Well, I've got to finish my chart."

"Good bye."

Obviously Stahr had put the pilots right up on the throne with him and let them rule with him for a while. Years later I travelled with one of those same pilots and he told me one thing Stahr had said.

He was looking down at the mountains.

"Suppose you were a railroad man," he said. "You have to send a train through there somewhere. Well, you get your surveyors' reports, and you find there's three or four or half a dozen gaps, and not one is better than the other. You've got to decide—on what basis? You can't test the best way—except by doing it. So you just do it."

The pilot thought he had missed something.

"How do you mean?"

"You choose some one way for no reason at all—because that mountain's pink or the blueprint is a better blue. You see?"

The pilot considered that this was very valuable advice. But he doubted if he'd ever be in a position to apply it.

"What I wanted to know," he told me ruefully, "is how he ever got to be Mr. Stahr."

I'm afraid Stahr could never have answered that one, for the embryo is not equipped with a memory. But I could answer a little. He had flown up very high to see, on strong wings when he was young. And while he was up there he had looked on all the kingdoms, with the kind of eyes that can stare straight into the sun. Beating his wings tenaciously—finally frantically—and keeping on beating them he had stayed up there longer than most of us, and then, remembering all he had seen from his great height of how things were, he had settled gradually to earth.

The motors were off and all our five senses began to readjust themselves for landing. I could see a line of lights for the Long Beach Naval Station ahead and to the left, and on the right a twinkling blur for Santa Monica. The California moon was out, huge and orange over the Pacific. However I happened to feel about these things—and they were home after all—I know that Stahr must have felt much more. These were the things I had first opened my eyes on, like the sheep on the back lot of the old Laemmle studio; but this was where Stahr had come to earth after that extraordinary illuminating flight where he saw which way we were going, and how we looked doing it, and how much of it mattered. You could say that this was where an accidental wind blew him but I don't think so. I would rather think that in a "long shot" he saw a new way of measuring our jerky hopes and graceful rogueries and awkward sorrows, and that he came here from choice to be with us to the end. Like the plane coming down into the Glendale airport, into the warm darkness.

Episodes 4 and 5

It was nine o'clock of a July night and there were still some extras in the drug store across from the studio—I could see them bent over the pin-games inside—as I parked my car. "Old" Johnny Swanson stood on the corner in his semi-cowboy clothes staring gloomily past the moon. Once he had been as big in pictures as Tom Mix or Bill Hart—now it was too sad to speak to him and I hurried across the street and through the front gate.

There is never a time when a studio is absolutely quiet. There is always a night shift of technicians in the laboratories and dubbing rooms and people on the maintenance staff dropping in at the commissary. But the sounds are all different—the padded hush of tires, the quiet tick of a motor running idle, the naked cry of a soprano singing into a nightbound microphone. Around a corner I came upon a man in rubber boots washing down a car in a wonderful white light—a fountain among the dead industrial shadows. I slowed up as I saw Mr. Marcus being hoisted into his car in front of the Administration Building, because he took so long to say anything, even goodnight—and while I waited I realized that the soprano was singing "Come! Come! I love you only" over and over; I remember this because she kept singing the same line during the earthquake. That didn't come for five minutes yet.

Father's offices were in the old building with the long balconies and iron rails with their suggestion of a perpetual tightrope. Father was on the second floor with Stahr on one side and Mr. Marcus on the other—this evening there were lights all along the row. My stomach dipped a little at the proximity to Stahr but that was in pretty good control now—I'd seen him only once in the month I'd been home.

There were a lot of strange things about Father's office but I'll make it brief. In the outer part were three poker-faced secretaries who had sat there like witches ever since I could remember—Birdy Peters, Maude something, and Rosemary Schmiel; I don't know whether this was her name but she was the Dean of the trio, so to speak, and under her desk was the kick-lock that admitted you to Father's throne room. All three of the secretaries were passionate capitalists and Birdy had invented the rule that if typists were seen eating together more than once in a single week they were hauled up on the carpet. At that time the studio feared mob rule.

I went on in. Nowadays all chief executives have huge drawing rooms but my father's was the first. It was also the first to have one-way glass in the big French windows and I've heard a story about a trap in the floor that would drop unpleasant visitors to an oubliette below but believe it to be an invention. There was a big painting of Will Rogers, hung conspicuously and intended, I think, to suggest Father's essential kinship with Hollywood's St. Francis; there was a signed photograph of Minna Davis, Stahr's dead wife, and photos of other studio celebrities and big chalk drawings of Mother and me. Tonight the one-way French windows were open and a big moon, rosy-gold with a haze around, was wedged helpless in one of them. Father and Jaques La Borwits and Rosemary Schmiel were down at the end around a big circular desk.

What did Father look like? I couldn't describe him except for once in New York when I met him where I didn't expect to; I was aware of a bulky, middle-aged man who looked a little ashamed of himself and I wished he'd move on—and then I saw he was Father. Afterward I was shocked at my impression. Father can be very magnetic—he has a tough jaw and an Irish smile.

But as for Jaques La Borwits I shall spare you. Let me just say he was an assistant producer which is something like a commissar, and let it go at that. Where Stahr picked up such mental cadavers or had them forced upon him—or especially how he got any use out of them—has always amazed me, as it amazed everyone fresh from the East who slapped up against them. Jaques La Borwits had his points, no doubt, but so have the sub-microscopic protozoa, so has a dog prowling for a bitch and a bone. Jaques La—oh, my!

From their expressions I was sure they had been talking about Stahr. Stahr had ordered something or forbidden something, or defied Father or junked one of La Borwits' pictures or something catastrophic and they were sitting there in protest at night in a community of rebellion and helplessness. Rosemary Schmiel sat pad in hand as if ready to write down their dejection.

"I'm to drive you home dead or alive," I told Father. "All those birthday presents rotting away in their packages!"

"A birthday!" cried Jaques in a flurry of apology. "How old? I didn't know."

"Forty-three," said Father distinctly.

He was older than that—four years—and Jaques knew it; I saw him note it down in his account book to use sometime. Out here these account books are carried open in the hand. One can see the entries being made without recourse to lip reading and Rosemary Schmiel was compelled in emulation to make a mark on her pad. As she rubbed it out the earth quaked under us.

We didn't get the full shock like at Long Beach where the upper stories of shops were spewed into the streets and small hotels drifted out to sea—but for a full minute our bowels were one with the bowels of the earth—like some nightmare attempt to attach our navel cords again and jerk us back to the womb of creation.

Mother's picture fell off the wall revealing a small safe—Rosemary and I grabbed frantically for each other and did a strange screaming waltz across the room. Jaques fainted or at least disappeared and Father clung to his desk and shouted "Are you all right?" Outside the window the singer came to the climax of "I love you only," held it a moment and then, I swear, started it all over. Or maybe they were playing it back to her from the recording machine.

The room stood still, shimmying a little. We made our way to the door, suddenly including Jaques who had reappeared, and tottered out dizzily through the ante-room on to the iron balcony. Almost all the lights were out and from here and there we could hear cries and calls. Momentarily we stood waiting for a second shock—then as with a common impulse we went into Stahr's entry and through to his office.

The office was big but not as big as Father's. Stahr sat on the side of his couch rubbing his eyes. When the quake came he had been asleep and he wasn't sure yet whether he had dreamed it. When we convinced him he thought it was all rather funny—until the telephones began to ring. I watched him as unobtrusively as possible. He was grey with fatigue while he listened to the phone and Dictograph but as the reports came in, his eyes began to pick up shine.

"A couple of water mains have burst," he said to Father, "—they're heading into the back lot."

"Gray's shooting in the French Village," said Father.

"It's flooded around the Station too and in the Jungle and the City Corner, what the hell—nobody seems to be hurt." In passing he shook my hands gravely. "Where've you been, Cecelia?"

"You going out there, Monroe?" Father asked.

"When all the news is in. One of the power lines is off too—I've sent for Robinson."

He made me sit down with him on the couch and tell about the quake again.

"You look tired," I said, cute and motherly.

"Yes," he agreed, "I've got no place to go in the evenings so I just work."

"I'll arrange some evenings for you."

"I used to play poker with a gang," he said thoughtfully. "Before I was married. But they all drank themselves to death."

Miss Doolan, his secretary, came in with fresh bad news.

"Robby'll take care of everything when he comes," Stahr assured Father. He turned to me. "Now there's a man—that Robinson. He was a trouble-shooter—fixed the telephone wires in Minnesota blizzards—nothing stumps him. He'll be here in a minute—you'll like Robby."

He said it as if it had been his life-long intention to bring us together, and he had arranged the whole earthquake with just that in mind.

"Yes, you'll like Robby," he repeated. "When do you go back to college?"

"I've just come home."

"You get the whole summer?"

"I'm sorry," I said. "I'll go back as soon as I can."

I was in a mist. It hadn't failed to cross my mind that he might have some intention about me but if it was so, it was in an exasperatingly early stage—I was merely "a good property." And the idea didn't seem so attractive at that moment—like marrying a doctor. He seldom left the studio before eleven.

"How long—" he asked my father, "—before she graduates from college? That's what I was trying to say."

And I think I was about to sing out eagerly that I needn't go back at all, that I was quite educated already—when the totally admirable Robinson came in. He was a bowlegged young redhead, all ready to go.

"This is Robby, Cecelia," said Stahr. "Come on, Robby."

So I met Robby. I can't say it seemed like fate—but it was. For it was Robby who later told me how Stahr found his love that night.

Episode 6

Under the moon the back lot was thirty acres of fairyland—not because the locations really looked like African jungles and French châteaux and schooners at anchor and Broadway by night, but because they looked like the torn picture books of childhood, like fragments of stories dancing in an open fire. I never lived in a house with an attic but a back lot must be something like that and at night of course in an enchanted distorted way, it all comes true.

When Stahr and Robby arrived clusters of lights had already picked out the danger spots in the flood.

"We'll pump it out into the swamp on Thirty-sixth Street," said

Robby after a moment. "It's city property—but isn't this an act of God? Say—look there!"

On top of a huge head of the god Siva, two women were floating down the current of an impromptu river. The idol had come un-loosed from a set of Burma and it meandered earnestly on its way, stopping sometimes to waddle and bump in the shallows with the other debris of the tide. The two refugees had found sanctuary along a scroll of curls on its bald forehead and seemed at first glance to be sightseers on an interesting bus-ride through the scene of the flood.

"Will you look at that, Monroe!" said Robby. "Look at those dames!"

Dragging their legs through sudden bogs they made their way to the bank of the stream. Now they could see the women looking a little scared but brightening at the prospect of rescue.

"We ought to let 'em drift out to the waste pipe," said Robby gallantly, "but De Mille needs that head next week."

He wouldn't have hurt a fly though and presently he was hip deep in the water fishing for them with a pole and succeeding only in spinning it in a dizzy circle. Help arrived and the impression quickly got around that one of them was very pretty and then that they were people of importance. But they were just strays and Robby waited disgustedly to give them hell while the thing was brought finally into control and beached.

"Put that head back!" he called up to them. "You think it's a souvenir?"

One of the women came sliding smoothly down the cheek of the idol and Robby caught and set her on solid ground; the other one hesitated and then followed. Robby turned to Stahr for judgement.

"What'll we do with them, chief?"

Stahr did not answer. Smiling faintly at him from not four feet away was the face of his dead wife, identical even to the expression. Across the four feet of moonlight the eyes he knew looked back at him, a curl blew a little on a familiar forehead, the smile lingered changed a little according to pattern, the lips parted—the same. An awful fear went over him and he wanted to cry aloud. Back from the still sour room, the muffled glide of the limousine hearse, the falling concealing flowers, from out there in the dark—here now warm and glowing. The river passed him in a rush, the great spot-lights swooped and blinked—and then he heard another voice speak that was not Minna's voice.

"We're sorry," said the voice. "We followed a truck in through a gate."

A little crowd had gathered—electricians, grips, truckers—and Robby began to nip at them like a sheep dog.

". . . get the big pumps on the tanks on Stage 4 . . . put a cable around this head . . . raft it up on a couple of two-by-fours . . . get the water out of the Jungle first for Christ's sake . . . that big A pipe lay it down, all that stuff is plastic. . . ."

Stahr stood watching the two women as they threaded their way after a policeman toward an exit gate. Then he took a tentative step to see if the weakness had gone out of his knees. A loud tractor came bumping through the slush and men began streaming by him—every second one glancing at him smiling speaking Hello Monroe . . . Hello Mr. Stahr . . . wet night Mr. Stahr . . . Monroe . . . Monroe . . . Stahr . . . Stahr . . . Stahr.

He spoke and waved back as the people streamed by in the dark-ness, looking I suppose a little like the Emperor and the Old Guard. There is no world so but it has its heroes and Stahr was the hero. Most of these men had been here a long time—through the begin-nings and the great upset when sound came and the three years of Depression he had seen that no harm came to them. The old loyal-ties were trembling now—there were clay feet everywhere—but still he was their man, the last of the princes. And their greeting was a sort of low cheer as they went by.

Episode 7

Between the night I got back and the quake I'd made many observations.

About Father, for example. I loved Father—in a sort of irregular graph with many low swoops—but I began to see that his strong will didn't fill him out as a passable man. Most of what he accom-plished boiled down to shrewd. He had acquired with luck and shrewdness a quarter interest in a booming circus—together with young Stahr. That was his life's effort—all the rest was an instinct to hang on. Of course he talked that double talk to Wall Street about how mysterious it was to make a picture but Father didn't know the ABC's of dubbing or even cutting. Nor had he learned much about the feel of America as a bar boy in Ballyhegan nor have any more than a drummer's sense of a story. On the other hand he didn't have concealed paresis like ———; he came to the studio before noon, and with a suspiciousness developed like a muscle it was hard to put anything over on him.

Stahr had been his luck—and Stahr was something else again. He was a marker in industry like Edison and Lumière and Griffith and Chaplin. He led pictures way up past the range and power of the theatre, reaching a sort of golden age before the censorship in 1933. Proof of his leadership was the spying that went on around him—not just for inside information or patented process secrets—but spying on his scent for a trend in taste, his guess as how things were going to be. Too much of his vitality was taken by the mere parrying of these attempts. It made his work secret in part, often devious, slow—and hard to describe as the plans of a general—where the psychological factors become too tenuous and we end by merely adding up the successes and failures. But I have determined to give you a glimpse of him functioning, which is my excuse for what follows. It is drawn partly from a paper I wrote in college on "A Producer's Day" and partly from my imagination. More often I have blocked in the ordinary events myself, while the stranger ones are true.

In the early morning after the flood, a man walked up to the outside balcony of the Administration Building. He lingered there some time according to an eyewitness, then mounted to the iron railing and dove head first to the pavement below. Breakage—one arm.

Miss Doolan, Stahr's secretary, told him about it when he buzzed for her at nine. He had slept in his office without hearing the small commotion.

"Pete Zavras!" Stahr exclaimed, "—the camera man?"

"They took him to a doctor's office. It won't be in the paper."

"Hell of a thing," he said, "I knew he'd gone to pot—but I don't know why. He was all right when we used him two years ago—why should he come here? How did he get in?"

"He bluffed it with his old studio pass," said Catherine Doolan. She was a dry hawk, the wife of an assistant director. "Perhaps the quake had something to do with it."

"He was the best camera man in town," Stahr said. When he had heard of the thousands dead at Long Beach he was still haunted by the abortive suicide at dawn. He told Catherine Doolan to trace the matter down.

The first Dictograph messages blew in through the warm morning. While he shaved and had coffee he talked and listened. Robby had left a message: "If Mr. Stahr wants me tell him to hell with it I'm in bed." An actor was sick or thought so; the Governor of California was bringing a party out; a supervisor had beaten up his wife for the prints and must be "reduced to a writer"—these three affairs were Father's job—unless the actor was under personal contract to Stahr. There was early snow on a location in Canada with the company already there—Stahr raced over the possibilities of salvage reviewing the story of the picture. Nothing. Stahr called Catherine Doolan.

"I want to speak to the cop who put two women off the back lot last night. I think his name's Malone."

"Yes, Mr. Stahr. I've got Joe Wyman—about the trousers."

"Hello Joe," said Stahr. "Listen—two people at the sneak preview complained that Morgan's fly was open for half the picture . . . of course they're exaggerating but even if it's only ten feet . . . no, we can't find the people but I want that picture run over and over until you find that footage. Get a lot of people in the projection room—somebody'll spot it."

> *Tout passe.—L'art robuste*
> *Seul a l'éternité.*

"And there's the Prince from Denmark," said Catherine Doolan. "He's very handsome." She was impelled to add pointlessly "—for a tall man."

"Thanks," Stahr said. "Thank you, Catherine, I appreciate it that I am now the handsomest small man on the lot. Send the Prince out on the sets and tell him we'll lunch at one."

"And Mr. George Boxley—looking very angry in a British way."

"I'll see him for ten minutes."

As she went out he asked:

"Did Robby phone in?"

"No."

"Call Sound and if he's been heard from call him and ask him this. Ask him this—did he hear that woman's name last night. Either of those women. Or anything so they could be traced."

"Anything else?"

"No, but tell him it's important while he still remembers. What were they? I mean what kind of people—ask him that too. I mean were they—"

She waited, scratching his words on her pad without looking.

"—oh, were they—questionable? Were they theatrical? Never mind—skip that. Just ask if he knows how they can be traced."

The policeman, Malone, had known nothing. Two dames and he had hustled 'em you betcha. One of them was sore. Which one? One of them. They had a car, a Chevvy, he thought of taking the license. Was it—the good looker who was sore? It was one of them.

Not which one—he had noticed nothing. Even on the lot here Minna was forgotten. In three years. So much for that then.

Episode 8

Stahr smiled at Mr. George Boxley. It was a kindly fatherly smile Stahr had developed inversely when he was a young man pushed into high places. Originally it had been a smile of respect toward his elders, then as his own decisions grew rapidly to displace theirs, a smile so that they should not feel it—finally emerging as what it was, a smile of kindness sometimes a little hurried and tired but always there, toward anyone who had not angered him within the hour. Or anyone he did not intend to insult aggressive and outright.

Mr. Boxley did not smile back. He came in with the air of being violently dragged though no one apparently had a hand on him. He stood in front of a chair and again it was as if two invisible attendants seized his arms and set him down forcibly into it. He sat there morosely. Even when he lit a cigarette on Stahr's invitation one felt that the match was held to it by exterior forces he disdained to control.

Stahr looked at him courteously.

"Something not going well, Mr. Boxley?"

The novelist looked back at him in thunderous silence.

"I read your letter," said Stahr. The tone of the pleasant young headmaster was gone. He spoke as to an equal but with a faint two-edged deference.

"I can't get what I write on paper," broke out Boxley. "You've all been very decent but it's a sort of conspiracy. Those two hacks you've teamed me with listen to what I say but they spoil it—they seem to have a vocabulary of about a hundred words."

"Why don't you write it yourself?" asked Stahr.

"I have. I sent you some."

"But it was just talk, back and forth," said Stahr mildly. "Interesting talk but nothing more."

Now it was all the two ghostly attendants could do to hold Boxley in the deep chair. He struggled to get up; he uttered a single quiet bark which had some relation to laughter but none to amusement, and said:

"I don't think you people read things. The men are dueling when the conversation takes place. At the end one of them falls into a well and has to be hauled up in a bucket."

He barked again and subsided.

"Would you write that in a book of your own, Mr. Boxley?"

"What? Naturally not."

"You'd consider it too cheap."

"Movie standards are different," said Boxley hedging.

"Do you ever go to them?"

"No—almost never."

"Isn't it because people are always dueling and falling down wells?"

"Yes—and wearing strained facial expressions and talking incredible and unnatural dialogue."

"Skip the dialogue for a minute," said Stahr. "Granted your dialogue is more graceful than what these hacks can write—that's why we brought you out here. But let's imagine something that isn't either bad dialogue or jumping down a well. Has your office got a stove in it that lights with a match?"

"I think it has," said Boxley stiffly, "—but I never use it."

"Suppose you're in your office. You've been fighting duels or writing all day and you're too tired to fight or write any more. You're sitting there staring—dull, like we all get sometimes. A pretty stenographer that you've seen before comes into the room and you watch her—idly. She doesn't see you though you're very close to her. She takes off her gloves, opens her purse and dumps it out on a table—"

Stahr stood up, tossing his key-ring on his desk.

"She has two dimes and a nickle—and a cardboard match box. She leaves the nickle on the desk, puts the two dimes back into her purse and takes her black gloves to the stove, opens it and puts them inside. There is one match in the match box and she starts to light it kneeling by the stove. You notice that there's a stiff wind blowing in the window—but just then your telephone rings. The girl picks it up, says hello—listens—and says deliberately into the phone 'I've never owned a pair of black gloves in my life.' She hangs up, kneels by the stove again, and just as she lights the match you glance around very suddenly and see that there's another man in the office, watching every move the girl makes—"

Stahr paused. He picked up his keys and put them in his pocket.

"Go on," said Boxley smiling. "What happens?"

"I don't know," said Stahr. "I was just making pictures."

Boxley felt he was being put in the wrong.

"It's just melodrama," he said.

"Not necessarily," said Stahr. "In any case nobody has moved violently or talked cheap dialogue or had any facial expression at all. There was only one bad line, and a writer like you could improve it. But you were interested."

"What was the nickle for?" asked Boxley evasively.

"I don't know," said Stahr. Suddenly he laughed, "Oh yes—the nickle was for the movies."

The two invisible attendants seemed to release Boxley. He relaxed, leaned back in his chair and laughed.

"What in hell do you pay me for?" he demanded. "I don't understand the damn stuff."

"You will," said Stahr grinning. "Or you wouldn't have asked about the nickle."

A dark saucer-eyed man was waiting in the outer office as they came out.

"Mr. Boxley, this is Mr. Mike Van Dyke," Stahr said. "What is it, Mike?"

"Nothing," Mike said. "I just came up to see if you were real."

"Why don't you go to work?" Stahr said. "I haven't had a laugh in the rushes for days."

"I'm afraid of a nervous breakdown."

"You ought to keep in form," Stahr said. "Let's see you peddle your stuff." He turned to Boxley. "Mike's a gag man—he was out here when I was in the cradle. Mike, show Mr. Boxley a double wing, clutch, kick and scram."

"Here?" asked Mike.

"Here."

"There isn't much room. I wanted to ask you about—"

"There's lots of room."

"Well," he looked around tentatively. "You shoot the gun."

Miss Doolan's assistant, Katie, took a paper bag, blew it open.

"It was a routine," Mike said to Boxley—"back in the Keystone days." He turned to Stahr. "Does he know what a routine is?"

"It means an act," Stahr explained. "Georgie Jessel talks about 'Lincoln's Gettysburg routine.' "

Katie poised the neck of the blown up bag in her mouth. Mike stood with his back to her.

"Ready?" Katie asked. She brought her hand down on the side. Immediately Mike grabbed his bottom with both hands, jumped in the air, slid his feet out on the floor one after the other, remaining in place and flapping his arms twice like a bird—

"Double wing," said Stahr.

—And then ran—out the screen door which the office boy held open for him and disappeared past the window of the balcony.

"Mr. Stahr," said Miss Doolan, "Mr. Hanson is on the phone from New York."

Ten minutes later he clicked his Dictograph and Miss Doolan came in. There was a male star waiting to see him in the outer office Miss Doolan said.

"Tell him I went out by the balcony," Stahr advised her.

"All right. He's been in four times this week. He seems very anxious."

"Did he give you any hint of what he wanted? Isn't it something he can see Mr. Brady about?"

"He didn't say. You have a conference coming up. Miss Meloney and Mr. White are outside. Mr. Broaca is next door in Mr. Rienmund's office."

"Send ———— in," said Stahr. "Tell him I can see him only for a minute."

When the handsome actor came in Stahr remained standing.

"What is it that can't wait?" he asked pleasantly.

The actor waited carefully till Miss Doolan had gone out.

"Monroe, I'm through," he said. "I had to see you."

"Through!" said Stahr. "Have you seen 'Variety'? Your picture's held over at Roxy's and did thirty-seven thousand in Chicago last week."

"That's the worst of it. That's the tragedy. I get everything I want and now it means nothing."

"Well, go on explain."

"There's nothing between Esther and me anymore. There never can be again."

"A row."

"Oh, no—worse—I can't bear to mention it. My head's in a daze. I wander around like a madman. I go through my part as if I was asleep."

"I haven't noticed it," said Stahr. "You were great in your rushes yesterday."

"Was I? That just shows you nobody ever guesses."

"Are you trying to tell me that you and Esther are separating?"

"I suppose it'll come to that. Yes—inevitably—it will."

"What was it?" demanded Stahr impatiently. "Did she come in without knocking?"

"Oh, there's nobody else. It's just—me. I'm through."

Stahr got it suddenly.

"How do you know?"

"It's been true for six weeks."

"It's your imagination," said Stahr. "Have you been to a doctor?"

The actor nodded.

"I've tried everything. I even—one day in desperation I went down to—to Claris. But it was hopeless. I'm washed up."

Stahr had an impish temptation to tell him to go to Brady about it. Brady handled all matters of public relations. Or was this private relations. He turned away a moment, got his face in control, turned back.

"I've been to Pat Brady," said the star, as if guessing the thought. "He gave me a lot of phoney advice and I tried it all but nothing doing. Esther and I sit opposite each other at dinner and I'm ashamed to look at her. She's been a good sport about it but I'm ashamed. I'm ashamed all day long. I think 'Rainy Day' grossed 25,000 in Des Moines and broke all records in St. Louis and did 27,000 in Kansas City. My fan mail's way up and there I am afraid to go home at night, afraid to go to bed."

Stahr began to be faintly oppressed. When the actor first came in Stahr had intended to invite him to a cocktail party but now it scarcely seemed appropriate. What would he want with a cocktail party with this hanging over him. In his mind's eye he saw him wandering haunted from guest to guest with a cocktail in his hand and his grosses up 28,000.

"So I came to you, Monroe. I never saw a situation where you didn't know a way out. I said to myself even if he advises me to kill myself I'll ask Monroe."

The buzzer sounded on Stahr's desk—he switched on the Dictograph and heard Miss Doolan's voice.

"Five minutes, Mr. Stahr."

"I'm sorry," said Stahr, "I'll need a few minutes more."

"Five hundred girls marched to my house from the high school," the actor said gloomily. "And I stood behind the curtains and watched them. I couldn't go out."

"You sit down," said Stahr. "We'll take plenty of time and talk this over."

In the outer office two members of the conference group had already waited ten minutes—Wylie White and Rose Meloney. The latter was a dried up little blonde of fifty about whom one could hear the fifty assorted opinions of Hollywood—"a sentimental dope," "the best writer on construction in Hollywood," "a veteran," "that old hack," "the smartest woman on the lot," "the cleverest plagiarist in the biz," and of course in addition a nymphomaniac, a virgin, a pushover, a lesbian and a faithful wife. Without being an old maid she was like most self-made women rather old maidish. She had ulcers of the stomach and her salary was over a hundred thousand a year. A complicated treatise could be written on whether she was "worth it" or more than that or nothing at all. Her value lay in such ordinary assets as the bare fact that she was a woman and adaptable, quick and trustworthy, "knew the game" and was without egotism. She had been a great friend of Minna's and over a period of years he had managed to stifle what amounted to a sharp physical revulsion.

She and Wylie waited in silence—occasionally addressing a remark to Miss Doolan. Every few minutes Rienmund the supervisor called up from his office where he and Broaca the director were waiting. After ten minutes Stahr's button went on and Miss Doolan called Rienmund and Broaca; simultaneously Stahr and the actor came out of Stahr's office with Stahr holding the man's arm. He was so wound up now that when Wylie White asked him how he was he opened his mouth and began to tell him then and there.

"Oh, I've had an awful time," he said but Stahr interrupted sharply.

"No you haven't. Now you go along and do the role the way I said."

"Thank you, Monroe."

Rose Meloney looked after him without speaking.

"Somebody been catching flies on him?" she asked, a phrase for stealing scenes.

"I'm sorry I kept you waiting," Stahr said. "Come on in."

Episode 9

It was noon already and the conferees were entitled to exactly an hour of Stahr's time. No less, for such a conference could only be interrupted by a director who was held up in his shooting; seldom much more because every eight days the company must release a production as complex and costly as Reinhardt's "Miracle."

Occasionally, less often than five years ago, Stahr would work all through the night on a single picture. But after such a spree he felt bad for days. If he could go from problem to problem there was a certain rebirth of vitality with each change. And like those sleepers who can wake whenever they wish, he had set his psychological clock to run one hour.

The cast assembled included besides the writers Rienmund, one of the most favored of the supervisors, and John Broaca, the picture's director.

Broaca, on the surface, was an engineer—large and without nerves, quietly resolute, popular. He was an ignoramus and Stahr often caught him making the same scenes over and over—one scene about a rich young girl occurred in all his pictures with the same action, the same business. A bunch of large dogs entered the room and jumped around the girl. Later the girl went to a stable and slapped a horse on the rump. The explanation was probably not Freudian; more likely that at a drab moment in youth he had looked through a fence and seen a beautiful girl with dogs and horses. As a trademark for glamor it was stamped on his brain forever.

Rienmund was a handsome young opportunist, with a fairly good education. Originally a man of some character he was being daily forced by his anomalous position into devious ways of acting and thinking. He was a bad man now, as men go. At thirty he had none of the virtues which either native Americans or Jews are taught to think admirable. But he got his pictures out in time and by manifesting an almost homosexual fixation on Stahr, seemed to have dulled Stahr's usual acuteness. Stahr liked him—considered him a good all around man.

Wylie White, of course, would have been recognizable in any country as an intellectual of the second order. He was civilized and voluble, both simple and acute, half dazed half saturnine. His jealousy of Stahr showed only in unguarded flashes, and was mingled with admiration and even affection.

"The production date for this picture is two weeks from Saturday," said Stahr. "I think basically it's all right—much improved."

Rienmund and the two writers exchanged a glance of congratulation.

"Except for one thing," said Stahr, thoughtfully. "I don't see why it should be produced at all and I've decided to put it away."

There was a moment of shocked silence—and then murmurs of protest, stricken queries.

"It's not your fault," Stahr said. "I thought there was something there that wasn't there—that was all." He hesitated, looking regretfully at Rienmund. "It's too bad—it was a good play. We paid fifty thousand for it."

"What's the matter with it, Monroe?" asked Broaca bluntly.

"Well, it hardly seems worth while to go into it," said Stahr.

Rienmund and Wylie White were both thinking of the professional effect on them. Rienmund had two pictures to his account this year—but Wylie White needed a credit to start his comeback to the scene. Rose Meloney was watching Stahr closely from little skull-like eyes.

"Couldn't you give us some clue?" Rienmund asked. "This is a good deal of a blow, Monroe."

"I just wouldn't put Margaret Sullavan in it," said Stahr. "Or Colman either. I wouldn't advise them to play it—"

"Specifically, Monroe," begged Wylie White. "What didn't you like? The scenes? the dialogue? the humor? construction?"

Stahr picked up the script from his desk, let it fall as if it were physically too heavy to handle.

"I don't like the people," he said. "I wouldn't like to meet them—if I knew they were going to be somewhere I'd go somewhere else."

Rienmund smiled but there was worry in his eyes.

"Well, that's a damning criticism," he said. "I thought the people were rather interesting."

"So did I," said Broaca. "I thought Em was very sympathetic."

"Did you?" asked Stahr sharply. "I could just barely believe she was alive. And when I came to the end I said to myself 'So what?' "

"There must be something to do," Rienmund said. "Naturally we feel bad about this. This is the structure we agreed on—"

"But it's not the story," said Stahr. "I've told you many times that the first thing I decide is the *kind* of story I want. We change in every other regard but once that is set we've got to work toward it with every line and movement. This is not the kind of a story I want. The story we bought had shine and glow—it was a happy story. This is all full of doubt and hesitation. The hero and heroine stop loving each other over trifles—then they start up again over trifles. After the first sequence you don't care if she never sees him again or he her."

"That's my fault," said Wylie suddenly. "You see, Monroe, I don't think stenographers have the same dumb admiration for their bosses they had in 1929. They've been laid off—they've seen their bosses jittery. The world has moved on, that's all."

Stahr looked at him impatiently, gave a short nod.

"That's not under discussion," he said. "The premise of this story is that the girl did have dumb admiration for her boss if you want to call it that. And there wasn't any evidence that he'd ever been jittery. When you make her doubt him in any way you have a different kind of story. Or rather you haven't anything at all. These people are extraverts—get that straight—and I want them to extravert all over the lot. When I want to do a Eugene O'Neill play I'll buy one."

Rose Meloney who had never taken her eyes off Stahr knew it
was going to be all right now. If he had really been going to abandon the picture he wouldn't have gone at it like this. She had been in
this game longer than any of them except Broaca with whom she
had had a three day affair twenty years ago.

Stahr turned to Rienmund.

"You ought to have understood from the casting, Rieny, what
kind of a picture I wanted. I started marking the lines that Carroll
and MacMurray couldn't say and got tired of it. Remember this in
future—if I order a limousine I want that kind of car. And the
fastest midget racer you ever saw wouldn't do. Now—" He looked
around. "Shall we go any farther? Now that I've told you I don't
even like the kind of picture this is? Shall we go on? We've got two
weeks. At the end of that time I'm going to put Carroll and Mac-
Murray into this or something else—is it worth while?"

"Well naturally," said Rienmund, "I think it is. I feel bad about
this. I should have warned Wylie. I thought he had some good
ideas."

"Monroe's right," said Broaca bluntly. "I felt this was wrong all
the time but I couldn't put my finger on it."

Wylie and Rose looked at him contemptuously and exchanged a
glance.

"Do you writers think you can get hot on it again?" asked Stahr,
not unkindly. "Or shall I try somebody fresh?"

"I'd like another shot," said Wylie.

"How about you, Rose?"

She nodded briefly.

"What do you think of the girl?" asked Stahr.

"Well—naturally I'm prejudiced in her favor."

"You better forget it," said Stahr warningly. "Ten million Americans would put thumbs down on that girl if she walked on the screen.
We've got an hour and twenty-five minutes on the screen—you show
a woman being unfaithful to a man for one-third of that time and
you've given the impression that she's one-third whore."

"Is that a big proportion?" asked Rose slyly, and they laughed.

"It is for me," said Stahr thoughtfully, "even if it wasn't for the

Hays office. If you want to paint a scarlet letter on her back it's all right but that's another story. Not this story. This is a future wife and mother. However—*however*—"

He pointed his pencil at Wylie White.

"—this has as much passion as that Oscar on my desk."

"What the hell!" said Wylie. "She's full of it. Why she goes to—"

"She's loose enough," said Stahr, "—but that's all. There's one scene in the play better than all this you cooked up and you've left it out. When she's trying to make the time pass by changing her watch."

"It didn't seem to fit," Wylie apologized.

"Now," said Stahr, "I've got about fifty ideas. I'm going to call Miss Doolan." He pressed a button. "—and if there's anything you don't understand speak up—"

Miss Doolan slid in almost imperceptibly. Pacing the floor swiftly Stahr began. In the first place he wanted to tell them what kind of a girl she was—what kind of a girl he approved of here. She was a perfect girl with a few small faults as in the play but a perfect girl not because the public wanted her that way but because it was the kind of girl that he, Stahr, liked to see in this sort of picture. Was that clear? It was no character role. She stood for health, vitality, ambition and love. What gave the play its importance was entirely a situation in which she found herself. She became possessed of a secret that affected a great many lives. There was a right thing and a wrong thing to do—at first it was not plain which was which but when it was she went right away and did it. That was the kind of story this was—thin, clean and shining. No doubts.

"She has never heard the word labor troubles," he said with a sigh. "She might be living in 1929. Is it plain what kind of girl I want?"

"It's very plain, Monroe."

"Now about the things she does," said Stahr. "At all times, at all moments when she is on the screen in our sight she wants to sleep with Ken Willard. Is that plain, Wylie?"

"Passionately plain."

"Whatever she does it is in place of sleeping with Ken Willard. If she walks down the street she is walking to sleep with Ken Willard, if she eats her food it is to give her strength to sleep with Ken Willard. *But* at no time do you give the impression that she would ever consider sleeping with Ken Willard unless they were properly sanctified. I'm ashamed of having to tell you these kindergarten facts but they have somehow leaked out of the story."

He opened the script and began to go through it page by page. Miss Doolan's notes would be typed in quintuplicate and given to them but Rose Meloney made notes of her own. Broaca put his hand up to his half closed eyes—he could remember "when a director was something out here," when writers were gag men or eager and ashamed young reporters full of whiskey—a director was all there was then. No supervisor—no Stahr.

He started wide awake as he heard his name.

"It would be nice, John, if you could put the boy on a pointed roof and let him walk around and keep the camera on him. You might get a nice feeling—not danger, not suspense, not pointing for anything—a kid on the roof in the morning."

Broaca brought himself back in the room.

"All right," he said. "—just an element of danger."

"Not exactly," said Stahr. "He doesn't start to fall off the roof. Break into the next scene with it."

"Through the window," suggested Rose Meloney. "He could climb in his sister's window."

"That's a good transition," said Stahr. "Right into the diary scene."

Broaca was wide awake now.

"I'll shoot up at him," he said. "Let him go away from the camera. Just a fixed shot from quite a distance—let him go away from the camera. Don't follow him. Pick him up in a close shot and let him go away again. No attention on him except against the whole roof and the sky." He liked the shot—it was a director's shot that didn't come up on every page any more. He might use a crane—it would be cheaper in the end than building the roof on the ground with a process sky. That was one thing about Stahr—the literal sky was the limit. He had worked with Jews too long to believe legends that they were small with money.

"In the third sequence have him hit the priest," Stahr said.

"What!" Wylie cried, "—and have the Catholics on our neck."

"I've talked to Joe Breen. Priests have been hit. It doesn't reflect on them."

His quiet voice ran on—stopped abruptly as Miss Doolan glanced at the clock.

"Is that too much to do before Monday?" he asked Wylie.

Wylie looked at Rose and she looked back not even bothering to nod. He saw their week-end melting away, but he was a different man from when he entered the room. When you were paid fifteen hundred a week emergency work was one thing you did not skimp, nor when your picture was threatened. As a "free lance" writer Wylie had failed from lack of caring but here was Stahr to care, for all of them. The effect would not wear off when he left the office—not anywhere within the walls of the lot. He felt a great purposefulness. The mixture of common sense, wise sensibility, theatrical ingenuity, and a certain half naive conception of the common weal which Stahr had just stated aloud, inspired him to do his part, to get his block of stone in place, even if the effort were foredoomed, the result as dull as a pyramid.

Out the window Rose Meloney watched the trickle streaming toward the commissary. She would have her lunch in her office and knit a few rows while it came. The man was coming at one-fifteen with the French perfume smuggled over the Mexican border. That was no sin—it was like prohibition.

Broaca watched as Rienmund fawned upon Stahr. He sensed that Rienmund was on his way up—not yet. He received seven hundred and fifty a week for his partial authority over directors, writers and stars who got much more. He wore a cheap English shoe he bought near the Beverly Wilshire and Broaca hoped they hurt his feet, but soon now he would order his shoes from Peal's and put away his little green alpine hat with a feather. Broaca was years ahead of him. He had a fine record in the war but he had never felt quite the same with himself since he had let Ike Franklin strike him in the face with his open hand.

There was smoke in the room and behind it, behind his great desk Stahr was withdrawing further and further, in all courtesy, still giving Rienmund an ear and Miss Doolan an ear. The conference was over.

"Any messages?"

"Mr. Robinson called in," Miss Doolan said, as he started for the commissary. "One of the women told him her name but he's forgotten it—he thinks it was Smith or Brown or Jones."

"That's a great help."

"And he remembers she says she just moved to Los Angeles."

"I remember she had a silver belt," Stahr said, "with stars cut out of it."

"I'm still trying to find out more about Pete Zavras. I talked to his wife."

"What did she say?"

"Oh, they've had an awful time—given up their house—she's been sick—"

"Is the eye trouble hopeless?"

"She didn't seem to know anything about the state of his eyes. She didn't even know he was going blind."

"That's funny."

He thought about it on the way to luncheon but it was as confusing as the actor's trouble this morning. Troubles about people's health didn't seem within his range—he gave no thought to his own. In the lane beside the commissary he stepped back as an open electric truck crammed with girls in the bright costumes of the regency came rolling in from the back lot. The dresses were fluttering in the wind, the young painted faces looked at him curiously and he smiled as it went by.

Episode 10

Eleven men and their guest Prince Agge sat at lunch in the private dining room of the studio commissary. They were the money men—they were the rulers and unless there was a guest they ate in broken silence, sometimes asking questions about each other's wives and children, sometimes discharging a single absorption from the forefront of their consciousness. Eight out of the ten were Jews—five of the ten were foreign born, including a Greek and an Englishman—and they had all known each other for a long time: there was a rating in the group, from old Marcus down to old Leanbaum who had bought the most fortunate block of stock in the business and never was allowed to spend over a million a year producing.

Old Marcus functioned with disquieting resilience. Some never-atrophying instinct warned him of danger, of gangings up against him—he was never so dangerous himself as when others considered him surrounded. His grey face had attained such immobility that even those who were accustomed to watch the reflex of the inner corner of his eye could no longer see it—nature had grown a little white whisker there to conceal it; his armor was complete.

As he was the oldest, Stahr was the youngest of the group—not by many years at this date, though he had first sat with most of these men when he was a boy wonder of twenty-two. Then, more than now, he had been a money man among money men. Then he had been able to figure costs in his head with a speed and accuracy that dazzled them—for they were not wizards or even experts in that regard, despite the popular conception of Jews in finance. Most of them owed their success to different and incompatible qualities. But in a group a tradition carries along the less adept, and they were content to look at Stahr for the sublimated auditing and experience a sort of glow as if they had done it themselves like rooters at a football game.

Stahr, as will presently be seen, had grown away from that par-ticular gift, though it was always there.

Prince Agge sat between Stahr and Mort Flieshacker the company lawyer and across from Joe Popolous the theatre owner. He was hostile to Jews in a vague general way that he tried to cure himself of. As a turbulent man, serving his time in the Foreign Legion, he thought that Jews were too fond of their own skins. But he was willing to concede that they might be different in America under different circumstances, and certainly he found Stahr was much of a man in every way. For the rest—he thought most business men were dull dogs—for final reference he reverted always to the blood of Bernadotte in his veins.

My father—I will call him Mr. Brady as Prince Agge did when he told me of this luncheon—was worried about a picture and when Leanbaum went out early he came up and took his chair opposite.

"How about the South America picture idea, Monroe?" he asked.

Prince Agge noticed a blink of attention toward them as distinct as if a dozen pair of eyelashes had made the sound of batting wings. Then silence again.

"We're going ahead with it," said Stahr.

"With that same budget?" Brady asked.

Stahr nodded.

"It's out of proportion," said Brady. "There won't be any miracle in these bad times—no 'Hell's Angels' or 'Ben-Hur' when you throw it away and get it back."

Probably the attack was planned, for Popolous, the Greek, took up the matter in a sort of double talk that reminded Prince Agge of Mike Van Dyke except that it tried to be and succeeded in being clear instead of confusing.

"It's not adoptable, Monroe, in as we wish adopt to this times in as it changes. It what could be done as we run the gamut of prosperity is scarcely conceptuable now."

"What do you think, Mr. Marcus?" asked Stahr.

All eyes followed his down the table but as if forewarned Mr. Marcus had already signalled his private waiter behind him that he wished to rise, and was even now in a basket-like position in the waiter's arms. He looked at them with such helplessness that it was hard to realize that in the evenings he sometimes went dancing with his young Canadian girl.

"Monroe is our production genius," he said. "I count upon Monroe and lean heavily upon him. I have not seen the flood myself."

There was a moment of silence as he moved from the room.

"There's not a two million dollar gross in the country now," said Brady.

"Is not," agreed Popolous. "Even as if so you could grab them by the head and push them by and in, is not."

"Probably not," agreed Stahr. He paused as if to make sure that all were listening. "I think we can count on a million and a quarter from the road-show. Perhaps a million and a half altogether. And a quarter of a million abroad."

Again there was silence—this time puzzled, a little confused. Over his shoulder Stahr asked the waiter to be connected with his office on the phone.

"But your budget?" said Flieshacker. "Your budget is seventeen hundred and fifty thousand, I understand. And your expectations only add up to that without profit."

"Those aren't my expectations," said Stahr. "We're not sure of more than a million and a half."

The room had grown so motionless that Prince Agge could hear a grey chunk of ash fall from a cigar in midair. Flieshacker started to speak, his face fixed with amazement, but a phone had been handed over Stahr's shoulder.

"Your office, Mr. Stahr."

"Oh yes—oh, hello Miss Doolan. I've figured it out about Zavras. It's one of these lousy rumors—I'll bet my shirt on it. . . . Oh, you did. Good. . . . Good. Now here's what to do—send him to my oculist this afternoon, Dr. John Kennedy, and have him get a report and have it photostated—you understand."

He hung up—turned with a touch of passion to the table at large.

"Did any of you ever hear a story that Pete Zavras was going blind?"

There were a couple of nods. But most of those present were poised breathlessly on whether Stahr had slipped on his figures a minute before.

"It's pure bunk. He says he's never even been to an oculist—never knew why the studios turned against him," said Stahr. "Somebody didn't like him or somebody talked too much and he's been out of work for a year."

There was a conventional murmur of sympathy. Stahr signed the check and made as though to get up.

"Excuse me, Monroe," said Flieshacker persistently, while Brady and Popolous watched, "I'm fairly new here and perhaps I fail to comprehend implicitly and explicitly." He was talking fast but the veins on his forehead bulged with pride at the big words from

N.Y.U. "Do I understand you to say you expect to gross a quarter million short of your budget?"

"It's a quality picture," said Stahr with assumed innocence.

It had dawned on them all now but they still felt there was a trick in it. Stahr really thought it would make money. No one in his senses—

"For two years we've played safe," said Stahr. "It's time we made a picture that'll lose some money. Write it off as good will—this'll bring in new customers."

Some of them still thought he meant it was a flyer and a favorable one but he left them in no doubt.

"It'll lose money," he said as he stood up, his jaw just slightly out and his eyes smiling and shining. "It would be a bigger miracle than 'Hell's Angels' if it broke even. But we have a certain duty to the public as Pat Brady says at Academy dinners. It's a good thing for the production schedule to slip in a picture that'll lose money."

He nodded at Prince Agge. As the latter made his bows quickly he tried to take in with a last glance the general effect of what Stahr said, but he could tell nothing. The eyes not so much downcast as fixed upon an indefinite distance just above the table were all blinking quickly now but there was not a whisper in the room.

Coming out of the private dining room they passed through a corner of the commissary proper. Prince Agge drank it in—eagerly. It was gay with gypsies and with citizens and soldiers with the sideburns and braided coats of the First Empire. From a little distance they were men who lived and walked a hundred years ago and Agge wondered how he and the men of his time would look as extras in some future costume picture.

Then he saw Abraham Lincoln and his whole feeling suddenly changed. He had been brought up in the dawn of Scandanavian socialism where Nicolay's biography was much read. He had been told Lincoln was a great man whom he should admire and he had hated him instead because he was forced upon him. But now seeing him sitting here, his legs crossed, his kindly face fixed on a forty cent dinner, including dessert, his shawl wrapped around him as if to protect himself from the erratic air-cooling—now Prince Agge, who was in America at last, stared as a tourist at the mummy of Lenin in the Kremlin. This then was Lincoln. Stahr had walked on far ahead of him, turned waiting for him—but still Agge stared.

—This then, he thought, was what they all meant to be.

Lincoln suddenly raised a triangle of pie and jammed it in his mouth and, a little frightened, Prince Agge hurried to join Stahr.

"I hope you're getting what you want," said Stahr feeling he had neglected him. "We'll have some rushes in half an hour and then you can go on to as many sets as you want."

"I should rather stay with you," said Prince Agge.

"I'll see what there is for me," said Stahr. "Then we'll go on together."

There was the Japanese consul on the release of a spy story which might offend the national sensibilities of Japan. There were phone calls and telegrams. There was some further information from Robby.

"Now he remembers the name of the woman was Smith," said Miss Doolan. "He asked her if she wanted to come on the lot and get some dry shoes and she said no—so she can't sue."

"That's pretty bad for a total recall—'Smith.' That's a great help." He thought a moment. "Ask the phone company for a list of Smiths that have taken new phones here in the last month. Call them all."

"All right."

For Episode 11

"How you, Monroe," said Red Ridingwood. "I'm glad you came down."

Stahr walked past him, heading across the great stage toward a set that would be used tomorrow. Director Ridingwood followed, realizing suddenly that Stahr walked a step or two ahead. He recognized the indication of displeasure—his own metier was largely the "delivery" of situations through mimetic business. He didn't know what the trouble was but he was a top director and not alarmed. Goldwyn had once interfered with him, and Ridingwood had led Goldwyn into trying to act out a part in front of fifty actors—with the result that he anticipated. His own authority had been restored.

Stahr reached the set and stared at it.

"It's no good," said Ridingwood. "I don't care how you light it—"

"Why did you call me about it?" Stahr asked standing close to him. "Why didn't you take it up with Art?"

"I didn't ask you to come down, Monroe."

"You wanted to be your own supervisor."

"I'm sorry, Monroe," said Ridingwood patiently. "But I didn't ask you to come down."

Stahr turned suddenly and walked back toward the camera set up. The eyes and open mouths of a group of visitors moved momentarily off the heroine of the picture, took in Stahr and then moved vacantly back to the heroine again. They were Knights of Columbus. They had seen the Host carried in procession but this was the dream made flesh.

Stahr stopped beside her chair. She wore a low gown which displayed the bright eczema of her chest and back. Before each take the blemished surface was plastered over with an emollient, which was removed immediately after the take. Her hair was of the color and viscosity of drying blood but there was starlight that actually photographed in her eyes.

Before Stahr could speak he heard a helpful voice behind him: "She's radiunt. Absolutely radiunt."

It was an assistant director and the intention was delicate compliment. The actress was being complimented so that she did not have to strain her poor skin to bend and hear. Stahr was being complimented for having her under contract. Ridingwood was being remotely complimented.

"Everything all right?" Stahr asked her pleasantly.

"Oh, it's fine," she agreed, "—except for the ——ing publicity men."

He winked at her gently.

"We'll keep them away," he said.

Her name had become currently synonymous with the expression "bitch." Presumably she had modelled herself after one of those queens in the Tarzan comics who rule mysteriously over a nation of blacks. She regarded the rest of the world as black. She was a necessary evil, borrowed for a single picture.

Ridingwood walked with Stahr toward the door of the stage.

"Everything's all right," the director said. "She's as good as she can be."

They were out of hearing range and Stahr stopped suddenly and looked at Red with blazing eyes.

"You've been photographing crap," he said. "Do you know what she reminds me of in the rushes—'Miss Foodstuffs.' "

"I'm trying to get the best performance—"

"Come along with me," said Stahr abruptly.

"With you? Shall I tell them to rest?"

"Leave it as it is," said Stahr, pushing the padded outer door.

His car and chauffeur waited outside. Minutes were precious most days.

"Get in," said Stahr.

Red knew now it was serious. He even knew all at once what was the matter. The girl had got the whip hand on him the first day with her cold lashing tongue. He was a peace-loving man and he had let her walk through her part cold rather than cause trouble.

Stahr spoke into his thoughts.

"You can't handle her," he said. "I told you what I wanted. I wanted her *mean*—and she comes out bored. I'm afraid we'll have to call it off, Red."

"The picture?"

"No. I'm putting Harley on it."

"All right, Monroe."

"I'm sorry, Red. We'll try something else another time."

The car drew up in front of Stahr's office.

"Shall I finish this take?" said Red.

"It's being done now," said Stahr grimly. "Harley's in there."

"What the hell—"

"He went in when we came out. I had him read the script last night."

"Now listen, Monroe—"

"It's my busy day, Red," said Stahr tersely. "You lost interest about three days ago."

It was a sorry mess Ridingwood thought. It meant he would have to do the next picture he was offered whether he liked it or not. It meant a slight, very slight loss of position—it probably meant that he could not have a third wife just now as he had planned. There wasn't even the satisfaction in raising a row about it—if you disagreed with Stahr you did not advertise it. Stahr was his world's great customer who was always—almost always right.

"How about my coat?" he asked suddenly. "I left it over a chair on the set."

"I know you did," said Stahr. "Here it is."

He was trying so hard to be charitable about Ridingwood's lapse that he had forgotten that he had it in his hand.

Episode 11

"Mr. Stahr's Projection Room" was a miniature picture theatre with four rows of overstuffed chairs. In front of the front row ran long tables with dim lamps, buzzers and telephones. Against the wall was an upright piano, left there since the early days of sound. The room had been redecorated and reupholstered only a year before but already it was ragged again with work and hours.

Here Stahr sat at two-thirty and again at six-thirty watching the lengths of film taken during the day. There was often a savage tensity about the occasion—he was dealing with *faits accomplis*—the net result of months of buying, planning, writing and rewriting, casting, constructing, lighting, rehearsing and shooting—the fruit alike of brilliant hunches or counsels of despair, of lethargy, conspiracy and sweat. At this point the tortuous manoeuvre was staged and in suspension—these were reports from the battle-line.

Besides Stahr there were present the representatives of all technical departments together with the supervisors and unit managers of the pictures concerned. The directors did not appear at these showings—officially because their work was considered done—actually because few punches were pulled here as money ran out in silver spools. There had evolved a delicate staying away.

The staff was already assembled. Stahr came in and took his place quickly and the murmur of conversation died away. As he sat back and drew his thin knee up beside him in the chair the lights in the room went out. There was the flare of a match in the back row—then silence.

On the screen a troop of French Canadians pushed their canoes up a rapids. The scene had been photographed in a studio tank and at the end of each take after the director's voice could be heard saying "Cut," the actors on the screen relaxed and wiped their brows and sometimes laughed hilariously—and the water in the tank stopped flowing and the illusion ceased. Except to name his choice from each set of takes and to remark that it was "a good process," Stahr made no comment.

The next scene, still in the rapids, called for dialogue between the Canadian girl (Claudette Colbert) and the *coureur du bois* (Ronald Colman) with her looking down at him from a canoe. After a few strips had run through Stahr spoke up suddenly.

"Has the tank been dismantled?"

"Yes, sir."

"Monroe—they needed it for—"

Stahr cut in peremptorily.

"Have it set up again right away. Let's have that second take again."

The lights went on momentarily. One of the unit managers left his chair and came and stood in front of Stahr.

"A beautifully acted scene thrown away," raged Stahr quietly. "It wasn't centered. The camera was set up so it caught the beautiful top of Claudette's head all the time she was talking. That's just what we want, isn't it? That's just what people go to see—the top of a beautiful girl's head. Tell Tim he could have saved wear and tear by using her stand-in."

The lights went out again. The unit manager squatted by Stahr's chair to be out of the way. The take was run again.

"Do you see now?" asked Stahr. "And there's a hair in the

picture—there on the right, see it? Find out if it's in the projector or the film."

At the very end of the take Claudette Colbert slowly lifted her head revealing her great liquid eyes.

"That's what we should have had all the way," said Stahr. "She gave a fine performance too. See if you can fit it in tomorrow or late this afternoon."

—Pete Zavras would not have made a slip like that. There were not six camera men in the industry you could entirely trust.

The lights went on; the supervisor and unit manager for that picture went out.

"Monroe, this stuff was shot yesterday—it came through late last night."

The room darkened. On the screen appeared the head of Siva, immense and imperturbable, oblivious to the fact that in a few hours it was to be washed away in a flood. Around it milled a crowd of the faithful.

"When you take that scene again," said Stahr suddenly, "put a couple of little kids up on top. You better check about whether it's reverent or not but I think it's all right. Kids'll do anything."

"Yes, Monroe."

A silver belt with stars cut out of it. . . . Smith, Jones or Brown. . . . Personal—will the woman with the silver belt who—?

With another picture the scene shifted to New York, a gangster story, and suddenly Stahr became restive.

"That scene's trash," he called suddenly in the darkness. "It's badly written, it's miscast, it accomplishes nothing. Those types aren't tough. They look like a lot of dressed up lollypops—what the hell is the matter, Mort?"

"The scene was written on the set this morning," said Mort Flieshacker. "Burton wanted to get all the stuff on Stage 6."

"Well—it's trash. And so is this one. There's no use printing stuff like that. She doesn't believe what she's saying—neither does Cary. 'I love you' in a close-up—they'll cluck you out of the house! And the girl's overdressed."

In the darkness a signal was given, the projector stopped, the lights went on. The room waited in utter silence. Stahr's face was expressionless.

"Who wrote the scene?" he asked after a minute.

"Wylie White."

"Is he sober?"

"Sure he is."

Stahr considered.

"Put about four writers on that scene tonight," he said. "See who we've got. Is Sidney Howard here yet?"

"He got in this morning."

"Talk to him about it. Explain to him what I want there. The girl is in deadly terror—she's stalling. It's as simple as that. People don't have three emotions at once. And Kapper—"

The art director leaned his head forward out of the second row.

"Yeah."

"There's something the matter with that set."

There were little glances exchanged all over the room.

"What is it, Monroe?"

"You tell *me*," said Stahr. "It's crowded. It doesn't carry your eye out. It looks cheap."

"It wasn't."

"I know it wasn't. There's not much the matter but there's something. Go over and take a look tonight. It may be too much furniture—or the wrong kind. Perhaps a window would help. Couldn't you force the perspective in that hall a little more?"

"I'll see what I can do." Kapper edged his way out of the row looking at his watch.

"I'll have to get at it right away," he said. "I'll work tonight and we'll put it up in the morning."

"All right. Mort, you can shoot around those scenes, can't you?"

"I think so, Monroe."

"I take the blame for this. Have you got the fight stuff?"

"Coming up now."

Stahr nodded. Kapper hurried out and the room went dark again. On the screen four men staged a terrific socking match in a cellar. Stahr laughed.

"Look at Tracy," he said. "Look at him go down after that guy. I bet he's been in a few."

The men fought over and over. Always the same fight. Always at the end they faced each other smiling, sometimes touching the opponent in a friendly gesture on the shoulder. The only one in danger was the stunt man, a pug who could have murdered the other three. He was in danger only if they swung wild and didn't follow the blows he had taught them. Even so the youngest actor was afraid for his face and the director had covered his flinches with ingenious angles and interpositions.

And then two men met endlessly in a door, recognized each other and went on. They met, they started, they went on. They did it wrong. Again they met, they started, they went on.

Then a little girl read underneath a tree with a boy reading on a limb of the tree above. The little girl was bored and wanted to talk to the boy. He would pay no attention. The core of the apple he was eating fell on the little girl's head.

A voice spoke up out of the darkness:

"It's pretty long, isn't it, Monroe?"

"Not a bit," said Stahr. "It's nice. It has nice feeling."

"I just thought it was long."

"Sometimes ten feet can be too long—sometimes a scene two hundred feet long can be too short. I want to speak to the cutter before he touches this scene—this is something that'll be remembered in the picture."

The oracle had spoken. There was nothing to question or argue. Stahr must be right always, not most of the time, but always—or the structure would melt down like gradual butter.

Another hour passed. Dreams hung in fragments at the far end of the room, suffered analysis, passed—to be dreamed in crowds, or else discarded. The end was signalled by two tests, a character man and a girl. After the rushes, which had a tense rhythm of their own, the tests were smooth and finished—the observers settled in their chairs—Stahr's foot slipped to the floor. Opinions were welcome. One of the technical men let it be known that he would willingly cohabit with the girl—the rest were indifferent.

"Somebody sent up a test of that girl two years ago. She must be getting around—but she isn't getting any better. But the man's good. Can't we use him as the old Russian Prince in 'Steppes'?"

"He *is* an old Russian Prince," said the casting director. "But he's ashamed of it. He's a Red. And that's one part he says he wouldn't play."

"It's the only part he could play," said Stahr.

The lights went on. Stahr rolled his gum into its wrapper and put it in an ash-tray. He turned questioningly to his secretary.

"The processes on Stage 2," she said.

He looked in briefly at the processes, moving pictures taken against a background of other moving pictures by an ingenious device. There was a meeting in Marcus' office on the subject of "Manon" with a happy ending and Stahr had his say on that as he had before—it had been making money without a happy ending for a century and a half. He was obdurate—at this time in the afternoon he was at his most fluent and the opposition faded into another subject—they would lend a dozen stars to the benefit for those the quake had made homeless at Long Beach. In a sudden burst of giving five of them all at once made up a purse of twenty-five thousand dollars. They gave well but not as poor men give. It was not charity.

At his office there was word from the oculist to whom he had sent Pete Zavras that the camera man's eyes were 20/19, approximately perfect. He had written a letter that Zavras was having photostated. Stahr walked around his office cockily while Miss Doolan admired him. Prince Agge had dropped in to thank him for his afternoon on the sets and while they talked a cryptic word came from a supervisor that some writers named Marquand had "found out" and were about to quit.

"These are good writers," Stahr explained to Prince Agge. "And we don't have good writers out here."

"Why you can hire anyone!" exclaimed his visitor in surprise.

"Oh we hire them but when they get out here they're not good writers—so we have to work with the material we have."

"Like what?"

"Anybody that'll accept the system and stay decently sober—we have all sorts of people—disappointed poets, one-hit playwrights, college girls—we put them on an idea in pairs and if it slows down we put two more writers working behind them. I've had as many as three pairs working independently on the same idea."

"Do they like that?"

"Not if they know about it. They're not geniuses—none of them could make as much any other way. But these Marquands are a husband and wife team from the East—pretty good playwrights. They've just found out they're not alone on the story and it shocks them—shocks their sense of unity—that's the word they'll use."

"But what does make the—the unity?"

Stahr hesitated—his face was grim except that his eyes twinkled.

"I'm the unity," he said. "Come and see us again."

He saw the Marquands. He told them he liked their work, looking at Mrs. Marquand as if he could read her handwriting through the typescript. He told them kindly that he was taking them from the picture and putting them on another where there was less pressure, more time. As he had half expected they begged to stay on the first picture, seeing a quicker credit even though it was shared with others. The system was a shame, he admitted—gross, commercial, to be deplored. He had originated it—a fact that he did not mention.

When they had gone Miss Doolan came in triumphant.

"Mr. Stahr, the lady with the belt is on the phone."

Stahr walked in to his office alone and sat down behind his desk and picked up the phone with a great sinking of his stomach. He did not know what he wanted. He had not thought about the matter as he had thought of the matter of Pete Zavras. At first he had only wanted to know if they were "professional" people, if the woman was an actress who had got herself up to look like Minna as he had once had a young actress made up like Claudette Colbert and photographed her from the same angles.

"Hello," he said.

"Hello."

As he searched the short, rather surprised word for a vibration of last night, the feeling of terror began to steal over him and he choked it off with an effort of will.

"Well—you were hard to find," he said. "*Smith*—and you moved here recently. That was all we had. And a silver belt."

"Oh yes," the voice said, still uneasy, unpoised, "I had on a silver belt last night."

Now, where from here?

"Who *are* you?" the voice said, with a touch of flurried bourgeois dignity.

"My name is Monroe Stahr," he said.

A pause. It was a name that never appeared on the screen and she seemed to have trouble placing it.

"Oh yes—yes. You were the husband of Minna Davis."

"Yes."

Was it a trick? As the whole vision of last night came back to him—the very skin with that peculiar radiance as if phosphorus had touched it, he thought if it were a trick to reach him from somewhere. Not Minna and yet Minna. The curtains blew suddenly into the room, the papers whispered on his desk and his heart cringed faintly at the intense reality of the day outside his window. If he could go out now this way what would happen if he saw her again—the starry veiled expression, the mouth strongly formed for poor brave human laughter.

"I'd like to see you. Would you like to come to the studio?"

Again the hesitancy—then a blank refusal.

"Oh, I don't think I ought to. I'm awfully sorry."

This last was purely formal, a brush off, a final axe. Ordinary skin-deep vanity came to Stahr's aid, adding persuasion to his urgency.

"I'd like to see you," he said. "There's a reason."

"Well—I'm afraid that—"

"Could I come and see you?"

A pause again not from hesitation, he felt, but to assemble her answer.

"There's something you don't know," she said finally.

"Oh, you're probably married." He was impatient. "It has nothing to do with that. I asked you to come here openly, bring your husband if you have one."

"It's—it's quite impossible."

"Why?"

"I feel silly even talking to you but your secretary insisted—I thought I'd dropped something in the flood last night and you'd found it."

"I want very much to see you for five minutes."

"To put me in the movies."

"That wasn't my idea."

There was such a long pause that he thought he had offended her.

"Where could I meet you?" she asked unexpectedly.

"Here? At your house?"

"No—somewhere outside."

Suddenly Stahr could think of no place. His own house—a restaurant. Where did people meet—a house of assignation, a cocktail bar?

"I'll meet you somewhere at nine o'clock," she said.

"That's impossible, I'm afraid."

"Then never mind."

"All right then nine o'clock, but can we make it near here? There's a drug store on Wilshire—"

It was quarter to six. There were two men outside who had come every day at this time only to be postponed. This was an hour of fatigue—the men's business was not so important that it must be seen to, nor so insignificant that it could be ignored. So he postponed it again and sat motionless at his desk for a moment thinking about Russia. Not so much about Russia as about the picture about Russia which would consume a hopeless half hour presently. He knew there were many stories about Russia, not to mention The Story, and he had employed a squad of writers and research men for over a year but all the stories involved had the wrong feel. He felt it could be told in terms of the American thirteen states but it kept coming out different, in new terms that opened unpleasant possibilities and problems. He considered he was very fair to Russia—he had no desire to make anything but a sympathetic picture but it kept turning into a headache.

"Mr. Stahr—Mr. Drummon's outside and Mr. Kirstoff and Mrs. Cornhill about the Russian picture."

"All right—send them in."

Afterwards from six-thirty to seven-thirty he watched the afternoon rushes. Except for his engagement with the girl he would ordinarily have spent the early evening in the projection room or the dubbing room but it had been a late night with the earthquake and he decided to go to dinner. Coming in through his front office he found Pete Zavras waiting, his arm in a sling.

"You are the Aeschylus and the Diogenes of the moving picture," said Zavras simply. "Also the Asclepius and the Menander."

He bowed.

"Who are they?" asked Stahr smiling.

"They are my countrymen."

"I didn't know you made pictures in Greece."

"You're joking with me, Monroe," said Zavras. "I want to say you are as dandy a fellow as they come. You have saved me one hundred percent."

"You feel all right now?"

"My arm is nothing. It feels like someone kisses me there. It was worth doing what I did if this is the outcome."

"How did you happen to do it here?" Stahr asked curiously.

"Before the oracle," said Zavras. "The solver of Eleusinian mysteries. I wish I had my hands on the son-of-a-bitch who started the story."

"You make me sorry I didn't get an education," said Stahr.

"It isn't worth a damn," said Pete. "I took my baccalaureate in Salonika and look how I ended up."

"Not quite," said Stahr.

"If you want anybody's throat cut anytime day or night," said Zavras, "my number is in the book."

Stahr closed his eyes and opened them again. Zavras' silhouette had blurred a little against the sun. He hung on to the table behind him and said in an ordinary voice:

"Good luck, Pete."

The room was almost black but he made his feet move following a pattern into his office and waited till the door clicked shut before he felt for the pills. The water decanter clattered against the table; the glass clacked. He sat down in a big chair waiting for the benzedrine to take effect before he went to dinner.

Episode 12

As Stahr walked back from the commissary a hand waved at him from an open roadster. From the heads showing over the back he recognized a young actor and his girl, and watched them disappear through the gate already part of the summer twilight. Little by little he was losing the feel of such things, until it seemed that Minna had taken their poignancy with her; his apprehension of splendor was fading so that presently the luxury of eternal mourning would depart. A childish association of Minna with the material heavens made him, when he reached his office, order out his roadster for the first time this year. The big limousine seemed heavy with remembered conferences or exhausted sleep.

Leaving the studio he was still tense but the open car pulled the summer evening up close and he looked at it. There was a moon down at the end of the boulevard and it was a good illusion that it was a different moon every evening, every year. Other lights shone in Hollywood since Minna's death: in the open markets lemons and grapefruit and green apples slanted a misty glare into the street. Ahead of him the stop-signal of a car winked violet and at another crossing he watched it wink again. Everywhere floodlights raked the sky. On an empty corner two mysterious men moved a gleaming drum in pointless arcs over the heavens.

In the drug store a woman stood by the candy counter. She was tall, almost as tall as Stahr, and embarrassed. Obviously it was a situation for her and if Stahr had not looked as he did—most considerate and polite—she would not have gone through with it. They said hello and walked out without another word, scarcely a glance— yet before they reached the curb Stahr knew: this was just exactly a pretty American woman and nothing more—no beauty like Minna.

"Where are we going?" she asked. "I thought there'd be a chauffeur. Never mind—I'm a good boxer."

"Boxer?"

"That didn't sound very polite." She forced a smile. "But you people are supposed to be such *horrors*."

The conception of himself as sinister amused Stahr—then suddenly it failed to amuse him.

"Why did you want to see me?" she asked as she got in.

He stood motionless, wanting to tell her get out immediately. But she had relaxed in the car and he knew the unfortunate situation was of his own making—he shut his teeth and walked around to get in. The street lamp fell full upon her face and it was difficult to believe that this was the girl of last night. He saw no resemblance to Minna at all.

"I'll run you home," he said. "Where do you live?"

"Run me home?" She was startled. "There's no hurry—I'm sorry if I offended you."

"No. It was nice of you to come. I've been stupid. Last night I had an idea that you were an exact double for someone I knew. It was dark and the light was in my eyes."

She was offended—he had reproached her for not looking like someone else.

"It was just that!" she said. "That's funny."

They rode in silence for a minute.

"You were married to Minna Davis, weren't you?" she said with a flash of intuition. "Excuse me for referring to it."

He was driving as fast as he could without making it conspicuous.

"I'm quite a different type from Minna Davis," she said, "—if that's who you meant. You might have referred to the girl who was with me. She looks more like Minna Davis than I do."

That was of no interest now. The thing was to get this over quick and forget it.

"Could it have been her?" she asked. "She lives next door."

"Not possibly," he said. "I remember the silver belt you wore."

"That was me all right."

They were northwest of Sunset, climbing one of the canyons

through the hills. Lighted bungalows rose along the winding road and the electric current that animated them sweated into the evening air as radio sound.

"You see that last highest light—Kathleen lives there. I live just over the top of the hill."

A moment later she said, "Stop here."

"I thought you said over the top."

"I want to stop at Kathleen's."

"I'm afraid I'm—"

"I want to get out here myself," she said impatiently.

Stahr slid out after her. She started toward a new little house almost roofed over by a single willow tree, and automatically he followed her to the steps. She rang a bell and turned to say good night.

"I'm sorry you were disappointed," she said.

He was sorry for her now—sorry for them both.

"It was my fault. Good night."

A wedge of light came out the opening door and as a girl's voice inquired "Who is it?" Stahr looked up.

There she was—face and form and smile against the light from inside. It was Minna's face—the skin with its peculiar radiance as if phosphorus had touched it, the mouth with its warm line that never counted costs—and over all the haunting jollity that had fascinated a generation.

With a leap his heart went out of him as it had the night before, only this time it stayed out there with a vast beneficence.

"Oh Edna you can't come in," the girl said. "I've been cleaning and the house is full of ammonia smell."

Edna began to laugh, bold and loud. "I believe it was you he wanted to see, Kathleen," she said.

Stahr's eyes and Kathleen's met and tangled. For an instant they made love as no one ever dares to do after. Their glance was closer than an embrace, more urgent than a call.

"He telephoned me," said Edna. "It seems he thought—" Stahr interrupted, stepping forward into the light.

"I was afraid we were rude at the studio, yesterday evening."

But there were no words for what he really said. She listened

closely without shame. Life flared high in them both—Edna seemed
at a distance and in darkness.

"You weren't rude," said Kathleen. A cool wind blew the brown
curls around her forehead. "We had no business there."

"I hope you'll both—," Stahr said, "—come and make a tour of
the studio."

"Who are you? Somebody important?"

"He was Minna Davis' husband, he's a producer," said Edna as if
it were a rare joke, "—and this isn't at all what he just told me. I
think he has a crush on you."

"Shut up, Edna," said Kathleen sharply.

As if suddenly realizing her offensiveness Edna said "Phone me,
will you?" and stalked away toward the road. But she carried their
secret with her—she had seen a spark pass between them in the
darkness.

"I remember you," Kathleen said to Stahr. "You got us out of the
flood."

—Now what? The other woman was more missed in her absence.
They were alone and on too slim a basis for what had passed
already. They existed nowhere. His world seemed far away—she
had no world at all except the idol's head, the half open door.

"You're Irish," he said, trying to build one for her.

She nodded.

"I've lived in London a long time—I didn't think you could tell."

The wild green eyes of a bus sped up the road in the darkness.
They were silent until it went by.

"Your friend Edna didn't like me," he said. "I think it was the
word Producer."

"She's just come out here too. She's a silly creature who means no
harm. *I* shouldn't be afraid of you."

She searched his face. She thought, like everyone, that he seemed
tired—then she forgot it at the impression he gave of a brazier out
of doors on a cool night.

"I suppose the girls are all after you to put them on the screen."

"They've given up," he said.

This was an understatement—they were all there, he knew, just
over his threshold, but they had been there so long that their clamor-

ing voices were no more than the sound of the traffic in the street. But his position remained more than royal—a king could make only one queen—Stahr, at least so they supposed, could make many.

"I'm thinking that it would turn you into a cynic," she said. "You didn't want to put me in the pictures."

"No."

"That's good. I'm no actress. Once in London a man came up to me in the Carlton and asked me to make a test but I thought awhile and finally I didn't go."

They had been standing nearly motionless, as if in a moment he would leave and she would go in. Stahr laughed suddenly.

"I feel as if I had my foot in the door—like a collector."

She laughed too.

"I'm sorry I can't ask you in. Shall I get my reefer and sit outside?"

"No." He scarcely knew why he felt it was time to go. He might see her again—he might not. It was just as well this way.

"You'll come to the studio?" he said. "I can't promise to go around with you, but if you come you must be sure to send word to my office."

A frown, the shadow of a hair in breadth, appeared between her eyes.

"I'm not sure," she said. "But I'm very much obliged."

He knew that, for some reason, she would not come—in an instant she had slipped away from him. They both sensed that the moment was played out. He must go, even though he went nowhere and left with nothing. Practically, vulgarly, he did not have her telephone number—or even her name, but it seemed impossible to ask for them now.

She walked with him to the car, her glowing beauty and her unexplored novelty pressing up against him, but there was a foot of moonlight between them when they came out of the shadow.

"Is this all?" he said spontaneously.

He saw regret in her face—but there was a flick of the lip also, a bending of the smile toward some indirection, a momentary dropping and lifting of a curtain over a forbidden passage.

"I do hope we'll meet again," she said almost formally.

"I'd be sorry if we didn't."

They were distant for a moment. But as he turned his car in the next drive and came back with her still waiting, and waved and drove on he felt exalted and happy. He was glad that there was beauty in the world that would not be weighed in the scales of the casting department.

But at home he felt a curious loneliness as his butler made him tea in the samovar. It was the old hurt come back, heavy and delightful. When he took up the first of two scripts that were his evening stint, that presently he would visualize line by line on the screen, he waited a moment, thinking of Minna. He explained to her that it was really nothing, that no one could ever be like she was, that he was sorry.

That was substantially a day of Stahr's. I don't know about the illness, when it started, etc., because he was secretive but I know he fainted a couple of times that month because Father told me. Prince Agge is my authority for the luncheon in the commissary where he told them he was going to make a picture that would lose money— which was something considering the men he had to deal with and that he held a big block of stock and had a profit sharing contract.

And Wylie White told me a lot which I believed because he felt Stahr intensely with a mixture of jealousy and admiration. As for me I was head over heels in love with him then and you can take what I say for what it's worth.

Episode 13

Fresh as the morning I went up to see him a week later. Or so I thought; when Wylie called for me I had gotten into riding clothes to give the impression I'd been out in the dew since early morning.

"I'm going to throw myself under the wheel of Stahr's car, this morning," I said.

"How about this car," he suggested. "It's one of the best cars Mort Flieshacker ever sold second hand."

"Not on your flowing veil," I answered like a book. "You have a wife in the East."

"She's the past," he said. "You've got one great card, Celia—your valuation of yourself. Do you think anybody would look at you if you weren't Pat Brady's daughter?"

We don't take abuse like our mothers would have. Nothing—no remark from a contemporary means much. They tell you to be smart they're marrying you for your money or you tell them. Everything's simpler. Or is it? as we used to say.

But as I turned on the radio and the car raced up Laurel Canyon to "The Thundering Beat of My Heart," I didn't believe he was right. I had good features except my face was too round and a skin they seemed to love to touch and good legs and I didn't have to wear a brassiere. I haven't a sweet nature but who was Wylie to reproach me for that.

"Don't you think I'm smart to go in the morning?" I asked.

"Yeah. To the busiest man in California. He'll appreciate it. Why didn't you wake him up at four?"

"That's just it. At night he's tired. He's been looking at people all day and some of them not bad. I come in in the morning and start a train of thought."

"I don't like it. It's brazen."

"What have you got to offer? And don't be rough."

"I love you," he said without much conviction. "I love you more than I love your money and that's plenty. Maybe your father would make me a supervisor."

"I could marry the last man tapped for Bones this year and live in Southampton."

I turned the dial and got either "Gone" or "Lost"—there were good songs that year. The music was getting better again. When I was young during the Depression it wasn't so hot and the best numbers were from the twenties like Benny Goodman playing "Blue Heaven" or Paul Whiteman with "When Day Is Done." There were only the bands to listen to. But now I liked almost everything except Father singing "Little Girl, You've Had a Busy Day" to try to create a sentimental father-and-daughter feeling.

"Lost" and "Gone" were the wrong mood so I turned again and

got "Lovely To Look At" which was my kind of poetry. I looked back as we crossed the crest of the foothills—with the air so clear you could see the leaves on Sunset Mountain two miles away. It's startling to you sometimes—just air, unobstructed, uncomplicated air.

"Lovely to look at—de—lightful to know-w-w," I sang.

"Are you going to sing for Stahr?" Wylie said. "If you do, get in a line about my being a good supervisor."

"Oh, this'll be only Stahr and me," I said. "He's going to look at me and think 'I've never really seen her before.' "

"We don't use that line this year," he said.

"—Then he'll say 'Little Celia' like he did the night of the earthquake. He'll say he never noticed I have become a woman."

"You won't have to do a thing."

"I'll stand there and bloom. After he kisses me as you would a child—"

"That's all in my script," complained Wylie. "And I've got to show it to him tomorrow."

"—he'll sit down and put his face in his hands and say he never thought of me like that."

"You mean you get in a little fast work during the kiss."

"I bloom, I told you. How often do I have to tell you I bloom."

"It's beginning to sound pretty randy to me," said Wylie. "How about laying off—I've got to work this morning."

"Then he says it seems as if he was always meant to be this way."

"Right in the industry. Producer's blood." He pretended to shiver. "I'd hate to have a transfusion of that."

"Then he says—"

"I know all his lines," said Wylie. "What I want to know is what you say."

"Somebody comes in," I went on.

"And you jump up quickly off the casting couch smoothing your skirts."

"Do you want me to walk out and get home?"

We were in Beverly Hills, getting very beautiful now with the tall Hawaiian pines. Hollywood is a perfectly zoned city so you know exactly what kind of people economically live in each section from executives and directors, through technicians in their bungalows right down to extras. This was the executive section and a very fancy lot of pastry. It wasn't as romantic as the dingiest village of Virginia or New Hampshire but it looked nice this morning.

"They asked me how I knew," sang the radio, "—my true love was true."

My heart was fire and smoke was in my eyes and everything but I figured my chance at about fifty-fifty. I would walk right up to him as if I was either going to walk through him or kiss him in the mouth—and stop a bare foot away and say Hello with disarming understatement.

And I did—though of course it wasn't like I expected. Stahr's beautiful dark eyes looking back into mine, knowing I am dead sure everything I was thinking—and not a bit embarrassed. I stood there an hour, I think, without moving and all he did was twitch the side of his mouth and put his hands in his pockets.

"Will you go with me to the ball tonight?" I asked.

"What ball?"

"The screen-writers' ball down at the Ambassador."

"Oh yes." He considered. "I can't go with you. I might just come in late. We've got a sneak preview in Glendale."

How different it all was than what you've planned. When he sat down I went over and put my head among his telephones like a sort of desk appendage and looked at him and his dark eyes looked back so kind and nothing. Men don't often know those times when a girl could be had for nothing. All I succeeded in putting into his head was:

"Why don't you get married, Celia?"

Maybe he'd bring up Robby again, try to make a match there.

"What could I do to interest an interesting man?" I asked him.

"Tell him you're in love with him."

"Should I chase him?"

"Yes," he said smiling.

"I don't know. If it isn't there it isn't there."

"I'd marry you," he said unexpectedly. "I'm lonesome as hell. But I'm too old and tired to undertake anything."

I went around the desk and stood beside him.

"Undertake me."

He looked up in surprise, understanding for the first time that I was in deadly earnest.

"Oh no," he said. He looked almost miserable for a minute. "Pictures are my girl. I haven't got much time—" He corrected himself quickly, "I mean any time. It'd be like marrying a doctor."

"You couldn't love me."

"It's not that," he said and—right out of my dream but with a difference, "I never thought of you that way, Celia. I've known you so long. Somebody told me you were going to marry Wylie White."

"And you had—no reaction."

"Yes, I did. I was going to speak to you about it. Wait till he's been sober for two years."

"I'm not even considering it, Monroe."

We were way off the track, and just as in my day-dream somebody came in—only I was quite sure Stahr had pressed a concealed button.

I'll always think of that moment, when I felt Miss Doolan behind me with her pad, as the end of childhood, the end of the time when you cut out pictures. What I was looking at wasn't Stahr but a picture of him I cut out over and over: the eyes that flashed a sophisticated understanding at you and then darted up too soon into his wide brow with its ten thousand plots and plans; the face that was ageing from within, so that there were no casual furrows of worry and vexation but a drawn asceticism as if from a silent self-set struggle—or a long illness. It was handsomer to me than all the rosy tan from Coronado to Del Monte. He was my picture, as sure as if he was pasted on the inside of my old locker in school. That's what I told Wylie White and when a girl tells the man she likes second best about the other one—then she's in love.

13 (continued)

I noticed the girl long before Stahr arrived at the dance. Not a pretty girl, for there are none of those in Los Angeles—one girl can be pretty but a dozen are only a chorus. Nor yet a professional beauty—they do all the breathing for everyone and finally even the men have to go outside for air. Just a girl, with the skin of one of Raphael's corner angels and a style that made you look back twice to see if it were something she had on.

I noticed her and forgot her. She was sitting back behind the pillars at a table whose ornament was a faded semi-star who, in hopes of being noticed and getting a bit, rose and danced regularly with some scarecrow males. It reminded me shamefully of my first party where Mother made me dance over and over with the same boy to keep in the spotlight. The semi-star spoke to several people at our table but we were busy being Cafe Society and she got nowhere at all.

From our angle it appeared that they all wanted something.

"You're expected to fling it around," said Wylie, "—like in the old days. When they find out you're hanging on to it they get discouraged. That's what all this brave gloom is about—the only way to keep their self respect is to be Hemingway characters. But underneath they hate you in a mournful way and you know it."

He was right—I knew that since 1933 the rich could only be happy alone together.

I saw Stahr come into the half-light at the top of the wide steps and stand there with his hands in his pockets looking around. It was late and the lights seemed to have burned a little lower, though they were the same. The floor show was finished except for a man who still wore a placard which said that at midnight in the Hollywood Bowl Sonja Henie was going to skate on hot soup. You could see the sign as he danced becoming less and less funny on his back. A few years before there would have been drunks around. The faded actress seemed to be looking for them hopefully over her partner's shoulder. I followed her with my eyes when she went back to her table—

—and there, to my surprise, was Stahr talking to the other girl. They were smiling at each other as if this was the beginning of the world.

Stahr had expected nothing like this when he stood at the head of the steps a few minutes earlier. The sneak preview had disappointed him and afterwards he had had a scene with Jaques La Borwits right in front of the theatre for which he was now sorry. He had started toward the Brady party when he saw Kathleen sitting in the middle of a long white table alone.

Immediately things changed. As he walked toward her the people shrank back against the walls till they were only murals; the white table lengthened and became an altar where the priestess sat alone. Vitality welled up in him and he could have stood a long time across the table from her, looking and smiling.

The incumbents of the table were crawling back—Stahr and Kathleen danced.

When she came close his several visions of her blurred; she was momentarily unreal. Usually a girl's skull made her real but not this time—Stahr continued to be dazzled as they danced out along the floor—to the last edge, where they stepped through a mirror into another dance with new dancers whose faces were familiar but nothing more. In this new region he talked, fast and urgently.

"What's your name?"

"Kathleen Moore."

"Kathleen Moore," he repeated.

"I have no telephone, if that's what you're thinking."

"When will you come to the studio?"

"It's not possible. Truly."

"Why isn't it? Are you married?"

"No."

"You're not married?"

"No, nor never have been. But then I may be."

"Someone there at the table."

"No." She laughed. "What curiosity!"

But she was deep in it with him, no matter what the words were. Her eyes invited him to a romantic communion of unbelievable intensity. As if she realized this she said, frightened:

"I must go back now. I promised this dance."

"I don't want to lose you. Couldn't we have lunch or dinner?"

"It's impossible." But her expression helplessly amended the words to "It's just possible. The door is still open by a chink if you could squeeze past. But quickly—so little time."

"I must go back," she repeated aloud. Then she dropped her arms, stopped dancing and looked at him, a laughing wanton.

"When I'm with you I don't breathe quite right," she said.

She turned, picked up her long dress, and stepped back through the mirror. Stahr followed until she stopped near her table.

"Thank you for the dance," she said. "And now really, good night."

Then she nearly ran.

Stahr went to the table where he was expected and sat down with the Cafe Society group—from Wall Street, Grand Street, Loudoun County Virginia, and Odessa Russia. They were all talking with enthusiasm about a horse that had run very fast and Mr. Marcus was the most enthusiastic of all. Stahr guessed that Jews had taken over the worship of horses as a super-symbol—for years it had been the Cossacks mounted and the Jews on foot. Now the Jews had horses and it gave them a sense of extraordinary well-being and power. Stahr sat pretending to listen and even nodding when something was referred to him, but all the time watching the table behind the pillars. If everything had not happened as it had, even to his connecting the silver belt with the wrong girl, he might have thought it was some elaborate frame-up. But the elusiveness was beyond suspicion. For there in a moment he saw that she was escaping again—the pantomime at the table indicated good bye. She was leaving, she was gone.

"There—" said Wylie White with malice, "—goes Cinderella. Simply bring the slipper to the Regal Shoe Co., 812 South Broadway."

Stahr overtook her in the long upper lobby where middle-aged women sat behind a roped-off space, watching the ballroom entrance.

"Am I responsible for this?" he asked.

"I was going anyhow." But she added almost resentfully, "They talked as if I'd been dancing with the Prince of Wales. They all stared at me. One of the men wanted to draw my picture and another one wanted to see me tomorrow."

"That's just what I want," said Stahr gently. "But I want to see you much more than he does."

"You insist so," she said wearily. "One reason I left England was that men always wanted their own way. I thought it was different here. Isn't it enough that I don't want to see you?"

"Ordinarily," agreed Stahr. "Please believe me, I'm way out of my depth already. I feel like a fool. But I must see you again and talk to you."

She hesitated.

"There's no reason for feeling like a fool," she said. "You're too good a man to feel like a fool. But you should see this for what it is."

"What is it?"

"You've fallen for me—completely. You've got me in your dreams."

"I'd forgotten you," he declared, "—till the moment I walked in that door."

"Forgotten me with your head perhaps. But I knew the first time I saw you that you were the kind that likes me—"

She stopped herself. Near them a man and woman from the party were saying good bye: "Tell her hello—tell her I love her dearly," said the woman, "you both—all of you—the children." Stahr could not talk like that, the way everyone talked now. He could think of nothing further to say as they walked toward the elevator except:

"I suppose you're perfectly right."

"Oh, you admit it?"

"No, I don't," he retracted. "It's just the whole way you're made. What you say—how you walk—the way you look right this minute—" He saw she had melted a little and his hopes rose. "Tomorrow is Sunday and usually I work on Sunday but if there's anything you're curious about in Hollywood, any person you want to meet or see, please let me arrange it."

They were standing by the elevator. It opened but she let it go.

"You're very modest," she said. "You always talk about showing me the studio and taking me around. Don't you ever stay alone?"

"Tomorrow I'll feel very much alone."

"Oh, the poor man—I could weep for him. He could have all the stars jumping around him and he chooses me."

He smiled—he had laid himself open to that one.

The elevator came again. She signalled for it to wait.

"I'm a weak woman," she said. "If I meet you tomorrow will you leave me in peace? No, you won't. You'll make it worse. It wouldn't do any good but harm so I'll say no and thank you."

She got into the elevator. Stahr got in too and they smiled as they dropped two floors to the hall cross-sectioned with small shops. Down at the end, held back by police was the crowd, their heads and shoulders leaning forward to look down the alley. Kathleen shivered.

"They looked so strange when I came in," she said, "—as if they were furious at me for not being someone famous."

"I know another way out," said Stahr.

They went through a drug store, down an alley and came out into the clear cool California night beside the car park. He felt detached from the dance now and she did too.

"A lot of picture people used to live down here," he said. "John Barrymore and Pola Negri in those bungalows. And Connie Talmadge lived in that tall thin apartment house over the way."

"Doesn't anybody live here now?"

"The studios moved out into the country," he said. "What used to be the country. I had some good times around here though."

He did not mention that ten years ago Minna and her mother had lived in another apartment over the way.

"How old are you?" she asked suddenly.

"I've lost track—almost thirty-five I think."

"They said at the table you were the boy wonder."

"I'll be that when I'm sixty," he said grimly. "You will meet me tomorrow, won't you?"

"I'll meet you," she said. "Where?"

Suddenly there was no place to meet. She would not go to a party at anyone's house, nor to the country, nor swimming though she hesitated, nor to a well-known restaurant. She seemed hard to please but he knew there was some reason. He would find out in time. It occurred to him that she might be the sister or daughter of someone well-known, who was pledged to keep in the background. He suggested that he come for her and they could decide.

"That wouldn't do," she said. "What about right here—the same spot."

He nodded—pointing up at the arch under which they stood.

He put her into her car which would have brought eighty dollars from any kindly dealer, and watched it rasp away. Down by the entrance a cheer went up as a favorite emerged, and Stahr wondered whether to show himself and say good night.

This is Cecelia taking up the narrative in person. Stahr came back finally—it was about half past three—and asked me to dance.

"How are you?" he asked me, just as if he hadn't seen me that morning. "I got involved in a long conversation with a man."

It was secret too—he cared that much about it.

"I took him to ride," he went on innocently. "I didn't realize how much this part of Hollywood had changed."

"Has it changed?"

"Oh yes," he said. "Changed completely. Unrecognizable. I couldn't tell you exactly but it's all changed—everything. It's like a new city." After a moment he amplified, "I had no idea how much it had changed."

"Who was the man?" I ventured.

"An old friend," he said vaguely. "Someone I knew a long time ago."

I had made Wylie try to find out quietly who she was. He had gone over and the ex-star had asked him excitedly to sit down. No—she didn't know who the girl was—a friend of a friend of someone—even the man who had brought her didn't know.

So Stahr and I danced to the beautiful music of Glenn Miller playing "I'm on a See-saw." It was good dancing now with plenty of room. But it was lonely—lonelier than before the girl had gone. For me, as well as for Stahr, she took the evening with her, took along the stabbing pain I had felt—left the great ball-room empty and without emotion. Now it was nothing and I was dancing with an absent minded man who told me how much Los Angeles had changed.

Section 14

They met, next afternoon, as strangers in an unfamiliar country. Last night was gone, the girl he had danced with was gone. A misty rose-and-blue hat with a trifling veil came along the terrace to him and paused, searching his face. Stahr was strange too in a brown suit and black tie that blocked him out more tangibly than a formal dinner coat, or when he was simply a face and voice in the darkness when they first met.

He was the first to be sure it was the same person as before—the upper half of the face that was Minna's, luminous, with creamy temples and opalescent brow—the coco-colored curly hair. He could have put his arm around her and pulled her close with an almost family familiarity—already he knew the down on her neck, the very set of her backbone, the corners of her eyes and how she breathed—the very texture of the clothes that she would wear.

"Did you wait here all night?" she said, in a voice that was like a whisper.

"I didn't move—didn't stir."

Still a problem remained, the same one—there was no special place to go.

"I'd like tea," she suggested, "—if it's some place you're not known."

"That sounds as if one of us had a bad reputation."

"Doesn't it?" she laughed.

"We'll go to the shore," Stahr suggested. "There's a place there where I got out once and was chased by a trained seal."

"Do you think the seal could make tea?"

"Well—he's trained. And I don't think he'll talk—I don't think his training got that far. What in *hell* are you trying to hide?"

After a moment she said lightly, "Perhaps the future," in a way that might mean anything or nothing at all.

As they drove away she pointed at her jalopy in the parking lot. "Do you think it's safe?"

"I doubt it. I noticed some black-bearded foreigners snooping around."

Kathleen looked at him alarmed.

"Really?" She saw he was smiling. "I believe everything you say," she said. "You've got such a gentle way about you that I don't see why they're all so afraid of you." She examined him with approval—fretting a little about his pallor, which was accentuated by the bright afternoon. "Do you work very hard? Do you really always work on Sundays?"

He responded to her interest—impersonal yet not perfunctory.

"Not always. Once we had—we had a house with a pool and all—and people came on Sunday. I played tennis and swam. I don't swim any more."

"Why not? It's good for you. I thought all Americans swam."

"My legs got very thin—a few years ago and it embarrassed me. There were other things I used to do—lots of things. I used to play handball when I was a kid, and sometimes out here—I had a court that was washed away in a storm."

"You have a good build," she said in formal compliment, meaning only that he was made with thin grace.

He rejected this with a shake of his head.

"I enjoy working most," he said. "My work is very congenial."

"Did you always want to be in movies?"

"No. When I was young I wanted to be a chief clerk—the one who knew where everything was."

She smiled.

"That's odd. And now you're much more than that."

"No, I'm still a chief clerk," Stahr said. "That's my gift, if I have one. Only when I got to be it I found out that no one knew where anything was. And I found out that you had to know why it was where it was, and whether it should be left there. They began throwing it all at me and it was a very complex office. Pretty soon I had all the keys. And they wouldn't have remembered what locks they fitted if I gave them back."

They stopped for a red light and a newsboy bleated at them: "Mickey Mouse Murdered! Randolph Hearst declares war on China!"

"We'll have to buy his paper," she said.

As they drove on she straightened her hat and preened herself. Seeing him looking at her she smiled.

She was alert and calm—qualities that were currently at a premium. There was lassitude in plenty—California was filling up with weary desperadoes. And there were tense young men and women who lived back East in spirit while they carried on a losing battle against the climate. But it was everyone's secret that sustained effort was difficult here—a secret that Stahr scarcely admitted to himself. But he knew that people from other places spurted a pure rill of new energy for a while.

They were very friendly now. She had not made a move or a gesture that was out of keeping with her beauty, that pressed it out of its contour one way or another. It was all proper to itself. He judged her as he would a shot in a picture. She was not trash, she was not confused but clear—in his special meaning of the word which implied balance, delicacy and proportion, she was "nice."

They reached Santa Monica where there were the stately houses of a dozen picture stars, penned in the middle of a crawling Coney Island. They turned down hill into the wide blue sky and sea and went on along the sea till the beach slid out again from under the bathers in a widening and narrowing yellow strand.

"I'm building a house out here," Stahr said. "Much further on. I don't know why I'm building it."

"Perhaps it's for me," she said.

"Maybe it is."

"I think it's splendid for you to build a big house for me without even knowing what I looked like."

"It isn't so big. And it hasn't any roof. I didn't know what kind of roof you wanted."

"We don't want a roof. They told me it never rained here. It—"

She stopped so suddenly that he knew she was reminded of something.

"Just something that's past," she said.

"What was it?" he demanded. "Another house without a roof?"

"Yes. Another house without a roof."

"Were you happy there?"

"I lived with a man," she said. "A long, long time—too long. It was one of those awful mistakes people make. I lived with him a long time after I wanted to get out but he couldn't let me go. He'd try but he couldn't. So finally I ran away."

He was listening, weighing but not judging. Nothing changed under the rose-and-blue hat. She was twenty-five or so. It would have been a waste if she had not loved and been loved.

"We were too close," she said. "We should probably have had children—to stand between us. But you can't have children when there's no roof to the house."

All right, he knew something of her. It would not be like last night when something kept saying, as in a story conference: "We know nothing about the girl. We don't have to know much—but we have to know something." A vague background spread behind her, something more tangible than the head of Siva in the moonlight.

They came to the restaurant, forbidding with many Sunday automobiles. When they got out the trained seal growled reminiscently at Stahr. The man who owned it said that the seal would never ride in the back seat of his car but always climbed over the back and up in front. It was plain that the man was in bondage to the seal, though he had not yet acknowledged it to himself.

"I'd like to see the house you're building," said Kathleen. "I don't want tea—tea is the past."

Kathleen drank a Coke instead and they drove on ten miles into a sun so bright that he took out two pairs of cheaters from a compartment. Five miles further on they turned down a small promontory and came to the fuselage of Stahr's house.

A headwind blowing out of the sun threw spray up the rocks and over the car. Concrete mixers, raw yellow wood and builders' rubble waited, an open wound in the sea-scape, for Sunday to be over. They walked around front where great boulders rose to what would be the terrace.

She looked at the feeble hills behind and winced faintly at the barren glitter, and Stahr saw—

"No use looking for what's not here," he said cheerfully. "Think of it as if you were standing on one of those globes with a map on it—I always wanted one when I was a boy."

"I understand," she said after a minute. "When you do that you can feel the earth turn, can't you."

He nodded.

"Yes. Otherwise it's all just mañana—waiting for the morning or the moon."

They went in under the scaffolding. One room, which was to be the chief salon, was completed even to the built-in book shelves and the curtain rods and the trap in the floor for the motion picture projection machine. And, to her surprise, this opened out to a porch with cushioned chairs in place and a ping-pong table. There was another ping-pong table on the newly laid turf beyond.

"Last week I gave a premature luncheon," he admitted. "I had some props brought out—some grass and things. I wanted to see how the place felt."

She laughed suddenly.

"Isn't that real grass?"

"Oh yes—it's grass."

Beyond the strip of anticipatory lawn was the excavation for a swimming pool, patronized now by a crowd of seagulls who saw them and took flight.

"Are you going to live here all alone?" she asked him. "Not even dancing girls?"

"Probably. I used to make plans but not any more. I thought this would be a nice place to read scripts. The studio is really home."

"That's what I've heard about American business men."

He caught a lilt of criticism in her voice.

"You do what you're born to do," he said gently. "About once a month somebody tries to reform me, tells me what a barren old age I'll have when I can't work any more. But it's not so simple."

The wind was rising. It was time to go and he had his car keys out of his pocket, absent mindedly jingling them in his hand. There was the silvery "Hey!" of a telephone, coming from somewhere across the sunshine.

It was not from the house and they hurried here and there around the garden like children playing warmer and colder—closing in finally on a tool shack by the tennis court. The phone, irked with delay, barked at them suspiciously from the wall. Stahr hesitated.

"Shall I let the damn thing ring?"

"I couldn't. Unless I was sure who it was."

"Either it's for somebody else or they've made a wild guess."

He picked up the receiver.

"Hello. . . . Long distance from where? Yes, this is Mr. Stahr."

His manner changed perceptibly. She saw what few people had seen for a decade—Stahr impressed. It was not discordant because he often pretended to be impressed but it made him momentarily a little younger.

"It's the President," he said to her, almost stiffly.

"Of your company?"

"No, of the United States."

He was trying to be casual for her benefit but his voice was eager.

"All right, I'll wait," he said into the phone, and then to Kathleen, "I've talked to him before."

She watched. He smiled at her and winked as an evidence that while he must give this his best attention he had not forgotten her.

"Hello," he said presently. He listened. Then he said "Hello" again. He frowned.

"Can you talk a little louder," he said politely, and then "Who? . . . What's that?"

She saw a disgusted look come into his face.

"I don't want to talk to him," he said. "No!"

He turned to Kathleen.

"Believe it or not, it's an orang-outang."

He waited while something was explained to him at length; then he repeated:

"I don't want to talk to it, Lew. I haven't got anything to say that would interest an orang-outang."

He beckoned to Kathleen and when she came close to the phone he held the receiver so that she heard odd breathing and a gruff growl. Then a voice:

"This is no phoney, Monroe. It can talk and it's a dead ringer for McKinley. Mr. Horace Wickersham is with me here with a picture of McKinley in his hand—"

Stahr listened patiently.

"We've got a chimp," he said after a minute. "He bit a chunk out of John Gilbert last year. . . . All right, put him on again."

He spoke formally as if to a child.

"Hello Orang-outang."

His face changed and he turned to Kathleen.

"He said hello."

"Ask him his name," suggested Kathleen.

"Hello Orang-outang—God, what a thing to be!—Do you know your name? . . . He doesn't seem to know his name. . . . Listen, Lew. We're not making anything like 'King Kong' and there is no monkey in 'The Hairy Ape.' . . . Of course I'm sure. I'm sorry, Lew, good bye."

He was annoyed with Lew because he had thought it was the President and changed his manner acting as if it were. He felt a little ridiculous but Kathleen felt sorry and liked him better because it had been an orang-outang.

SECTION 14 (2nd part)

They started back along the shore with the sun behind them. The house seemed kindlier when they left it, as if warmed by their visit—the hard glitter of the place was more endurable if they were not bound there like people on the shiny surface of a moon. Looking back from a curve of the shore, they saw the sky growing pink behind the indecisive structure and the point of land seemed a friendly island, not without promise of fine hours on a further day.

Past Malibu with its gaudy shacks and fishing barges they came into the range of human kind again, the cars stacked and piled along the road, the beaches like ant hills without a pattern, save for the dark drowned heads that sprinkled the sea.

Goods from the city were increasing in sight—blankets, matting, umbrellas, cookstoves, reticules full of clothing—the prisoners had laid out their shackles beside them on this sand. It was Stahr's sea if he wanted it, or knew what to do with it—only by sufferance did these others wet their feet and fingers in the wild cool reservoirs of man's world.

Stahr turned off the road by the sea and up a canyon and along a hill road and the people dropped away. The hill became the outskirts of the city. Stopping for gasoline he stood beside the car.

"We could have dinner," he said almost anxiously.

"You have work you could do."

"No—I haven't planned anything. Couldn't we have dinner?"

He knew that she had nothing to do either—no planned evening or special place to go.

She compromised.

"Do you want to get something in that drug store across the street?"

He looked at it tentatively.

"Is that really what you want?"

"I like to eat in American drug stores. It seems so queer and strange."

They sat on high stools and had tomato broth and hot sandwiches. It was more intimate than anything they had done and they both felt a dangerous sort of loneliness and felt it in each other. They shared in varied scents of the drug store, bitter and sweet and sour, and the mystery of the waitress with only the outer part of her hair dyed and black beneath, and when it was over, the still life of their empty plates—a sliver of potato, a sliced pickle and an olive stone.

It was dusk in the street, it seemed nothing to smile at him now when they got into the car.

"Thank you so much. It's been a nice afternoon."

It was not far from her house. They felt the beginning of the hill and the louder sound of the car in second was the beginning of the end. Lights were on in the climbing bungalows—he turned on the headlights of the car. Stahr felt heavy in the pit of his stomach.

"We'll go out again."

"No," she said quickly as if she had been expecting this. "I'll write you a letter. I'm sorry I've been so mysterious—it was really a compliment because I like you so much. You should try not to work so hard. You ought to marry again."

"Oh, that isn't what you should say," he broke out protestingly. "This has been you and me today. I may have meant nothing to you—it meant a lot to me. I'd like time to tell you about it."

But if he were to take time it must be in her house for they were there and she was shaking her head as the car drew up to the door.

"I must go now. I do have an engagement. I didn't tell you."

"That's not true. But it's all right."

He walked to the door with her and stood in his own footsteps of that other night while she felt in her bag for the key.

"Have you got it?"

"I've got it," she said.

That was the moment to go in but she wanted to see him once more and she leaned her head to the left, then to the right trying to catch his face against the last twilight. She leaned too far and too long and it was natural when his hand touched the back of her upper arm and shoulder and pressed her forward into the darkness of his throat. She shut her eyes feeling the bevel of the key in her tight clutched hand. She said "Oh" in an expiring sigh and then "Oh" again as he pulled her in close and his chin pushed her cheek around gently. They were both smiling just faintly and she was frowning too as the inch between them melted into darkness.

When they were apart she shook her head still but more in wonder than in denial. It came like this then, it was your own fault, how far back, when was the moment. It came like this and every instant the burden of tearing herself away from them together, from it, was heavier and more unimaginable. He was exultant; she resented and could not blame him but she would not be part of his exultation for it was a defeat. So far it was a defeat. And then she thought that if she stopped it being a defeat, broke off and went inside, it was still not a victory. Then it was just nothing.

"This was not my idea," she said. "Not at all my idea."

"Can I come in?"

"Oh no—no."

"Then let's jump in the car and drive somewhere."

With relief she caught at the exact phrasing—to get away from here immediately, that was accomplishment or sounded like one—as if she were fleeing from the spot of a crime. Then they were in the car going down hill with the breeze cool in their faces and she came slowly to herself. Now it was all clear in black and white.

"We'll go back to your house on the beach," she said.

"Back there?"

"Yes—we'll go back to your house. Don't let's talk. I just want to ride."

Section 14 (Part iii)

When they got to the coast again the sky was grey and at Santa Monica a sudden gust of rain bounced over them. Stahr halted beside the road, put on a raincoat and lifted the canvas top. "We've got a roof," he said.

The windshield wiper ticked domestically as a grandfather clock. Sullen cars were leaving the wet beaches and starting back into the city. Further on they ran into fog—the road lost its boundaries on either side and the lights of cars coming toward them were stationary until just before they flared past.

They had left a part of themselves behind, and they felt light and free in the car. Fog fizzed in at a chink and Kathleen took off the rose-and-blue hat in a calm, slow way that made him watch tensely, and put it under a strip of canvas in the back seat. She shook out her hair and, when she saw that Stahr was looking at her, she smiled.

The trained seal's restaurant was only a sheen of light off toward the ocean. Stahr cranked down a window and looked for landmarks but after a few more miles the fog fell away and just ahead of them the road turned off that led to his house. Out here a moon showed behind the clouds. There was still a shifting light over the sea.

The house had dissolved a little back into its elements. They found the dripping beams of a doorway and groped over mysterious waist-high obstacles to the single finished room, odorous of sawdust and wet wood. When he took her in his arms they could just see each other's eyes in the half darkness. Presently his raincoat dropped to the floor.

"Wait," she said.

She needed a minute. She did not see how any good could come from this and though this did not prevent her from being happy and desirous she needed a minute to think how it was, to go back an hour and know how it had happened. She waited in his arms, moving her head a little from side to side as she had before, only more slowly, and never taking her eyes from his. Then she discovered that he was trembling.

He discovered it at the same time and his arms relaxed. Immediately she spoke to him coarsely and provocatively and pulled his face down to hers. Then, with her knees she struggled out of something, still standing up and holding him with one arm, and kicked it off beside the coat. He was not trembling now and he held her again as they knelt down together and slid to the raincoat on the floor.

Afterwards they lay without speaking and then he was full of such tender love for her that he held her tight till a stitch tore in her dress. The small sound brought them to reality.

"I'll help you up," he said, taking her hands.

"Not just yet. I was thinking of something."

She lay in the darkness thinking irrationally that it would be such a bright, indefatigable baby, but presently she let him help her up. . . . When she came back into the room, the room was lit from a single electric fixture.

"A one-bulb lighting system," he said. "Shall I turn it off?"

"No. It's very nice. I want to see you."

They sat in the wooden frame of the window seat with the soles of shoes touching.

"You seem far away," she said.

"So do you."

"Are you surprised?"

"At what?"

"That we're two people again. Don't you always think—hope that you'll be one person and then find you're still two?"

"I feel very close to you."

"So do I to you," she said.

"Thank you."

"Thank *you*."

They laughed.

"Is this what you wanted?" she asked. "I mean last night."

"Not consciously."

"I wonder when it was settled," she brooded. "There's a moment when you needn't and then there's another moment when you know nothing in the world could keep it from happening."

This had an experienced ring and to his surprise he liked her even more. In his mood which was passionately to repeat yet not recapitulate the past it was right that it should be that way.

"I *am* rather a trollop," she said following his thoughts. "I suppose that's why I didn't get on to Edna."

"Who is Edna?"

"The girl you thought was me. The one you phoned to—who lived across the road. She's moved to Santa Barbara."

"You mean she was a tart?"

"So it seems. She went to what you call call-houses."

"That's funny."

"If she had been English I'd have known right away. But she seemed like everyone else. She only told me just before she went away."

He saw her shiver and got up, putting the raincoat around her shoulders. He opened a closet and a pile of pillows and beach mattresses fell out on the floor. There was a box of candles and he lit them around the room, attaching the electric heater where the bulb had been.

"Why was Edna afraid of me?" he asked suddenly.

"Because you were a producer. She had some awful experience or a friend of hers did. Also I think she was extremely stupid."

"How did you happen to know her?"

"She came over. Maybe she thought I was a fallen sister. She seemed quite pleasant. She said 'Call me Edna' all the time. 'Please call me Edna'—so finally I called her Edna and we were friends."

She got off the window seat so he could lay pillows along it and behind her.

"What can I do?" she said. "I'm a parasite."

"No, you're not." He put his arms around her. "Be still. Get warm."

They sat for a while quiet.

"I know why you liked me at first," she said. "Edna told me."

"What did she tell you?"

"That I looked like—Minna Davis. Several people have told me that."

He leaned away from her and nodded.

"It's here," she said, putting her hands on her cheekbones and distorting her cheeks slightly. "Here and here."

"Yes," said Stahr. "It was very strange. You look more like she actually *look*ed than how she was on the screen."

She got up, changing the subject with her gesture as if she were afraid of it.

"I'm warm now," she said. She went to the closet and peered in, came back wearing a little apron with a crystalline pattern like a snowfall. She stared around critically.

"Of course we've just moved in," she said, "—and there's a sort of echo."

She opened the door of the verandah and pulled in two wicker chairs, drying them off. He watched her move, intently yet half afraid that her body would fail somewhere and break the spell. He had watched women in screen tests and seen their beauty vanish second by second as if a lovely statue had begun to walk with meagre joints of a paper doll. But Kathleen was ruggedly set on the balls of her feet—the fragility was, as it should be, an illusion.

"It's stopped raining," she said. "It rained the day I came. Such an awful rain—so loud—like horses weeing."

He laughed.

"You'll like it. Especially if you've got to stay here. Are you going to stay here? Can't you tell me now? What's the mystery?"

She shook her head.

"Not now—it's not worth telling."

"Come here then."

She came over and stood near him and he pressed his cheek against the cool fabric of the apron.

"You're a tired man," she said putting her hand in his hair.

"Not that way."

"I didn't mean that way," she said hastily. "I meant you'll work yourself sick."

"Don't be a mother," he said.

"All right. What shall I be?"

Be a trollop, he thought. He wanted the pattern of his life broken. If he was going to die soon, like the two doctors said, he wanted to stop being Stahr for a while and hunt for love like men who had no gifts to give, like young nameless men who looked along the streets in the dark.

"You've taken off my apron," she said gently.

"Yes."

"Would anyone be passing along the beach? Shall we put out the candles?"

"No, don't put out the candles."

Afterwards she lay half on a white cushion and smiled up at him.

"I feel like Venus on the half shell," she said.

"What made you think of that?"

"Look at me. Isn't it Botticelli?"

"I don't know," he said smiling. "It is if you say so."

She yawned.

"I've had such a good time. And I'm very fond of you."

"You know a lot, don't you?"

"What do you mean?"

"Oh, from little things you've said. Or perhaps the way you say them."

She deliberated.

"Not much," she said. "I never went to a university if that's what you mean. But the man I told you about knew everything and he had a passion for educating me. He made out schedules and made me take courses at the Sorbonne and go to museums. I picked up a little."

"What was he?"

"He was a painter of sorts and a hell-cat. And a lot besides. He wanted me to read Spengler—everything was for that. All the history and philosphy and harmony was all so I could read Spengler and then I left him before we got to Spengler. At the end I think that was the chief reason he didn't want me to go."

"Who was Spengler?"

"I tell you we didn't get to him," she laughed. "And now I'm forgetting everything very patiently because it isn't likely I'll ever meet anyone like him again."

"Oh, but you shouldn't forget it," said Stahr shocked. He had an intense respect for learning, a racial memory of the old shuls. "You shouldn't forget."

"It was just in place of babies."

"You could teach your babies," he said.

"Could I?"

"Sure you could. You could give it to them while they were young. When I want to know anything I've got to ask some drunken writer. Don't throw it away."

"All right," she said getting up, "I'll tell it to my children. But it's so endless—the more you know the more there is just beyond and it keeps on coming. This man could have been anything if he hadn't been a coward and a fool."

"But you were in love with him."

"Oh yes—with all my heart." She looked through the window, shading her eyes. "It's light out there. Let's go down to the beach."

He jumped up exclaiming:

"Why, I think it's the grunion!"

"What?"

"It's tonight. It's in all the papers." He hurried out the door and she heard him open the door of the car. Presently he returned with a newspaper.

"It's at ten-sixteen. That's five minutes."

"An eclipse or something?"

"Very punctual fish," he said. "Leave your shoes and stockings and come with me."

It was a fine blue night. The tide was at the turn and the little silver fish rocked off shore waiting for 10:16. A few seconds after the time they came swarming in with the tide and Stahr and Kathleen stepped over them barefoot as they flicked slip-slop in the sand. A Negro man came along the shore toward them collecting the grunion quickly like twigs into two pails. They came in twos and threes and platoons and companies, relentless and exalted and scornful around the great bare feet of the intruders, as they had come before Sir Francis Drake had nailed his plaque to the boulder on the shore.

"I wish for another pail," the Negro man said, resting a moment.

"You've come a long way out," said Stahr.

"I used to go to Malibu but they don't like it those moving picture people."

A wave came in and forced them back, receded swiftly leaving the sand alive again.

"Is it worth the trip?" Stahr asked.

"I don't figure it that way. I really come out to read some Emerson. Have you ever read him?"

"I have," said Kathleen. "Some."

"I've got him inside my shirt. I got some Rosicrucian literature with me too but I'm fed up with them."

The wind had changed a little—the waves were stronger further down and they walked along the foaming edge of the water.

"What's your work?" the Negro asked Stahr.

"I work for the pictures."

"Oh." After a moment he added, "I never go to movies."

"Why not?" asked Stahr sharply.

"There's no profit. I never let my children go."

Stahr watched him and Kathleen watched Stahr protectively.

"Some of them are good," she said, against a wave of spray, but he did not hear her. She felt she could contradict him and said it again and this time he looked at her indifferently.

"Are the Rosicrucian brotherhood against pictures?" asked Stahr.

"Seems as if they don't know what they *are* for. One week they for one thing and next week for another."

Only the little fish were certain. Half an hour had gone and still they came. The Negro's two pails were full and finally he went off over the beach toward the road, unaware that he had rocked an industry.

Stahr and Kathleen walked back to the house and she thought how to drive his momentary blues away.

"Poor old Sambo," she said.

"What?"

"Don't you call them poor old Sambo?"

"We don't call them anything especially." After a moment he said, "They have pictures of their own."

In the house she drew on her shoes and stockings before the heater.

"I like California better," she said deliberately. "I think I was a bit sex-starved."

"That wasn't quite all was it?"

"You know it wasn't."

"It's nice to be near you."

She gave a little sigh as she stood up so small that he did not notice it.

"I don't want to lose you now," he said. "I don't know what you think of me or whether you think of me at all. As you've probably guessed my heart's in the grave—" He hesitated, wondering if this was quite true, "—but you're the most attractive woman I've met since I don't know when. I can't stop looking at you. I don't know now exactly the color of your eyes but they make me sorry for everyone in the world—"

"Stop it, stop it!" she cried laughing. "You'll have me looking in the mirror for weeks. My eyes aren't any color—they're just eyes to see with and I'm just as ordinary as I can be. I have nice teeth for an English girl—"

"You have beautiful teeth."

"—but I couldn't hold a candle to these girls I see here—"

"*You* stop it," he said. "What I said is true and I'm a cautious man."

She stood motionless a moment—thinking. She looked at him, then she looked back into herself, then at him again—then she gave up her thought.

"We must go," she said.

Now they were different people as they started back. Four times they had driven along the shore road today, each time a different pair. Curiosity, sadness and desire were behind them now; this was a true returning—to themselves and all their past and future and the encroaching presence of tomorrow. He asked her to sit close in the car and she did but they did not seem close because for that you have to seem to be growing closer. Nothing stands still. It was on his tongue to ask her to come to the house he rented and sleep there tonight—but he felt that it would make him sound lonely. As the car climbed the hill to her house Kathleen looked for something behind the seat cushion.

"What have you lost?"

"It might have fallen out," she said, feeling through her purse in the darkness.

"What was it?"

"An envelope."

"Was it important?"

"No."

But when they got to her house and Stahr turned on the dashboard light she helped take the cushions out and look again.

"It doesn't matter," she said as they walked to the door. "What's your address where you really live?"

"Just Bel-Air. There's no number."

"Where is Bel-Air?"

"It's a sort of development near Santa Monica. But you'd better call me at the studio."

"All right . . . good night, Mr. Stahr."

"*Mister* Stahr," he repeated, astonished.

She corrected herself gently.

"Well then, good night, Stahr. Is that better?"

He felt as though he had been pushed away a little.

"As you like," he said. He refused to let the aloofness communicate itself. He kept looking at her and moved his head from side to side in her own gesture, saying without words "you know what's happened to me." She sighed. Then she came into his arms and for a moment was his again completely. Before anything could change Stahr whispered good night and turned away and went to his car.

Winding down the hill he listened inside himself as if something by an unknown composer, powerful and strange and strong, was about to be played for the first time. The theme would be stated presently but because the composer was always new, he would not recognize it as the theme right away. It would come in some such guise as the auto-horns from the technicolor boulevards below or be barely audible, a tattoo on the muffled drum of the moon. He strained to hear it, knowing only that music was beginning, new music that he liked and did not understand. It was hard to react to what one could entirely compass—this was new and confusing, nothing one could shut off in the middle and supply the rest from an old score.

Also, and persistently, and bound up with the other, there was the Negro on the sand. He was waiting at home for Stahr with his pails of silver fish, and he would be waiting at the studio in the morning. He had said that he did not allow his children to listen to Stahr's story. He was prejudiced and wrong and he must be shown somehow, some way. A picture, many pictures, a decade of pictures, must be made to show him he was wrong. Since he had spoken, Stahr had thrown four pictures out of his plans—one that was going into production this week. They were borderline pictures in point of interest but at least he submitted the borderline pictures to the Negro and found them trash. And he put back on his list a difficult picture that he had tossed to the wolves, to Brady and Marcus and the rest, to get his way on something else. He rescued it for the Negro man.

When he drove up to his door the porch lights went on and his Filipino came down the steps to put away the car. In the library Stahr found a list of phone calls.

La Borwits
Marcus
Harlow
Rienmund
Fairbanks
Brady
Colman
Skouras
Flieshacker

The Filipino came into the room with a letter.
"This fell out of the car," he said.

"Thanks," said Stahr, "I was looking for it."

"Will you be running a picture tonight, Mr. Stahr?"

"No thanks—you can go to bed."

The letter, to his surprise, was addressed to Monroe Stahr, Esq. He started to open it—then it occurred to him that she had wanted to recapture it, and possibly to withdraw it. If she had had a phone he would have called her for permission before opening it. He held it for a moment. It had been written before they met—it was odd to think that whatever it said was now invalidated; it possessed the interest of a souvenir by representing a mood that was gone.

Still he did not like to read it without asking her. He put it down beside a pile of scripts and sat down with the top script in his lap. He was proud of resisting his first impulse to open the letter. It seemed to prove that he was not "losing his head." He had never lost his head about Minna even in the beginning—it had been the most appropriate and regal match imaginable. She had loved him always and just before she died all unwilling and surprised his tenderness had burst and surged toward her and he had been in love with her. In love with Minna and death together—with the world into which she looked so alone that he wanted to go with her there.

But "falling for dames" had never been an obsession—his brother had gone to pieces over a dame, or rather over dame after dame after dame. But Stahr, in his younger days, had them once and never more than once—like one drink. He had quite another sort of adventure reserved for his mind—something better than a series of emotional sprees. Like many brilliant men he had grown up dead cold. Beginning at about twelve probably with the total rejection common to those of extraordinary mental powers, the "see here—this is all wrong—a mess—all a lie—and a sham—" he swept it all away, everything, as men of his type do and then instead of being a son-of-a-bitch as most of them are he looked around at the barrenness that was left and said to himself "*This* will never do." And so he had learned tolerance, kindness, forbearance, and even affection like lessons.

The Filipino boy brought in a carafe of water and bowls of nuts and fruit and said good night. Stahr opened the first script and began to read.

He read for three hours—stopping from time to time, editing without a pencil. Sometimes he looked up, warm from some vague happy thought that was not in the script, and it took him a minute each time to remember what it was. Then he knew it was Kathleen and looked at the letter—it was nice to have a letter.

It was three o'clock when a vein began to bump in the back of his hand signalling that it was time to quit. Kathleen was really far away now with the waning night—the different aspects of her telescoped into the memory of a single thrilling stranger bound to him only by a few slender hours. It seemed perfectly all right to open the letter.

Dear Mr. Stahr:

In half an hour I will be keeping my date with you. When we say good bye I will hand you this letter. It is to tell you that I am to be married soon and that I won't be able to see you after today.

I should have told you last night but it didn't seem to concern you. And it would seem silly to spend this beautiful afternoon telling you about it and watching your interest fade. Let it fade all at once—now. I will have told you enough to convince you that I am Nobody's Prize Potato. (I have just learned that expression—from my hostess of last night who called and stayed an hour. She seems to believe that everyone is Nobody's Prize Potato—except you. I think I am supposed to tell you she thinks this, so give her a job if you can.)

I am very flattered that anyone who sees so many lovely women I can't finish this sentence but you know what I mean. And I will be late if I don't go to meet you right now.

With All Good Wishes
Kathleen Moore.

Stahr's first feeling was like fear; his first thought was that the letter was invalidated—she had even tried to retrieve it. But then he remembered "Mister Stahr" just at the end, and that she had asked him his address—she had probably already written him another letter, which would also say good bye. Illogically he was shocked by the letter's indifference to what had happened later. He read it again realizing that it foresaw nothing. Yet in front of the house she had decided to let it stand, belittling everything that had happened, curving her mind away from the fact that there had been no other man in her consciousness that afternoon. But he could not even believe this now and the whole adventure began to peel away even as he recapitualted it searchingly to himself. The car, the hill, the hat, the music, the letter itself blew off like the scraps of tar paper from the rubble of his house. And Kathleen departed, packing up her remembered gestures, her softly moving head, her sturdy eager body, her bare feet in the wet swirling sand. The skies paled and faded—the wind and rain turned dreary, washing the silver fish back to sea. It was only one more day, and nothing was left except the pile of scripts upon the table.

He went upstairs. Minna died again on the first landing and he forgot her lingeringly and miserably again, step by step to the top. The empty floor stretched around him—the doors with no one sleeping behind. In his room Stahr took off his tie, untied his shoes and sat on the side of his bed. It was all closed out except for something that he could not remember; then he remembered, her car was still down in the parking lot of the hotel. He set his clock to give him six hours' sleep.

Section 15 (first part)

This is Cecelia taking up the story. I think it would be most interesting to follow my own movements at this point, as this is a time in my life that I am ashamed of. What people are ashamed of usually makes a good story.

When I sent Wylie White over to Martha Dodd's table he had no success in finding out who the girl was, but it had suddenly become my chief interest in life. Also I guessed—correctly—that it would be Martha Dodd's: to have had at your table a girl who is admired by royalty, who may be tagged for a coronet in our little feudal system—and not even know her name.

I had only a speaking acquaintance with Martha and it would be too obvious to approach her directly, but I went out to the studio Monday and dropped in on Rose Meloney.

Rose Meloney was quite a friend of mine. I thought of her rather as a child thinks of a family dependent. I knew she was a writer but I grew up thinking that writer and secretary were the same except that a writer usually smelled of cocktails and came more often to meals. They were spoken of the same way when they were not around—except for a species called playwrights who came from the East. These were treated with respect if they did not stay long—if they did they sank with the others into the white collar class.

Rose's office was in the "old writers' building." There was one on every lot, a row of iron maidens left over from silent days and still resounding the dull moans of cloistered hacks and bums. There was the story of the new producer who had gone down the line one day and then reported excitedly to the head office.

"Who are those men?"

"They're supposed to be writers."

"I thought so. Well, I watched them for ten minutes and there were two of them that didn't write a line."

Rose was at her typewriter about to break off for lunch. I told her frankly that I had a rival.

"It's a dark horse," I said. "I can't even find out her name."

"Oh," said Rose. "Well, maybe I know something about that. I heard something from somebody."

The somebody, of course, was her nephew Ned Sollinger, Stahr's office boy. He had been her pride and hope. She had sent him through New York University where he played on the football team. Then in his first year at medical school after a girl turned him down he dissected out the least publicized section of a lady corpse and sent it to the girl. Don't ask me why. In disgrace with fortune and men's eyes he had begun life at the bottom again, and was still there.

"What do you know?" I asked.

"It was the night of the earthquake. She fell into the lake on the back lot and he dove in and saved her life. Someone else told me it was his balcony she jumped off of and broke her arm."

"Who was she?"

"Well, that's funny too—"

Her phone rang and I waited restlessly during a long conversation she had with Joe Rienmund. He seemed to be trying to find out over the phone how good she was or whether she had ever written any pictures at all. And she was reputed to have been on the set the day Griffith invented the close-up! While he talked she groaned silently, writhed, made faces into the receiver, held it all in her lap so that the voice reached her faintly—and kept up a side chatter to me.

"What is *he* doing—killing time between appontments? . . . He's asked me every one of these questions ten times . . . that's all on a memorandum I sent him. . . ."

And into the phone:

"If this goes up to Monroe it won't be my doing. I want to go right through to the end."

She shut her eyes in agony again.

"Now he's casting it . . . he's casting the minor characters . . . he's going to have Buddy Ebsen. . . . My God he just hasn't anything to do . . . now he's on Harry Davenport—he means Donald Crisp . . . he's got a big casting directory open in his lap and I can hear him turn the pages . . . he's a big important man this morning, a second Stahr, and for Christ sake I've got two scenes to do before lunch."

Rienmund quit finally or was interrupted at his end. A waiter came in from the commissary with Rose's luncheon and a Coca-Cola for me—I wasn't lunching that summer. Rose wrote down one sentence on her typewriter before she ate. It interested me the way she wrote. One day I was there when she and a young man had just lifted a story out of "The Saturday Evening Post"—changing the characters and all. Then they began to write it making each line answer the line before it, and of course it sounded just like people do in life when they're straining to be anything—funny or gentle or brave. I always wanted to see that one on the screen but I missed it somehow.

I found her as lovable as a cheap old toy. She made three thousand a week, and her husbands all drank and beat her nearly to death. But today I had an axe to grind.

"You don't know her name?" I persisted.

"Oh—" said Rose "—*that*. Well, he kept calling her up afterwards and he told Katy Doolan it was the wrong name after all."

"I think he found her," I said. "Do you know Martha Dodd?"

"Hasn't that little girl had a tough break though!" she exclaimed with ready theatrical sympathy.

"Could you possibly invite her to lunch tomorrow?"

"Oh, I think she gets enough to eat all right. There's a Mexican—"

I explained that my motives were not charitable. Rose agreed to cooperate. She called Martha Dodd.

15 (second part)

We had lunch next day at the Bev Brown Derby, a languid restaurant patronized for its food by clients who always look as if they'd like to lie down. There is some animation at lunch where the women put on a show for the first five minutes after they eat but we were a tepid threesome. I should have come right out with my curiosity. Martha Dodd was an agricultural girl who had never quite understood what had happened to her and had nothing to show for it except a washed out look about the eyes. She still believed that the life she had tasted was reality and this was only a long waiting.

"I had a beautiful place in 1928," she told us. "Thirty acres, with a miniature golf course and a pool and a gorgeous view. All spring I was up to my ass in daisies."

I ended by asking her to come over and meet Father. This was pure penance for having had "a mixed motive" and being ashamed of it. One doesn't mix motives in Hollywood—it is confusing. Everybody understands, and the climate wears you down. A mixed motive is conspicuous waste.

Rose left us at the studio gate, disgusted by my cowardice. Martha had worked up inside to a pitch about her career—not a very high pitch because of seven years of neglect but a sort of nervous acquiescence and I was going to speak strongly to Father. They never did anything for people like Martha who had made them so much money at one time. They let them slip away into misery eked out with extra work—it would have been kinder to ship them out of town. And Father was being so proud of me this summer. I had to keep him from telling everybody just how I was brought up to produce such a perfect jewel. And Bennington—oh what an exclusive—dear God my heart. I assured him there was the usual proportion of natural born skivies and biddies tastefully concealed by throw overs from Sex, Fifth Avenue; but Father had worked himself up to practically an alumnus. "You've had everything," he used to say happily. Everything included roughly the two years in Florence where I managed against heavy odds to be the only virgin in school, and the courtesy debut in Boston, Massachusetts. I was a veritable flower of the fine old cost-and-gross aristocracy.

So I knew he would do something for Martha Dodd and as we went into his office I had great dreams of doing something for Johnny Swanson the cowboy too and Evelyn Brent and all sorts of discarded flowers. Father was a charming and sympathetic man—except for that time I had seen him unexpectedly in New York—and there was something touching about his being my father. After all he was *my* father—he would do anything in the world for me.

Only Rosemary Schmiel was in the outer office and she was on Birdy Peters' phone. She waved for me to sit down but I was full of my plans and telling Martha to take it easy I pressed the clicker under Rosemary's desk and went toward the opened door.

"Your father's in conference," Rosemary called. "Not in conference but I ought to—"

By this time I was through the door and a little vestibule and another door and caught Father in his shirt sleeves, very sweaty and trying to open a window. It was a hot day but I hadn't realized it was that hot and thought he was ill.

"No, I'm all right," he said. "What is it?"

I told him. I told him the whole theory of people like Martha Dodd, walking up and down his office. How he could use them and guarantee them regular employment. He seemed to take me up excitedly and kept nodding and agreeing, and I felt closer to him than I had for a long time. I came close and kissed him on his cheek. He was trembling and his shirt was soaked through.

"You're not well," I said. "Or you're in some sort of stew."

"No, I'm not at all."

"What is it?"

"Oh it's Monroe," he said. "That God damn little Vine Street Jesus! He's in my hair night and day!"

"What's happened?" I asked, very much cooler.

"Oh, he sits like a little God damn priest or rabbi and says what he'll do and he won't do. I can't tell you now—I'm half crazy. Why don't you go along."

"I won't have you like this."

"Go along I tell you!" I sniffed but he never drank.

"Go and brush your hair," I said. "I want you to see Martha Dodd."

"In here! I'd never get rid of her."

"Out there then. Go wash up first. Put on another shirt."

With an exaggerated gesture of despair he went into the little bathroom adjoining. It was hot in the office as if it had been closed for hours and maybe that was making him sick so I opened two more windows.

"You go along," Father called from behind the closed door of the bathroom. "I'll be there presently."

"Be awfully nice to her," I said. "No charity."

As if it were Martha speaking for herself a long low moan came from somewhere in the room. I was startled—then transfixed as it came again not from the bathroom where Father was, not from outside but from a closet in the wall across from me. How I was brave enough I don't know but I ran across to it and opened it and Father's secretary Birdy Peters tumbled out stark naked—just like a corpse in the movies. With her came a gust of stifling, stuffy air. She flopped sideways on the floor with the one hand still clutching some clothes and lay on the floor bathed in sweat—just as Father came in from the bathroom. I could feel him standing behind me and without turning I knew exactly how he looked, for I had surprised him before.

"Cover her up," I said, covering her up myself with a rug from the couch. "Cover her *up!*"

I left the office. Rosemary Schmiel saw my face as I came out and responded with a terrified expression. I never saw her again or Birdy Peters either. As Martha and I went out Martha asked

"What's the matter dear?"—and when I didn't say anything, "You did your best. Probably it was the wrong time. I'll tell you what I'll do. I'll take you to see a very nice English girl. Did you see the girl that Stahr danced with at our table the other night?"

So at the price of a little immersion in the family drains I had what I wanted.

I don't remember much about our call. She wasn't at home was one reason. The screen door of her house was unlocked and Martha went in calling "Kathleen" with bright familiarity. The room we saw was bare and formal as a hotel; there were flowers about but they did not look like sent flowers. Also Martha found a note on the table which said, "Leave the dress. Have gone looking for a job. Will drop by tomorrow."

Martha read it twice but it didn't seem to be for Stahr, and we waited five minutes. People's houses are very still when they are gone. Not that I expect them to be jumping around but I leave the observation for what it's worth. Very still. Prim almost with just a fly holding down the place and paying no attention to you, and the corner of a curtain blowing.

"I wonder what kind of a job," said Martha. "Last Sunday she went somewhere with Stahr."

But I was no longer interested. It seemed awful to be here—producer's blood, I thought in horror. And in quick panic I pulled her out into the placid sunshine. It was no use—I felt just black and awful. I had always been proud of my body—I had a way of thinking of it as geometric which made everything it did seem all right and there was probably not any kind of place, including churches and offices and shrines, where people had not embraced—but no one had ever stuffed me naked into a hole in the wall in the middle of a business day.

Episode 16, First Part

"If you were in a drug store," said Stahr "—having a prescription filled—"

"You mean a chemist?" Boxley asked.

"If you were in a chemist's," conceded Stahr, "and you were getting a prescription for some member of your family who was very sick—"

"—Very ill?" queried Boxley.

"Very ill. *Then* whatever caught your attention through the window, whatever distracted you and held you would probably be material for pictures."

"A murder outside the window, you mean."

"There you go," said Stahr smiling. "It might be a spider working on the pane."

"Of course—I see."

"I'm afraid you don't, Mr. Boxley. You see it for *your* medium but not for ours. You keep the spiders for yourself and you try to pin the murders on us."

"I might as well leave," said Boxley. "I'm no good to you. I've been here three weeks and I've accomplished nothing. I make suggestions but no one writes them down."

"I want you to stay. Something in you doesn't like pictures, doesn't like telling a story this way—"

"It's such a damned bother," exploded Boxley. "You can't let yourself go—"

He checked himself. He knew that Stahr, the helmsman, was finding time for him in the middle of a constant stiff blow—that they were talking in the always creaking rigging of a ship sailing in great awkward tacks along an open sea. Or else—it seemed at times—they were in a huge quarry where even the newly cut marble bore the tracery of old pediments, half obliterated inscriptions of the past.

"I keep wishing you could start over," Boxley said. "It's this mass production."

"That's the condition," said Stahr. "There's always some lousy condition. We're making a life of Rubens—suppose I asked you to do portraits of rich dopes like Pat Brady and me and Gary Cooper and Marcus when you wanted to paint Jesus Christ! Wouldn't you feel you had a condition? Our condition is that we have to take people's own favorite folklore and dress it up and give it back to them. Anything beyond that is sugar. So won't you give us some sugar, Mr. Boxley?"

Boxley knew he could sit with Wylie White tonight at the Troc raging at Stahr, but he had been reading Lord Charnwood and he recognized that Stahr like Lincoln was a leader carrying on a long war on many fronts; almost single-handed he had moved pictures sharply forward through a decade, to a point where the content of the "A productions" was wider and richer than that of the stage. Stahr was an artist only as Mr. Lincoln was a general, perforce and as a layman.

"Come down to La Borwits' office with me," said Stahr. "They sure need some sugar there."

In La Borwits' office two writers, a shorthand secretary and a supervisor sat in a tense smokey stalemate where Stahr had left them three hours before. He looked at the faces one after another and found nothing. La Borwits spoke with awed reverence for his defeat.

"We've just got too many characters, Monroe."

Stahr snorted affably.

"That's the principal idea of the picture."

He took some change out of his pocket, looked up at the suspended light and tossed up half a dollar which clanked into the bowl. He looked at the coins in his hands and selected a quarter.

La Borwits watched miserably; he knew this was a favorite idea of Stahr's and he saw the sands running out. At the moment everyone's back was toward him. Suddenly he brought up his hands from their placid position under the desk and threw them high in the air, so high that they seemed to leave his wrists—and then he caught them neatly as they were descending. After that he felt better. He was in control.

One of the writers had taken out some coins also and presently rules were defined. "You have to toss your coin through the chains without hitting them. Whatever falls into the light is the kitty."

They played for half an hour—all except Boxley who sat aside and dug into the script, and the secretary who kept tally. She calculated the cost of the four men's time, arriving at a figure of sixteen hundred dollars. At the end La Borwits was winner by $5.50 and a janitor brought in a step-ladder to take the money out of the light.

Boxley spoke up suddenly.

"You have the stuffings of a tuhkey here," he said.

"What!"

"It's not pictures."

They looked at him in astonishment. Stahr concealed a smile.

"So we've got a real picture man here!" exclaimed La Borwits.

"A lot of beautiful speeches," said Boxley boldly. "But no situations. After all, you know, it's not going to be a novel: and it's too long. I can't exactly describe how I feel but it's not quite right. And it leaves me cold."

He was giving them back what had been handed him for three weeks. Stahr turned away, watching the others out of the corner of his eye.

"We don't need *less* characters," said Boxley. "We need *more*. As I see it that's the idea."

"That's the idea," said the writers.

"Yes—that's the idea," said La Borwits.

Boxley was inspired by the attention he had created.

"Let each character see himself in the other's place," he said. "The policeman is about to arrest the thief when he sees that the thief actually has *his* face. I mean show it that way. You could almost call the thing 'Put Yourself in My Place.' "

Suddenly they were at work again—taking up this new theme in turn like hepcats in a swing band and going to town with it. They might throw it out again tomorrow but life had come back for a moment. Pitching the coins had done it as much as Boxley. Stahr had recreated the proper atmosphere—never consenting to be a driver of the driven, but feeling like and acting like and sometimes even looking like a small boy getting up a show.

He left them, touching Boxley on the shoulder in passing—a deliberate accolade—he didn't want them to gang up on him and break his spirit in an hour.

Episode 16 (Part 2)

Doctor Baer was waiting in his inner office. With him was a colored man with a portable cardiograph like a huge suitcase. Stahr called it the lie detector. He stripped to the waist and the weekly examination began.

"How've you been feeling?"

"Oh—the usual," said Stahr.

"Been hard at it? Getting any sleep?"

"No—about five hours. If I go to bed early I just lie there."

"Take the sleeping pills."

"The yellow one gives me a hangover."

"Take two red ones then."

"That's a nightmare."

"Take one of each—the yellow first."

"All right—I'll try. How've *you* been?"

"Say—I take care of myself, Monroe. I save myself."

"The hell you do—you're up all night sometimes."

"Then I sleep all next day."

After ten minutes Baer said:

"Seems O.K. The blood pressure's up five points."

"Good," said Stahr. "That's good isn't it?"

"That's good. I'll develop the cardiograms tonight. When are you coming away with me?"

"Oh, some time," said Stahr lightly. "In about six weeks things'll ease up."

Baer looked at him with a genuine looking that had grown over three years.

"You got better in thirty-three when you laid up," he said. "Even for three weeks."

"I will again."

No he wouldn't, Baer thought. With Minna's help he had enforced a few short rests years ago and lately he had hinted around trying to find who Stahr considered his closest friends. Who could take him away and keep him away. It would almost surely be useless. He was due to die very soon now. Within six months one could say definitely. What was the use of developing the cardiograms? You couldn't persuade a man like Stahr to stop and lie down and look at the sky for six months. He would much rather die. He said differently but what it added up to was the definite urge toward total exhaustion that he had run into before. Fatigue was a drug as well as a poison and Stahr apparently derived some rare almost physical pleasure from working lightheaded with weariness. It was a perversion of the life force he had seen before but he had almost stopped trying to interfere with it. He had cured a man or so—a hollow triumph of killing and preserving the shell.

"You hold your own," he said.

They exchanged a glance. Did Stahr know? Probably. But he did not know when—he did not know how soon now.

"If I hold my own I can't ask more," said Stahr.

The colored man had finished packing the apparatus.

"Next week same time?"

"O.K., Bill," said Stahr. "Good bye."

As the door closed Stahr switched open the Dictograph. Miss Doolan's voice came through immediately.

"Do you know a Miss Kathleen Moore?"

"What do you mean?" he asked startled.

"A Miss Kathleen Moore is on the line. She said you asked her to call."

"Well, my God!" he exclaimed. He was swept with indignant rapture. It had been five days—this would never do at all.

"She's on now?"

"Yes."

"Well, all right then."

In a moment he heard the voice up close to him.

"Are you married?" he asked, low and surly.

"No, not yet."

His memory blocked out her face and form—as he sat down she seemed to lean down to his desk keeping level with his eyes.

"What's on your mind?" he asked in the same surly voice. It was hard to talk that way.

"You did find the letter?" she asked.

"Yes. It turned up that night."

"That's what I want to speak to you about."

He found an attitude at length—he was outraged.

"What is there to talk about?" he demanded.

"I tried to write you another letter but it wouldn't write."

"I know that too."

There was a pause.

"Oh cheer up!" she said surprisingly. "This doesn't sound like you. It *is* Stahr, isn't it? That very nice Mr. Stahr?"

"I feel a little outraged," he said almost pompously. "I don't see the use of this. I had at least a pleasant memory of you."

"I don't believe it's you," she said. "Next thing you'll wish me luck." Suddenly she laughed. "Is this what you planned to say? I know how *aw*ful it gets when you plan to say anything—"

"I never expected to hear from you again," he said with dignity; but it was no use, she laughed again—a woman's laugh that is like a child's, just one syllable, a crow and a cry of delight.

"Do you know how you make me feel?" she demanded. "Like one day in London during a caterpillar plague when a hot furry thing dropped in my mouth."

"I'm sorry."

"Oh please wake up," she begged. "I want to see you. I can't explain things on the phone. It was no fun for me either, you understand."

"I'm very busy. There's a sneak preview in Glendale tonight."

"Is that an invitation?"

"George Boxley, the English writer, is going with me." He surprised himself. "Do you want to come along?"

"How could we talk?"

She considered. "Why don't you call for me afterwards," she suggested. "We could ride around."

Miss Doolan on the huge Dictograph was trying to cut in a shooting director—the only interruption ever permitted. He flipped the button and called "wait" impatiently into the machine.

"About eleven?" Kathleen was saying confidently.

The idea of "Riding around" seemed so unwise that if he could have thought of the words to refuse her he would have spoken them but he did not want to be the caterpillar. Suddenly he had no attitude left except the sense that the day, at least, was complete. It had an evening—a beginning, a middle and an end.

He rapped on the screen door, heard her call from inside, and stood waiting where the level fell away. From below came the whir of a lawn mower—a man was cutting his grass at midnight. The moon was so bright that Stahr could see him plainly a hundred feet off and down as he stopped and rested on the handle before pushing it back across his garden. There was a midsummer restlessness abroad—early August with imprudent loves and impulsive crimes. With little more to expect from summer one tried anxiously to live in the present—or, if there was no present, to invent one.

She came at last. She was all different and delighted. She wore a suit with a skirt that she kept hitching up as they walked down to the car with a brave gay, stimulating reckless air of "Tighten up your belt, baby. Let's get going—to any pole." Stahr had brought his limousine with the chauffeur, and the intimacy of the four walls whisking them along a new curve in the dark took away any strangeness at once. In its way the little trip they made was one of the best times he had ever had in life. It was certainly one of the times when, if he knew he was going to die, it was not tonight.

She told him her story. She sat beside him cool and gleaming for a while, spinning on excitedly, carrying him to far places with her, meeting and knowing the people she had known. The story was vague at first. "This Man" was the one she had loved and lived with. "This American" was the one who had rescued her when she was sinking into a quicksand.

"Who is he—the American?"

Oh, names—what did they matter? No one important like Stahr, not rich. He had lived in London and now they would live out here. She was going to be a good wife, a real person. He was getting a divorce—not just on account of her—but that was the delay.

"But the first man?" asked Stahr. "How did you get into that?"

Oh, that was a blessing at first. From sixteen to twenty-one the thing was to eat. The day her stepmother presented her at Court they had one shilling to eat with so as not to feel faint. Sixpence apiece but the stepmother watched while she ate. After a few months the stepmother died and she would have sold out for that shilling but she was too weak to go into the streets. London can be harsh—oh quite.

Was there nobody?

There were friends in Ireland who sent butter. There was a soup kitchen. There was a visit to an uncle who made advances to her when she had a full stomach, and she held out and got fifty pounds out of him for not telling his wife.

"Couldn't you work?" Stahr asked.

"I worked. I sold cars. Once I sold a car."

"But couldn't you get a regular job?"

"It's hard—it's different. There was a feeling that people like me forced other people out of jobs. A woman struck me when I tried to get a job as chambermaid in a hotel."

"But you were presented at Court?"

"That was my stepmother who did that—on an off chance. I was nobody. My father was shot by the Black and Tans in twenty-two when I was a child. He wrote a book called 'Last Blessing.' Did you ever read it?"

"I don't read."

"I wish you'd buy it for the movies. It's a good little book. I still get a royalty from it—ten shillings a year."

Then she met "The Man" and they travelled the world around. She had been to all the places that Stahr made movies of, and lived in cities whose names he had never heard. Then The Man went to seed, drinking and sleeping with the housemaids and trying to force her off on his friends. They all tried to make her stick with him. They said she had saved him and should cleave to him longer now, indefinitely, to the end. It was her duty. They brought enormous pressure to bear. But she had met The American, and so finally she ran away.

"You should have run away before."

"Well, you see it was difficult." She hesitated, and plunged. "You see I ran away from a king."

His moralities somehow collapsed—she had managed to top him. A confusion of thoughts raced through his head—one of them a faint old credo that all royalty was diseased.

"It wasn't the King of England," she said. "My king was out of job as he used to say. There are lots of kings in London." She laughed—then added almost defiantly, "He was very attractive until he began drinking and raising hell."

"What was he king of?"

She told him—and Stahr visualized the face out of old newsreels.

"He was a very learned man," she said. "He could have taught all sorts of subjects. But he wasn't much like a king. Not nearly as much as you. None of them were."

This time Stahr laughed.

"They were the standard article," he said.

"You know what I mean. They all felt old fashioned. Most of them tried so hard to keep up with things. They were always advised to keep up with things. One was a Syndicalist for instance. And one used to carry around a couple of clippings about a tennis tournament when he was in the semi-finals. I saw those clippings a dozen times."

They rode through Griffith Park and out past the dark studios of Burbank, past the airports and along the way to Pasadena past the neon signs of roadside cabarets. Up in his head he wanted her but it was late and just the ride was an overwhelming joy. They held hands and once she came close in to his arms saying, "Oh you're *so* nice. I *do* like to be with you." But her mind was divided—this was not his night as the Sunday afternoon had been his. She was absorbed in herself, stung into excitement by telling of her own adventures; he could not help wondering if he was getting the story she had saved up for The American.

"How long have you known The American?" he asked.

"Oh I knew him for several months. We used to meet. We understand each other. He used to say 'It looks like a cinch from now on.' "

"Then why did you call me up?"

She hesitated.

"I wanted to see you once more. Then too—he was supposed to arrive today but last night he wired that he'd be another week. I wanted to talk to a friend—after all you *are* my friend."

He wanted her very much now but one part of his mind was cold and kept saying: she wants to see if I'm in love with her, if I want to marry her. Then she'd consider whether or not to throw this man over. She won't consider it till I've committed myself.

"Are you in love with The American?" he asked.

"Oh yes. It's absolutely arranged. He saved my life and my reason. He's moving half way around the world for me. I insisted on that."

"But are you in love with him?"

"Oh yes, I'm in love with him."

The "Oh yes" told him she was not—told him to speak for himself—that she would see. He took her in his arms and kissed her deliberately on the mouth and held her for a long time. It was so warm.

"Not tonight," she whispered.

"All right."

They passed over suicide bridge with the high new wire.

"I know what it is," she said, "but how stupid. English people don't kill themselves when they don't get what they want."

They turned around in the driveway of a hotel and started back. It was a dark night with no moon. The wave of desire had passed and neither spoke for a while. Her talk of kings had carried him oddly back in flashes to the pearly White Way of Main Street in Erie, Pennsylvania when he was fifteen. There was a restaurant with lobsters in the window and green weeds and bright light on a shell cavern and behind a red curtain the terribly strange brooding mystery of people and violin music. That was just before he left for New York. This girl reminded him of the fresh iced fish and lobsters in the window. She was Beautiful Doll. Minna had never been Beautiful Doll.

They looked at each other and her eyes asked "Shall I marry The American?" He did not answer. After a while he said:

"Let's go somewhere for the week-end."

She considered.

"Are you talking about tomorrow?"

"I'm afraid I am."

"Well, I'll tell you tomorrow," she said.

"Tell me tonight. I'd be afraid—"

"—find a note in the car?" she laughed. "No there's no note in the car. You know almost everything now."

"Almost everything."

"Yes—almost. A few little things."

He would have to know what they were. She would tell him tomorrow. He doubted—or he wanted to doubt—if there had been a maze of philandering—a fixation had held her to The Man, the king, firmly and long. Three years of a highly anomalous position—one foot in the Palace and one in the background. "You had to laugh a lot," she said. "I learned to laugh a lot."

"He could have married you—like Mrs. Simpson," Stahr said in protest.

"Oh, he was married. And he wasn't a romantic." She stopped herself.

"Am I?"

"Yes," she said unwillingly, as if she were laying down a trump. "Part of you is. You're three or four different men but each of them out in the open. Like all Americans."

"Don't start trusting Americans too implicitly," he said, smiling. "They may be out in the open but they change very fast."

She looked concerned.

"Do they?"

"Very fast and all at once," he said. "And nothing ever changes them back."

"You frighten me. I always had a great sense of security with Americans."

She seemed suddenly so alone that he took her hand.

"Where will we go tomorrow?" he said. "Maybe up in the mountains. I've got everything to do tomorrow but I won't do any of it. We can start at four and get there by afternoon."

"I'm not sure. I seem to be a little mixed up. This doesn't seem to be quite the girl who came out to California for a new life."

He could have said it then, said "It is a new life" for he knew it was, he knew he could not let her go now, but something else said to sleep on it as an adult, no romantic. And tell her tomorrow. Still she was looking at him her eyes wandering from his forehead to his chin and back again, and then up and down once more with that odd slowly waving motion of her head.

. . . It is your chance, Stahr. Better take it now. This is your girl. She can save you, she can worry you back to life. She will take looking after and you will grow strong to do it. But take her now—tell her and take her away. Neither of you knows it but far away over the night The American has changed his plans. At this moment his train is speeding through Albuquerque; the schedule is accurate. The engineer is on time. In the morning he will be here.

. . . The chauffeur turned up the hill to Kathleen's house. It seemed warm even in darkness—wherever he had been near her was by way of being enchanted place for Stahr: this limousine—the rising house at the beach, the very distances they had already covered together over the sprawled city. The hill they climbed now gave forth a sort of glow, a sustained sound that struck his soul alert with delight.

As he said good bye he felt again that it was impossible to leave her, even for a few hours. There was only ten years between them but he felt that madness about it akin to the love of an ageing man for a young girl. It was a deep and desperate time-need, a clock ticking with his heart, and it urged him against the whole logic of his life to walk past her into the house now—and say "This is forever."

Kathleen waited, irresolute herself—pink and silver frost waiting to melt with spring. She was a European, humble in the face of power, but there was a fierce self-respect that would only let her go so far. She had no illusions about the considerations that swayed princes.

"We'll go to the mountains tomorrow," said Stahr. Many thousands of people depended on his balanced judgement—you can suddenly blunt a quality you have lived by for twenty years.

He was very busy the next morning, Saturday. At two o'clock when he came from luncheon there was a stack of telegrams—a company ship was lost in the Arctic, a star was in disgrace, a writer was sueing for one million dollars, Jews were dead miserably beyond the sea. The last telegram stared up at him:

I WAS MARRIED AT NOON TODAY GOODBYE, and on a sticker attached *Send your answer by Western Union Telegram.*

Episode 17

I knew nothing about any of this. I went up to Lake Louise and when I came back didn't go near the studio. I think I would have started East in mid-August—if Stahr hadn't called me up one day at home.

"I want you to arrange something, Cecelia—I want to meet a Communist Party member."

"Which one?" I asked, somewhat startled.

"Any one."

"Haven't you got plenty out there?"

"I mean one of their organizers—from New York."

The summer before I had been all politics—I could probably have arranged a meeting with Harry Bridges. But my boy had been killed in an auto accident after I went back to college and I was out of touch with such things. I had heard there was a man from "The New Masses" around somewhere.

"Will you promise him immunity?" I asked, joking.

"Oh yes," Stahr answered seriously. "I won't hurt him. Get one that can talk—tell him to bring one of his books along."

He spoke as if he wanted to meet a member of the "I AM" cult.

"Do you want a blonde, or a brunette?"

"Oh, get a man," he said hastily.

Hearing Stahr's voice cheered me up—since I barged in on Father it had all seemed a paddling about in thin spittle. Stahr changed everything about it—changed the angle from which I saw it, changed the very air. He was like a brazier out of doors on a cool night.

"I don't think your father ought to know," he said. "Can we pretend the man is a Bulgarian musician or something?"

"Oh, they don't dress up any more," I said.

It was harder to arrange than I thought—Stahr's negotiations with the Writers Guild, which had continued over a year, were approaching a dead end. Perhaps they were afraid of being corrupted, and I was asked what Stahr's "proposition" was. Afterwards Stahr told me that he prepared for the meeting by running off the Russian Revolutionary Films that he had in his film library at home. He also ran off "Doctor Caligari" and Salvador Dali's "Un Chien Andalou," possibly suspecting that they had a bearing on the matter. He had been startled by the Russian Films back in the twenties and on Wylie White's suggestion he had had the script department get him up a two-page "treatment" of the "Communist Manifesto."

But his mind was closed on the subject. He was a rationalist who did his own reasoning without benefit of books—and he had just managed to climb out of a thousand years of Jewry into the late eighteenth century. He could not bear to see it melt away—he cherished the parvenu's passionate loyalty to an imaginary past.

The meeting took place in what I called the "processed leather room"—it was one of six done for us by a decorator from Sloane's years ago, and the term stuck in my head. It was *the* most decorator's room—an angora wool carpet the color of dawn, the most delicate grey imaginable—you hardly dared walk on it; and the silver panelling and leather tables and creamy pictures and slim fragilities looked so easy to stain that we could not breathe hard in there, though it was wonderful to look into from the door when the windows were open and the curtains whimpered querulously against the breeze. It was a lineal descendant of the old American parlor that used to be closed except on Sunday. But it was exactly the room for the occasion and I hoped that whatever happened would give it character and make it henceforth part of our house.

Stahr arrived first. He was white and nervous and troubled —except for his voice which was always quiet and full of consideration. There was a brave personal quality in the way he would meet you—he would walk right up to you and put aside something that was in the way, and grow to know you all over as if he couldn't help himself. I kissed him for some reason, and took him into the processed leather room.

"When do you go back to college?" he asked.

We had been over this fascinating ground before.

"Would you like me if I were a little shorter?" I asked. "I could wear low heels and plaster down my hair."

"Let's have dinner tonight," he suggested. "People will think I'm your father but I don't mind."

"I *love* old men," I assured him. "Unless the man has a crutch I feel it's just a boy and girl affair."

"Have you had many of those?"

"Enough."

"People fall in and out of love all the time, don't they."

"Every three years so Fanny Brice says. I just read it in the paper."

"I wonder how they manage it," he said. "I know it's true because I see them. But they look so con*vinced* every time. And then suddenly they don't look convinced. But they get convinced all over."

"You've been making too many movies."

"I wonder if they're as convinced the second time or the third time or the fourth time," he persisted.

"More each time," I said. "Most of all the last time."

He thought this over and seemed to agree.

"I suppose so. Most of all the last time."

I didn't like the way he said this and I suddenly saw that under the surface he was miserable.

"It's a great nuisance," he said. "It'll be·better when it's over."

"Wait a *min*ute! Perhaps pictures are in the wrong hands."

Brimmer, the Party Member, was announced and going to meet him I slid over to the door on one of those gossamer throw-rugs and practically into his arms.

He was a nice-looking man, this Brimmer—a little on the order of Spencer Tracy but with a stronger face and a wider range of reactions written up in it. I couldn't help thinking as he and Stahr smiled and shook hands and squared off, that they were two of the most alert men I had ever seen. They were very conscious of each other immediately—both as polite to me as you please but with a softening of the ends of their sentences when they turned in my direction.

"What are you people trying to do?" demanded Stahr. "You've got my young men all upset."

"That keeps them awake, doesn't it?" said Brimmer.

"First we let half a dozen Russians study the plant," said Stahr. "As a model plant, you understand. And then you try to break up the unity that makes it a model plant."

"The unity?" Brimmer repeated. "Do you mean what's known as the company spirit?"

"Oh, not that," said Stahr, impatiently. "It seems to be *me* you're after. Last week a writer came into my office—a drunk—a man who's been floating around for years just two steps out of the bughouse—and began telling me my business."

Brimmer smiled.

"You don't look to me like a man who could be told his business, Mr. Stahr."

They would both have tea. When I came back Stahr was telling a story about the Warner brothers and Brimmer was laughing with him.

"I'll tell you another one," Stahr said. "Balanchine the Russian dancer had them mixed up with the Ritz Brothers. He didn't know which ones he was training and which ones he was working for. He used to go around saying 'I cannot train those Warner Brothers to dance.' "

It looked like a quiet afternoon. Brimmer asked him why the producers didn't back the Anti-Nazi League.

"Because of you people," said Stahr. "It's your way of getting at the writers. In the long view you're wasting your time. Writers are children—even in normal times they can't keep their minds on their work."

"They're the farmers in this business," said Brimmer pleasantly. "They grow the grain but they're not in at the feast. Their feeling toward the producer is like the farmers' resentment of the city fellow."

I was wondering about Stahr's girl—whether it was all over between them. Later when I heard the whole thing from Kathleen, standing in the rain in a wretched road called Goldwyn Terrace, I figured out that this must have been a week after she sent him the telegram. She couldn't help the telegram. The man got off the train unexpectedly and walked her to the registry office without a flicker of doubt that this was what she wanted. It was eight in the morning and Kathleen was in such a daze that she was chiefly concerned in how to get the telegram to Stahr. In theory you could stop and say "Listen I forgot to tell you but I met a man." But this track had been laid down so thoroughly, with such confidence, such struggle, such relief that when it came along suddenly cutting across the other she found herself on it like a car on a closed switch. He watched her write the telegram, looking directly at it across the table, and she hoped he couldn't read upside down. . . .

When my mind came back into the room they had destroyed the poor writers—Brimmer had gone so far as to admit they were "unstable."

"They are not equipped for authority," said Stahr. "There is no substitute for will. Sometimes you have to fake will when you don't feel it at all."

"I've had that experience."

"You have to say 'It's got to be like this—no other way'—even if you're not sure. A dozen times a week that happens to me. Situations where there is no real reason for anything. You pretend there is."

"All leaders have felt that," said Brimmer. "Labor leaders, and certainly military leaders."

"So I've had to take an attitude in this Guild matter. It looks to me like a try for power and all I am going to give the writers is money."

"You give some of them very little money. Thirty dollars a week."

"Who gets that?" asked Stahr surprised.

"The ones who are commodities and easy to replace."

"Not on my lot," said Stahr.

"Oh yes," said Brimmer. "Two men in your shorts department get thirty dollars a week."

"Who?"

"Man named Ransome—man named O'Brien."

Stahr and I smiled together.

"Those are not writers," said Stahr. "Those are cousins of Cecelia's father."

"There are some in other studios," said Brimmer.

Stahr took his teaspoon and poured himself some medicine from a little bottle.

"What's a fink?" he asked suddenly.

"A fink? That's a strike breaker or a Company Tec."

"I thought so," said Stahr. "I've got a fifteen hundred dollar writer that every time he walks through the commissary keeps saying 'Fink!' behind other writers' chairs. If he didn't scare hell out of them it'd be funny."

Brimmer laughed.

"I'd like to see that," he said.

"You wouldn't like to spend a day with me over there?" suggested Stahr.

Brimmer laughed with genuine amusement.

"No, Mr. Stahr. But I don't doubt but that I'd be impressed. I've heard you're one of the hardest working and most efficient men in the entire West. It'd be a privilege to watch you but I'm afraid I'll have to deny myself."

Stahr looked at me.

"I like your friend," he said. "He's crazy but I like him." He looked closely at Brimmer. "Born on this side?"

"Oh yes. Several generations."

"Many of them like you?"

"My father was a Baptist minister."

"I mean are many of the Reds. I'd like to meet this big Jew that tried to blow over the Ford factory. What's his name—"

"Frankensteen?"

"That's the man. I guess some of you believe in it."

"Quite a few," said Brimmer dryly.

"Not you," said Stahr.

A shade of annoyance floated across Brimmer's face.

"Oh yes," he said.

"Oh no," said Stahr. "Maybe you did once."

Brimmer shrugged his shoulders.

"Perhaps the boot's on the other foot," he said. "At the bottom of your heart, Mr. Stahr, you know I'm right."

"No," said Stahr, "I think it's a bunch of tripe."

"—you think to yourself 'He's right' but you think the system will last out your time."

"You don't really think you're going to overthrow the government."

"No, Mr. Stahr. But we think perhaps you are."

They were nicking at each other—little pricking strokes like men do sometimes. Women do it too but it is a joined battle then with no quarter, but it is not pleasant to watch men do it because you never know what's next. Certainly it wasn't improving the tonal associations of the room for me and I moved them out the French window into our golden-yellow California garden.

It was midsummer but fresh water from the gasping sprinklers made the lawn glitter like spring. I could see Brimmer look at it with a sigh in his glance—a way they have. He opened up big outside—inches taller than I thought and broad-shouldered. He reminded me a little of Superman when he takes off his spectacles. I thought he was as attractive as men can be who don't really care about women as such. We played a round robin game of ping-pong and he handled his bat well. I heard Father come into the house singing that damn "Little Man, You've Had a Busy Day" and then breaking off as if he remembered we weren't speaking any more. It was half past six—my car was standing in the drive and I suggested we go down to the Trocadero for dinner.

Brimmer had that look that Father O'Ney had that time in New York when he turned his collar around and went with Father and me to the Russian Ballet. He hadn't quite ought to be here. When Bernie the photographer, who was waiting there for some big game or other, came up to our table he looked trapped—Stahr made Bernie go away, and I would like to have had the picture.

Then, to my astonishment, Stahr had three cocktails one after the other.

"Now I know you've been disappointed in love," I said.

"What makes you think that, Cecelia?"

"Cocktails."

"Oh, I never drink, Cecelia. I get dyspepsia—I never have been tight."

I counted them. "—two—*three*."

"I didn't realize. I couldn't taste them. I thought there was something the matter."

A silly glassy look darted into his eye—then passed away.

"This is my first drink in a week," said Brimmer. "I did my drinking in the navy."

The look was back in Stahr's eye—he winked it fatuously at me and said:

"This soapbox son-of-a-bitch has been working on the navy."

Brimmer didn't know quite how to take this. Evidently he decided to include it with the evening for he smiled faintly and I saw Stahr was smiling too. I was relieved when I saw it was safely in the great American tradition and I tried to take hold of the conversation but Stahr seemed suddenly all right.

"Here's my typical experience," he said very succinctly and clearly to Brimmer. "The best director in Hollywood—a man I never interfere with—has some streak in him that wants to slip a pansy into every picture or something on that order. Something offensive. He stamps it in deep like a watermark so I can't get it out. Every time he does it the Legion of Decency moves a step forward and something has to be sacrificed out of some honest film."

"Typical organization trouble," agreed Brimmer.

"Typical," said Stahr. "It's an endless battle. So now this director tells me it's all right because he's got a Directors Guild and I can't oppress the poor. That's how you add to my troubles."

"It's a little remote from us," said Brimmer smiling. "I don't think we'd make much headway with the directors."

"The directors used to be my pals," said Stahr proudly.

It was like Edward the VII's boast that he had moved in the best society in Europe.

"But some of them have never forgiven me," he continued, "—for bringing out stage directors when sound came in. It put them on their toes and made them learn their jobs all over but they never did really forgive me. That time we imported a whole new hogshead full of writers and I thought they were great fellows till they all went Red."

Gary Cooper came in and sat down in a corner with a bunch of men who breathed whenever he did and looked as if they lived off him and weren't budging an inch. A woman across the room looked around and turned out to be Carole Lombard—I was glad that Brimmer was at least getting an eyeful.

Stahr ordered a whiskey and soda and, almost immediately, another. He ate nothing but a few spoonfuls of soup and he said all the awful things about everybody being lazy so-and-so's and none of it mattered to *him* because he had lots of money—it was the kind of talk you heard whenever Father and his friends were together. I think Stahr realized that it sounded pretty ugly outside of the proper company—maybe he had never heard how it sounded before. Anyhow he shut up and drank off a cup of black coffee. I loved him and what he said didn't change that but I hated Brimmer to carry off this impression. I wanted him to see Stahr as a sort of technological virtuoso and here Stahr had been playing the wicked overseer to a point he would have called trash if he had watched it on the screen.

"I'm a production man," he said as if to modify his previous attitude. "I like writers—I think I understand them. I don't want to kick anybody out if they do their work."

"We don't want you to," said Brimmer pleasantly. "We'd like to take you over as a going concern."

Stahr nodded grimly.

"I'd like to put you in a roomful of my partners. They've all got a dozen reasons for having Fitts run you fellows out of town."

"We appreciate your protection," said Brimmer with a certain irony. "Frankly we *do* find you difficult, Mr. Stahr—precisely because you are a paternalistic employer and your influence is very great."

Stahr was only half listening.

"I never thought," he said, "—that I had more brains than a writer has. But I always thought that his brains be*longed* to me—because I knew how to use them. Like the Romans—I've heard that they never invented things but they knew what to do with them. Do you see? I don't say it's right. But it's the way I've always felt—since I was a boy."

This interested Brimmer—the first thing that had interested him for an hour.

"You know yourself very well, Mr. Stahr," he said.

I think he wanted to get away. He had been curious to see what kind of man Stahr was and now he thought he knew. Still hoping things would be different I rashly urged him to ride home with us but when Stahr stopped by the bar for another drink I knew I'd made a mistake.

It was a gentle, harmless, motionless evening with a lot of Saturday cars. Stahr's hand lay along the back of the seat touching my hair. Suddenly I wished it had been about ten years ago. I would have been nine. Brimmer about eighteen and working his way through some mid-western college and Stahr twenty-five just having inherited the world and full of confidence and joy. We would both have looked up to Stahr so, without question. And here we were in an adult conflict to which there was no peaceable solution, complicated now with exhaustion and drink.

We turned in at our drive and I drove around to the garden again.

"I must go along now," said Brimmer. "I've got to meet some people."

"No, stay," said Stahr. "I never have said what I wanted. We'll play ping-pong and have another drink and then we'll tear into each other."

Brimmer hesitated. Stahr turned on the floodlight and picked up his ping-pong bat and I went into the house for some whiskey—I wouldn't have dared disobey him.

When I came back they were not playing but Stahr was batting a whole box of new balls across to Brimmer who turned them aside. When I arrived he quit and took the bottle and retired to a chair just out of the floodlight, watching in dark dangerous majesty. He was pale—he was so transparent that you could almost watch the alcohol mingle with the poison of his exhaustion.

"Time to relax on Saturday night," he said.

"You're not relaxing," I said.

He was carrying on a losing battle with his instinct toward schizophrenia.

"I'm going to beat up Brimmer," he announced after a moment. "I'm going to handle this thing personally."

"Can't you pay somebody to do it?" asked Brimmer.

I signalled him to keep quiet.

"I do my own dirty work," said Stahr. "I'm going to beat hell out of you and put you on a train."

He got up and came forward and I put my arms around him, gripping him.

"Please *stop* this!" I said. "Oh, you're being so bad."

"This fellow has an influence over you," he said darkly. "Over all you young people. You don't know what you're doing."

"Please go home," I said to Brimmer.

Stahr's suit was made of slippery cloth and suddenly he slipped away from me and went for Brimmer. Brimmer retreated backward around the table. There was an odd expression in his face and afterwards I thought it looked as if he were saying, "Is *this* all? This frail half sick *person* holding up the whole thing."

Then Stahr came close, his hands going up. It seemed to me that Brimmer held him off with his left arm a minute and then I looked away—I couldn't bear to watch.

When I looked back Stahr was out of sight below the level of the table and Brimmer was looking down at him.

"Please go home," I said to Brimmer.

"All right." He stood looking down at Stahr as I came around the table. "I always wanted to hit ten million dollars but I didn't know it would be like this."

Stahr lay motionless.

"Please go," I said.

"I'm sorry. Can I help—"

"No. Please go. I understand."

He looked again, a little awed at the depths of Stahr's repose which he had created in a split second. Then he went quickly away over the grass and I knelt down and shook Stahr. In a moment he came awake with a terrific convulsion and bounced up on his feet.

"Where is he?" he shouted.

"Who?" I asked innocently.

"That American. Why in hell did you have to marry him, you damn fool."

"Monroe—he's gone. I didn't marry anybody."

I pushed him down in a chair.

"He's been gone half an hour," I lied.

The ping-pong balls lay around in the grass like a constellation of stars. I turned on a sprinkler and came back with a wet handkerchief but there was no mark on Stahr—he must have been hit in the side of the head. He went off behind some trees and was sick and I heard him kicking up some earth over it. After that he seemed all right but he wouldn't go into the house till I got him some mouthwash so I took back the whiskey bottle and got a mouthwash bottle. His wretched essay at getting drunk was over. I've been out with college freshmen but for sheer ineptitude and absence of the Bacchic spirit it unquestionably took the cake. Every bad thing happened to him but that was all.

We went in the house; the cook said Father and Mr. Marcus and Flieshacker were on the verandah so we stayed in the "processed leather room." We both sat down in a couple of places and seemed to slide off and finally I sat on a fur rug and Stahr on a footstool beside me.

"Did I hit him?" he asked.

"Oh, yes," I said. "Quite badly."

"I don't believe it." After a minute he added, "I didn't want to hurt him. I just wanted to chase him out. I guess he got scared and hit me."

If this was his interpretation of what had happened it was all right with me.

"Do you hold it against him?"

"Oh no," he said. "I was drunk." He looked around. "I've never been in here before—who did this room—somebody from the studio?"

"Somebody from New York."

"Well, I'll have to get you out of here," he said in his old pleasant way. "How would you like to go out to Doug Fairbanks' ranch and spend the night? He asked me—I know he'd love to have you."

That's how the two weeks started that he and I went around together. It only took one of them for Louella to have us married.

SELECTED FITZGERALD WORKING
NOTES: FACSIMILES

F. Scott Fitzgerald accumulated more material than he could incorporate in *The Love of the Last Tycoon*. His use of the notes during the process of composition has been described by Frances Kroll Ring (see Introduction, p. xlviii).

The Princeton University Library holds more than two-hundred pages of Fitzgerald's notes covering the gestation and composition of the novel: character lists, character sketches, outlines of action, plot ideas, dialogue, description, strippings from short stories, notes on Irving Thalberg and M-G-M, background on the movie industry and the Writers Guild, and marked typescripts of posthumously published Hollywood stories ("Last Kiss" and "Director's Special"). Most of the pages are in typescript and were either typed from Fitzgerald's holograph notes or dictated by him. The pages are undated, and they have been reshuffled whenever a researcher has handled them. The facsimile pages have been ordered by the editor: planning memos are followed by work-in-progress or writing notes. The rationale for selection of pages was to include notes that reveal Fitzgerald's thinking about the evolving novel—particularly those that bear on the unwritten episodes—and notes that assist in editing *The Love of the Last Tycoon*.

The handwritten letters on some pages refer to sections of Fitzgerald's notebooks (see "Appendix: Loose Notes" in *The Notebooks of F. Scott Fitzgerald*). Frances Kroll Ring thinks that the numbers at the heads of some original pages (1P, 1, 2P, 10, 10P) may refer to segments of the episodes.

Edmund Wilson's 1941 edition of *The Last Tycoon* provided thirty typeset pages of his edited selections from the notes, as well as material from Fitzgerald's manuscripts. In addition to correcting spelling and punctuation, Wilson abridged and conflated Fitzgerald's notes. Another selection, of twenty-eight printed pages of notes, is appended to "*The Last of the Novelists*." The pages presented here are selected from the 140 pages of notes facsimiled in *F. Scott Fitzgerald Manuscripts, V: The Last Tycoon*, Part I. These sixty-eight pages are facsimiled in their entirety. The facsimile method was decided on because transcription of the original notes distorts them.

a brilliant producer, Stahr, has everything, but has lost his wife whom he loved. He meets her image, falls for her, finding in mid-channel that he is breaking up a good marriage.

He leaves her, takes up with another girl and is plunged into a growing row in his business which gets worse and finally strikes him down in Washington. On his return his ambitious partner has done some dirty tricks. Stahr calls him and in his disgust throws over the man's daughter, returns to the girl and tries for a divorce.

His enemy strikes by going to the jealous husband. Stahr takes counter-measures then seeing it makes him as low as what he is fighting he gives up and goes away — with no future that he sees. The plane falls.

Bradogue and Stahr are actually great friends but Bradogue wants him out — Schwartz tries to warn him. Stahr meets the English wife of a cutter and is haunted by her. He meets her half secretly at the football — everywhere except at his office. There is absolutely no privacy and the seduction finally takes place at Malibu in his unfinished house.

Cecelia knows all this and it breaks her heart. But nobody knows, including her, who the girl really is. She inadvertently tells her father who discovers who the girl is and immediately sees his chance — he goes to Stahr, Threatening him in a pleasant way and suggesting he marry Cecelia but Stahr counters with what he knows about Bradogue (the affair of the girls husband murdered — Stahr has found it out from his wifes trained nurse whom he drew). Stahrs problem is whether to quit or go on in the face of inevitable discovery. He and Thalia are taking breathless chances. Now the storm breaks and everyone he had counted on turns against him. He plays with the idea of marrying Cecelia as the best way of getting out and is seen everywhere with her. The reds see him as a conservative — Wall Street as a red. He has one last fling with Thalia, tells Cecelia about it — throws her over and goes to Washington where he falls sick with worry.

Meanwhile Bradogue gets the news to the cutter who has long suspected something. Robinson (who is Savvy) feels it's the perfect anti-semetic smear gets backing and prepares the bomb.

Knowing nothing of this Stahr gets word of the salary cuts and comes west sick. Thalia gets word to him. He goes to work and crushes the whole thing by doing just what Bradogue did — plan to have Robinson killed. The clock has gone around. He leaves Hollywood, plan alibi — in the air he decides against it. The plane falls. Thalia is ruined. She never went inside a studio.

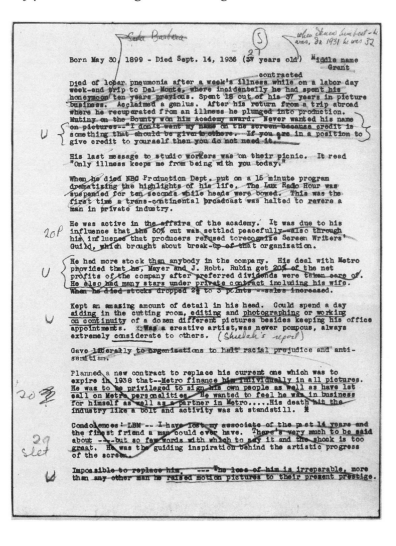

Santa Barbara

(S)   when Jones kim best - he
                                was, in 1931 he was 32

Born May 30, 1899 - Died Sept. 14, 1936 (37 years old) Middle name
                                                    Grant

                                    contracted
Died of lobar pneumonia after a week's illness while on a labor day
week-end trip to Del Monte, where incidentally he had spent his
honeymoon ten years previous. Spent 18 out of his 37 years in picture
business. Acclaimed a genius. After his return from a trip abroad
where he recuperated from an illness he plunged into production.
Mutiny on the Bounty won him Academy award. Never wanted his name
on pictures--"I don't want my name on the screen because credit is
something that should be given to others. If you are in a position to
give credit to yourself then you do not need it."

His last message to studio workers was on their picnic. It read
"Only illness keeps me from being with you today."

When he died NBC Production Dept. put on a 15 minute program
dramatizing the highlights of his life. The Lux Radio Hour was
suspended for ten seconds while heads were bowed. This was the
first time a trans-continental broadcast was halted to revere a
man in private industry.

He was active in the affairs of the academy. It was due to his
influence that the 50% cut was settled peacefully--also through
his influence that producers refused to recognize Screen Writers'
Guild, which brought about break-up of that organization.

He had more stock than anybody in the company. His deal with Metro
provided that he, Mayer and J. Robt. Rubin get 20% of the net
profits of the company after preferred dividends were taken care of.
He also had many stars under private contract including his wife.
When he died stocks dropped 2½ to 3 points --sales increased.

Kept an amazing amount of detail in his head. Could spend a day
aiding in the cutting room, editing and photographing or working
on continuity of a dozen different pictures besides keeping his office
appointments. He was a creative artist, was never pompous, always
extremely considerate to others. (Sheilah's report)

Gave liberally to organisations to halt racial prejudice and anti-
semitism.

Planned a new contract to replace his current one which was to
expire in 1938 that--Metro finance him individually in all pictures.
He was to be privileged to sign his own people as well as have let
call on Metro personalities. He wanted to feel he was in business
for himself as well as a partner in Metro.....His death hit the
industry like a bolt and activity was at standstill.

Condolences: LBM -- I have lost my associate of the past 14 years and
the finest friend a man could ever have. There's very much to be said
about --,but so few words with which to say it and the shock is too
great. He was the guiding inspiration behind the artistic progress
of the screen.

Impossible to replace him. --- The loss of him is irreparable, more
than any other man he raised motion pictures to their present prestige.

20P

20½

20

29
Slet

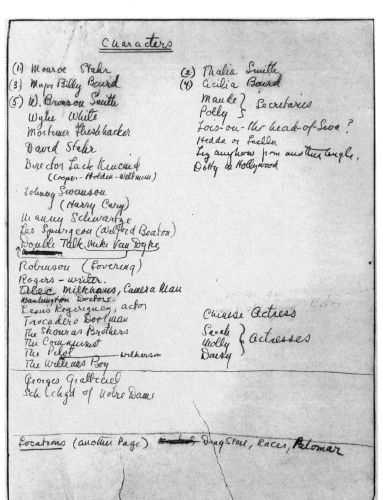

Characters

(1.) Monroe Stahr
(3) Major Billy Baird
(5) W. Bronson Smith
  Wylie White
  Mortimer Fleishhacker
  David Stahr
  Director Jack Kincaid
    (Cooper-Holden-Wellman)
· Johnny Swanson
    (Harry Cary)
  Manny Schwartze
  Lee Spurgeon (Welford Beaton)
  Double Talk Mike Van Dyke

Robinson (Covering)
Rogers - writer.
Alec milkhaus, Camera Man
Washington Doctors.
Jesus Rodriquez, actor
Trocadero Doorman
The Skouras Brothers
The Communist
The Pilot ——— wilkerson
The Williams Boy

Georges Gralbeciel
Sch Cchgd of Notre Dame

(2.) Thalia Smith
(4) Cecilia Baird
  Maude ⎫ Secretaries
  Polly ⎬
  Lois-on-the head-of-Siva ?
  Hedda or Luella
  Liz anyhow from another angle.
  Dotty de Hollywood

Chinese Actress
Sarah ⎫
Molly ⎬ actresses
Daisy

Locations (another page) ~~———~~ Drug Store, Races, Patomar

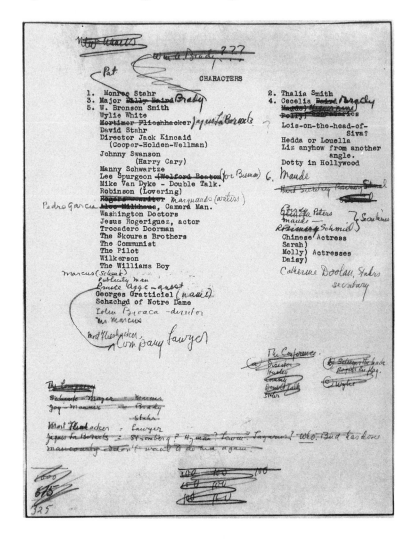

CHARACTERS

1. Monroe Stahr
3. Major ~~Billy Baird~~ Brady
5. W. Bronson Smith
   Wylie White
   ~~Mortimer Flieschhacker~~ Jacques La Borwde ?
   David Stahr
   Director Jack Kincaid
   (Cooper-Holden-Wellman)
   Johnny Swanson
          (Harry Cary)
   Manny Schwartze
   Lee Spurgeon ~~(Welford Beaton)~~ for Bruman)
   Mike Van Dyke - Double Talk.
   Robinson (Lovering)
   ~~Rogers   writer~~ Marquauds (writers)
   Pedro Garcia ~~Alex Millhaus~~, Camera Man.
   Washington Doctors
   Jesus Rogeriguez, actor
   Trocadero Doorman
   The Skouras Brothers
   The Communist
   The Pilot
   Wilkerson
   The Williams Boy
   Marcus (Schenk)
        Publicity man
        Ernice (agge - guest)
   Georges Gratticiel (namiel)
   Schzchgd of Notre Dame
   Iolm Broaca - director
   Mr. Marcus
   Mort Fleshpacker
          Company Lawyer

2. Thalia Smith
4. Cecelia ~~Baird~~ Brady
   ~~Maude) Minnerham)~~
   ~~Polly)   ceries~~
   Lois-on-the-head-of-
                    Siva?
   Hedda or Louella
   Liz anyhow from another
                    angle.
   Dotty in Hollywood

6. Maude
   ~~Hard Secretary Birchan, Carol~~

   Glenda Peters
   Maude —   } Secretaries
   Rosemary Schmid)
   Chinese Actress
   Sarah)
   Molly) Actresses
   Daisy)
   Catherine Doolan, Stahrs
             secretary

The Conference.
a Director   b Schenk for trade
  Hanley   Roger the flag.
  County
  Double Talk   c Wyler
  Stahr

~~The Company~~
Schenck - Mayer = Marcus
Joy - Mannix = Brady
                  Stahr
Mort Fleshacker = Lawyer
Jacques La Borwds = Stromberg ? Hyman? Leavr Sagovais? Webb, Bud Casdow
mancounty editor - wan't to do him again.

000
675
325

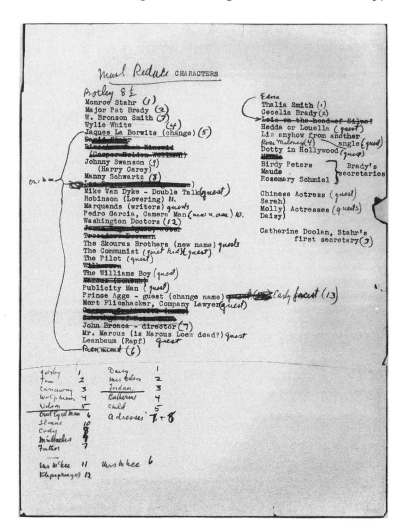

must Reduce CHARACTERS

Brotley 8½

Monroe Stahr (1)
Major Pat Brady (2)
W. Bronson Smith (3)
Wylie White (4)
Jaques La Borwits (change) (5)
~~Donald Glover~~
~~Rienzi — Jack Edwould~~
(Cooper-Weldon-Wollman)
Johnny Swanson (9)
(Harry Carey)
Manny Schwartz (8)
~~on her~~
~~Lee ————————————~~
Mike Van Dyke - Double Talk (guest)
Robinson (Lovering) 11.
Marquands (writers) guests
Pedro Garcia, Camera Man (new name) 10.
Washington Doctors (12)
~~Jesus ——————— door~~
~~Trocadero-Doorman~~
The Skouras Brothers (new name) guests
The Communist (guest kid)(guest) guests
The Pilot (guest)
~~Williamson~~
The Williams Boy (guest)
~~Marcus (Schenk)~~
Publicity Man (guest)
Prince Agge - guest (change name) ~~————————~~ Carly fascist (13)
Mort Flieshacker, Company Lawyer (guest)
~~Queens-Goolaison ——————~~
~~Schwabacher & Nussbaum~~
John Broaca - director (7)
Mr. Marcus (is Marcus Loew dead?) guest
Leanbaum (Rapf) guest
~~Benmund~~ (6)

Edna
Thalia Smith (1)
Cecelia Brady (2)
~~Lois on the head of Silva?~~
Hedda or Louella (guest)
Liz anyhow from another
(Rose Meloney) (4) angle (guest)
Dotty in Hollywood (guest)
~~Martha~~
Birdy Peters ⎫
Maude ⎬ Brady's secretaries
Rosemary Schmiel ⎭

Chinese Actress (guest)
Sarah)
Molly) Actresses (guests)
Daisy)

Catherine Doolan, Stahr's
first secretary (3)

Gatsby   1   Daisy   1
Tom   2   Mrs Wilson   2
Carraway   3   Jordan   3
Wolfshiem   4   Catherine   4
Wilson   5   child   5
Owl Eyed Man 6   Adresses 7 + 8
Sloane   10
Cody   8
Michaelis   9
Father   7

Mrs McKee   11   Mrs McKee 6
Klipspringer 12

MUST REDUCE CHARACTERS

Monroe Stahr
Major Pat Brady
W. Bronson Smith
Wylie White
Jaques La Borwits (change)
Rienmund
John Broaca – director
Manny Schwartz
Boxley
Johnny Swanson
    (Harry Carey)   *Greek*
Pedro Garcia, Camera Man (new name)
Robinson (Lovering)
Washington Doctors
Prince Agge – guest (change name)
                        Early fascist
Mike Van Dyke – Double Talk (guest)
Marquands (writers) guests
The Skouras Brothers (new name) guests
The Communist (quiet kid) guest
The Pilot (guest)
The Williams Boy (guest)
Publicity Man (guest)
Mort Flieshacker, Company Lawyer (guest) *Change name.*
Mr. Marcus (is Marcus Loew dead?) guest
Leanbaum (Rapf)(guest)
The Star
"Red" Redingwood (director)

Thalia Smith
Cecelia Brady
Catherine Doolan, Stahr's
    first secretary
Rose Meloney
Edna
Hedda or Louella (guest)
Liz anyhow from another
        angle (guest)
Dotty in Hollywood (guest)
Birdy Peters   )
Maude   ) Brady's
Rosemary Schmiel) secretaries
Chinese Actress (guest)
Sarah)
Molly) Actresses (guests)
Daisy)
Bitch

U.

~~Boston, July 11, 1921~~   *For Schwartze*

A midnight frolic of four years ago at Mishawum Manor, a roadhouse
in Woburn said to be conducted by a woman known as Brownie Kennedy,
whose guests included several motion picture producers was described
today at the hearing on a petition for the removal of Nathan A. Tufts,
District Attorney of Middlesex. Attorney General Weston Allen
preferred charges that Tufts was concerned in a conspiracy by which
the motion picture men paid $100,000 to escape prosecution threatened
on account of their presence at this dinner party.

The affair took place on March 6, 1917. It followed a dinner
to Fatty Arbuckle at the Copley Plaza . 20 or 25 people were
at this party and there were 10 or 12 women at the house. The
company remained from midnight until 4 a.m. The bill was $1050.
Abrams who was president of the New England Baseball League said
he paid it.

The affair was referred to as "drunken affair". There was a
conference at Tufts' office. Coakly, Boston Attorney, said if
he could prove the men were innocent he hoped Tufts would drop it.
District Attorney said that if complainents could be gotten off
his back he would not prosecute them. Lasky, Zukor, Walter Green,
Abe Berman were present at the "drunken affair". It was agreed
that all the complainants would be satisfied and the lawyers fees
for $100,000 would be paid. They wanted to have time to prove
the men were innocent. Tufts agreed to grant the time.

Two checks of $85,000 were investigated. They were said to be
paid in full settlement of a case growing out of this incident.
There were releases signed which were submitted to Zukor and Lasky
and Abrams who denied recognition of the signatures on the releases.

There was no trace that Tufts got any of the $100,000 to hush
up this affair and it was finally settled.

How Brady got his start?

CHAPTER I

3rd Episode:-

This will be based on a conversation that I had
with Stahr the first time I was alone with him in 1927,
the day that he said a thing about railroads. As near
as I can remember what he said was this:

We sat in the old commissary at Metro and he said,
"Scottie, supposing there's got to be a road through a
mountain--a railroad and two or three surveyors and people
come to you and you believe some of them and some of them
you don't believe, but all in all, there seem to be half a
dozen possible roads through those mountains, each one of
which so far as you can determine, is as good as the other.
Now suppose you happen to be the top man, there's a point
where you don't exercise the faculty of judgment in the
ordinary way, but simply the faculty of arbitrary decision.
You say, 'Well, I think we will put the road there' and
you trace it with your finger and you know in your secret
heart and no one else knows, that you have no reason for
putting the road there rather than in several other different
courses, but you're the only person that knows that you
don't know why you're doing it and you've got to stick to
that and you've got to pretend that you know and that you
did it for specific reasons, even though you're utterly
assailed by doubts at times as to the wisdom of your decision because all these other possible decisions keep
echoing in your ear. But when you're planning a new
enterprise on a grand scale, the people under you mustn't
ever know or guess that you're in any doubt because they've
all got to have something to look up to and they mustn't
ever dream that you're in doubt about any decision.
Those things keep occurring."

At that point, some other people came into the
commissary and sat down and the first thing I knew there
was a group of four and the intimacy of the conversation
was broken, but I was very much impressed by the shrewdness
of what he said--something more than shrewdness--by the
largeness of what he thought and how he reached it at the
age of 26, which he was then.

So I think that this last episode will be when Stahr
goes up and sits with the pilot up in front and rides beside the pilot, and the pilot recognizes in Stahr someone
who in his own field must be just as sure, just as determined,
just as courageous as he himself is. Very few words are
exchanged between Stahr and the pilot--in fact, it is an
episode that we may see entirely through the eyes of Cecelia
peeping in, of the stewardness reporting to Cecelia what
she saw peeping through the cockpit or Schwartz still trying
to get to Stahr before they get to Los Angeles. It is
quite possible that we may not be alone with Stahr through
this entire episode down to the very end, but at the very
end I want to go into that strong feeling that I had in
that undeveloped note about the motor shutting off and the
plane settling down to earth and the lights of Los Angeles
and for a minute there, I want to give an all fireworks
illumination of the intense passion in Stahr's soul, his

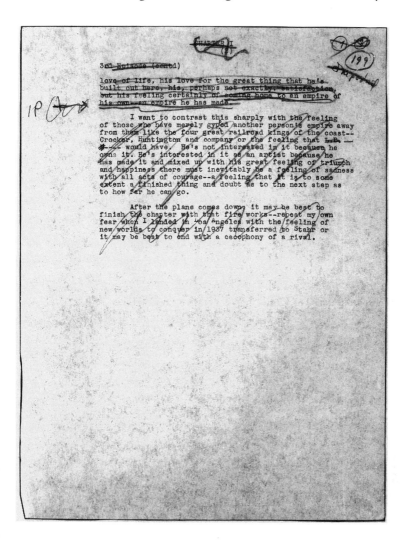

3rd Episode (contd)

love of life, his love for the great thing that he's
built out here, his, perhaps not exactly satisfaction,
but his feeling certainly of coming home to an empire of
his own--an empire he has made

    I want to contrast this sharply with the feeling
of those who have merely gyped another person's empire away
from them like the four great railroad kings of the coast--
Crocker, Huntington and company or the feeling that L.B.
-- would have. He's not interested in it because he
owns it. He's interested in it as an artist because he
has made it and mixed up with his great feeling of triumph
and happiness there must inevitably be a feeling of sadness
with all acts of courage--a feeling that it is to some
extent a finished thing and doubt as to the next step as
to how far he can go.

    After the plane comes down it may be best to
finish the chapter with that fire works--repeat my own
fear when I landed in Los Angeles with the feeling of
new worlds to conquer in 1937 transferred to Stahr or
it may be best to end with a cacophony of a rival.

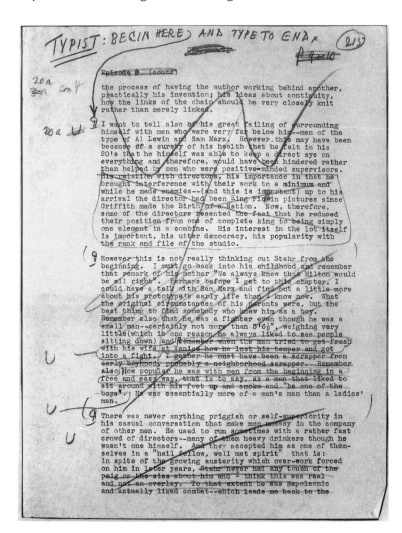

TYPIST: BEGIN HERE) AND TYPE TO END x   215

Episode B. (cont'd)

the process of having the author working behind another,
practically his invention; his ideas about continuity,
how the links of the chain should be very closely knit
rather than merely linked.

I want to tell also of his great failing of surrounding
himself with men who were very far below him--men of the
type of Al Lewin and Sam Marx. However, this may have been
because of a surety of his health that he felt in his
20's that he himself was able to keep a direct eye on
everything and therefore, would have been hindered rather
than helped by men who were positive-minded supervisors.
His relation with directors, his importance in that he
brought interference with their work to a minimum and
while he made enemies--(and this is important) up to his
arrival the director had been King Pin in pictures since
Griffith made the Birth of a Nation. Now, therefore,
some of the directors resented the fact that he reduced
their position from one of complete king to being simply
one element in a combine. His interest in the lot itself
is important, his utter democracy, his popularity with
the rank and file of the studio.

However this is not really thinking out Stahr from the
beginning. I must go back into his childhood and remember
that remark of his mother "We always knew that Milton would
be all right". Perhaps before I get to this chapter, I
could have a talk with Sam Marx and find out a little more
about his prototype's early life than I know now. What
the original circumstances of his parents were, but the
best thing to find somebody who knew him as a boy.
Remember also that he was a fighter even though he was a
small man--certainly not more than 5'6½", weighing very
little(which is one reason he always liked to see people
sitting down) and remember when the man tried to get fresh
with his wife at Venice how he lost his temper and got
into a fight. I gather he must have been a scrapper from
early boyhood, probably a neighborhood scrapper. Remember
also how popular he was with men from the beginning in a
free and easy way, that is to say, as a man that liked to
sit around with his feet up and smoke and "be one of the
boys". He was essentially more of a man's man than a ladies'
man.

There was never anything priggish or self-superiority in
his casual conversation that make men uneasy in the company
of other men. He used to run sometimes with a rather fast
crowd of directors--many of them heavy drinkers though he
wasn't one himself. And they accepted him as one of themselves in a "hail fellow, well met spirit" that is:
in spite of the growing austerity which over-work forced
on him in later years, Stahr never had any touch of the
prig or the siss about him and I think this was real
and not an overlay. To that extent he was Napoleonic
and actually liked combat--which leads me back to the

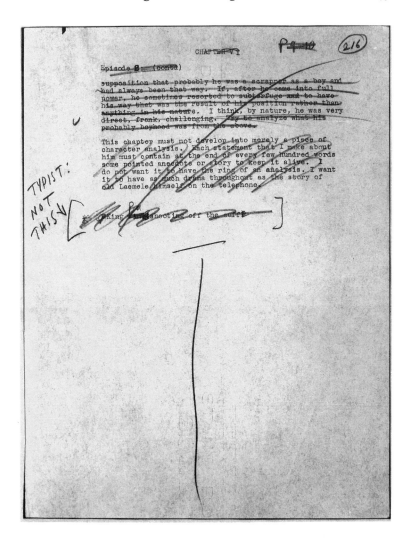

CHAPTER VI   P 4 10   (216)

Episode 8: (cont'd)

supposition that probably he was a scrapper as a boy and had always been that way. If, after he came into full power, he sometimes resorted to subterfuge and to have his way that was the result of his position rather than anything in his nature. I think, by nature, he was very direct, frank, challenging. Try to analyze what his probably boyhood was from the above.

This chapter must not develop into merely a piece of character analysis. Each statement that I make about him must contain at the end of every few hundred words some pointed anecdote or story to keep it alive. I do not want it to have the ring of an analysis. I want it to have as much drama throughout as the story of old Laemele himself on the telephone.

TYPIST:
NOT
THIS ✓   [talking shooting off the cuff]

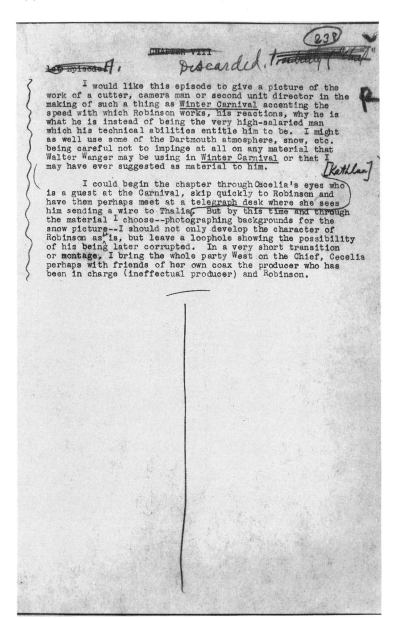

CHAPTER VIII

238

Discarded.

Episode A.

[Kathleen]

I would like this episode to give a picture of the
work of a cutter, camera man or second unit director in the
making of such a thing as <u>Winter Carnival</u> accenting the
speed with which Robinson works, his reactions, why he is
what he is instead of being the very high-salaried man
which his technical abilities entitle him to be. I might
as well use some of the Dartmouth atmosphere, snow, etc.
being careful not to impinge at all on any material that
Walter Wanger may be using in <u>Winter Carnival</u> or that I
may have ever suggested as material to him.

I could begin the chapter through Cecelia's eyes who
is a guest at the Carnival, skip quickly to Robinson and
have them perhaps meet at a telegraph desk where she sees
him sending a wire to Thalia. But by this time and through
the material I choose--photographing backgrounds for the
snow picture--I should not only develop the character of
Robinson as is, but leave a loophole showing the possibility
of his being later corrupted. In a very short transition
or montage, I bring the whole party West on the Chief, Cecelia
perhaps with friends of her own coax the producer who has
been in charge (ineffectual producer) and Robinson.

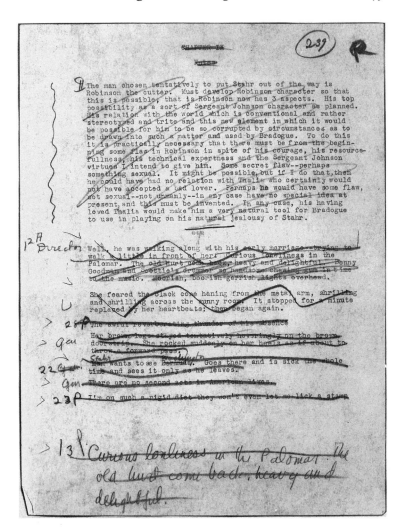

CHAPTER IX

(239)

¶ The man chosen tentatively to put Stahr out of the way is
Robinson the cutter. Must develop Robinson character so that
this is possible, that is Robinson now has 3 aspects. His top
possibility as a sort of Sergeant Johnson character as planned.
His relation with the world which is conventional and rather
stereotyped and trite and this new element in which it would
be possible for him to be so corrupted by circumstances as to
be drawn into such a matter and used by Bradogue. To do this
it is practically necessary that there must be from the beginning some flaw in Robinson in spite of his courage, his resource-
fullness, his technical expertness and the Sergeant Johnson
virtues I intend to give him. Some secret flaw--perhaps
something sexual. It might be possible, but if I do that, then
he could have had no relation with Thalia who certainly would
not have accepted a bad lover. Perhaps he would have some flaw,
not sexual--not unmanly--in any case have no special idea at
present, and this must be invented. In any case, his having
loved Thalia would make him a very natural tool for Bradogue
to use in playing on his natural jealousy of Stahr.

12 A Director Well, he was walking along with his early marriage trying to
walk a little in front of her. Curious lonelinesss in the
Palomar. The old hurt come back, heavy and delightful. Benny
Goodman and Scottie's drummer so handsome chewing gum in time
to the music. Moorish, boorish garrish lights overhead.

She feared the black cone haning from the metal arm, shrilling
and shrilling across the sunny room. It stopped for a minute
replaced by her heartbeats; then began again.

28 p The awful reverberating thunder of his absence

9 am Her brown legs stayed tentatively, hoveringly on the brown
doorbrick. She rocked suddenly on her heels as if about to
throw a forward pass.

22 G Stahr wants to see Bermuda. Goes there and is sick the whole
time and sees it only as he leaves.

9 m There are no second acts in American lives.

23 p I'm on such a rigid diet they won't even let me lick a stamp

13 Curious lonliness in the Palomar. The
old hurt come back, heavy and
delightful.

Thalia's Previous Life (Discard) 240

CHAPTER IV (but see 3d page for note)

K

R

1st Episode:

THALIA was born in 1908 in Newfoundland.

She was married in '29 to a rich man who came to Newfoundland as a tourist and loved her. She came of very humble parents, father was captain of a fishing snack and it was a run-away marriage. She married this wealthy man who had a place there. They had an awful time about their marriage because he was married. She had to live with him a year before he could divorce his wife and marry her.

One of the children of the first marriage died. It was blamed on her because if the divorce had not occurred and she hadn't appeared, it would not have happened. Her husband went all to pieces, lost all his money and she is still taking care of him in a vague way and he is perhaps in a sanitarium in the East and perhaps dead.

She came to California as a companion of the wife (KIKI) who is divorced and who leans on her altogether and at times is very grateful to her and sometimes turns on her for breaking up her home. She has become a great friend of this wife--both of whom love this man--and has stepped in and helped by giving up her own plans and what money there was. The wife is kind of a broken neurotic who has dabbled in dope and Thalia is haunted by the idea that she has broken up this home and doesn't know what her position is--she did it for love, etc., but she did break up this home, she feels.

The first wife has a little girl left from the marriage. She takes care of this woman part of the time and also does part time work in her mornings, but has never considered the studios and when she meets Stahr it is absolutely unimportant.

Her position in the home has gradually drifted into that of an upper servant because she unfortunately was too generous in a moment of feeling of atonement. She has been having an affair intermittant of which she is half ashamed, with the character whom I have called Robinson the cutter who is in his: (and this is very important) professional life an extraordinarily interesting and subtle character on the idea of Sergeant Johnson in the army or that cutter at United Artists whom I so admired or any other person of the type of trouble shooter or film technician--and I want to contrast this sharply with his utter conventionality and acceptance of banalities in the face of what might be called the cultural urban world. Women can twist him around their little finger. He might be able to unravel the most twisted skein of wires in a blinding snowstorm on top of a sixty foot telephone pole in the dark with no more tools than an imperfect pair of pliers made out of the nails of his boots, but faced with the situation which the most ignorant and useless person would handle with urbanity he would seem helpless and gauky--so much

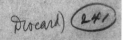

CHAPTER IV
(contd)

so as to give the impression of being a Babbitt or of being
a stupid, gawky, inept fellow.

This contrast at some point in the story is recognized
by Stahr who must at all points, when possible, be pointed
up as a man who sees below the surface into reality.

Her attitude towards this man has been that even
in the niceties of love-making she has had to be his master
and his deep gratitude to her is allied to his love for
her though throughout the story he always feels that she
is inevitably the superior person. Stahr at some point
points it out to her that this is nonsense and I want to
show here something different in mens' and women's points
of view: particularly that women are prone to cling to
an advantage or rather have less human generosity in points
of character than men have, or do I mean a less wide point
of view?

THE AFFAIR

Benchley's - the smile and the belt --the wrong girl.
The Screen Writers' Dance - at the table (The Chinese girl)
Eddie Mayer phoning--his words--the dinner--the Clover Club.
The glimpse of her at Benchley's.
The Anti-Nazi Ball--at Parker's--the car - at the movie - at
the ball itself.

Reaction--my wire--her phone.

The evening with Scottie.

ONE WEEK
         SAN FRANCISCO
         The phone call
         The movie with Benchley

ANOTHER WEEK
         CAROLINA
         The letter

RENEWAL UP TO THE DONEGAL LETTER. END OF STAGE I.

The quarrels - up to Chicago.

1. Drug Store (use the belt)
2. House high on hill (Use the glimpse and the table). A week
                                                      passes.
3. Gets Wylie to take her to ball--he can't go (invent why)
    but gets there late. Use the dinner, and the car. A week
    passes. The letter and the phone.
4. Football and seduction. Four days.
5. Her wedding.

Query -- where is the man for these 3 weeks. Getting his
           divorce.

Query -- why does Thalia after meeting a man of great power,
           and falling for him violently so that she sleeps with
           him then marry another man?

Answer -- she actually knows Stahr only a week after she falls
           in love with him and during that time resolutely
           considers it as a romance just as he does. In fact
           the letter impells the phone and the seduction is a
           surprise.

           Even so why does she not now stop the other thing?
           Ans. - Some pure circumstance intervenes--Stahr's
           moral doubts about her are a factor that let him
           neglect her at one important moment, his work keeps
           him from calling her. The moment it is too late he
           is desperate.

The Hollywood producers have not had
the early advantages which are ~~considered~~ standard —
and it is not very kindly nor
Christian to mock at them. ~~But they~~
~~low grade men are such delirium~~ they are
~~determinedly low~~ ~~accept mockery~~
and ~~hatred as their share and~~ ~~#~~
~~to it our ~~grow~~ to unconfortable comes~~ as less than
~~than~~ people & I have never heard a writer or
playwright or an ~~actress~~ or a novelist
say a nice thing about a producer ~~unless~~ except
~~possibly the one they are~~ ~~it was~~ working for ~~them~~ — from Dorothy
Parkers exhibit who was "only a
ponys bottom" — on up. They ~~cannot~~ is too much
~~be pleasant~~ to ask that they have pleasant natures
for it is a "filthy job to debauch
a nation — even though the nation wallows
in the spew.

~~On~~ their side they have their
money and their ~~strident~~ molls and

They accept mockery and hatred
as their share. They do not mind —
They link it up with the oppressions
visited upon their parents in
Oddessa and Loty — they are
having their moment among the
fleshpots before returning to the
darker and bloodier ghettos that
lie ahead.

12.

Plant his anonymity--his many plans. Your contributions can't
be measured. They have to pay in statue. On his deathbed
that haunts him. Maybe a statue.

I must not alienate the reader from her at the beginning, but
must give the feeling that "well, I don't like this girl much,
but I am going to stick around and see what she has to say because
she has let drop a few things that make me think that given the
right circumstances she might have been worthwhile."

Nevertheless, the first episode must close with something
definitely arresting or shocking about herself.

Very, very fine--pilot. Unbeknownst--pilot.

At M.I.T., he studied birth control, flood control, self control
and remote control.

She admired him; she was used to clasping her hands together in
his wake and heaving audible signs.

We had a professor in Freshman who taught us the technique of novels
in one month, of plays in another and was going to devote a whole
week to moving pictures at the end. She asked me to get her a script
of a real picture to serve as her text and I did--but after a week
she handed it back to me without comment and didn't mention the picture
pat of the course again.

It was a pale, even spiritual face lit reverently with great brown
eyes, but the pointed ears and the corners of the mouth were puckish
and grotesque and the smile with which he greeted Josephine said
plainly enough that they were all three characters in a ghastly joke,
and that he was glad she understood it from the beginning. "One of
those crazy men," she thought to herself--"
The smell of old dialogue in the writer's building.

To his golden touch with stars and stories Metro's amazing profits
were almost universally ascribed (fortune)

Change Brady name.

Action is character.

Consider transferring strong scenes to rear.

Fitzgerald you keep on as if that class still existed, etc..
From a Review and Auden quotation.

Naming the sections.

Cannot the characters express themselves more--I mean psychologically,
not didactically.

He had to leave school on account of illness and took a job at
his grandfather's dept. store, where he taught himself to type
in his spare time. He then felt ready for bigger things and put
an ad in the paper for a job. "Situation wanted--secretary, stenographer, Spanish, English. Highschool education. Inexperienced.$15."
He got four answers and took a job in an importing company.

1P

When he came down out of the sky he saw the Glendale airport
below him, bright, warm. The moon was straight ahead above the
Pacific that was the lands of the Long Beach Naval Reserves; further
down there was Huntington Park and on the right, the great mutual
blur of Santa Monica. Stahr loves these clusters of lights as if
they were something he had set up himself as an electrician.
"And this I shall black-out, and this I will lay my hand on,
reluctantly, cruelly, definitely, and squeeze and squeeze, and
squeeze, and something dark, something I don't know--something
I may have left behind me in the dark. But these lights, this
brightness, these clusters of human hope, of wild desire--I shall
takes these lights in my fingers. I shall make them bright, and
whether they shine or not, it is these fingers that they shall
succeed or fail."
The plane bumped lower, lower; the engines stopped breathing--then
round softly and down. It was always very exciting to get there.

Important that he knew the business side first. His submission of
a scenario was probably a very quaking venture on his part--very
timorous. He must have had no more aesthetic education after
finishing secondary school than I did. He had to pick the whole
thing up out of the air not even by reading though probably he did
some--still in all he probably learned pictures from pictures and
naturally got his sense of realities from acute observation and
men. He was therefore as unliterate a man as you can imagine in
regard to formative influence.

1½

I want to write scenes that are frightening and inimitable. I don't want to be as intelligible to my contemporaries as Ernest who as Gertrude Stein said, is bound for the Museums. I am sure I am far enough ahead to have some small immortality if I can keep well.

For names see nonsense and stray phrases.

Cecelia does not tell the story though I write it as if she does whenever I can get the effect of looking out.

2P

She was eighteen with such a skin as the Italian painters of
the decadence used for corner angels.

Feel a girl's skull and she becomes a human being.

I'm one of those people who would just as soon starve in a
garret with a man--if I didn't have to.

They're Swell people--an essay on softness.

While he was on the make Stahr was as shrewd, ruthless, and
opportunistic as the next man, but he arrived quickly after only
a short breathless struggle, and once arrived he found it easier
to be fair and generous and honorable than not to be. So he granted
the premises on which he was founded--he was a better man than most
of us, less bruised, less fearful, and less corrupt.

When Laemmle went to Europe he left--in charge. When pay day came
around they found he was too young to sign the checks. Cables
crackled across the ocean and things were finally straightened out
to save the new young director from embarrassment

3P

Characteristic slant missing in Stahr. His point of view overwhelming. Also he must be _for_ somebody--not one class but two
or three.

~~You changed all that. You could do it because you looked less
like a driver and organizer. You looked just like a little boy
starting up a show.~~

Stahr's wife.

Both hardy and sensitive.

Stahr had arrived young, etc. (that was oo note) (can't find)
Was private secretary to Laemmle, Sr., then director of production.
Remained in that capacity for two years and then joined IBM as
production manager--Boy Wonder...

She first discovered love in her throat.

6P

The head was fifty times life-size.

Bracing their heels upon such irregularities as they could find.

They looked at the idol which, finding no channel deep enough to continue its progress on, lingered near, regarding the scene with huge impersonal eyes.

A Railway station which had seen the meetings and partings of lovers from Vladivestok to Kalamazoo.

"Did it rock you, Mr. Stahr?"
"It scared hell out of me." This was a lie but off duty Stahr found it simpler to have democratic emotions.

The morale of the studio, Stahr's morale, had survived the expansion, the arrival of sound and, up to this point, the crash and the depression. Other studios had lost identity, changed personal, changed policies, wavered in subjection to Eastern stockholders, or meekly followed the procession. But Stahr's incalculable prestige had created an optimism only equalled by that of the River Rouge plant in its great days.

It's size and luxury had not evolved from vanity but from his doctor's opinion that he conferred too long in rooms full of cigarette smoke and exhaust air. There was the great room thirty feet by forty and in addition a dining room, waiting room, a bathroom, secretaries' room and ante-room.

Her skin had a peculiar radiance as if phosphorous had touched it. In her eyes was that triangular veiled expression sometimes described as "starry".

She must have a faint brogue from her first speech.

We were just looking at the----and then the waters came swirling and we climbed up on the statue. It was hard to tell you.

MGM's technicians are more highly paid than those of MGM's competitors (Fortune)

Fox Studio by moonlight--French chateaux, Southern mansion, Jungle, City of Algiers, plaster walls, junk, colt on bazarre clothes-- Stahr can only get into outer lot himself even though it is his studio; the first time he tries to take Thalia on lot he is so conscientious that he let's the policeman keep him out.

₢ 7

Rich mauve drapes which seemed always stirring in a little wind.

Old timers regretted the old smoky intimate office in the other wing "where his great pictures were born".

Bieman seems the most excited.

Father used to have great scraps with the Jews over Jewish and Irish tricks. The Jews claimed he always oversold his points. Father thought he was just right. For instance weeping trick. Morgan might be funnier.

No one could intereept conference except a shooting director.

Sly for shrewd; Schley for name.

It is usually not much before ten o'clock hen Mr. Thalberg arrives and by this time there are people all over the lot who want words with him. (Fortune)

Some of the conversation in the long day more sexy in tone. Not too much and in good taste.

For Stahr: Call from a red-head (35 yrs. old) His refusal. I think this is necessary if it is not sordid.

Change Garcia to a Greek

Stahr's health.

Twenty-three Metro producers.

"Sure--you did a sequence for Collins with a watch face and some little cardboard silhouettes. It was very interesting.

Impossible to replace him--the loss of him is irreparable, more than any other man he raised motion pictures to their present prestige. (*Tribune*)

He used to run sometimes with a rather fast crowd of directors-- many of them heavy drinkers though he wasn't one himself. And they accepted him as one of themselves in a "hail fellow, well met spirit" that is: in spite of the growing austerity which over-work forced on him in later years.

The Vanity Case (for Morgan Fly episode.)

Impotent actor says to Stahr, "You own me, don't you, you ought to care".

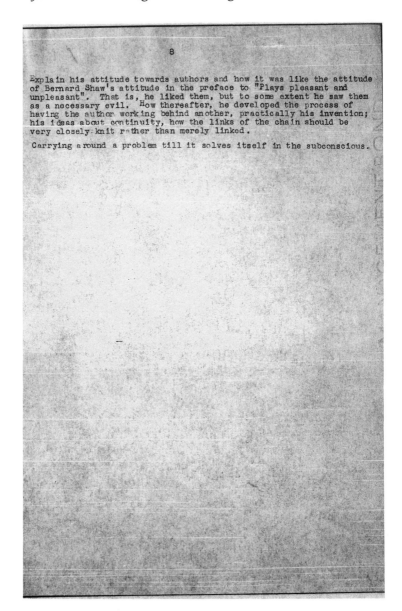

8

Explain his attitude towards authors and how it was like the attitude
of Bernard Shaw's attitude in the preface to "Plays pleasant and
unpleasant". That is, he liked them, but to some extent he saw them
as a necessary evil. How thereafter, he developed the process of
having the author working behind another, practically his invention;
his ideas about continuity, how the links of the chain should be
very closely knit rather than merely linked.

Carrying around a problem till it solves itself in the subconscious.

⇒ 8P

This, however, is the old fashioned seed-corn prester m'chester.

~~The tone that one of a popular young headmaster pleasant warm~~
~~and the dead, say that it worked a complementary mood in the~~
listeners.

Plot about people in the bus.

Very funny scene of Aldous Huxley trying to be a regular scenario
writer and Sidney Franklin against. Huxley quoting Wells whom
he thinks of as a popular writer ("Wells--he's had some success
here hasn't he?") Quotes: "Wells says in some early novel we're
all Hegelians in spite of ourselves and perhaps the 31st member
is a communist and the 4th is double talk man..

Tracing Stahr biologically through a day in terms of blood
pressure. Did he take coffee? Was it all will? Did he rest well?

More work in a Persian rug than in Leonardo's last supper but
who wants to work on a Persian rug.

Affable for Stahr. Speak soft but carry a big stick.

The guy that played Sergeant Quirt in Romeo and Juliet.

How popular he was with men from the beginning in a free and easy
way. There was never anything priggish or self-superiority in
his casual conversation that make men uneasy in the company of
other men.

And then exhibited herself as an ornament on his desk bending
her head forward among the phones.

She expired gently and gracefully from the room.

If we have to change the script and have him play it in an iron
lung.

For actor Golden bronze head. Make him beautiful.

A dark saucer-eyed man.

The left part of his hair flying (used? for Mike Van Dyke)

Must describe Thalia definitely the first time he really sees her.

Show Stahr hiding in retreat or surrounded or avoiding people
without hurting them.

~~Roxxxxwxxxxxburkxxquxxqmxxxx~~
La Borwitz. Joe Mank---pictures smell of rotten bananas.

It was amazing what simple things had to be explained to them.
Last year you said no Arizona
That was because we had just done Arizona, New Mexico and Idaho.
Understand?---(for Very stupid producer.
Yes.

10

Gross revenue from film rentals has been consistently higher than that of other studios.

Loew's was the only one of the five integrated "majors" to weather the depression without bankruptcy, reorganization, or shake-up of any kind.

First picture company (1926) able to sell long-term debentures on the New York Stock Exchange.

An atmosphere of courage and inventiveness can be just as vital to a studio as a chestful of contracts.

Metro financed him individually in all pictures. He was to be privileged to sign his own people as well as have first call on Metro personalities. He wanted to feel he was in business for himself as well as a partner in Metro...His death hit the industry like a bolt and activity was at standstill.

There was a picture known in the studio simply as Stahr's picture because its name changed too often to remember.

The idea of a certain great film which Stahr has long planned--a very rough subject or irreligious. An original. And have the censor interfere.

Be sure the solution of the director incident is not too neat. Keep the coat thing but somehow remove the smarty superman element with a little irony.

Firing director seems a small thing to do unless someone else is scared, or director is fierce and brutal.

10P

Profit-sharing contract--Important. Stahr had that sort of contract and yet did the Good Earth.

To return to Metro their negative costs.

I'm getting tired of Cinderella. I want to have some fun.

The renting of stars by one studio to another.

Dave who preserved democratic forms.

He had more stock than anybody in the company. His deal with Metro provided that he, Mayer and J. Robt. Rubin get 20% of the net profits of the company after preferred dividends were taken care of. He also had many stars under private contract including his wife.

He was under no illusion about success--the varying components of its make up. For instance he was right a little more often than most men but this was trebly reinforced by his habit of saying things in an utterly assured way, no less forceful for being soft. He knew that the intuitional proportion of superior rightness in his thoughts was simply incalculable importance--he knew also that it might cease at any time but this was something he did not like to think about.

General low autocracy a la Louis XI with observers (le barbier) Acute attention and quick weighing. Quite pleasant without warmth. Knows the value of praise. Distrusts theatrics--hence Nunnally's success with him.

Tests are for make-up men," said Jim, impatiently. "I seldom believe a good test. And I always suspect a bad one."

Stahr tells someone a plot half in Yiddish.

What is missing Ridingwood scene is imagination etc. What an extraordinary thing that it should all have been there for Ridingwood and then not there.

Correction: Ridingwood Sceme insert--
Ridinghood followed Stahr back across the stage, again trying to keep up again falling behind. The assistant director spoke to him. "Just hold it," Red said frowning, and six hundred thousand of dollars were immobolized--interest at twenty dollars a minute. More here.
In the car Stahr had control of his temper. He spoke regretfully. "I'm afraid it's no go, Red. She's putting it over on you. She's loafing. It's not just my opinion."

Correction: Ridingwood Scene--
You didn't want to work with Lewin did you King?
I couldn't stand it Monroe.
You didn't want these scenes rewritten.
If I can have my own man. I don't want some writer like X who doesn't know his ass about pictures sit here and kibitz.
Stahr's face flexed. He reached out suddenly and tore open King's blouse the great buttons bursting off to the floor. (one button?)

~~10 P~~

~~Story of Tony Gaudio. Calls department heads. Calls Tony's Occulist, photostat. Letters. Warner Bros.~~

Brothers--their wearing out people.

Company lawyer as well as publicity man.

For Guest - Died: Prince Aage of Denmark, 52 veteran officer in the French Foreign Legion; after brief illness; in Taza, French Morocco. Cousin of King George V, Tsar Nicholas II, King ChristianX of Denmark, King Haakon VII of Norway, King Constantine of Greece, he renounced his rights to the Danish throne when he was 26. Said he then: "It wasn't such a sacrifice." Don't divulge who he is until far in the scene.

As a money man dealing with the big shots.

Charles Emmet Rogers and his flags.

~~After name...Charles...phone...and...follow...into the...tomorrow. The old brother...same...work in shifts...and wear you down...x~~
~~I think I...sent...want...to borrow...x~~

"~~He only hands his son~~. One of the Bauberg brothers is waiting in Mr. Brady's office. It's either Jefferson or Moe."
Stahr chuckled.
"It's Jefferson--that was Moe on the phone. This afternoon Charles'll phone and I'll run into Abe tomorrow. The old brother game--work in shifts and wear you down--"
"I think they want to borrow--"

Attitude of the 12 men to the Prince. They don't know who he is. Straighten him out throughout chapter.

~~New name for Thalia and Smith.~~

In 1932 average cost of Metro-Goldwyn-Mayer pictures runs slightly under $500,000. This is at least $150,000 more per picture than other companies pend. (Fortune)

Stahr's earnings of $500,000 a year--actual salary is now only $110,000 (Fortune.

~~Miss Foodstores.~~

Phrase for gross the "take".

About Garcia. " Too bad," said Brady, who had a public relations conscience.

Take it easy, won't you boys and girls, don't bring it back all snarled up.

There was style still to work on.

The left side of his hair was always flying (Broaca)

~~Dollars through the chandelier.~~

13

If you think there are a lot of attractive young men around Hollywood you are wrong. There are handsome males but even when their names are Brown or Jones or Robinson they seem like the type you can find on any cheap beach in Italy. Like the oranges and lemons they are plentiful and large but they have no taste. That's why I went with Wylie White. He was a southerner and at his worst he had a code to violate. It was fun to watch him doing it.

I was in such a good humor that when a bug flew into my eye I was sorry for the bug.

A thing called the Grand Canyon Symphony which seemed to me to lean heavily on Horses Horses Horses.

The faded star who had togo to the Film Guild Ball with the Electrician's brother.

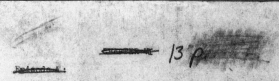

13 p

This will concern itself with Cecelia's love for
Stahr and the episode will concern itself with her discovery
of her father.

(·a) This episode begins with Cecelia taking up the story
directly and describing an affair she was having with a
young man. Have her describe it just as women do when
they feel that they will be more convincing by telling almost everything and leaving out the main thing rather than
the second method which, of course, is wiser for women not
to mention anything or any incident about which they are
not prepared to reveal the whole truth. That is, she tells
our listener, our reader, our recorder a lot about this
affair which was engrossing her attention at this time,
but always casually reassuring him that while there had
been a lot of struggling, she had preserved her "virtue"
Have her make a great emphasis on this enough so that
perhaps the wisest of the readers may think "she does
protest too much". Nevertheless let her in a burst of
conventional self-righteousness think that she has convinced
the reader that her relations with this undetermined man
are essentially not most extreme. Now at this point,
either by an accidental meeting on her way to see her
father on the lot or perhaps because Stahr has sent for
her thinking she could do something for Thalia --something
he has planned for Thalia, perhaps something in the nature
of a job or some sort of work that Thalia's interested
in.

In the scene that takes place, she, Cecelia the narrator,
should realize the depth of her love for this man at its
fullest and I would like to do some very strong, quiet
writing there to describe her feelings. In the writing,
Cecelia should appear at her best and at her most profound.
It is rather her feeling about Stahr that I want to describe
than an objective picture of Stahr at this particular point.
I want to find some new method of describing this. Some
method in which everything that surrounds him assumes a
magical touch, a magical quality without resorting to any
of the old dodges of her touching the objects that he
touches. I want her feelings to soar to the highest pitch
of which she is capable and I want her in this episode to,
for the benefit of the reader, to set away everything tawdry
or superficial in her nature. This should be one of the
strongest episodes in the book.

Now when the episode with Stahr is over, I want her to leave
his office and have outside his office, a tremendous reaction
from this exaltation and in this reaction I want her to tell
the reader or the recorder the truth about the fact that
she had given herself to this other man the night before--
whom she has no intention of marrying, perhaps an almost
experimental gesture.

13P

Beatrice D's first frightening experience.

She turns a man down in narrative, then to readers' surprise:
Except that I did sleep with him--that afternoon. I'd rather
you'd put that in too.

Jane Hall and her wiles (Cecelia)

The music was getting better again. When I was young during the
depression it wasn't so much. The best was the old songs like
Blue Heaven played hot--but now there were the bands.

<u>Music May 1934-Oct 1935</u> - Lost; Gone; Beat of my Heart; See-saw;
Smoke gets in Your Eyes; Lovely to Look At; Busy Day (her father)

Charlie MacArthur kicks the man downstairs.

I went to the screen actors ball. I shall not describe it. Suffice
to say the lights shone over fair women and brave, not very brave
men.

It had started out to be such a lovely day.

If the ball room of the Ambassador that night had been the Sistine
Chapel Stahr could have covered it with innumerable figures like
Michael Angelo.

Scotty comes up to people when she meets them as if she were
going to kiss them on the mouth, or walk right thru them, looking
them straight in the eye--then stops a bare foot away and says
her Hello, in a very disarming understatement of a voice. This
approach is her nearest to Zelda's personality. Zelda's was
always a vast surprise. (Celia imitates another girl in this)

I gave him a side smile, half of my face, like a small white cliff.

Girls pushed by their arm in movies.

14.

Shaken by the flare-up they go back, she still thinking she can
withdraw. She could not bear to think. It was tonight. It is
a murky rainy dusk, a dreary day (change former time to sunset)
They left the hotel a little more than three hours ago but it
seemed a long time. Get them there quickly. Odd effect of
the place like a set. The mood should be two people--free--He
has an overwhelming urge toward the girl who promises to give life
back to him--though he has no idea yet of marriage--she is the
heart of hope and freshness. He seduces her because she is slipping
away--she lets herself be seduced because of overwhelming admiration
(the phone call). Once settled it is sexual, breathless, immediate.
Then gentle and tender for awhile.

Pink + Silver Frost

14P

This girl had a life--it was very seldom he met anyone whose life did not depend in some way on him or hope to depend on him.

Cut the heart in the grave.

I have had five tumultuous years that were about one part ecstacy to four parts misery and I want to settle down as a good wife and a real person. The man I am going to marry will never be an important man like you. We will not move in your sphere and probably it wouldn't please him to know I had gone out with such a "big shot" before he arrived. The man I am going to marry saved my reason such as it is, took me out of an impossible situation and sent me here to California.

Letter could be a "please-it-means-so-much-to-me-so-little-to-you". Also gratitude motif to man is left out.

Vivid as a tongue of fire even against the bright out-doors.

Reinforce sense of a deep rich past with Minna--he brusquely says to Kathleen that it can never be the same. Her reaction is in spunkily saying the same, but knowing it's comparatively in a minor key.

Dark glass cheaters.

14P

Her eyes, dark and intimate, seemed to have wakened at the
growing brilliance of the illuminations overhead; there was
the promise of excitement in them now, like the promise of the
cooling night.

With the Los Angeles County immense distances--three hours a day
in an automobile is not exceptional.

Where will the warmth come from in this. Why does he think she's
warm. Warmer than the voice in Farewell. My girls were all so
warm and full of promise. The sea at night. What can I do to
make it honest and different?

14P

I spend most of my time concealing how little I know. They
think I know everything now.

~~A woman's laughter when it's like a child--just one syllable,~~
~~eager and approving, a crow and a cry of delight,~~

It was fine hearing Nora say that she never looked behind.

The nineteen wild green eyes of a bus were coming up to them
through the dark.

~~The intimacy of the car, its four walls whisking them along~~
~~toward a new adventure, had drawn them together,~~

Porch at Loos, halls full of prints, Kleenex in bathrooms.
Empty unfinished Emerson house. Book shelves, record shelves.

Anything added to beauty has to be paid for, that is, the qualities
that pass as substitutes can be liabilities when added to beauty
itself.

She always carried space around into which one could step and be
alone with her

Skin of the corner angel. (used?)

Her voice and the drooping of her eyes when she finished speaking
like a sort of exercise in control, fascinated him. He had felt
that they both tolerated something, that each knew half of some
secret about people and life, and that if they rushed toward each
other there would be a romantic communion of almost unbelievable
intensity. It was this element of promise and possibility that
had haunted him for a fortnight and was now dying away. (half used)

Wise and fond and chokingly sweet as it had been with Minna when
sometimes they had gone for many days.

Diminished sound of the sea.

If there had been misgivings in the long hour nothing showed in
her friendly smile.

Physical attraction not clear. Time lapses wrong. Indicate desire
and confidence and have it grow.

Must plant stove--etc., and that it's a covered room, etc. Wooden
window seat.

She is beautiful in the drug store--her smile. (Time of Day.)

Time: 4.30 - 5.15 Drive out.
      5.15 - 5.45 House
             6.15 Dinner
             7.00 Passion (Sunset)
             7.45 House . Twilight.

Which was excitement, friendliness, stimulous, fascination.

14P

She let the familiar lift and float and flow of love close
around them, pulling him back from his far-away uniqueness.

The Grunion (mood of transition)

The Ride back (two moods)

They ran here and there exhilerated by the spray shouting "Here
they are."

Sheilah and Frances hate the letter and both miss more emotion
or something after seduction. The talk about Edna seems cold.
They would like to develop negro and Stahr's reaction. They do
not understand that the girl is not in the market--suspect her
of leading him on. But he must not know the truth so perhaps the
reader should.

Had a false front with a door marked bathroom.

~~He had not realized that flashing fairness could last so far
into the twenties.~~

Women having only one role, their own charm--all the rest is mimicry.

Probably should describe a bunch of actors and actresses sitting
there or dancing--the ones I've noticed.

Kathleen is physically attracted. Also playing with idea that she
might marry him right away. But her debt makes her dismiss this.

He is struck again by her beauty which must be redescribed, her
manner, her gestures, way of talking, style, content. It becomes
apparent to Stahr that she has a great deal of culture--from the
Baron-Goldbeck man.

She says something smart and he sees it's in another world and gets
her to say it again and again. She fascinates him like some writers.
She thinks what a long way she's come. I'd better like it and it
starts maybe a certain jealousy.

The phone in the workman's shed actually rings and she catches
a glimpse of his power which he hadn't intended. It fascinates
her. He represents action. He hadn't intended to answer the phone.

She rather expects him to make some pass and when he doesn't she
is a little offended.

They tell each other stories. Edna--tells him about call house.
He is shocked.

She felt nice and cool after a dip in the lake, felt her pink
dress where it touched her, frothy as pink soda water, all fresh
in the new wind. When Roger appeared, she would make him sorry for
his haughtiness of the last twenty-four hours.

15

About Birdy, etc.: It was hard to fit girls for the secretarial
who read books unless they were imported from New England.
Out here, though the bookstores were bulging, reading was becoming
a mere skill in the middle income brackets--a sort of technological
accomplishment.

Lots and foliage in Bel-air.

Rose was a burlesque queen.

This is Celia taking up the story. I should probably explain why
I spent so much of the summer hanging around the studio. Well,
for one thing I was too big to keep out now and I knew how to do
it without bothering people. I had had a difference with Wylie
White about who had the say about my body so there was --- ---,
whom I didn't intend to marry who was playing the man who almost
got the girl in three pictures at once and had to be on the lot.
And thirdly, most important I had nothing else to do. (Finish
with description of Hollywood boys.)

15   ~~CHAPTER VI~~

~~Episode 3: (e)~~

The Bradogue character, to be a convincing villain
must, like Joe Mank--- have some attractive exterior facets.
The reason that louses from "Pretty Boy" Floyd all the way
down to Whitney, the stockbroker have been able to get
away with their chacaneries is that they have had external
facets which are very pleasing so Bradogue must be a very
handsome man. This attractiveness whatever it is--looks
or manners--he has managed to half sell to his daughter.
She knows pragmatically and by observation that he is an
unscrupulous man, yet the charm must have touched her so
that when she comes from Stahr's office in this exalted
mood, it is half in her mind to ask her father if he
thinks that Stahr will ever marry again. In other words,
if she has a chance to get Stahr. (Cecelia is either
divorced or motherless or has a stepmother)

Cecelia comes to her father's office full of the idea that
perhaps Stahr might marry again, perhaps by some wile,
from use of her youth that she could "get him", full of
complete exaltation and wanting to tell her father about
it simply because her father is the nearest person to her
and because that charm--which I will have to create in
Bradogue--has fooled her at times into thinking that he
is a decent and sympathetic person and going through the
outer offices (which must be very protective and elaborate--
something like the entrance to the Stromberg-Hyman bungalow)
she notices that one of the outside secretaries(create a
minor caricature giving this girl some special characteristic)
--look through list of characters-- is in a state of agitation.
However, it is nothing to what she finds when after pressing
the secret catch to her father's office(I must interrupt by
saying that the secretary has assured her that her father
is not in conference and then contradicts herself and then
re-contradicts herself) in which she finds her father, his
coat, tie and vest are off and he is perspiring profusely
and seems terrifically upset.

Cecelia is so absorbed in her story that on receiving the
formal answer that "No, he is not busy, not busy at all",
she launches into her own affairs and only after some
moments does she perceive that her father is really in
some kind of stew, made sympathetic by her own passion
for Stahr, she comes close to him and starts to put her
arm on his shoulder and he shrinks away from her. He
launches suddenly into a tirade against Stahr which
shocks her--the tirade is based perhaps on the quarrel
he had with Stahr at luncheon in the commissary about
making the expensive picture. In any case, it is purely
a business attack upon what he considers Stahr's bogus
idealism and of course has no effect on Cecelia. But
the vehemence with which he talks is of the kind that if
he had been a drinking man would have made her think he
was drinking.

16

The break between Stahr and Thalia has been of Stahr's making. I
may or may not show the scene in which this occurs, but Stahr's
motive is roughly: "I am not going to marry this girl. My plans
do not include marrying again. She hasn't the particular shine,
glamor, poise, cultural background that would make her the fitting
match for this high destiny toward which I seem to be going or
this position in which I find myself; therefore, I am really indulg-
ing myself by cutting her off from Robinson who is obviously a fine
fellow, who adores her and would be a good provider and a good
husband."

She thought of electric fans in little restaurants with lobsters
on ice in the windows, and of pearly signs glittering and revolving
against the obscure, urban sky, the hot, dark sky. And pervading
everything, a terribly strange, brooding mystery of roof tops and
empty apartments, of white dresses in the paths of parks, and fingers
for stars and faces instead of moons, and people with strange people
scarcely knowing one another's names.

At first, for some hours, they share an overwhelming joy. They
eat together and make love, cling together at times, each cannot
bear to let the other out of his sight. The reunion has been so
strong in its emotional implications that it seems to the reader
as well as to Stahr and Thalia that it is the prelude to an immediate
marriage and almost a fade out and a happy ending. At some point
though, during that same evening or perhaps the next morning which
would be necessarily then a Sunday, something happens (invent some
detail or small instant) which gives Stahr the idea: After all, this
is not what I intended. I didn't intend to marry this girl. It is
against the logic of my life. The premises that I set out for
myself when I was young do not include this. The cold part of
Stahr has crept in a little, not the cold emotion, but the cold
part of his mind and almost at the instant in which he realizes and
shows it perhaps by some flicker of his expression, Thalia who by
now is as close to him as if she had lived with him for fifty years,
knows it and makes up her mind what to do.

It's such a useless mistake--when there's so many mistakes you have
to make--because you get sorry for people, or you love them.

Frances finds 16 marred by the calculation.

Stahr counting on the long pull like Rhett Butler. He begins to
have a tremendous affection. Can't conceive of another man. It
would be nothing.

She asks him at Burbank if the studios are a long way apart.

17.

Some very dramatic and rather shocking fact about herself such as her views on sexual morality.

"A dump with neon lights".

Memory of a fist blow--a mere sensory impression--a sudden bitter taste in the mouth.

"You're a stubborn man," she said, "When we first met you put me in the undesirable class. Why?" She tossed her shoulders despairingly, "Because I was an inch too tall for you. Darling--I'd have gone into low heels and glued down my hair. But you'd made up your mind."

She sat full of promise, her hands clasped in her lap.

"A man offered to cut somebody's throat for me last week," said Stahr. "You're just drunk with power."
Stahr was amused. That was the way Wylie White talked to him but no girl had ever talked to him like that before.

"You people don't fight fair," said Stahr, "but you expect us to,"
"The strongest man always wants to fight fair'," said Brimmer, "You've got the courts on your side so of course you want to fight fair."

A grin on his face.

Listen, I'm an ignorant man. I know it. Except about pictures. But over there I have to pretend to know everything.

He saw it through the dark magnificent blindness of his own life.

Dark mysterious power.

Final Form for the Brimmer Episode
More indication of Stahr's state. In trouble.
Why he went over their heads--realizing the "little bit more" approach. Department of Justice. Sat full of promise.

I want to get a couple of you fellows on our side.
The old days--getting drunk with the brave conceited male stars.

I pointed them out to Brimmer who stared but said he had no autograph book. Stahr asked him if he lost it in Russia but Brimmer said no he'd never had one but once he had a stamp collection. It was all like that now--nobody's night.

who w

18

The theatre.

Climax is the discovery of Smith.

18. (3 short episodes)

The Cummerbund
The Dubbing Room
The Theatre

He liked Sam Goldwyn - you always knew where you stood with
Goldwyn - nowhere.

The actor hasn't been acting well. Stahr talks to him. After
lunch actor waves. He has seduced a script girl.

The body gets down and crouches in a corner of itself and
says 'You're doing this to me. I'll make you pay' and you
say never mind--stay down there.

Montgomery for flowers.

20.

Come in! Come in!
And have a Micky Finn.

A truck was throwing a humming cone of white against a side wall
of the costume building.

Watertowers on Metro.

Junior writers $300.
Minor poets--$500. a week.
Broken novelists - $850. - $1000.
One play dramatists - $1500.
Sucks - $2000. -- Wits - $2500.

Dick Scheyer and the sword.

Stahr remembered how they had used the three freaks back in 1927.
X was being bothered by a really appalling woman. The day before
the case came to trial he sent a dwarf, and X and X to her with
messages. his counsel opened by stating that the woman was crazy.
On the stand she told about her visitors--the jury shook their
heads, winked at each other and aquitted.

Wylie's effect by creating an atmosphere of menace, even torture--
then relieving it with a laugh for a character.

Ernest Hemingway and Ernest Lubitsch--Dotty "We're all shits."

It is doubtful if any of these head men read through a single
work of the imagination in a year. And Stahr who had no time
whatever to read and must depend on synopses began to doubt that
any of his supervisors read more than what was ordered; he doubted
that his casting people (note for a character here) covered the
range he would have wanted them to. A show played a year and a
half in San Francisco--the speciality in it was discovered only
after it reached Los Angeles where the young beats of a girl
show drew a tired satiated audience and the specialty was in a
boom market within a week. And had to be paid for against important
budgets where alertness would have bought it for nothing.

Huckleberry Finn--how a girl changed the life of a Missouri boy.
Jim Creelman doing King Kongs and Tarzans.

In thirty-four and thirty-five the party line crept into everything except the Sears Roebuck Catalogue.

See Renan, 102 for Jewish character Stahr. For Stallings or
Herman to say to him.

There was once a moving picture magnate who was shipwrecked on
a desert island with nothing but two dozen cans of film.

Stahr as a sort of Rimbeau. Precocity and irony which is born
young.

Drinking gives a sort of steely completion.

Writer telling producer they're not easy to work for--they're
temperamental, excitable, unstable, etc.

Stahr and Rogers--They're all drunks and they're all lazy, but
we just can't do without them.

Stahr finds that Rogers has established himself in his inner
sanctum and has been amusing himself by giving orders which he
pretends are eminating from Stahr himself. Stahr's feeling is
of extreme annoyance. He has once told Rogers that if he ever
got drunk again he could never come on the lot and his immediate
assumption is that Rogers is drunk to have done such a thing.
Rogers assures him he is not drunk. Stahr tries to find out what
has been done. Various confused calls come in from different
departments showing that he has had a very busy fifteen minutes
rather like a monkey in a cocoanut tree. Stahr is angry--tells
Rogers he has to get off the lot and stay off. Rogers stalls
that he must go to his office and get various possessions, pictures
of his children, wife, etc. Stahr says he will go with him. For
a moment, it looks as if Rogers is going to threaten Stahr of
whom he is very fond. Stahr is also fond of Rogers. Stahr is
not physically afraid at all. Nevertheless, when they get out
on one of the streets of the lot, he signals to a company policeman to follow them at 20 paces. They go up to Roger's office
to collect his belongings. Follow the conversation.
The chapter can end either by Stahr carrying out his intention
of putting Rogers off the lot (though secretly intending to hire
him back) or else by Stahr realizing that Rogers is not drunk
and that the mischief which he did springs from some curious
suppressed phenomenon in himself which is valuable when turned
into useful channels. This in itself interests Stahr's active
intelligent and curious mind. This should give an opportunity
to work in whatever wit and comment on pictures that I want
from Rogers in this chapter.

21.

Origin of "fair play" as it began to extend to the bourgeoise.
and the proletariat (about 1840 then 1880). It was formerly
exclusive to chivalry.
Stahr accepting it with the American tradition. Bradogue not.
Bradogue a mere survival morality--slums of Dublin or Manx.
Like Sicily.

Wires crossed

Great masses of wires on floor can hear everyone thru dictaphone.
An actress comes in in the middle of a conference.

The cleverly expressed opposite of any generally accepted human
idea is worth a fortune to somebody.

Wylie calls Stahr on why not a story about the vigilantes. Look up.

The valuable lust zum fabulieren, expressed mostly in yes-ing and
no-ing the suggestions of others, fugitive and vague yet mystically
linked with the tastes and dreams of all the chambermaids and
yokels in the world. (Fortune) (Wylie reads it).

Next I'll see you down on Hollywood Boulevard with an oil well angle--
and your hat pulled over your eyes.

In Hollywood you play by the rules--'the convict code' Jim used to
call it. There'll be people here who've done first degree murder.

Dotty-Parker-like statement. He doesn't deserve any great credit for
that. Only additional dialogue.

Attitude like Portrait of Artist.

2.V.22P   21

Stahr overhearing a conversation between gentiles about Jews.
A sharp cutting scene. The effect on him in toto.

Stahr: Those men won't want to make good pictures after I'm gone--

Stahr didn't die of overwork--he died of a certain number of
forces allied against him.

Stahr's memory of Dartmouth where he never went--delirium.

Question of girl using the phrase S---house of the world.
Possibly make this half heard. Stahr turns around hardly
believing, thinking it's someone else. It haunts him--later
makes her pronounce it.

"Against my better judgment," he would say, having no judgment
and "obviously" and "precisely". (Stahr's Doctor)

"There's no use looking at things, because you don't like things,"
remarked Raines, in answer to his polite interest.
"No," said Charlie frankly, "I don't." (No--the opposite)
"You like only rhythms, with things marking the beats, and now
your rhythm is broken." (Stahr denies what doctor says)

When a writer tells how he could make so much more--Stahr says
how he could too, as a banker. He left only 10,000 after all.
Even then, he says, interest divided.

Max Perkins didn't want to leave himself lying around.

A cadence started in his head like a motor warming up. That was
one way--to get something to it--the word, the name, the shape
of the sky get it quickly. The other way was to start with the
thing, to be profoundly affected by it, until it stretched
elongated, stood up and walked.

When you once get to the point where you don't care whether you
live or die--as I did--it's hard to come back to life. Compton
McKenzie for instance. It's hard to believe in yourself again--
you have slain part of yourself.

Men who have been endowed with unusual powers for work or analysis
or ingredients that go to make big personal successes, seem to
forget as soon as they are rich that such abilities are not evenly
distributed among the other men of their kind. So when the suggestion of a Union springs out of this act of Baird's Stahr seems to
reverse his form, join the other side and almost to ally himself
with Baird. Note also in the epilogue that I want to show that
Stahr left certain harm behind him just as he left good behind him.
That some of his reactionary creations such as the Screen Playwrights
existed long after his death just as so much of his valuable
creative work survived him.

My blue dream of being in a basket like a kite held by a rope
against the wind.

The blue-green unalterable dream.

⊕ ⊸Ω. 21

The trained nurse stood gazing into the medicine closet. "I wonder what the hell medicine to give him," she muttered to herself. "They all look like the same old horse poison to me." She wishes the labels were written in American so she could tell what the drugs were for. She considered shutting her eyes and picking one at random with a pointing finger but some might be poison and she did not dare.

Stahr wants to see Washington. Goes there and is sick the whole time and sees it only as he leaves.

A great friend says something bitter to him about his race. It makes him think. He goes hence to a conference and examines Lubin, Selig, etc.

I have never wished there was a God to call on--I have often wished there was a God to thank.

After every experience we should go off and die, thought Stahr, like widow spiders. Why do we want to continue, to repeat, to satiate--then to weaken from repletion, to tire, be lonely--and whine because we do not want sympathy.

Before death thoughts from crack-up. Do I look like death (in mirror at 6 p.m.)

One man felt suffering as with his fingers, felt its rough shape. Another seemed to hold it against his cheek. Sickness has sensitized Stahr.

"Right away--hi!" sang the central in a mad cheer. He laughed.

A move wedding. Ushers were Harold Lloyd, Victor Varconi, Ronald Coleman, and Donald Duck.

Better Hollywood's bizaare variations on the normal, with George Collins on the phone ordering twelve girls for dinner, none over eighteen.

Dream of Joe M--1050 word continuity, cost too much to type. Sorry His face. He compliments me on other work. Too many montages-- can't afford them.

Prayers are punctuations and reminders.

Dignity for Stahr--portentiousness--some one's head hangs on it.

Sidney Franklin's dance. Another suggestion is a real story to be shown developing later.

In a seventeenth century powder puff of a costume.

If we have to change the script and have him play it in an iron lung.

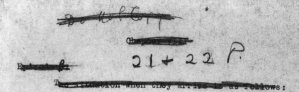

21 + 22 P.

Bradogue who is great on the horses and has long
rebelled against what he thinks of as Stahr's idealism
and extravagance in the picture business, seeing cuts made
in other industries is taking advantage of a special situation. The situation is that Stahr who is in the East has
fallen ill and has succumbed to a complete nervous and
physical breakdown affecting his heart so that what he
thought would be a four or five day trip devoted largely
to discussion with certain blocks of stockholders has become a conference around a sickbed. Stahr who has previously
been in general good health, though conscious of a growing
fatigue, has the natural rebellion of an active man and of
what the doctor says and asks for a specialist. The specialist
confirms what the doctor said and gives Stahr what amounts to
an ultimatum: That is a death sentence unless he stops here
and now and rests himself in some quiet way. He suggests a
trip around the world or a year off or anything that will
divorce him from work.

The idea fills Stahr with a horror that I must write
a big scene to bring it off. Such a scene as has never been
written. The scene that to Stahr is the equivalent to that
of an amorous man being told that he is about to be castrated.
In other words, the words of the doctor fill Stahr with a
horror that I must be able to convey to the laziest reader--
the blow to Stahr and the utter unwillingness to admit that
at this point, 35 years old, his body should refuse to serve
him and carry on these plans which he has built up like a
pyramid of fairy skyscrapers in his imagination.

He has survived the talkies, the depression, carried
his company over terrific obstacles and done it all with a
growing sense of kingliness--of some essential difference
which he could not help feeling between himself and the
ordinary run of man and now from the mere accident of one
organ of his body refusing to pull its weight, he is incapa-
citated from continuing. Let him go through every stage of
revolt.

Meanwhile, however, the stockholders are meeting around
his bed and only by certain things that he lets slip to them
does he divulge what is going on inside himself. However,
enough has been divulged so that there have been telephone
calls to Bradogue and Bradogue himself has gotten in touch
with both doctors and in his winning way, posing as Stahr's
friend, found out the truth that Stahr is definitely an
unwell man. All this Cecelia finds out from her father on
her return. Once again, we see Cecelia at her best, not as
a very effectual character, but again as a person who under
certain circumstances might have been quite a person.
She tells the recorder or the reader how she got in touch

~~Chapter VIII~~

22   21 + 22 (con't)

Episode 2: (contd)

with Rogers and was rather surprised to find that Rogers
had been re-hired before Stahr left (she has heard, of
course, about how Stahr found him in his office, in fact
she has heard everything that is told in the book).
Rogers knows that the whole lot is in a ferment and that
various meetings are being called.

> We are going to cut at this
> point to the meeting of camera
> men (cutters) at which Robinson
> will be present.

Episode ~~B~~ C.

This meeting will be very briefly summarized--these
men being only medium salaried and as a rule not very
thoughtful men or very articulate men and are very easily
bamboozled into taking this 50% cut that Bradogue is going
to put over in Stahr's absence. At the end of the meeting,
Robinson should be summoned from the meeting or called
aside in almost a mysterious way suggesting to the reader
that there is some significance in his being called away
though this is a fact that will not be explained at this
time. We will go from here to what I hope will be a big
scene in which Bradogue asks the directors, writers, supervisors to accept a 50% cut which he says he is going to
accept himself, using as his argument, to their surprise
and rather to their confusion, the specious argument that
by accepting this they will save those in the lower salary
brackets --the secretaries from $12. a week up and the prop
boys, etc., to whom the drastic cut would mean a terrible
hardship. He gets over his idea for two reasons--one because
the amorphous unions-though the name is not used--which are
called into being among workers with common interest such
as directors and writers are split by jealousies and factual
disagreements, certain of them for example, have never even
thought of themselves as workers and some are haunted by
the old fashioned dream of communism and Bradogue is wise
enough to use every stop on the organ including personal
ties to increase these differences and to rule by dividing.
In any case, he wins his point to the great disgust of those
of the writers who are the more politically advanced or the
shrewdest and who detect in this a very definite manifesta-
tion of a class war reaching Hollywood.

Episode D ←——— We will go from here, by the very quickest way, to
an office where Cecelia is talking to a secretary who
happens to be a personal friend who has helped her as
a reader and who was called to the office of the chief
of secretaries and now we learn that the whole thing has
been a frame-up--that a great proportion of the secretaries
are going to be laid-off without warning, that extensive
cuts are to be made in their pay of 40% instead of 50%

CHAPTER VII

-6-

21-22

Episode *d*; (contd)

but still the very things that he has made his point
by promising to avoid, are going to happen. Women
with families to support are going to find that
they have scarcely enough with which to buy bread
and that they are without jobs and no chance to get
a job in any other studio for to a certain extent,
other studios have waited for this studio to start
cutting and then take the same steps.

22,

During his illness Deanna Durbin and Fred Astaire were tested
at Culver City and turned down.

Minna burned in a fire.

But he never forgot--he was forever haunted by the picture of the
girl floating slowly out over the city at dusk, buoyed up by
delicious air, by a quintessence of golden hope, like a soaring
and unstable stock issue.

When Stahr is sick he keeps saying give it back to the directors
again. Don't leave it with these men. Give it back. I took it
away from etc. (Rearrange)

The sailor boy story--Stahr's hatred of lieing.

Girls slept beside their own vomit in Beverly Hills.

When Stahr is drunk he is silly.

Puts Croton oil in the sandwich mayonnaise.

Tremendous American generosity, without comment.

She feared the black cone hanging from the metal arm, shrilling
and shrilling across the sunny room. It stopped for a minute
replaced by her heartbeats; then began again.

The two young men quit jobs as hotel clerks and lay around the beach all summer on nine dollars a week unemployment insurance. One of them turned down a job at forty but he had fun. But the old barber who had mental troubles and physical troubles and financial troubles oh and everything in hell the matter with him--they told him to scram out of there quick.

On the set, how much he interfered and didn't interfere.

Explain angle.

A character like Wilford Beaton who really knows and won't cooperate and is always trying to see Stahr. See Chateaubriand. p. 175.

Sitting in the projection room Stahr, etc.,--dreamed and watched technically blooming in dissolves. Dissolves that were like the bloom of a rose to him--white dissolves startling as the first snow fall of the year. Not at Rushes.

Stahr treats both actors and themes with a fine eye for contour and polish. (fortune)

The Breen Family.

Exigent overlord ship

Not one survived the castration.

Don Stewart and double exposure.

Bernie Hyman like Zero--looks like nothing, acts like nothing-- add him to anything and he decreases it.

Joe: As a writer you're an amateur--you smooth everything. Any actor would rather have a cacophony and dissonance. That's why in Hollywood dialogue by several writers often plays better than dialogue by one. It takes an old hand to change keys. Now all the characters answer each other--before they had a little inner life of their own.

Scenario hacks having removed all life from a story substituting the stink of life--a loose joke, a dirty jeer. How they do it.

The blind luck that had attended the industry, and he knew the croupiers who raked in the earnings of that vast gambling house. And he knew that the Europeans were impressed with it as they were impressed with the sky-scrapers, as something without human rhythm or movement. He was tired of his own rhythm and the rhythms of the people in Hollywood. He wanted to see people with more secrets than the necessity of concealing a proclivity for morphine.

Hunt's--run the gamut. (for gauntlet)

The man who never read the books and Stahr.

And then we get Bang! Bang! Bang!

Distressed by the cloactal imagry of Briskin.

His own dictation is wrong.

His talent is not exactly thin, like Dotty's and so many Jewish and Irish talents--it is simply infrequent. He needs years to dream. (Broken poets).

"No brilliant idea was ever born in a conference room," he assured the Dane. "But a lot of silly ideas have died there," said Stahr.

Trouble with bad pictures he had conceived, as one problem.

Spurgeon doesn't know what pride is--there's not much of it around here."

"We've had that problem before with stage plays," said Stahr, "In 'Tattersall' we took all the hints of what had gone before and even shot two thousand feet of it. Finally we cut it all-- that's why it was such a short picture. Sherwood knew when he wanted to start his play and he was right. When you extend a play with a prelude you're asking for it--you're including a lot of situations the playwright has already rejected. That's why he's reduced them to a mention. Why should we take that mention like one of those dried fish from Iceland and dip in water. You can make it swell but you can't bring it to life."

Stahr explaining why he let a certain bad picture go through. It's complications--like Lee

Stahr had a working of technics but because he had been head man for so long and so many apprentices had grown up during his sway more knowledge was attributed to him than he possessed. He accepted this as the easiest way and was an adept though cautious bluffer. In the dubbing room, which was for sound what the cutting room was for sight he worked by ear alone and was often lost amid the chorus of ever newer terms and slang (get this up). So on the stages. He watched the new processes of faking animated backgrounds. Moving pictures taken against the background of other moving pictures, with a secret child's approval. He could have understood easily enough often he preferred not to preserve a sensual acceptance when he saw the scene unfold in the rushes. There were smart young men about--Rienmund was one--who phrased their remarks toconvey the impression that they understood everything about pictures. Not Stahr. When he interfered it was always from his own point of view not from theirs. Thus his function was different from Griffith in the early days who had been all things to every finished frame of film.

Close to you could see white wigs with the rubber elastic touching the grease paint.

 23.

Trusts technicians most.

Likes directors all right--they're more like it was once. Like a lot of little boys getting up a show.

John Chas. Rogers' American Flag.

Miss Barnes having tea.

I'm on such a rigid diet they won't even let me lick a stamp.

Baird and Stahr go into terrible row about pay-out and at the same time all his writer friends desert him on the Film Guild issue.

What would I be as Stahr's wife--another Mrs. Rich Bitch of Beverly Hills. I could promote him from Beverly Hills to Pasadena except he wouldn't want to be promoted.

Perhaps repeat story conference in pay off way.

24.

I'll pay for passion--so will the public. But it's rare, and it doesn't consist of being born on Grand Street, and sometimes it wears out.

Shipping out the papers in her possession by means of the little granddaughter who innocently lights a stuffed candle at church every Sunday evening.

The Warner Bros. narrative writing and the Metro dramatic packed cut back and forth writing from Stahr.

Joke about "shoot it both ways."

There's this to be said for the happy ending: a healthy man goes along from love to love, doesn't he? You ought to know, Wylie. What's the matter with it? Sometimes the boys think they only have to get unpleasant at the end to have a great drama."

All those phrases like "knock your teeth down your throat", etc. kidded some way. Have them sound formidable. Then show that they're uttered by yellow bellies and faggots. Kid the whole school.

He turned courteously to the woman as if he had read her handwriting through the typescript.

Your audience imagination is working for you here if you let it."

About your second sequence. How're you going to photograph Aunt Georgia looking quaint? What does that mean, Wylie? Do you know how that's going to come out. We'll cast a character woman and she'll play herself and we won't have anything at all."

Politely and maliciously he took a sheet from his folio and gave it to Stahr.

Incident of Stahr calmly telling off an agent he was an overgrown errand boy. Implication, you can get away with it with writers who are soft but not with him. Something like quarrel of Knopf with Swanie.

It is ballet school. Two girls want to strike each other with wet towels and running to wet the towels at the wash stand they collide and are knocked out.

Somebody repeats: Baby, I tore him in two.
A bored man: (later) Did you partition him?

The pulp writer--that superficial hysteria which he substitutes for emotion.

Man showing some children vanishing coin, accidentally intercepts coin from passerby. Serves ice cream cones made out of snow.

There is a place for a hint somewhere of a big agent to complete the picture. Myron or Berg though--no mercy for Swanson.

Crack at Grover Jones and John Gilbert.

25.

The people of Hollywood are not very nice outwardly--there is too much unwelcome familiarity, too much casual snootiness. (the agent who picked up paper in the office).

In order to forgive Stahr for what he did that afternoon it should be remembered that he came out of the old Hollywood that was rough and tough and where the wildest bluffs hold. He had manufactured gloss and polish and contour of new Hollywood but occasionally he liked to tear it apart just to see if it was there.

The Lunar Rainbow.

The pool lights don't work. A flood got in the cellar and there's no electricity.

George knew how the pool lights worked, having seen them installed in broad daylight.

28,

If their souls are alive they no longer speak or perhaps it
is that I have grown deaf.

Suddenly outdated he dies. (accidentally, naturally, murdered)

And they build the Stahr Building.

There was a flurry of premature snow in the air and the stars
looked cold. Staring up at them he saw that they were his stars
as always--symbols of ambition, struggle and glory. The wind blew
through them, trumpeting that high white note for which he always
listened, and the thin-brown clouds, stripped for battle, passed
in review. The scene was of an unparalleled brightness and
magnificence, and only the practiced eye of the commander saw that
one star was no longer there.

28

Past the Garden of Allah Hotel--then as the remembered Rubiat.

At the end all his toys are broken.

The Junk about Garbo laughs, Chaplin talks, Harpo talks (a publicity man)

Never wanted his name on pictures--"I don't want my name on the screen because credit is something that should be given to others. If you are in a position to give credit to yourself then you do not need it."

I wouldn't go to a war--unless it was in Morocco--or the Khyber Pass.

28

It was all small change, incessant nickles and dimes of conversation.

A feeling of having had life pass virtually and endlessly before their eyes like a motion picture reel and give it that much attention.

Producers on plane. Their realization of a small status out of their world and in, and then their refuge in the transcendental thought of their bigness in that little corner, how complete the world was there.

The situation on the big lot was that every producer, director, and scenarist there could adduce proof that he was a money maker. With the phenomenal rise of the industry, the initial distrust of it by business, the stage and literature changing with the weeding out of better men from the needs of speed, with the emphasis as in a mining camp on the lower virtues; then with the growing complication of technique and the exclusiveness it created and finally with the grand consolidation and trashification whose finest flower was block booking--it could be fairly said of all and by all of those who remained that they had made money-- despite the fact that most directors had been reduced by the talkies to mere putters on, that not a third of the producers or one twentieth of the writers could have earned their living in the East. That like the Boers army in the 19th century operating against ill-armed savages, scarcely a general, a colonel or a major was not one of these men, no matter how low grade and incompetent a fellow who could not claim to have participated largely in success. This made difficulty in dealing with them.

The stewardesses on air lines.

Mountains of the Saw (Sierra Nevadas)

Plot's new life.

Drawing away from the little valley, past pink pines and fresh, diamond-strewn snow.

The coming of the talkies. Great technical scene--Stahr thinking back.

He was active in the affairs of the academy. It was due to his influence that the 50% cut was settled peacefully--also through his influence that producers refused to recognize Screen Writers' Guild, which brought about break-up of that organization.

Loved to discuss political economy. He had great ideas of the relation between business and government and the conducting of a government on a thorough business basis.

UNCLASSIFIED

There was, for example, a man who in all seriousness asked him
this favor: Stahr was to say "Hello Tim", and slap him on the
back in front of the commissary one morning. Stahr had the man's
record traced and then slapped him on the back. The man ascended
into heaven.

Ge was taken into one of the best agencies--which is what George
Gershwin referred to when he said "it's nice work if you can get it."
He sits there today. He has his nails manicured at the Beverly
Hills Hotel and his life is one long happy dream.

Marie Prevost.

Someone asks Stahr: Do you know the Cartridges there?

Norbert and Kitty in the snow.

mention "Lovely Helen Hayes & Norma Scheerer

"I want her to change her name to Boots."
"I thought you said Toots," the girl laughed.
"Toots or Boots. It's the oo-oo sound. Cutie shoots Toots. Judge
Hoots. No conviction possible. Pamela is English. Her real name
is Sybil Higgins."

She's the one who looks out the studio gate and wishes she was them.

Sheilah, tell me about yourself. I'm thinner, aren't I. - For Yale
boy to begin chapter with.

Leger's Ballet Mechanique

It is the custom now to look back ourselves on the boom days with
a disapproval that approaches horror. But it had its virtues, that
old boom: Life was a great deal larger and gayer for most people,
and the stampede to the spartan virtues in times of war and famine
shouldn't make us too dizzy to remember its hilarious glory. There
were so many good things. These eyes have been hallowed by watching
a man order champagne for his two thousand guests, by listening
while a woman ordered a whole staircase from the greatest sculptor
in the world, by seeing a man tear up a good check for eight hundred
thousand dollars.

Sid Howard's communist who never had the film with him.

She's a one-girl jazz age.

Virginia had lovely puffed straw hair and the grey eyes of home--
she was a late developer, an awkward duckling at twenty-one, but
learning a whole series of things that unmarried women don't. At
twenty-seven her charm was in full flower.

Mrs. Whitney phoning Virginia about her thoroughbreds--twenty
thousand dollars a day.

Mike Romanoff at the Troc door--fake Mike Romanoff.

UNCLASSIFIED

Brady killed Stahr. The Academy dream. <u>Artists get more than bosses.</u>
The phone companies trying to milk them. <u>Collective bargaining.</u>
How Warner protracted salary cuts. "You trying to tell me how to
run my business". Collecting from him. His revenge--wrecking the
Academy. Stahr not making pictures at the end--only going through
the motions. Lying low--his own company. He was in Europe when
the banks were closed and the committee met agreeing to the cuts.
Mayer's company did not need the cut. Smaller companies would have
gone broke. He used to faint all the time toward the end. His
political opinions(?) Grousing about taxes. His selfishness.

Brothers —like Schenks, Warners, Skouras.

Organizing the thoughtless.

All you comics want to play Hamlet once. Next we'll have the
Ritz comrades.

If you have an inconvenient opinion they name it like a disease
and quarantine you.--"I'm a <u>what</u>?"

For Mankiewicz--the ten days that shook down the world.

The writers at Ted Paramore's were all in low gear, temporarily
or permanently.

Hean Harloe, Marie Prevost, Pauline Frederick, Barbara LaMarr,
Barbara Frederic - Marie Lamotte, Pauline Brevost.

Mike Van Dyke a commie.

These blows hit Stahr all at once. But at first he has them in
control. It is not till they hit his great picture which should
be planted back in 10., that he realizes what they mean. He should
quarrel with the writers in such a way as to effect the great pictures.

Schwartze knows that Brady is after Stahr and writes him a letter.
His lawyer offers to seel him the letter. All about the 1917 scandal.

Get the movie dialogue from files.

Necrology: Ruth Roland, Pearl White, Thelma Todd, Alice Brady,
Marie Dressler. Lillian Tashman - Prevost, Frederick, Harlow,
Lamarr.   -   Connoley, Fairbanks, Gilbert, Valentino, Meighan,
Mix, Rogers, Healy(Ted)

For she has a good forgetting apparatus. That's why she's so
popular, why she can have a heart like a hotel. If she couldn't
forget, there wouldn't be any room. (Cecelia)

Attractive people are always getting into cars in a hurry or
standing still and statuesque, or out of sight.

Scottie: "mousing around" (in regard to a quiet couple.)

Like a Yale boy registering "Superman and wife" at the Commodore
Hotel (for Cecelia)

Having an unsuspecting drink with the agent who had contrived his
ruin.

UNCLASSIFIED

Marcus arriving.

You drew people right up close to you and held them there, not able to move either way.

Moving on to hot seat in theatre. (for Cecelia)

The flickering patches of white on the jockeys made it look like a flight of birds.

And went down to the lake for a dip, swimming on an unreal surface that existed between a world of water like mist and a drizzling firmament of air.

The table clothes blew around the pillars. They blew and blew and blew. The flags twisted around the red chairs like live things, the banners were ragged, the corners of the tables tore off through the burbling, billowing ends of the cloths.

Scrabble.

Tragedy of these men was that nothing in their lives had really bitten deep at all.

Bald ᴴemingway characters.

One was an agent who hated him and always referred to him, so Stahr was told as "the Vine Street Jesus"--"the Walking Oscar" or the "Back house Napoleon".

Discuss Hollywood as a mongrel world.

Trusts technicians most.

We can't just let our worlds crash around us like a lot of dropped trays.

Paradox about Stahr the artist standing for reaction and corruption and--, and the people who stood for all the good things were horrible.

Drifting towards some ignoble destiny they could not evade.

He was so old, so wise that he looked forward only to his anticipations. Oh God give me good anticipations.

Gloom of 1931--fear of 1932--Panic of 1933--N.R.A. of 1934-- Guilds of 1935--Smashing them of 1936

Had brought over German players.

Talk with Eisenstein.

Has Stahr a friend

Some time passes slower for Stahr because of a quick heart and pulse. These seem more crowded days (like after the split)

Commissar Stewart.

UNCLASSIFIED

That day--I thought I saw Mr. Marcus driving a Chevy jalopy but I knew
I was wrong--he'd no more be seen without his Lincoln than his
father would be seen without his pushcart!

The day Stahr read the Communist Manifesto and disagreed about women.

Stahr and the Bride Wore Red. Says knowing La Borwits understands
only money. The nerve of you to play with $600,000 etc.

For Boxley--They think because you can write you know, poor fools,
that you can give them the good life.

In the late afternoon Stahr and Margaret Doolan slowed up like
exhausted clock-work and rested a few minutes without comment.
He lay on the couch, his hand over his eyes. Miss Doolan leaned
back, looking out the French windows, her dictation book still
open. Along the cat walk she saw the boy turn into the
projection room with the last rushes of the day.
"What happened next door?" Stahr asked suddenly, "--early in the
week."
Miss Doolan did not answer. From a cement gully off and down
somewhere a shout of laughter pierced up into the room.
"I mean what became of those girls of Brady's?" Stahr took his hand
off his eyes, "Do you know?"
"I can imagine," she said.
"Why two of them? It seems rather immoderate. They were good
girls--Rosemary did some work for me."

The day Stahr died everyone on the lot (including the Marx Brothers)
were crying and trying to see who was watching them. "Trash", I
could hear him say, "Trash."

Strong women wept into their vichysoisse.

In life too much luck, in drama too much destiny.

If you keep people's blood in their heads it won't be where it
should be for making love.

See the first notes in H.

"Perfectly respectable girl but only been drinking that day.
No matter how long she lives she'll always know she's killed somebody."

The Casting room.

The supervisor stays with the picture till it's in the can.

With your practically brilliant faculty for supposing that whatever
isn't in the foreground of your conscience has ceased to exist.

Dolly had done her worst suffering on the boat in an economical way
she had, it was weeks before George saw her eyes silvery clear in
the morning.

Director's Special.

UNCLASSIFIED

A scene where a communist insults Stahr intolerably, belittles his whole life.

Sam Wood and the house in life   See some photographs.

Which Vanderbilt--the one with the beat mouth, the horse and the scrambled teeth.

Idea about Basil and Josephine.

Rex Ingram

Turkey Burger (Gerald)

His house finished for late meeting.

Some Myrmydons--Production manager; assistant production manager; production secretary; location manager; camera men; flack--publicity man; company grip and assistants; construction superintendant; sound mixer; studio police chief.

The brilliant but ailing Franklin and also Lubitch.

The lumiere man

Let us take a day and some weather and go to Rose Meloney's office.

The Love of the Last Tycoon
   A Western
      by
F. Scott Fitzgerald

Ping pong

Bugsy Siegel

He had met the two Lindbergs and thought them dazed and tragic spooks. and...and. .

To establish official liason work in an infantry division and realized in the process that an uneducated trouble shooter was worth a dozen college graduates dignified as signal officers (Robinson)

The kind of man who stamps just before he laughs or shoves forward his chair with each change of emotion.

He's got four-legged caviar in his pantry.

There is undoubtedly something funny about not being a lady, or rather about being a gold digger. You've got to laugh a lot like Constance Talmadge and Ruth. (Half used)

Joe's "You know what I say about him every time--what is it I say about him every time--what is it?" The answer, "That you like him." Flieshacker.

His coordination

UNCLASSIFIED

Margaret Bishop's conversational meglomania. The woman star didn't engage Character actress.

Remember my summing up in Crazy Sunday--don't give the impression that these are bad people.

Hollywood child--the little hard face of a successful streetwalker (prostitute) on a jumping jack's body, the clear cultured whine of the voice.

The fulgitutinous palps like Mike Romanoff and Elsa Maxwell.

"Oh, I have lots of tact. We learn it at Bennington "
"Do you really. Oh, I'd so love to take that."

She wore a little summer number from Saks, about $18.98 and a pink and blue hat that had been stepped on on one side.

Talking grosses

Roy the superboy

You're all the songs

Father kicked upstairs.

These are the picture people. Do not blame them too much. I am sure you would do much better in their place if you had all that money to spend and that strange story of what happened to--to produce. We all have one story. But what would you do after that and that and that day after day after dozens hundreds thousands and ten thousands of time.

Most of us could be photographed from the day of our birth to the day of our death and the film shown without producing any emotion except boredom and disgust. It would all just look like monkeys scratching. How do you feel about your friends' home movies of their baby or their trip. Isn't it a God awful bore?

He did not love anyone at all because the dead did not count. It was not fair to love the dead.

Behaviorism--the only guide to the validity of emotion.

Get from the library the books on movies and go through them. First get list of titles of such books.

Like many men he did not like flowers except a few weedy ones--they were too highly evolved and self conscious. But he liked leaves and horse chestnuts and peeled twigs and even acorns, unripe, ripe and wormy fruit.

I always liked the horse chestnuts and leaves better than flowers.

Beat of my Heart.

Norbert and the boy in the snow for Kitty.

1P

De Mille Book: note--Look from 157 on ---p. 148, 60, 113, 122, 100.

I'm one of the few people who know who killed William Dean Taylor but I'll always consider it a trade secret.

Let the glamor show as from far away. Cling to reality, for any departure from a high pitch of reality at which the Jews live leads to farce in which the Christians live. Hollywood is a Jewish holiday, a gentiles tragedy. Stahr should be half Jewish like Hunt. Or is this a compromise. I think it is.

Coming home to an empire of his own--an empire he has made.

Motor shutting off and the plane settling down to earth.

Give the pilot some kind of special if only physical characteristic that will make him vivid to the reader.

Rowland saying afterwards that he died with silent pictures.

The moon of California

In a strange atmosphere of a mining town in Lotus land.

Landing at Glendale--and there it was again the bright California moon. (work out description of the hush of the motors, lights, etc., as elaborate settling down in the warm California night.)

I went to Vassar for 3 years because that's what my father said I had to do, because that was supposed to make me more desirable, because he said men weren't going to marry that other type.

Schwartz typifies the excitement of going to this mining town the same way that some unidentified people might typify a lot of miners approaching gold settled in Alaska. It is necessary that this episode shall have that and also a definitely sexual touch again without compromising Cecelia in the reader's eyes.

The man who has struggled madly for a pot of gold and had his finger tips on it and it has slipped away and now he has gone a little bit crazy in his attempts to catch up with it and that very intensity (typified by his trying to meet this man who is in the private compartment and who will later develop as Stahr) is making a pot of gold more and more inaccessible to him.

The red and white lights of the city from the cabarets.

Cecelia has Maude with her a friend who is to present her Philly. Has the girl coming for summer. Girl is a Bennington number utterly unlike Peaches. Bargain as per Mannix--Ordway, me-and-Pinney.

Maude - pink nostril beauty--Gretha Garson.

INVENTORY OF DRAFTS

This inventory identifies the layers of Fitzgerald's working drafts in the order of composition. The chapter and episode groupings are keyed to Fitzgerald's latest outline facsimiled on pp. xlvi–xlvii.

The first column provides the editor's draft designations as utilized in this Cambridge edition, as well as in *"The Last of the Novelists"*: F. Scott *Fitzgerald and The Last Tycoon* and in *F. Scott Fitzgerald Manuscripts V: The Last Tycoon*. An asterisk identifies a draft that is one of the base-texts for this edition. The "§" symbol indicates that the draft is facsimiled in *F. Scott Fitzgerald Manuscripts V*.

The second column provides a description of the documents with their paginations. The manuscript pages are written in pencil on 8½" × 11" or 8½" × 13" leaves; all typed pages are 8½" × 11". "MS" designates a document in Fitzgerald's hand; "TS" designates a ribbon copy of a typed document; "CC" designates a carbon copy of a typed document. The symbol "R" for "revised" is restricted to Fitzgerald's own holograph (hand-written) revisions or annotations on a typed draft. "Wilson" in the description column identifies a typed draft that Edmund Wilson altered and incorporated in the text he submitted to Scribners; his marks on the typescripts are not described as revisions. "FK" indicates that the document bears corrections, notes, or shorthand by Frances Kroll, Fitzgerald's secretary.

The third column provides the heading that appears—in Fitzgerald's hand or typed—on the first page of the document.

The fourth column provides the version number(s) noted—in Fitzgerald's hand or in typescript—on the draft pages; these numbers were often changed or omitted in accordance with Fitzgerald's method of writing by accretion.

The single right-hand bracket indicates the direction of change: 2 [3 signifies that Fitzgerald changed his designation of version 2 to version 3. Paired square brackets indicate inferred pagination: [1] 2–25. Italic brack-eted digits designate the total of unnumbered pages: [*11*] signifies 11 pages that Fitzgerald did not number. Angle brackets indicate crossed-out Fitzger-ald headings: ⟨(Episodes 1, 2, 3)⟩. Page numbers within parentheses indicate that Fitzgerald assigned two or more numbers to an inserted page: (54–55).

Thus, under *Outline Chapter I; Episodes 1–3* the draft designated * I §

is the base-text for that section of the Cambridge edition and is facsimiled in *F. Scott Fitzgerald Manuscripts V.* This draft is the latest secretarial typescript and is revised in Fitzgerald's hand; it consists of an unnumbered first page followed by pages numbered 2–25. Draft * I § also bears Wilson's holograph alterations and was incorporated in the edition he delivered to Scribners. Draft * I § is headed "CHAPTER I" with "(Episodes 1, 2, 3)" crossed out. Fitzgerald designated it "v. 4".

See "Fitzgerald's Revisions, Corrections, and Annotations on the Latest Typescripts" and "Wilson's Alterations on the Latest Typescripts" for full lists of holograph marks on the latest RTS drafts.

Inventory of Drafts

Draft Designation	Description	FSF Heading	FSF Version Number
Outline Chapter I; Episodes 1–3			
A §	MS & RTS [1] 2–54 (54–55) 56–66	Chapter I	
B §	RTS & MS [1] 2–13 [14–15] 16–32	CHAPTER I	1
C §	RCC/shorthand— FK [1] 2–4 [2] 5–6 [1] 7–13 [1] 14– 25	CHAPTER I	1
D §	RTS & MS [1] 2–8 [1] 9–10, 10½–21, 21½ [1] 22–24, 24½	CHAPTER I	2 [(v.3)
E	CC [1] 2–25	CHAPTER I	2;1
F	TS [1] 2–17, 17A, 18–24	CHAPTER I	(v.3)
G	CC 2–17, 17A, 18– 24	CHAPTER I (Episodes 1, 2, 3)	(v.3)

Draft Designation	Description	FSF Heading	FSF Version Number
H §	RCC & MS [1] 2–17, 17A, 18–19, 19½, 20–24	CHAPTER I	v.3 [v.4
* I §	Latest RTS [1] 2–25. Wilson.	CHAPTER I ⟨⟨Episodes 1, 2, 3⟩⟩	v.4

Variant opening: —It was still "roses, roses all the way" . . . .

J §	MS 4–6 [7]	Chapter I	
K §	CC 5–7	CHAPTER I	1.

Outline Chapter II; Episodes 4–6

A §	MS & RTS [1–13]	Chapter II	
B §	RTS & RCC/ shorthand—FK [26] 27–29, 29½ (30–31) [1] 32, insert A, insert B, 33–34, 36, 36½, 36½A, 37–39	CHAPTER II	
C	TS [26] 27–29, 31–38	CHAPTER II	2;1
D	RCC [33]–34	OLD CHAP II (Restaurant Scene	2
E §	MS & RCC 1, 1½, 2, 2½, 3, 3½	Chapter II	v2
F §	RTS, RCC, MS [1] 2–9	CHAPTER II	2
G	RTS 25–31	⟨CHAPTER II⟩	v.2
H §	MS & RTS 1–5	Chapter II	2 [3

Draft Designation	Description	FSF Heading	FSF Version Number
I	RTS—FK [25] 26–33	CHAPTER II	3
J §	MS & RTS 1–7 [11]		2
K	CC—FK [25] 26–33	CHAPTER II	3.
L	CC—FK [25] 27–33	CHAPTER II	3.
M §	RTS [1] 2–4, 6, 5, 6–9	CHAPTER II	v.1.n.c./4 [v.2
N	CC [25] 26–30. 3 copies.	CHAPTER II	4.
O	RCC/shorthand—FK 29–36 [2] 37–38		
P	CC [1–4]		
Q §	MS g–k		
R	MS 1–12		
S §	RTS 20, 33–38		
T §	MS [17]	Chap II (Part III)	
U §	TS 1–5	Unclassified	
V	RTS 40		
W §	MS 1–20	Episodes 4 and 5	
X §	RCC 1–6	Episodes 4 and 5.	
* Y §	Latest RTS 1–6. Wilson.	Episodes 4 and 5.	

Draft Designation	Description	FSF Heading	FSF Version Number

Outline Chapter III; Episode 7

Z	CC 1–3	Episode 6	
* AA §	Latest RTS 1–3. Wilson.	Episode 6	
A §	MS [1] 2–12	Episode 8	
B §	RCC 1–6	Episode 8 [7	
* C §	Latest RTS 1–5. Wilson.	Episode 8 [7	

Outline Chapter III; Episode 8

A §	MS & RTS 1–5, 4, 5–13	Episode 9	
B §	RCC 1–9	Episode 9 [8	
* C §	Latest RTS 1–9. Wilson.	Episode 9 [8	

Rejected Episode 9: Stahr, Agge & Van Dyke at story conference

A §	MS 1–7	Episode 9.	
B	CC 1–4	Episode 9.	
C	RTS 1–4	Episode 9.	

Outline Chapter III; Episode 9

A §	MS & RTS 1–19	Episode 10 [9	
B §	RCC 1–11	Episode 9	
* C §	Latest RTS 1–11. Wilson.	⟨Episode 9⟩	

Draft Designation	Description	FSF Heading	FSF Version Number

Rejected Episode 10: Stahr & Agge at story conference; Carlson

A§	MS 1, 9–17 [3 inserts for 18] 18–19	Episode 10 ⟨Second Confer- ence⟩	
B	CC 1–11	Episode 10	
C §	RTS [1–3] 4–11	⟨Episode 10⟩	

Outline Chapter III; Episode 10

A §	MS 1–11	Episode 11	
B	CC 1–7	Episode 11 [10	
* C §	Latest RTS 1–7. Wilson.	Episode 11 [10	

Outline Chapter III; Episode 10 continuation

A §	MS 1, 1a, 1b, 1c, 2–5	Episode 12 (1st part)	
B	CC 1–5	Episode 12 (1st part)	
C	RTS & MS 7–10	Episode 10 Con- tinuation	

Outline Chapter III; Episode 10 insert

A §	MS [1] 2–6	Episode 11 [For Episode 10	
B	CC 1, 1–4	*Correction for 10;* For Episode 10 [11	
* C §	Latest TS 1, 1–4. Wilson.	⟨*Correction for 10*⟩; ⟨For Episode 10⟩	

Draft Designation	Description	FSF Heading	FSF Version Number
Outline Chapter IV; Episode 11			
A §	MS & RTS [1] 2–21	Episode 11	
B	RCC 1–13	Episode 11	
* C §	RTS 1–13. Wilson.	Episode 11	
Outline Chapter IV; Episode 12			
A §	MS 1–10, 10½, 11	Episode 13	
B	CC 1–5	Episode 13	
C §	RTS 1–5	Episode 13	
D	CC 1–5	Episode 13	
E §	MS & RTS 1–11	Episode 13	
F	RCC 1–8	Episode 13 [12	
* G §	Latest RTS 1–8. Wilson.	Episode 13 [12	
Outline Chapter IV; Episode 12			
A §	MS [1]	End of 12	
B	CC [1]	(End of 12)	
* C §	Latest TS [1]. Wilson.	(End of 12)	
Outline Chapter V; Episode 13			
A §	MS 1–11	13. (1st part)	

Draft Designation	Description	FSF Heading	FSF Version Number
B	CC 1–6	Episode 13	
* C §	Latest TS 1–6. Wilson.	Episode 13	
D	MS 1–5, 5½, 6–16	13 (continued)	
E	CC 1–9	13 (continued)	
* F §	Latest TS 1–9. Wilson.	13 (continued)	

Outline Chapter V; Episode 14

Draft Designation	Description	FSF Heading	FSF Version Number
A §	MS 1–3, 3½, 4–6, insert 6, 7–13, 13½	Section 14	
B §	MS 8–11	(Attach to Section 14, Part I)	
C	CC 1–10	Section 14	
* D §	Latest TS 1–10. Wilson.	Section 14	
E §	MS 1–9	Section 14 (2nd part)	
F	CC 1–4	Section 14 (2nd part)	
* G §	Latest TS 1–4. Wilson.	Section 14 (2nd part)	
H §	MS [1] 2–15 [10] 12–18, 18½, 19–20, 20½, 21–23	Section 14 (Part III)	
I	RTS 11		
J	CC 11–13		

Draft Designation	Description	FSF Heading	FSF Version Number
K	CC 1–17	Section 14 (Part III)	
* L §	Latest RTS 1–17. Wilson.	Section 14 (Part III)	

Outline Chapter V; Episode 15

A §	MS 1–2, 2½, 3–7	*Section 15* (first part)	
B	CC 1–4	*Section 15* (first part)	
* C §	Latest TS 1–4. Wilson.	*Section 15* (first part)	
D §	MS 1–8	15. (Second part)	
E	CC 1–5	15 (second part)	
* F §	Latest TS 1–5. Wilson.	15 (second part)	

Outline Chapter V; Episode 16

A §	MS [1] 2–5	Episode 16, 1st Part.	
B	CC 1–4	*Episode 16, First Part*	
* C §	Latest TS 1–4. Wilson.	*Episode 16, First Part*	
D §	MS [1] 2–5, 5½, 6– 15, 15½, 16–21	Episode 16 (Part 2)	
E	CC 1–12	Episode 16 (Part 2)	
* F §	Latest TS 1–12. Wilson.	Episode 16 (Part 2)	

Draft Designation	Description	FSF Heading	FSF Version Number

Outline Chapter VI; Episode 17

Draft Designation	Description	FSF Heading	FSF Version Number
A §	MS & RTS 1–4, 4½, 5–6, 6½, 7–8, 8½, 9, 9½, 10–15, 15½, 16–17 [1] 17½, 18–26	Episode 17	
B §	RCC 1–17	Episode 17	
* C §	Latest RTS 1–17. Wilson.	Episode 17	

Sanitarium Frame

Draft Designation	Description	FSF Heading	FSF Version Number
A §	RTS [1] 2–3		3.
B	CC [1] 2–3		3.
C §	RTS [1] 2–3		4.
D	CC [1] 2–3		4.
E §	RTS 1–4		5.
F	TS 1–3		6.
G	CC [1] 2–3. Wilson appendix.		6.

TEXTUAL APPARATUS

EDITORIAL EMENDATIONS IN THE BASE-TEXTS; TEXTUAL NOTES

The Emendations List stipulates the editorial departures from the base-texts with a record of the variant readings from selected documents. This list is not a historical collation: it does not trace the evolution of textual variants through every stage of the manuscripts and pre–base-texts typescripts. Differences between MSS and the latest TS are reported here when the MS reading has been restored in the Cambridge text. A historical collation of all the manuscripts and revised typescripts would require a separate volume and would be a poor substitute for the published facsimiles of the documents.

Since the text edited by Edmund Wilson has been the basis for all previous editions of the novel, his alterations on the base-texts pages and the transmission of the Wilson text to the retyped Scribners setting copy and to the first printing have been identified in the Emendations List when an emendation in the Cambridge edition is involved. The post–base-texts alterations have no authority but have been recorded to establish the genesis of the first-printing text. The complete record of Wilson's alterations and their transmission is provided in "Wilson's Alterations on the Latest Typescripts" and "Variants in the Scribners Setting Copy and the First Printing."

Base-texts for the Cambridge edition are the latest typescripts for Chapter I and part of Chapter II and each subsequent episode as revised by Fitzgerald. The first reading in each entry provides the emended reading in this edition; it is followed by a left-pointing bracket ( ]) and the source of the emendation. Following the emendation source and a separating semicolon, the rejected reading or readings and their documents are stipulated. Thus at 61.10 the editor has provided "Diogenes" for Fitzgerald's incorrect MS and TS reading "Diocenes"; Wilson altered the TS to "Euripides," and this reading was retained in the Scribners setting copy and in the first printing. The symbols used in the Emendations List are explained below.

A *stet* entry indicates the editor's decision not to emend in a case where an emendation is possible. Daggers indicate readings for which there are Explanatory Notes.

An emendation entry includes a Textual Note only when clarification is required. Certain passages with complex transmission histories are identified in the list of Editorial Emendations (see 94.16–95.2). In these Textual Notes *manuscript* refers to a document; *holograph* refers to handwriting. Thus pages in Fitzgerald's hand constitute a *manuscript;* but a typescript page is revised by Fitzgerald in *holograph.*

It is not always clear when Fitzgerald wrote a capital letter (Premiers/ premiers) or whether he wrote an *e* or an *i* (oases/oasis). In these instances the manuscript is not cited as the basis for emendation.

Key to Symbols

~	the same word
∧	omitted punctuation
¶	new paragraph
ed	an emendation made by the editor of this volume
MS	a draft in Fitzgerald's holograph; however, for Episodes 8, 9, 11, 12, and 17 the draft identified as MS includes typescript or revised typescript interpolations. The actual form (handwritten or typed) of each reading is not stipulated. To enable readers to find specific readings in the published facsimiles, the MS symbol is accompanied by an identification of that draft as catalogued in the "Inventory of Drafts." Thus: MS(II-W) refers to the 20-page MS for Episodes 4 and 5 of Chapter II designated draft W.
CCH	Chapter I, draft H (revised carbon copy of TS draft F, which *precedes* the latest TS of Chapter I). Draft H is cited because there is no complete MS draft for these episodes.
RCC	Fitzgerald's holograph revision on CCH
TS	latest unrevised secretarial ribbon typescript
RTS	Fitzgerald's holograph revision on the TS
W	Edmund Wilson's alteration on the base-texts; cited only when it affects an emendation made in the Cambridge edition (see "Wilson's Alterations in the Latest Typescripts")
SC	retyped Scribners setting copy (the reading noted here is the latest reading in SC; see "Variants in the Scribners Setting Copy and the First Printing")
B	first printing of the first edition, edited by Wilson (*The Last Tycoon* [New York: Scribners, 1941]).

Silent Emendations

See Introduction, pp. lxxxvi–vii, for regularization of characters' names.

The placement of punctuation with quotation marks has been made to conform with the rules of typography.

Spelling corrections—except for names or possible ambiguities in meaning—are not recorded.

Spelled numbers (twenty-two) and fractions (one-half) have been hyphenated.

Ellipsis periods have been treated as a typographical convention and have been normalized in accordance with the three/four rule.

Fitzgerald's *awhile* has been normalized to *a while* when part of a prepositional phrase.

Father has been capitalized when used as a name.

East and *West* have been capitalized when they refer to a place rather than a direction.

title   *The Love of The Last Tycoon: A Western*
          See Introduction, pp. xiv–xvii, for discussion of Fitzgerald's
          working titles.
1.1   brought] CCH, SC, B; brough TS (torn)
1.5   Producer's] ed; Producers CCH, TS; *Producer's* W, SC, B
† 1.14, 10.22, 14.18–19   Bennington] B; Smith CCH, TS, SC
          Cecelia's college is written as 'Bennington' in MS(15-D) and
          typed as 'Bennington' in TS(15-F) for 103.2. See Sheilah Graham
          to Wilson (Introduction, p. xviii): "Later he changed it to Benning-
          ton, and it was the latter that he wanted."
1.15   products∧] ed; ~, CCH, TS, SC, B
1.29–30   men. *space break* ¶ The] *stet* RCC, TS, SC; men. *no break* ¶
          The B
          The space break was lost in B because the paragraph following
          the break started a new page.
† 4.1   junior] B; Junior CCH, TS, SC
† 4.5, 5.6   Depression] ed; depression CCH, TS, SC, B
4.21   to—] B; ~, CCH, TS, SC
† 4.25   or a Nembutal] ed; or a nembutal CCH; or nembutal TS, SC, B
5.5   west] SC; West CCH, TS, B
5.10   Mother] ed; mother CCH, TS, SC, B

5.11 stewardess.] B; ~, CCH, TS, SC

5.22 upstream] ed; up stream CCH, TS, SC, B

5.34 stewardess.] W, SC, B; ~, CCH, TS

6.3 *Brady*] W, B; *Brad*ogue CCH, TS; *Brady* SC

6.4 him.] B; ~, CCH, TS, SC

6.24 up.] ed; ~, CCH, TS; ~: W, SC, B

6.29 *night?*] SC, B; night? CCH; *night?* TS

7.11 Schwartze∧] ed; ~, CCH, TS; Schwartz, W; ~∧ SC, B

7.14 White.] W, SC, B;~, CCH, TS

7.25 she] ed; he CCH, TS, SC, B

7.25 said Mr. Schwartze] CCH; said Schwartze TS; said Schwartz W, SC, B

7.36 oases] W, SC, B; oasis CCH, TS

8.9 premieres] ed; Premiers CCH, TS; premiers W, SC; premières B

8.17 farm house] ed; farmhouse CCH, TS, SC, B

8.17 Bennington] B; Northhampton RCC, TS, SC
   Bennington College is in Bennington, Vermont; Smith College is in Northhampton, Massachusetts. See 3.14.

† 8.19 "Top Hat"] ed; ∧~~∧ RCC, TS; ∧*Top Hat*∧ W, SC, B

† 8.19 "Cheek to Cheek"] ed; ∧~~~∧ RCC, TS; ∧*Cheek to Cheek*∧ W, SC, B

8.20 hand] RCC; hands CCH, TS, SC, B

8.35 half ∧ past] ed; ~-~ CCH, TS, SC, B

8.36 White.] B; ~, CCH, TS, SC

9.2 The] ed; the CCH, TS, W, SC, B

9.7 *he's*] RCC, B; *he*'s TS, SC

9.13 said.] ed; ~, CCH, TS, SC, B

9.17 him.] W, SC, B; ~, CCH, TS

9.19 he,] W, SC, B; ~∧ CCH, TS

9.22 Wylie.] W, SC, B; ~, CCH, TS

9.29 Negro] ed; negro RCC, TS, SC, B

9.31 warm∧ fresh,] ed; ~, ~∧ CCH, TS; ~, ~, W, SC, B
   In the typescript (I-D) preceding CCH, Fitzgerald revised 'fresh∧ warm∧' to 'warm∧ fresh,'.

9.32 Negro] ed; negro CCH, TS, SC, B

10.18 me.] ~, CCH, TS; ~: W, SC, B

10.18 Cecelia,] ed; ~∧ CCH, TS; Cecilia∧ W, SC; Cecilia, B

10.20 lie] W, SC, B; lay CCH, TS

10.21 Celia?] ed; ~. CCH, TS, SC, B

† 10.24 'Esquire'] ed; ∧~∧ RCC, TS; ∧*Esquire*∧ CCH, W, SC, B

10.25   juniors] B; Juniors CCH, TS, SC
10.29   said.] W, SC, B; ~, TS; ~∧ RCC
11.2   you.' "] ed; ~." CCH; ~'." RCC; ~!." TS; ~! W, SC; ~!' " B
11.11   Schwartze?] ed; ~, CCH, TS; Schwartz, W, SC, B
11.37   smugly.] W, SC, B; ~, CCH, TS
12.4   eastern] W, SC, B; Eastern CCH, TS
12.17   president] W, SC, B; President CCH, TS
12.21   said.] B; ~, CCH, TS, SC
12.34   Mannie] ed; Manny CCH, TS, SC, B
13.8–9 in. And] RCC; ~, and TS, SC, B
13.17   surprise.] W, SC, B; ~, CCH, TS
13.18   smiling.] W, SC, B; ~, CCH, TS
13.27   Mannie] CCH; Manny TS, SC, B
13.33   one] RCC, SC, B; on TS
13.34–35   head. *space break* ¶ Of] RCC; ~. *no break* ¶ ~ TS, SC, B
         The space break was lost in TS because the paragraph following
         the break started a new page.
14.2   eastern] ed; Eastern CCH, TS, SC, B
14.4   iron maidens] ed; Iron Maidens CCH, TS, SC, B
15.6   time,] B; ~∧ CCH, TS, SC
15.15   and,] W, SC, B; ~∧ CCH, TS
15.19   knew how] CCH, SC, B; ~ ho TS
16.2–7 He looked . . . mouth.] *stet* RCC, TS, SC, B
         Graham informed Maxwell Perkins on 11 January 1941 (see
         Introduction, p. lxix) that Fitzgerald intended to delete this de-
         scription of Stahr's Bronx boyhood. See 115.23 where Stahr's
         boyhood in Erie, Pennsylvania, is noted.
16.18   Monro] *stet* CCH, TS; Monroe W, SC, B
16.23   MANNIE] CCH; MANNY TS, SC; Mᴀɴɴʏ B
16.26   said.] W, SC, B; ~, CCH, TS
16.31   Wylie.] W, SC, B; ~, CCH, TS
17.1   said.] W, SC, B; ~, CCH, TS
17.8   Wylie.] W, SC, B; ~, CCH, TS
17.15   Stahr.] W, SC, B; ~, RCC, TS
17.16   judgement] RCC; judgment TS, SC, B
17.19   No.' "] ed; No'." CCH; No!." TS; No!' " W, SC, B
17.32   Pat] ed; Billy CCH, TS, SC, B
         Brady's first name is provided as 'Pat' beginning in typescript
         for 48.15, except for 106.34, where it is 'Bill'.
18.24   course∧] B; ~, CCH, TS, SC

18.26   pictures—] W, SC, B; ~, RCC, TS

18.26   example,] W, SC, B; ~∧ CCH, TS

19.3   said.] B; ~, CCH, TS, SC

19.5   interest.] ed; ~, CCH, TS, SC; ~: B

19.22   volunteered. "Up] ed; ~, "~ CCH, TS; ~∧ "—up W; ~. "—Up SC; ~, "∧up B

19.24   name. "] W, SC; ~.∧ CCH, TS; ~—" B

19.30   mentality,] W, SC, B; ~∧ CCH, TS

19.35   said,] W, SC, B; ~∧ RCC, TS

20.6   Good bye."] ed; Goodbye." CCH, W, SC, B; ~.∧ TS

20.24–21.14   ¶ "What. . . . darkness.
        This passage was retyped from a typescript page revised by Fitzgerald.

21.15   Episodes 4 and 5] *stet* MS(II-W); Episodes 4 and 5. TS; Chapter 2 W; CHAPTER 2 SC; CHAPTER II B
        After combining Episodes 4 and 5 Fitzgerald stopped designating chapters. All chapter divisions subsequent to Chapter I in the published book were provided by Wilson from Fitzgerald's outline-plan. Fitzgerald's episode or section designations have been retained in this edition.

21.17   drug store] ed; ~-~ MS(II-W), TS, SC, B

21.18   car.] SC, B; ~∧ RTS
        See "Fitzgerald's Revisions."

† 21.21   Bill Hart] W, SC, B; Bill Harte MS(II-W); Bell Harte TS

21.32   Administration Building] ed; administration building MS(II-W), TS, SC, B

† 21.34   Come! Come!] ed; ~∧ come∧ MS(II-W), TS; *Come, come,* W, SC, B

22.12, 17   Birdy] B; Glenola MS(II-W), TS, SC
        This secretary's name becomes 'Birdy' in MS(15-D) and TS(15-F) for 103.19.

22.15   speak,] W, SC, B; ~∧ MS(II-W), TS

22.28   Mother] ed; mother MS(II-W), TS, SC, B

23.7   protozoa] *stet* MS(II-W), TS, SC, B
        Protozoa are not sub-microscopic. A correct term would be *microbes* or *viruses.*

23.15   Father. "All] B; father, "All MS(II-W); ~, "all TS, SC

23.17   apology.] W, SC, B; ~, MS(II-W), TS

† 24.13   Dictograph] ed; dictographs MS(II-W), TS; dictograph RTS, SC, B

24.20　gravely.] ed; ~, MS(II-W), TS; ~; W; ~: SC, B

24.30　thoughtfully. "Before] ed; ~, "~ MS(II-W), TS; ~, "before SC, B

24.32　Doolan] W, SC, B; Dolan MS(II-W), TS
　　　　This is the only point at which Stahr's secretary's surname is
　　　　'Dolan' in MS and TS; it is 'Doolan' in all other appearances.

25.4　repeated.] W, SC, B; ~, MS(II-W), TS

25.8　said.] B; ~, MS(II-W), TS, SC

25.15　college?] ed; ~. MS(II-W), TS, SC, B

25.18　redhead] B; red-head MS(II-W); ~∧~ TS, SC

25.24　Episode 6] *stet* TS; Episode 6 (7 is out) MS(II-W); *omitted* W, SC,
　　　　B

25.27　châteaux] W, B; chateaux MS(II-W); Chateaux TS, SC

25.34　Thirty-sixth Street] ed; thirty-sixth street MS(II-W), TS; Thirty-
　　　　Sixth Street W, SC, B

26.1　moment.] W, SC, B; ~, MS(II-W), TS

† 26.3　god] ed; Godess MS(II-W); Goddess TS, SC, B

26.10　Robby.] B; ~, MS(II-W), TS, SC

† 26.16　De Mille] W; Demille MS(II-W), TS; DeMille SC, B

26.24　them.] W, SC, B; ~, MS(II-W), TS

26.28　judgement] MS(II-W); judgment TS, SC, B

26.29　them,] W, SC, B; ~∧ MS(II-W), TS

27.4　voice.] W, SC, B; ~, MS(II-W), TS

27.6　truckers—] ed; ~∧ MS(II-W), TS; ~, W, SC, B

27.9　two-by-fours] ed; ~∧~∧~ MS(II-W), TS, SC, B

27.10　Jungle] ed; jungle MS(II-W), TS, SC, B

27.10　sake . . . that] W, SC, B; ~ ∧ ~ MS(II-W), TS

27.11　plastic. . . ."] B; ~ . . . MS(II-W), TS; ~" . . . W, SC

† 27.20　Old Guard] B; old guard MS(II-W), TS, SC

† 27.24　Depression] ed; depression MS(II-W), TS, SC, B

27.25　now—there were clay feet everywhere—] ed; ~∧~~~~~∧
　　　　MS(II-W), TS; ~∧~~~~~, W, SC; ~, ~~~~~; B
　　　　Fitzgerald inserted 'there were clay feet everywhere' inter-
　　　　lineally in MS without punctuation.

27.28　Episode 7] *stet* RTS; ~ 8 MS(7-A), TS; Chapter 3 W; CHAPTER
　　　　3 SC; CHAPTER III B
　　　　Fitzgerald's note '(Episode 7 is out)' at the top of this TS page
　　　　was crossed out by an unidentifiable hand.

28.1　shrewdness∧] W, SC, B; ~, MS(7-A), TS

28.5　ABCs] MS(7-A); ABC's TS, SC, B

† 28.12　Lumière] W, SC, B; Lumiere MS(7-A), TS

28.14–15 censorship in 1933. Proof] MS(7-A); censorship. ¶ Proof TS, SC, B

28.29 eyewitness] MS(7-A), B; eye witness TS, SC

29.11 Dictograph] ed; dictograph MS(7-A), TS, SC, B

29.24 "Yes, Mr. Stahr. I've] *stet* RTS, SC, B; "All right. I called about Pedro Garcia—he tried to kill himself in front of Warner Brothers last week. Mr Brown says he's going blind . . . I've MS(7-A), TS
   Because of this Fitzgerald revision there is no previous reference to the vision problem when Stahr asks at 44.16: "Is the eye trouble hopeless?"

29.25 Stahr.] W, SC, B; ~, MS(7-A), TS

† 29.31–32 ∧*Tout passe.—L'art robuste / Seul a l'éternité.*∧] ed; ∧*Toute passe—l'art seule dure a l'eternite.*∧ MS(7-A), TS; ∧*Tout passe*∧*—l'art seul dure à l'éternité.*∧ W, SC; *"Tout passe.—L'art robuste / Seul a l'éternité."* B

29.32 *l'éternité.*∧ space break ¶ "And] W, SC; *l'eternite.*∧ space break ¶ "And MS(7-A), TS; *l'éternité.*" no break ¶ "And B

30.6–7 asked: ¶ "Did] ed; turned. ¶ "~ MS(7-A), TS; asked. ¶ "~ RTS; asked: "~ W, SC, B

30.7 "Did Robby phone in?"] *stet* MS(7-A), TS, SC, B
   Robby left a message for Stahr at 29.12–14.

30.9 Sound] ed; sound MS(7-A), TS, SC, B

30.12 else?] W, SC, B; ~. MS(7-A), TS

30.14 too.] W, SC, B; ~? MS(7-A), TS

30.22 sore?] W, SC, B; ~∧ MS(7-A); ~. TS

30.24–26 then. / Episode 8 / ¶ Stahr] ed; then. *space break* ¶ Stahr RTS, SC, B
   Fitzgerald deleted the Agge material at the end of typescript for Episode 7 and revised the paragraph after his space break to introduce Boxley; but he retained the Episode 8 designation between the first two paragraphs of the Boxley-Stahr meeting. See "Fitzgerald's Revisions."

30.34–31.1 outright. ¶ Mr.] W, SC, B; outright. / Episode 8 / ¶ Mr. RTS
   See "Fitzgerald's Revisions."

31.14 Boxley.] W, SC, B; ~, MS(8-A), TS

31.18 yourself?] B; ~, MS(8-A), TS, SC

31.20 mildly.] W, SC, B; ~, MS(8-A), TS

31.37 wells?] W, SC, B; ~. MS(8-A), TS

32.3 Stahr.] W, SC, B; ~, MS(8-A), TS

32.21 stove.] W, SC, B; ~∧ RTS
    See "Fitzgerald's Revisions."
32.29 smiling.] W, SC, B; ~, MS(8-A), TS
32.30 Stahr.] MS(8-A), W, SC, B; ~, TS
32.33 Stahr.] B; ~, MS(8-A), TS, SC
33.6 demanded.] W, SC, B; ~, MS(8-A), TS
33.8 grinning. "Or] ed; ~, "~ MS(8-A), TS; ~, "or W, SC, B
33.12 Boxley,] W, SC, B; ~∧ MS(8-A), TS
33.12 said.] W, SC, B; ~, MS(8-A), TS
33.12 it,] W, B; ~∧ MS(8-A), TS, SC
33.14 said.] W, SC, B; ~∧ MS(8-A); ~, TS
33.15 said.] W, SC, B; ~, MS(8-A), TS
33.18 said.] W, SC, B; ~, MS(8-A), TS
33.19 Boxley.] ed; ~, MS(8-A), TS; ~; SC; ~: W, B
33.21–34.9 and scram. . . . There
    MS(8-A) for this passage consists of two typescript pages which
    Fitzgerald revised in holograph.
33.24 room.] W, SC, B; ~∧ MS(8-A), TS
33.24–34 room. . . . side
    MS(8-A) for this passage consists of a TS page Fitzgerald re-
    vised in holograph.
33.27 Katie] *stet* MS(8-A), TS, SC; Katy B
    Catherine Doolan is referred to at 101.36 as 'Katy'; naming her
    assistant 'Katie' causes possible confusion, but there is no evi-
    dence for emendation.
33.29 Stahr.] ed; ~∧ MS(8-A); ~, TS; ~: W, SC, B
33.30 explained.] W, SC, B; ~, MS(8-A), TS
33.34 hand] ed; hands MS(8-A), TS, W, SC, B
34.8 Dictograph] ed; dictagraph MS(8-A), TS; dictograph W, SC, B
34.19 Send _____ in] *stet* MS(8-A), TS; Send ____ in W; Send
    _____ in SC; Send Mr. Roderiguez in B
    Fitzgerald did not name this character. The name "Jesus Rogeri-
    guez, actor" is deleted on two of Fitzgerald's character lists.
34.19 Stahr.] W, SC, B; ~, MS(8-A), TS
34.24 said.] W, SC, B; ~, MS(8-A), TS
34.25 Stahr.] W, SC, B; ~, MS(8-A), TS
† 34.25 'Variety'?] ed; ∧~.∧ MS(8-A), TS; ∧~?∧ W, SC; ∧*Variety*?∧ B
34.25 picture's] W, SC, B; picture s MS(8-A); pictures TS
35.1 Stahr.] W, SC, B; ~, MS(8-A), TS
35.4 separating?] SC, B; ~. MS(8-A), TS

35.6   impatiently.] W, SC, B; ~, MS(8-A), TS

35.20   thought.] W, SC, B; ~, MS(8-A), TS

35.24   'Rainy Day'] ed; ∧~ ~∧ MS(8-A), TS, SC; ∧*Rainy Day*∧ B

36.1–2   Dictograph] ed; dictograph MS(8-A), TS, SC, B

36.6   gloomily. "And] ed; ~, "~ MS(8-A), TS; ~, "and W, SC, B

36.8   Stahr.] W, SC, B; ~, MS(8-A), TS

36.11   Rose] *stet* MS(8-A), TS, SC; Jane B
         See Introduction, pp. lxxiii–iv.

36.12–26 dried. . . . revulsion.
         Fitzgerald transferred the description of Rose Meloney from
         Episode 9. The MS(8-A) for this paragraph reads: 'In the outer
         office two members of the conference group had already waited
         ten minutes—Wylie White and Rose Meloney the latter was a
         (insert description from 1 + 2 Episode 9.' See also Graham to
         Perkins, 11 January 1941 (Introduction, p. lxviii).

36.28–29 Rienmund∧ . . . Broaca∧] MS(8-A); ~, . . . ~, TS; Rein-
         mund, . . . ~, W, SC, B
         Rienmund and Broaca are identified again at 37.20–22.

37.8   Episode 9] *stet* MS(9-A), TS; *omitted* W, SC, B

† 37.13   "Miracle."] ed; ∧~.∧ MS(9-A), TS; ∧*Miracle.*∧ W, SC, B

37.16   bad] ed; badly MS(9-A), TS, SC, B

37.18   wish,] MS(9-A), W, SC, B; ~∧ TS

37.20   besides] W, SC, B; beside RTS
         See "Fitzgerald's Revisions."

37.21   supervisors, and John Broaca,] W, SC, B; supervisors; Broaca
         MS(9-A), TS; supervisors and John Broaca, RTS

38.5   native Americans] *stet*
         Fitzgerald was referring to native-born American gentiles.

38.10–11 course, would have been recognizable in any country as] ed;
         course, in any country would have been recognizable in any
         country as RTS; course, in any country would have been recog-
         nizable as SC, B
         See "Fitzgerald's Revisions."

38.11   order. He] SC, B; ~. he RTS
         See "Fitzgerald's Revisions."

38.16   Stahr.] W, SC, B; ~, MS(9-A), TS

38.19   thoughtfully.] W, SC, B; ~, MS(9-A), TS

38.23   said.] W, SC, B; ~, MS(9-A), TS

38.25   Rienmund.] ed; ~, MS(9-A), TS; Reinmund; W; ~: SC, B

38.27   it,] B; ~∧ MS(9-A), TS, SC

38.34 clue?] ed; ~, MS(9-A), TS, SC, B
38.36 Stahr.] W, SC, B; ~, MS(9-A), TS
† 38.37 Colman] W, SC, B; Coleman MS(9-A), TS
39.3 desk,] W, SC, B; ~∧ MS(9-A), TS
39.3 if it were] SC, B; if were MS(9-A), TS
39.5 said.] W, SC, B; ~, MS(9-A), TS
39.10 Broaca.] W, SC, B; ~, MS(9-A), TS
39.11 sharply.] W, SC, B; ~, MS(9-A), TS
39.13 what?'∧"] W, SC, B; ~?'." MS(9-A), TS
39.14 said.] W, SC, B; ~, MS(9-A), TS
39.16 Stahr.] W, SC, B; ~, MS(9-A), TS
39.25 suddenly.] W, SC, B; ~, MS(9-A), TS
39.25 see, Monroe,] W, SC, B; ~∧ ~∧ MS(9-A), TS
39.30 said.] W, SC, B; ~, MS(9-A), TS
† 40.8–9, 14–15 Carroll and MacMurray] ed; Carrol and McMurray
          MS(9-A), TS, SC; Corliss and McKelway B
          See Introduction, p. lxxiii.
40.9–10 in future] MS(9-A); in the future TS, SC, B
40.12 around. "Shall] ed; ~, "~ MS(9-A), TS; ~, "shall W, SC; ~.
          "—shall B
40.19 bluntly.] W, SC, B; ~, MS(9-A), TS
40.24 unkindly.] W, SC, B; ~, MS(9-A), TS
40.24 fresh?] B; ~. MS(9-A), TS, SC
40.26 you,] W, SC, B; ~∧ MS(9-A), TS
40.30 warningly.] W, SC, B; ~, MS(9-A), TS
40.33 to a man] W, SC, B; to man MS(9-A), TS
† 41.1 Hays] B; Hayes MS(9-A), TS, SC
41.6 Wylie.] W, SC, B; ~, MS(9-A), TS
41.20 he,] W, SC, B; ~∧ MS(9-A), TS
41.29 sigh.] W, SC, B; ~, MS(9-A), TS
41.32 Stahr.] B; ~, MS(9-A), TS, SC
42.15–43.4 could. . . . them."
          MS(9-A) for this passage consists of a typescript page Fitzgerald
          revised in holograph.
42.17 danger,] W, SC, B; ~∧ MS(9-A), TS
42.23 Meloney.] MS(9-A), W, SC, B; ~, TS
42.25 Stahr.] W, SC, B; ~, MS(9-A), TS
43.19 foredoomed,] W, SC, B; fordoomed, MS(9-A); foredoomed∧ TS
43.26 fawned] MS(9-A), W, SC, B; fauned TS
43.27 up—not yet. He] *stet* MS(9-A), TS, SC; up. He B

† 43.31   Peal's] ed; Peels MS(9-A), TS; Peel's W, SC, B

  44.2–4   over. *space break* ¶ "Any messages?" ¶ "Mr.] *stet* RTS; over. ¶ "Mr. TS

      MS(9-A) for Episode 9 ends with 'over.' Fitzgerald continued the episode (44.4–27) with material he revised from the opening of Rejected Episode 10. Wilson inserted the passage about Mr. Marcus printed in B (43.29–44.17) from Fitzgerald's Rejected Episode 10. See "Wilson's Alterations" and Introduction, p. xlix.

  44.28   Episode 10] *stet* RTS; ~ 11 MS(10-A), TS; *omitted* W, SC, B

  44.29   guest⋀] MS(10-A); ~, TS, SC, B

  44.29   Agge⋀] MS(10-A); ~, TS, SC, B

  44.32   sometimes asking questions about] W, SC, B; sometimes asking questions sometimes about MS(10-A), TS

      Fitzgerald first wrote 'asking questions sometimes about' and then inserted 'sometimes' before 'asking' without deleting the original 'sometimes'.

  45.4   Englishman—] MS(10-A); ~⋀ TS; ~; W, SC, B

  45.9   functioned with] ed; functioned, as has been said, with MS(10-A), TS; still managed to function with W, SC, B

      Marcus's 'resilience' has not been previously mentioned; but his slipping mind is noted in Rejected Episode 10: 'the once brilliant steel trap mind of Mr Marcus which was intermittently slipping.'

  45.12   grey] MS, B; gray TS, SC

  45.30   Flieshacker⋀] ed; Flieshhacker⋀ MS; Flieshhacker, TS; Fleishhacker, W; Fleishacker, SC, B

  45.31   lawyer⋀] MS(10-A); ~, TS, SC, B

  45.33   Foreign Legion] B; foriegn legion MS(10-A); foreign legion TS, SC

  46.6   Monroe?] W, SC, B; ~, MS(10-A), TS

† 46.14   'Hell's Angels'] ed; ⋀Hells ~⋀ MS(10-A); ⋀Hell's ~⋀ TS; ⋀*Hell's Angels*⋀ W, SC, B

† 46.14   'Ben-Hur'] ed; ⋀~⋀~⋀ MS(10-A), TS; ⋀*Ben*⋀*Hur*⋀ W, SC, B

  46.16   Popolous] ed; Populous MS(10-A), TS; Populos W; Popolos SC, B

  46.17–19   double talk that reminded Prince Agge of Mike Van Dyke except that it tried to be and succeeded in being clear instead of confusing.] *stet* MS(10-A), TS; double talk. W, SC, B

      The MS passage in which Pops Carlson (Mike Van Dyke) confuses Agge with double talk is in Rejected Episode 9.

46.25   signalled] MS(10-A), B; signaled TS, SC

46.30   said.] W, SC, B; ~, MS(10-A), TS

46.35   Popolous.] ed; Skouras, MS(10-A); Popolous, TS; Popolos. W, SC, B

47.14   amazement,] W, SC, B; ~∧ MS(10-A), TS

47.19   do—] ed; ~∧ MS(10-A), TS; ~, SC; ~: B

47.20   Kennedy,] ed; ~∧ MS(10-A), TS; ~— W, SC, B

47.29   Stahr.] W, SC, B; ~, MS(10-A), TS

48.7   Stahr.] W, SC, B; ~, MS(10-A), TS

48.12   up,] W, SC, B; ~ ∧ MS(10-A), TS

48.13   shining] MS(10-A), W, SC, B; shing TS

48.14   'Hell's Angels'] ed; ∧Hells ~∧ MS(10-A); ∧Hell's ~∧ TS; ∧Hell's Angels∧ W, SC, B

48.15   says] ed; say MS(10-A); said TS; has said W, SC, B

        In MS Fitzgerald revised 'as I hear Mr Brady' to 'as Pat Brady' but neglected to revise the following verb 'say'.

48.19   downcast] W, SC, B; down cast MS(10-A), TS

48.21–22   room. *space break* ¶ Coming] *stet*

        The MS for Episode 10 (10-A) ends with 'room.' The MS for the material after the space break starts a new episode headed 'Episode 12 (1st part)' (10 Continuation-A). Fitzgerald revised the TS (10 Continuation-C), changing the heading to 'Episode 10 Continuation'. The first 1½ pages of this TS were then retyped as the end of Episode 10 (10-C). The rest of 10 Continuation-C was interpolated into MS(11-A) for Episode 11. See chart below.

MS (10 Continuation-A)

┌─── TS (10 Continuation-C) ───┐

first 1½ pages	last 3½ pages
revised and retyped	revised and inserted
as end of TS for	in MS for Episode 11
Episode 10 (TS 10-C)	(MS 11-A)

48.25   sideburns] W, SC, B; side burns MS(10 Continuation-A), TS

† 48.25   First Empire] W, SC, B; first empire MS(10 Continuation-A), TS

† 48.31   Nicolay's] W, SC, B; Moolay's TS

        MS (10 Continuation-A) reads 'Schwartztrube's', which was typed as 'Schwietztrube's' (10 Continuation-C); Fitzgerald revised the first typescript to 'Nicolay's', but the typist misread it and typed 'Moolay's' in the second typescript (10-C).

48.31   biography] W, SC, B; Biography MS(10 Continuation-A), TS

48.32–33   he had hated] MS(10 Continuation-A); he hated TS, SC, B

48.36   Agge,] W, SC, B; ~/\ MS(10 Continuation-A), TS
49.8   him.] W, SC, B; ~, MS(10 Continuation-A), TS
49.21   moment.] ed; ~, TS; ~: W, SC, B
49.25   For Episode 11] RTS; ~ ~ 10 MS(Insert for 10-A), TS; CHAPTER
        4 SC; CHAPTER IV B

> Fitzgerald altered TS '10' to '11'; but this scene comes between
> Episodes 10 and 11, and it is not clear whether he intended to
> retain it. He wrote at the head of the typed page: 'No good——I
> think, <u>out</u>'. His note on MS for the opening (49.26–50.6) of this
> episode reads: 'Copy this once as is. Then copy this page as it was
> before I crossed it out—marking it *Correction for 10*'. He did not
> indicate his preference between the two openings. Wilson pub-
> lished the *Correction for 10,* changing the heading to 'Chapter 4',
> inserting 'outplay' in the space on the TS between 'not' and 'him',
> and making other alterations. The TS text without Wilson's alter-
> ations follows:

> "How are you, Monroe," said Red Ridingwood. "I'm glad you
> came down."
> Stahr walked past him, heading across the great stage toward
> the set of a brilliant room that would be used tomorrow. Director
> Ridingwood followed, realizing after a moment that however fast
> he walked Stahr managed to be a step or two ahead. He recog-
> nized the indication of displeasure—he had used it himself. He
> had had his own studio once and he had used everything. There
> was no stop Stahr could pull that would surprise him. His task
> was delivery of effects and was the delivery of situations and Stahr
> by effective business could not ⟨space for missing word⟩ him on
> his own grounds. Goldwyn had once interfered with him, and
> Ridinghood had led Goldwyn into trying to act out a part in front
> of fifty people and the result had been as he anticipated. His own
> authority had been restored.
> Stahr reached the brilliant set and stopped.
> "It's no good," said Ridingwood, "No imagination.

49.26   How you] *stet* MS(Insert for 10-A), TS; How are you W, SC, B

> The typist added the word 'are' when typing the *Correction for
> 10.*

49.26   Ridingwood.] MS(Insert for 10-A); ~, TS
50.5   Ridingwood.] ed; Ridinghood, MS (Insert for 10-A); Ridingwood,
        TS
50.7   asked/\ ] MS(Insert for 10-A); ~, TS, SC, B
50.8   him.] W, SC, B; ~, MS(Insert for 10-A), TS

† 50.8   Art] W, SC, B; art MS(Insert for 10-A), TS

50.11   sorry,] B; ~∧ MS(Insert for 10-A), TS, SC

50.11   patiently. "But] ed; ~, "~ MS(Insert for 10-A), TS; ~, "but W, SC, B

50.17   Host] MS(Insert for 10-A); host TS, SC, B

50.21   emollient] W, SC, B; emolument MS(Insert for 10-A), TS

50.26   radiunt. . . . radiunt] *stet* MS(Insert for 10-A), TS, B; radiant. . . . radiant SC

50.33   ——ing] *stet* MS(Insert for 10-A), TS, B; ____ing SC
       Fitzgerald wrote '——ing' in MS, indicating that he did not ex-
       pect to print the word. Bowers to Bruccoli, 8 February 1990: "You
       are editing a period piece. Stay in its period. Otherwise a clash of
       sensibilities." The word 'fucking' had appeared in Ernest Heming-
       way's *To Have and Have Not* (New York: Scribners, 1937).

51.6   said.] B; ~, MS(Insert for 10-A), TS, SC

51.10   said.] SC, B; ~, MS(Insert for 10-A), TS

51.24   said.] W, SC, B; ~, MS(Insert for 10-A), TS

51.26   it] MS(Insert for 10-A), SC, B; if TS

51.32   take?] SC, B; ~, MS(Insert for 10-A), TS

51.33   Stahr∧] MS(Insert for 10-A), B; ~, TS, SC

51.33   grimly.] W, SC, B; ~, MS(Insert for 10-A), TS

52.1   Stahr∧] MS(Insert for 10-A); ~, TS, SC, B

52.1   tersely.] W, SC, B; ~, MS(Insert for 10-A), TS

52.3–5   have to do the next picture he was offered whether he liked it or
       not. It meant a slight] MS(Insert for 10-A); have slight TS, SC, B
       The omission in TS was the result of secretarial eyeskip in typ-
       ing the MS.

52.10   suddenly.] W, SC, B; ~, MS(Insert for 10-A), TS

52.15   Episode 11] *stet* MS(11-A), TS; *omitted* W, SC, B

† 53.17   *coureur du bois*] ed; *courrier de bois* MS(11-A), TS; *courrier du
       bois* W, SC, B

53.18   Colman] W, SC, B; Coleman MS(11-A), TS

53.28   quietly.] W, SC, B; ~, MS(11-A), TS

53.36   Stahr.] W, SC, B; ~, MS(11-A), TS

54.5   Stahr.] W, SC, B; ~, MS(11-A), TS

54.18   put] W, SC, B; Put MS(11-A), TS

54.25   story,] W, SC, B; ~∧ MS(11-A), TS

54.26   darkness.] W, SC, B; ~, MS(11-A), TS

54.29   Mort] *stet* MS(11-A), TS, SC; Lee B
       Mort Flieshacker is a lawyer, not a production man, and would

not be viewing the rushes or shooting other scenes. The first edition replaces him with Lee Kapper, the art director, who is present.

54.31   Flieshacker.] ed; Flieshacker, MS(11-A), TS; Fleishacker. W, SC; Kapper. B

54.31   Stage 6] B; stage six MS(11-A), TS, SC

54.34   close-up] ed; ~∧~ MS(11-A), TS, SC, B

55.8   said.] SC, B; ~, MS(11-A), TS

55.14   leaned his head forward] MS(11-A); leaned forward TS, SC, B

55.28   said.] W, SC, B; ~, MS(11-A), TS

56.1   said.] W, SC, B; ~, MS(11-A), TS

56.6   man,] W, SC, B; ~∧ MS(11-A), TS

56.9   had] W, SC, B; has MS(11-A), TS

56.12–13 They did it wrong. Again they met, they started, they went on.] *stet* MS(11-A), TS; *omitted* SC, B

56.19   it,] W, SC, B; ~∧ MS(11-A), TS

56.25   picture."] W, SC, B; ~.∧ MS(11-A), TS

57.2   good. ∧Can't] W, SC, B; good," said Stahr, "Can't MS(11-A), TS; good, "Can't RTS

57.3   'Steppes'?] ed; ∧~∧. MS(11-A), TS; ∧*Steppes*∧. W; ∧*Steppes*∧? SC, B

57.4   director. "But] ed; ~∧ "~ MS(11-A); ~, "~ TS; ~, "but SC, B

57.13   device] W, SC, B; devise MS(11-A), TS

† 57.14   "Manon"] ed; *Manon* MS(11-A), TS, SC, B

57.24   20/19] ed; 19-20 MS(11-A), TS, SC, B

57.29   Marquand] *stet* MS(11-A), TS, SC; Tarleton B
        See Introduction, pp. lxxiii–iv.

57.31–58.19 ¶ "These are. . . . where there was
        MS(11-A) for this passage consists of a typed page revised in Fitzgerald's holograph which he transferred from Episode 7.

57.31   Agge. "And] W, SC; ~, "~ MS(11-A), TS; ~, "and B

57.33   anyone!] W, SC, B; ~? MS(11-A), TS

58.2   playwrights,] ed; playrights, MS(11-A); playwrights— TS, SC, B

58.14–15 again." *space break* ¶ He] MS(11-A); ~." *no break* ¶ ~ TS, SC, B
        The space break was lost in TS because the paragraph following the break started a new page.

58.20   picture,] W, SC, B; ~∧ MS(11-A), TS

58.24–60.20 ¶ When. . . . Wilshire—"
        MS(11-A) for this passage consists of 3½ typed pages revised in Fitz-

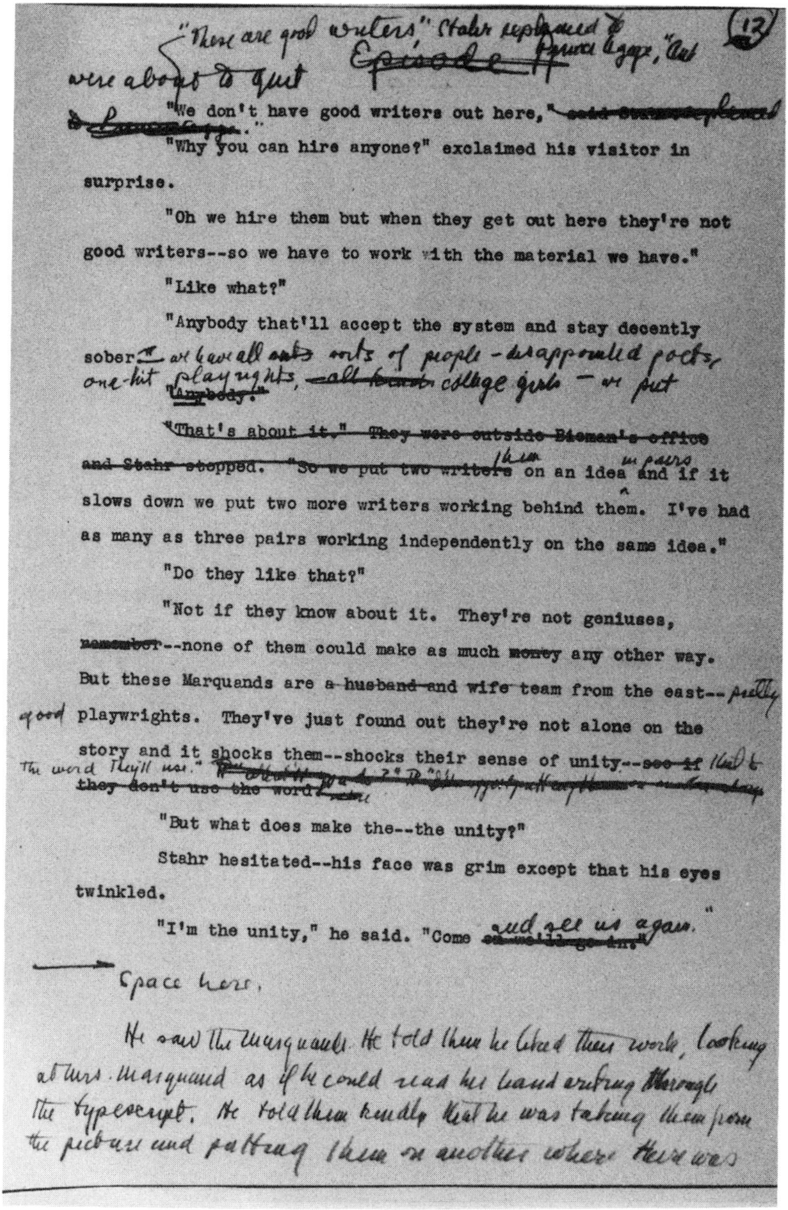
(13)

"These are good writers," Stahr explained to Prince Agge, "but were about to quit
~~Episode 11~~

"We don't have good writers out here," ~~said Stahr explained to Boxley~~.

"Why you can hire anyone?" exclaimed his visitor in surprise.

"Oh we hire them but when they get out here they're not good writers--so we have to work with the material we have."

"Like what?"

"Anybody that'll accept the system and stay decently sober--we have all sorts of people--disappointed poets, one-hit playwrights, ~~all kinds~~ college girls--we put ~~"Anybody?"~~

~~"That's about it." They were outside Bieman's office and Stahr stopped. "So we put two writers~~ them on an idea in pairs and if it slows down we put two more writers working behind them. I've had as many as three pairs working independently on the same idea."

"Do they like that?"

"Not if they know about it. They're not geniuses, ~~remember~~--none of them could make as much ~~money~~ any other way. But these Marquands are a ~~husband and wife~~ team from the east--pretty good playwrights. They've just found out they're not alone on the story and it shocks them--shocks their sense of unity--~~see if~~ that's the word they'll use." ~~they don't use the word~~ [illegible]

"But what does make the--the unity?"

Stahr hesitated--his face was grim except that his eyes twinkled.

"I'm the unity," he said. "Come and see us again." ~~[illegible]~~

→ Space here.

He saw the Marquands. He told them he liked their work, looking at Mrs. Marquand as if he could read her handwriting through the typescript. He told them kindly that he was taking them from the picture and putting them on another where there was

See *The Love of the Last Tycoon*, pp. 57–58.

gerald's holograph which he transfered from 'Episode 10 Continuation' (draft 10 Continuation-C). See Textual Note on 48.21–22.

58.25   Stahr,] B; ~∧ MS(11-A), TS, SC

58.28   wanted.] W, SC, B; ~? MS(11-A), TS

59.3   said.] B; ~, MS(11-A), TS, SC

59.15   trick?] W, SC, B; ~. MS(11-A), TS

59.16–17   peculiar . . . touched it] *stet* MS(11-A), TS, SC, B
     Fitzgerald repeated this phrase at 64.21–22.

59.27–28   skin-deep] B; ~∧~ MS(11-A), TS, SC

59.29   said.] W, SC, B; ~, MS(11-A), TS

59.35   married." He] ed; ~," he MS(11-A), TS, SC, B

60.10   you?] W, SC, B; ~, MS(11-A), TS

60.19   here?] SC, B; ~. MS(11-A), TS

60.20   drug store] ed; drugstore MS(11-A), TS, SC; drug-store B

60.21   was quarter] MS(11-A); was a quarter TS, SC, B

60.24   ignored.] MS(11-A), SC, B; ~∧ TS

61.10   Diogenes] ed; Diocenes MS(11-A), TS; Euripides W, SC, B
     Fitzgerald was referring to Diogenes of Sinopé (fourth century B.C.), the celebrated Cynic philosopher. Wilson's emendation to Euripides, the Athenian tragic poet, is unnecessary and inappropriate. As a graduate of the University of Salonika, Zavras would have a correct knowledge of Greek classical civilization. The spelling errors in this passage are Fitzgerald's—not Zavras's.

61.10   picture] MS(11-A), W, SC, B; pictures TS

61.11   simply.] W, SC, B; ~, MS(11-A), TS

61.11   Asclepius] ed; Esculpias MS(11-A), TS; Aristophanes W, SC, B
     Wilson's emendation to Aristophanes, the Greek comic dramatist, is imperceptive: since Stahr has "cured" Zavras's blindness, it is appropriate for Stahr to be compared to Asclepius, the Greek god of medicine (Latin form: Aesculapius).

61.11   Menander] W, SC, B; Minanorus MS(11-A), TS
     Fitzgerald was probably referring to Menander, the Greek comic dramatist. Mimnermus, the seventh-century B.C. author of elegies and love poems, is less likely.

61.16   Zavras.] W, SC, B; Garcia, MS(11-A), TS

61.19   now?] W, SC, B; ~. MS(11-A), TS

61.23   the oracle] *stet* MS(11-A), TS; the Delphic oracle W, SC, B

61.23   Zavras.] W, SC, B; Garcia, MS(11-A), TS

† 61.23–24   The solver of Eleusinian mysteries.] ed; ~ ~ ~ Elusianian ~. MS(11-A), TS; *omitted* W, SC; The Oedipus who solved the riddle. B

61.27   Pete.] SC, B; Pedro, MS(11-A), TS; Pedro. W

61.31   my] W, SC, B; My MS(11-A), TS

61.32   Zavras'] B; Garcia's MS(11-A), TS; Zavra's W, SC

61.34   voice:] ed; ~∧ MS(11-A); ~. TS, SC, B

62.6   Episode 12] *stet* RTS; ~ 13 MS(12-E), TS; *omitted* W, SC, B
       MS(12-E) for Episode 12 begins with three typed pages heavily re-
       vised in Fitzgerald's holograph which correspond to 62.7–64.14.

62.28   drug store] ed; ~-~ MS(12-E), TS, SC, B

63.1   asked.] W, SC, B; ~, MS(12-E), TS

63.4   polite.] W, B; ~, MS(12-E), TS, SC

63.4   smile.] W, SC, B; ~, MS(12-E), TS

63.9   her get] *stet* MS(12-E), TS; her to get W, SC, B

63.15   said.] W, SC, B; ~, MS(12-E), TS

63.16   startled.] W, SC, B; ~, MS(12-E), TS

63.26   intuition.] W, SC, B; ~, MS(12-E), TS

63.33   asked.] W, SC, B; ~, MS(12-E), TS

63.34   said.] W, SC, B; ~, MS(12-E), TS

64.13–14   good night] MS(12-E), B; goodnight TS, SC

64.27   said.] W, SC, B; ~, MS(12-E), TS

64.32   closer] *stet* MS(12-E), TS; slower SC, B

64.34   Edna.] W, SC, B; ~, MS(12-E), TS

65.4   forehead.] W, SC, B; ~, MS(12-E), TS

65.16   Stahr.] W, SC, B; ~, MS(12-E), TS

65.27   said.] MS (12-E), W, SC, B; ~, TS

66.19   said.] W, SC, B; ~, MS(12-E), TS

66.28   and left with] ed; and left him with MS(12-E), TS; and it left him
       with W, SC, B

66.31   car,] W, SC, B; ~; MS(12-E), TS
       When Fitzgerald revised MS 'pressed' to 'pressing' he neglected
       to change the punctuation.

67.16   illness,] W, SC, B; ~∧ MS(End of 12-A), TS

67.26   Episode 13] *stet* TS; 13. (1st part) MS(13-A); Chapter 5 W;
       CHAPTER 5 SC; CHAPTER V B

67.32   suggested.] W, SC, B; ~, MS(13-A), TS

68.1   book.] W, SC, B; ~, MS(13-A), TS

68.2   East] W, SC, B; east MS(13-A), TS

† 68.11   "The Thundering Beat of My Heart,"] ed; ∧~ ~ ~ ~ my ~,∧
       MS(13-A); ∧~ ~ ~ ~ My ~,∧ TS; ∧*The Thundering Beat of
       My Heart,*∧ W, SC, B

68.18   four?] SC, B; ~. MS(13-A), TS

68.23   offer?] W, SC, B; ~. MS(13-A), TS

68.24   conviction.] ed; ∼, MS(13-A), TS, SC, B

† 68.28   Southampton] B; Southhampton MS(13-A), TS, SC

68.29   "Gone" or "Lost"] ed; "*Gone*" or "*Lost*" MS(13-A), TS; ∧*Gone*∧ or ∧*Lost*∧ W, SC, B

68.31   Depression] ed; depression MS(13-A), TS, SC, B

68.35   Girl,] ed; girl∧ MS(13-A); Girl∧ TS; *Girl*∧ W, SC; *Girl,* B

68.37   "Lost" and "Gone"] ed; ∧∼∧ ∼ ∧∼∧ MS, TS; ∧*Lost*∧ ∼ ∧*Gone*∧ W, SC, B

† 69.1   "Lovely To Look At∧"] ed; ∧∼ to ∼ at∧∧ MS(13-A); ∧∼ to ∼ At∧∧ TS; ∧*Lovely to Look At,*∧ W, SC, B

† 69.3   Mountain] W, SC, B; mountain MS(13-A), TS

69.4   sometimes] W, SC, B; sometime MS(13-A), TS

69.6   know-w-w] MS(13-A); know - w TS; know—w W, SC; *know-w* B

69.7   Stahr?] W, SC, B; ∼, MS(13-A), TS

69.7   said.] W, SC, B; ∼, MS(13-A), TS

69.7   do,] W, SC, B; ∼∧ MS(13-A), TS

69.9   said.] SC, B; ∼, MS(13-A), TS

69.12   Celia] MS(13-A); Cecelia TS; Cecilia W, SC, B
Fitzgerald wrote 'Ceci' and revised to 'Celia' in MS.

69.17   Wylie. "And] ed; ∼, "∼ MS(13-A), TS; ∼, "and W, SC, B

69.23   Wylie.] W, SC, B; ∼, MS(13-A), TS

69.27   shiver.] W, SC, B; ∼, MS(13-A), TS

69.34   "Do you want me to walk out and get home?"] *stet* MS(13-A), TS, SC, B
The transposal of words was deliberate.

69.35–36   Beverly Hills. . . . Hollywood] *stet*
Beverly Hills is a city; Hollywood is part of the city of Los Angeles.

70.8   fifty-fifty] W, SC, B; ∼∧∼ MS(13-A), TS

70.16   pockets] ed; pocket MS(13-A), TS, SC, B

70.17   tonight?] SC, B; ∼, MS(13-A), TS

70.20   considered.] B; ∼, MS(13-A), TS, SC

70.28   married,] W, SC, B; ∼∧ MS(13-A), TS

70.29   Robby] W, SC, B; Robbie MS(13-A), TS

70.33   Yes,] W, SC, B; ∼. MS(13-A), TS

70.35   unexpectedly.] W, SC, B; ∼, MS(13-A), TS

71.4   minute.] W, SC, B; ∼, MS(13-A), TS

71.6   It'd be like marrying a doctor.] *stet* MS(13-A), TS, SC; *omitted* B
Possibly deleted in proof because of repetition of phrase at 25.12.

71.9   way,] W, SC, B; ~∧ MS(13-A), TS

71.15   as in my] W, SC, B; as my MS(13-A), TS

71.31   13 (continued)] *stet* TS; *13 (continued)* MS(13-D); *omitted* W, SC, B

72.9   Mother] ed; mother MS(13-D), TS, SC, B

72.22   pockets] W, SC, B; pocket MS(13-D), TS

† 72.26 Henie] W, SC, B; Hienie MS(13-D); Heine TS

72.27   less and less funny] ed; less and funny MS(13-D); less funny TS, SC, B

72.36   ∧sneak∧preview∧] ed; "~∧~" W, SC, B; "~-~" MS(13-D), TS

73.9–10 smiling. ¶ The] *stet* TS, SC, B

         It is impossible to be certain whether Fitzgerald's paragraph symbol in MS(13-D) is deleted.

73.29   laughed.] W, SC, B; ~, MS(13-D), TS

73.29   curiosity!] W, SC, B; ~? MS(13-D), TS

73.36   It's] W, SC, B; it's MS(13-D), TS

74.6   said. "And] ed; ~, "~ MS(13-D), TS; ~, "and W, SC, B

† 74.10 Loudoun] W, SC; Louden MS(13-D), TS; Loudon B

74.22   there∧] MS(13-D), W, SC, B; ~, TS

74.23   good bye] MS(13-D); goodbye TS, SC, B

74.26   Co.,] ed; Co∧, MS(13-D); Company, TS, SC, B

74.34   gently. "But] ed; ~, "~ MS(13-D), TS; ~, "but W, SC, B

74.36   wearily.] MS(13-D), W, SC, B; ~, TS

75.3   Stahr.] W, SC, B; ~, MS(13-D), TS

75.4   depth] W, SC, B; depths TS

         It is impossible to determine whether MS(13-D) reads 'depth' or 'depths'.

75.18   good bye] MS(13-D); goodbye TS, SC, B

75.24   retracted.] W, SC, B; ~, MS(13-D), TS

75.31   said.] W, SC, B; ~, MS(13-D), TS

75.32   alone?] W, SC, B; ~. MS(13-D), TS

76.2   said.] W, SC, B; ~, MS(13-D), TS

76.13   drug store] MS(13-D); drugstore TS, SC; drug-store B

76.16   said.] B; ~, MS(13-D), TS, SC

76.20   said. "What] ed; ~, "~ MS(13-D), TS; ~, "—what W, SC, B

76.27   grimly.] W, SC, B; ~, MS(13-D), TS

76.28   tomorrow,] W, SC, B; ~∧ MS(13-D), TS

76.28   you?] W, SC, B; ~. MS(13-D), TS

76.33   would find out] W, SC, B; would out MS(13-D), TS

77.1   said.] MS(13-D), W, SC, B; ~, TS

77.9   three—] W, SC, B; ~∧ MS(13-D), TS
77.14   innocently.] W, SC, B; ~, MS(13-D), TS
77.17   said. "Changed] ed; ~, "~ MS(13-D), TS; ~, "—changed W, SC, B
77.22   vaguely. "Someone] ed; ~, "~ MS(13-D), TS; ~, "—someone W, SC, B
† 77.28 Glenn] ed; Glen MS(13-D), TS, SC, B
78.1   Section 14] *stet* MS(14-A), TS; *omitted* W, SC, B
78.4   veil∧] W, SC, B; ~, MS(14-A), TS
78.6   and black] MS(14-A); and a black TS, SC, B
78.9   person as before] W, SC, B; person before MS(14-A), TS
78.11   brow] *stet* MS(14-A), TS, SC; brown B
78.11   coco-colored] *stet* MS(14-A), TS; coca-~ SC; cool-~ B
78.16   night?] ed; ~, MS(14-A), TS, SC, B
79.14   things.] ed; ~∧ MS(14-A), TS; ~: W, SC, B
79.20   said.] W, SC, B; ~, MS(14-A), TS
79.26   said.] W, SC, B; ~, MS(14-A), TS
79.32–33 back." ¶ They stopped] *stet* TS, SC, B
        It is unclear whether Fitzgerald decided to retain the lines in MS(14-A) between 'back." ' and '¶ They stopped. . . .' He crossed out: '¶ "Success story." ¶ "I spend most of my time concealing how little I know. They think I know everything now." ' He marked the second paragraph to be copied for his notes but also wrote *stet* in the margin beside it.
79.33   them] MS(14-A); him TS, SC, B
80.4   East] W, SC, B; east MS(14-A), TS
80.8–9   a while. ¶ They] ed; awhile. ~ MS(14-A); ~. ¶ ~ TS, SC, B
80.20   said. "Much] ed; ~, "~ MS(14-A), TS; ~, "—much W, SC, B
80.32   demanded. "Another] ed; ~, "~ MS(14-A), TS; ~, "—another W, SC, B
80.32   roof?] W, SC, B; ~. MS(14-A), TS
80.35   said. "A] ed; ~, "~ MS(14-A), TS; ~, "a W, SC, B
81.4   rose-and-blue] ed; ~∧~∧~ MS(14-A), TS, SC, B
81.6   said.] W, SC, B; ~, MS(14-A), TS
81.21   Kathleen.] W, SC, B; ~, MS(14-A), TS
81.23   Coke] ed; coke MS(14-A), TS, SC, B
81.34   said∧] MS(14-A), B; ~, TS, SC
81.34   cheerfully.] W, SC, B; ~, MS(14-A), TS
82.1   minute.] B; ~, MS(14-A), TS, SC
82.4   mañana] W, SC; manana MS(14-A), TS; *mañana* B

82.9   And,] MS(14-A); ~∧ TS, SC, B

82.10   a ping-pong] B; a ping∧pong MS(14-A), TS, SC

82.11   another ping-pong] MS(14-A), B; ~ ~∧~ TS, SC

82.11   laid turf beyond] ed; laid beyond MS(14-A), TS; laid sod beyond W, SC, B

        MS has deleted 'grass' replaced by deleted 'turn'. Graham's note on TS reads: 'ORIGINALLY HAD "GRASS" BUT HAD CROSSED IT OUT WITHOUT SUBSTITUTING NEW WORD S. G.'

82.12   admitted.] W, SC, B; ~, MS(14-A), TS

82.21   him. "Not] ed; ~, "~ MS(14-A), TS; ~, "—not W, SC, B

82.22   girls?] W, SC, B; ~. MS(14-A), TS

82.26   lilt] MS; tilt TS, SC, B

82.32   Hey] MS(14-B); hey TS, SC, B

83.1   ring?] SC, B; ~. MS(14-B), TS

83.26, 30   orang-outang] W, SC, B; orangatang MS(14-B); orangutang TS

84.1   said∧] MS(14-B); ~, TS, SC, B

84.1   minute.] W, SC, B; ~, MS(14-B), TS

84.4   Orang-outang] ed; Orangatang MS(14-B); orangutang TS; orang-outang W, SC, B

84.8   Orang-outang] ed; Oranatang MS(14-B); orangutang TS; orang-outang W, SC, B

† 84.10   'King Kong'] ed; ∧~ ~∧ MS(14-B), TS; ∧*King Kong*∧ W, SC, B

† 84.11   'The Hairy Ape.'] ed; ∧the Hairy Ape.∧ MS(14-B), TS; ∧*The Hairy Ape.*∧ W, SC, B

84.12   good bye] MS(14-B); goodbye TS, SC, B

84.16   orang-outang] W, SC, B; oranatang MS(14-B); orangutang TS

84.17   Section 14 (2nd part)] *stet* MS(14-E), TS; *omitted* W, SC, B

84.29   matting] MS(14-E), W, SC, B; malting TS

        Graham's note on the TS reads: 'MATTING S.G.'

85.10   drug store] MS(14-E); drugstore TS, SC; drug-store B

85.14   drug stores] MS(14-E); drugstores TS, SC; drug-stores B

85.18   They shared] *stet* TS, SC, B; Then shared MS(14-E)

85.19   drug store] ed; ~-~ MS(14-E), TS, SC, B

85.19   sour,] W, SC, B; ~∧ MS(14-E), TS

85.29   headlights] W, SC, B; head lights MS(14-E), TS

85.31   this.] W, SC, B; ~, MS(14-E), TS

85.36   I] *stet* MS(14-E), TS; It SC, B

86.12   touched] W, SC, B; toughed MS(14-E), TS

86.15–16 then "Oh"] W, SC, B; ~ ∧oh∧ MS(14-E), TS
86.20 how] MS(14-E); now TS, SC, B
86.23 exultant;] W, SC, B; ~∧ MS(14-E), TS
86.26 inside,] W, SC, B; ~∧ MS(14-E), TS
86.28 said. "Not] ed; ~, "~ MS(14-E), TS; ~, "—not W; ~, "∧~ SC, B
87.4 Section 14 (Part III)] *stet* MS(14-H), TS; *omitted* W, SC, B
87.7 raincoat∧] MS(14-H); ~, TS, SC, B
87.9 grandfather] ed; grandfathers MS(14-H); grandfather's TS, SC, B
87.18 her,] W, SC, B; ~∧ MS(14-H), TS
87.28 raincoat] ed; rain coat MS(14-H), TS, SC, B
88.17 room,] W, SC, B; ~∧ MS(14-H), TS
88.19 said.] B; ~, MS(14-H), TS, SC
88.22 of shoes] MS(14-H); of their shoes TS, SC, B
       Fitzgerald wrote 'their shoes' and revised to 'the soles of shoes' in MS.
88.34 asked.] W, SC, B; ~, MS(14-H), TS
89.1 brooded.] W, SC, B; ~, MS(14-H), TS
89.7 thoughts.] W, SC, B; ~, MS(14-H), TS
89.15 English] SC, B; Brittish MS(14-H); British TS
       Graham to Wilson, 11 January 1941: " . . . the word 'English' for British. I was his technical adviser on the English stuff and would have told him to make that change." Graham emended TS 'British' to 'ENGLISH'.
89.29 Edna'—] ed; ~'∧ MS(14-H), TS; ~,' W, SC, B
89.32 said.] B; ~, MS(14-H), TS, SC
89.33 not.] B; ~, MS(14-H), TS, SC
89.33 her.] W, SC, B; ~, MS(14-H), TS
89.36 said.] W, SC, B; ~, MS(14-H), TS
90.6 slightly.] MS(14-H), W, SC, B; ~, TS
90.9 up,] MS(14-H), B; ~∧ TS, SC
90.16 verandah] MS(14-H); veranda TS, SC, B
90.23 said.] W, SC, B; ~, MS(14-H), TS
90.33 hair.∧] MS(14-H), SC, B; ~." TS
91.9 beach?] W, SC, B; ~. MS(14-H), TS
91.15 me. Isn't] ed; ~, ~ MS(14-H); ~, isn't TS; ~—~ W, SC, B
91.16 smiling.] W, SC, B; ~, MS(14-H), TS
91.24 said.] W, SC, B; ~, MS(14-H), TS
91.36 laughed. "And] ed; ~, "~ MS(14-H); ~, "and TS, SC, B
92.4 learning,] MS(14-H), W, SC, B; ~∧ TS

† 92.4   shuls] ed; schules MS(14-H), TS, SC; *schules* B

92.18   eyes.] W, SC, B; ~, MS(14-H), TS

92.30   10:16] ed; 10.16 MS(14-H), TS, SC, B

92.33   Negro] W, SC; negro MS(14-H), TS, B

† 92.33–34   collecting the grunion quickly like] W, SC; collecting quickly
    them like MS(14-H); collecting quickly like TS; collecting the
    grunion quickly, like B
        This sentence is heavily rewritten in MS.

93.1   plaque] MS(14-H), W, SC, B; plague TS

93.1   boulder] W, SC, B; bouder MS(14-H); bounder TS
        The reading should be *stake;* it is impossible to drive a nail into
    a boulder. Graham's note on the TS reads: 'ORIGINALLY "TO
    THE PINE TREE" S.G.' In MS Fitzgerald first wrote 'pine tree',
    which he revised to 'bounder' and then to 'bouder'.

93.3   Negro] W, SC; negro MS(14-H), TS, B

† 93.13, 26   Rosicrucian] W, SC, B; Rosocrucian MS(14-H); Rosecrucian
    TS

93.17   work?] ed; ~, MS(14-H), TS, SC, B

93.17   Negro] W, SC; negro MS(14-H), TS, B

93.23   spray,] ed; ~∧ MS(14-H), TS; ~; W, SC, B

93.31   Negro's] MS(14-H), W, SC; negro's TS, B

94.7   deliberately.] W, SC, B; ~, MS(14-H), TS

94.14   said.] W, SC, B; ~, MS(14-H), TS

94.17–95.2   I've. . . . but
        The differences between MS(14-H) and the extant TS for this
    passage reveal that the original typescript pages corresponding to
    seven MS pages were heavily revised and cut by Fitzgerald and
    retyped as TS page 11; the original typescript pages are not extant.

94.21   laughing.] W, SC, B; ~∧ MS(14-H); ~, TS

94.23   as] MS(14-H), W, SC, B; an TS

95.17   said∧] MS(14-H); ~, TS, SC, B

95.17   door.] W, SC, B; ~, MS(14-H), TS

† 95.19, 20   Bel-Air] ed; Belle∧air MS(14-H); Bel-air TS, SC, B

95.21   development∧] MS(14-H); ~, TS, SC, B

95.24   *Mister*] MS(14-H); *Mister* TS, SC, B

95.34   inside∧] MS(14-H), W, SC, B; ~, TS

96.9   persistently,] MS(14-H), W, SC, B; ~∧ TS

96.9   other,] W, SC, B; ~∧ MS(14-H), TS

96.10   Negro] W, SC; negro MS(14-H), TS, B

96.10   Stahr∧] MS(14-H); ~, TS, SC, B

96.11   fish,] MS(14-H), W, SC, B; ~∧ TS

96.14   of pictures,] MS(14-H), W, SC, B; ~ ~∧ TS

96.19   Negro] W, SC; negro MS(14-H), TS, B

96.21   rest,] W, SC, B; ~∧ MS(14-H), TS

96.22   Negro] W, SC; negro MS(14-H), TS, B

96.24, 35   Filipino] ed; Phillipino MS(14-H), TS; Philippino B

96.34–35   Flieshacker ¶ The] *stet* TS; Fleishacker ¶ The W, SC;
           Fleishacker," *etc.* ¶ The B

           Following this name in MS(14-H) is a note typed in TS as '(etc.
           whole cast)'—indicating that Fitzgerald intended to augment this
           list of messages.

97.4   Esq.] W, SC, B; esq. MS(14-H), TS

97.18   toward her and] ed; toward and MS(14-H); foward and TS;
        forward and SC, B

        TS seems to have an 'f' strike-over on the 't'.

97.31   son-of-a-bitch] B; ~∧~∧~∧ ~ MS(14-H), TS, SC

97.33–34   forbearance,] W, SC, B; forebearance, MS(14-H); ~∧ TS

97.34–35   lessons. ¶ The

           MS(14-H) and TS have Fitzgerald's note '(Now the idea about
           young and generous)' at the end of the paragraph.

97.35   Filipino] ed; Phillipino MS(14-H), TS; Philippino B

98.5   and looked] MS(14-H); and he looked TS, SC, B

98.12   *Stahr:*] MS(14-H); *Stahr.* TS; Stahr. W, SC, B

98.13–14   *good bye*] MS(14-H); *goodbye* TS; goodbye W, SC, B

98.32   written him another] MS(14-H); written another TS, SC, B

98.33   letter,] MS(14-H); ~∧ TS, SC, B

98.33   good bye] ed; goodbye MS(14-H), TS, SC, B

99.19   hours'] W, SC, B; ~∧ MS(14-H), TS

99.20   Section 15 (first part)] ed; *Section 15* (first part) MS(15-A), TS;
        omitted W, SC, B

99.25   Wylie White over] MS(15-A); Wylie over TS, SC, B

99.25   Martha Dodd's] *stet* TS, SC, B; Lois Wilson's MS(15-A)

        Fitzgerald changed 'Lois Wilson' to 'Martha Dodd' in MS for
        101.37 and 'Lois' to 'Martha Dodd' in MS for 102.6. (Lois Wil-
        son portrayed Daisy in the 1926 silent movie version of *The Great
        Gatsby*.)

99.26   was,] MS(15-A), W, SC, B; ~∧ TS

100.8   writers'] W, SC, B; writer's MS(15-A), TS

100.20 Rose.] W, SC; ~, MS(15-A), TS; Jane. B

100.22 nephew∧] MS(15-A); ~, TS, SC, B

100.27   why.] ed; ~? MS(15-A), TS, SC, B

100.36–37   conversation∧ she] MS(15-A), SC, B; ~.~ TS

101.3   close-up] W, SC, B; ~∧~ MS(15-A), TS

101.8   him. . . ."] ed; ~. . . . MS(15-A); ~. . . TS; ~" . . . W; ~." . . SC; ~." . . . B

† 101.14   Ebsen] ed; Ebson MS(15-A), TS, SC, B

† 101.15   Harry] ed; Walter MS(15-A), TS, SC, B

101.17   morning,] W, SC, B; ~∧ MS(15-A), TS

101.18   Stahr,] W, SC, B; ~∧ MS(15-A), TS

101.21–22   Coca-Cola] B; cola∧cola MS(15-A); coca∧~ TS, SC

† 101.25   "The Saturday Evening Post"] ed; ∧the ~ ~ ~∧ MS(15-A), TS; ∧*The Saturday Evening Post*∧ W, SC, B

101.28   gentle] W, SC, B; gentile MS(15-A), TS
        The sense requires *gentle*.

101.35   Rose∧] MS(15-A); ~, TS, SC; Jane, B

101.35   *that*] MS(15-A); that TS, SC, B

101.37   said.] W, SC, B; ~, MS(15-A), TS

102.7   15 (second part)] *stet* TS; 15. (second part) MS(15-D); *omitted* W, SC, B

102.18   us. "Thirty] ed; ~, "~ MS(15-D), TS; ~, "—thirty W, SC, B

102.19   spring] W, SC, B; Spring MS(15-D), TS

† 103.4   Sex] MS(15-D); sex TS, SC, B

103.19   Peters'] ed; Peter's MS(15-D), TS, SC, B

103.22   called.] W, SC, B; ~, MS(15-D), TS

103.28   said.] W, SC, B; ~, MS(15-D), TS

103.30   Dodd,] W, SC, B; Scott∧ MS(15-D); Dodd∧ TS

103.30   he could] *stet* MS(15-D), TS; could he SC, B

103.35   said. "Or] ed; ~, "~ MS(15-D), TS; ~, "or W, SC, B

104.2   said.] W, SC, B; ~, MS(15-D), TS

104.8   have] *stet* TS, SC, B
        MS(15-D) is unclear; possibly 'leave'.

104.9   along] MS(15-D), B; a long TS, SC

104.10   said.] W, SC, B; ~, MS(15-D), TS

104.19   bathroom.] W, SC, B; ~, MS(15-D), TS

104.26   secretary∧] MS(15-D); ~, TS, SC, B

104.26   Peters∧] MS(15-D); ~, TS, SC, B

104.34   couch.] W, SC, B; ~, MS(15-D), TS

105.1   dear?] W, SC, B; ~∧ MS(15-D), TS

105.5   immersion] W, SC, B; emulsion MS(15-D), TS

105.12   said,] ed; ~∧ MS(15-D), TS; ~: W, SC, B

105.20   Martha.] W, SC, B; ~, MS(15-D), TS
105.26–27   right∧ and] MS(15-D); ~. And TS, SC, B
105.28   shrines,] ed; ~∧ MS(15-D), TS, SC, B
105.31   Episode 16, First Part] ed; *Episode 16, 1ˢᵗ Part.* MS(16-A);
          Episode 16, First Part TS; *omitted* W, SC, B
105.32   Stahr∧] MS(16-A); ~, TS, SC, B
106.10   smiling.] W, SC, B; ~, MS(16-A), TS
106.28   inscriptions] MS(16-A), W, SC, B; conscriptions TS
106.30   said.] MS(16-A), W, SC, B; ~, TS
106.32   Stahr.] W, SC, B; ~, MS(16-A), TS
106.34   Pat] ed; Bill MS(16-A), TS, SC, B
106.37   people's] W, SC, B; peoples' MS(16-A), TS
107.9   only∧] MS(16-A); ~, TS, SC, B
107.13–14   a supervisor] MS(16-A); a hushed supervisor TS, SC, B
          The typist retained MS deleted 'hushed'.
107.14   stalemate] W, SC, B; stale-mate MS(16-A), TS
107.29   wrists] ed; wrist MS(16-A), TS, SC, B
107.34   kitty] MS(16-A), W, SC, B; Kitty TS
107.37   time,] W, SC, B; ~∧ MS(16-A), TS
108.5   tuhkey] *stet* MS(16-A), TS, SC; turkey B
          Boxley speaks with an English accent. Fitzgerald marked this
          word in MS: 'follow spelling'. See Introduction, p. lxix.
108.10   boldly. "But] ed; ~, "~ MS(16-A), TS; ~, "but W, B; ~, ∧~
          SC
108.11   novel: and] MS(16-A); ~. And TS, SC, B
108.22   said.] W, SC, B; ~, MS(16-A), TS
108.31–32   and sometimes even looking] ed; and even sometimes even
          looking MS(16-A); and even sometimes looking TS, SC, B
          Fitzgerald inserted 'even' after 'sometimes' in MS but did not
          delete the 'even' he had already written.
109.1   Episode 16 (Part 2)] *stet* MS(16-D), TS; *omitted* W, SC, B
109.4   He stripped] ed; Stahr ~ TS, SC, B
          Fitzgerald crossed out 'Stahr' in MS(16-D) without substitu-
          tion when he inserted 'With . . . detector.'
109.16   Monroe.] ed; ~, MS(16-D), TS, SC, B
109.21   Stahr.] W, SC, B; ~, MS(16-D), TS
109.22   cardiograms] ed; cardiographs MS(16-D), TS, SC, B
109.26   looking] *stet* MS(16-D), TS; liking W, SC, B
          Graham's note on TS reads: 'LOOKING IS THE WORD IN
          PENCIL COPY. BUT THINK HE MEANT LIKING S.G.'

109.28 said.] W, SC, B; ~, MS(16-D), TS

110.12 know?] W, SC, B; ~. MS(16-D), TS

110.17 Good bye] MS(16-D); Goodbye TS, SC, B

110.18 Dictograph] ed; dictograph MS(16-D), TS, SC, B

110.20 Moore?] W, SC, B; ~. MS(16-D), TS

111.9 pompously.] W, SC, B; ~, MS(16-D), TS

111.12 laughed.] ed; ~, MS(16-D), TS; ~: W, SC, B

111.17 demanded.] W, SC, B; ~, MS(16-D), TS

111.18 one] MS(16-D); a TS, SC, B

111.21 begged.] W, SC, B; ~, MS(16-D), TS

111.22 either,] B; ~∧ MS(16-D), TS, SC

111.27 himself.] W, SC, B; ~, MS(16-D), TS

111.29 considered.] W, SC, B; ~, MS(16-D), TS

111.30 suggested.] W, SC, B; ~, MS(16-D), TS

111.31 Dictograph] ed; dictor graph MS(16-D); dictograph TS, SC, B

111.31–32 cut in a shooting] ed; cut in shooting MS(16-D); cut in on the line with a shooting TS, SC, B
The typist retained MS crossed-out 'on the line with a'.

111.34 confidently] MS(16-D); confidentially TS, SC, B

111.35 idea of "Riding] ed; idea "Riding MS(16-D), TS; idea of "riding W, SC, B

112.2 beginning,] W, SC, B; ~∧ MS(16-D), TS

112.15 going—to any pole.] stet MS(16-D), TS; going. W, SC, B

112.15 brought] MS(16-D), W, SC, B; brough TS

112.19 in life] stet MS(16-D), TS; in his life W, SC, B
Fitzgerald crossed out 'his' in MS.

112.34 stepmother] B; step-mother MS(16-D), TS, SC

112.36 apiece] W, SC, B; a piece MS(16-D), TS

112.36 stepmother] MS(16-D), B; step-mother TS, SC

113.1 stepmother] B; step mother MS(16-D); ~-~ TS, SC

113.16 stepmother] ed; step mother MS(16-D); ~-~ TS, SC, B

† 113.17 Black∧and∧Tans] ed; ~-~-tans MS(16-D), TS; ~-~-Tans W, SC, B

113.25 names] ed; name MS(16-D), TS, SC, B

114.1 king] W, SC, B; King MS(16-D), TS

114.1–2 of job] stet MS(16-D), TS; of a job W, SC, B

114.7 said.] W, SC, B; ~, MS(16-D), TS

114.11 ¶ "They were the standard article," he said.] stet TS, SC; ¶ "~ ~ ~ ~ ~," ~ ~∧ MS(16-D); *omitted* B

114.14 Syndicalist] MS(16-D); syndicalist TS, SC, B

114.22   in to] MS(16-D); into TS, SC, B
114.22   saying,] W, SC, B; ~∧ MS(16-D), TS
114.34   too] MS(16-D); *too* TS, SC, B
114.35   another week] MS(16-D), W, SC, B; another a week TS
115.10   "Oh yes"] ed; ∧~ ~∧ MS(16-D), TS; "~, ~" W, SC, B
115.18   they don't get] *stet* TS, SC, B; they get MS(16-D)
115.21   kings] W, SC, B; Kings MS(16-D), TS
115.24   light] MS(16-D); lights TS, SC, B
115.25   and behind] ed; and behyond behind MS(16-D); and betrayed
          behind TS; and beyond behind W, SC, B
115.28   Beautiful Doll. Minna] *stet* TS, SC, B; Beautiful. Minna MS(16-
          D)
          The words 'Doll—she was Beautiful Doll' are crossed out
          after 'Beautiful' in MS.
116.1   laughed.] SC, B; ~, MS(16-D), TS
116.8   anomalous] W, SC, B; analymous MS(16-D), TS
116.19   said,] MS(16-D); ~∧ TS, SC, B
116.19   smiling.] W, SC, B; ~∧ MS(16-D); ~, TS
116.23   said.] "And] ed; ~, "~ MS(16-D), TS; ~, "and W, SC, B
116.28   said.] B; ~, MS(16-D), TS, SC
116.33   It] W, SC, B; it MS(16-D), TS
116.35   And tell her tomorrow] ed; And tell her till tomorrow MS(16-
          D), TS; And not to tell her till tomorrow W, SC, B
                              as an adult, no romantic. And tell her
          MS reads: 'sleep on it∧ ~~(poor phrase.)~~ till tomorrow.'
          Fitzgerald's intention is clear; Wilson's emendation is unnecessary.
117.5   grow] MS(16-D), W, SC, B; grown TS
117.6   knows] W, SC, B; know MS(16-D), TS
117.11   her] MS(16-D); here TS, SC, B
117.12   being enchanted] *stet* MS(16-D), TS; being an enchanted W, B;
          being an enchanged SC
117.17   good bye] MS(16-D); goodbye TS, SC, B
117.19   akin] MS(16-D), W, SC, B; a kin TS
117.20   time-need,] W, SC, B; ~-~∧ MS(16-D), TS
117.21   heart,] W, SC, B; ~∧ MS(16-D), TS
117.22   life∧] ed; ~, MS(16-D), TS, SC, B
117.22   now—] MS(16-D); ~∧ TS, SC, B
117.26   power,] W, SC, B; ~∧ MS(16-D), TS
117.30   judgement] MS(16-D); judgment TS, SC, B

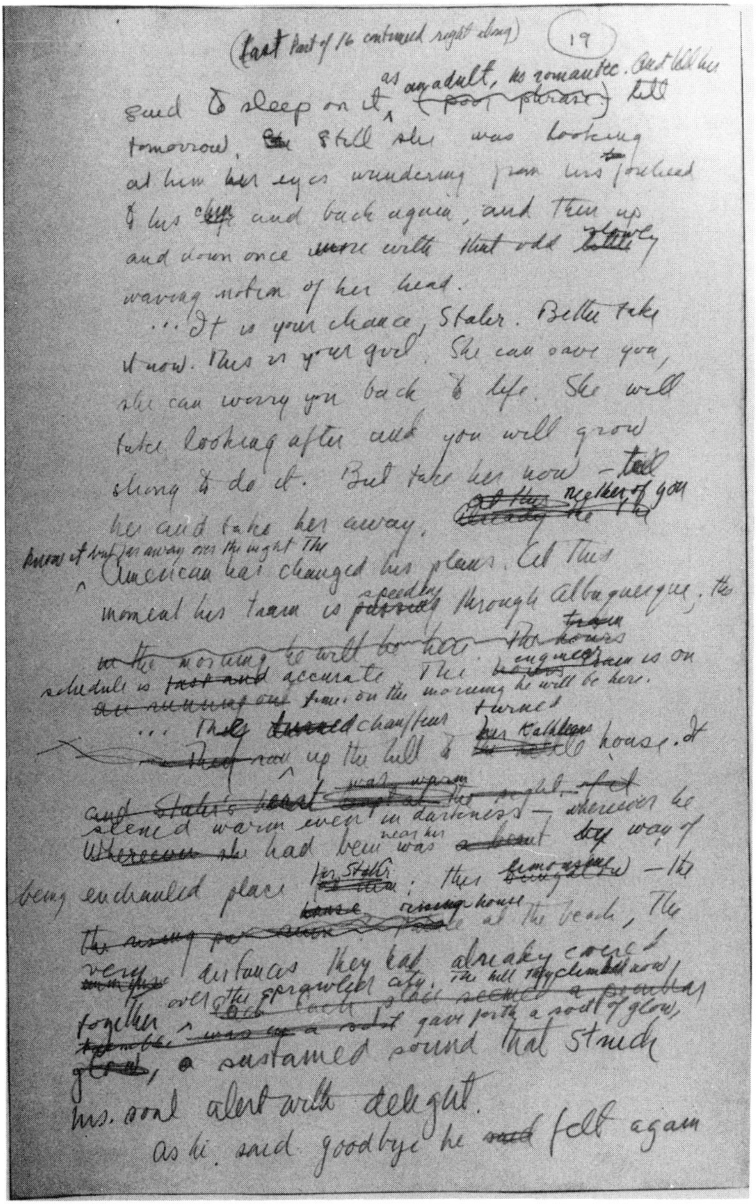

See pp. 116–17.

117.35   dollars,] MS(16-D); ~. TS, SC, B

118.1   I WAS MARRIED AT NOON TODAY GOODBYE] ed; *I was
married at noon today. Goodbye* MS(16-D), TS, SC, B
Telegrams were typed in full capitals.

118.2   attached∧] MS(16-D); ~, TS, SC, B

118.2   *Send*] MS(16-D), W, SC, B; *send* TS

118.3   Episode 17] *stet* MS(17-A), TS; Chapter 6 W; CHAPTER 6
SC; CHAPTER VI B
Fitzgerald rewrote MS pages 1–3 (corresponding to 118.4–
119.35: leather room"), but his rewritten pages do not survive.

† 118.17–18   "The New Masses"] ed; ∧*The New Masses*∧ TS, SC, B

118.20   seriously.] W, SC, B; ~, TS

† 118.22   AM] ed; am TS, SC, B

118.28–29   He was like a brazier out of doors on a cool night.] *stet* TS,
SC; *omitted* B
Possibly omitted in proof because this description also ap-
pears at 65.32–33.

118.30   said.] W, SC, B; ~, TS

† 119.1   Writers∧ Guild] ed; writers' guild TS; Writers' Guild W, SC, B

† 119.6   "Doctor Caligari"] ed; ∧~ Caliagarri∧ TS; ∧*Doctor Caligari*∧ W, SC, B

119.6   Salvador] ed; Salvatore TS; Salvator W, SC, B

† 119.6   "Un Chien Andalou,"] ed; ∧Le Chien D'Analou,∧ TS; ∧*Le
Chien d'Analou,*∧ W, SC; ∧ *Le Chien Andalou,*∧ B

119.10   "Communist Manifesto."] ed; ∧~ ~ .∧ TS, SC; ∧*Communist
Manifesto.*∧ B

120.2   asked.] ed; ~, MS(17-A), TS, SC, B

120.4   suggested.] W, SC, B; ~, MS(17-A), TS

120.6   him.] W, SC, B; ~∧ MS(17-A); ~, TS

120.12   said.] W, SC, B; ~, MS(17-A), TS

120.18   said.] W, SC, B; ~, MS(17-A), TS

120.23   said.] W, SC, B; ~, MS(17-A), TS

120.25   Member,] W, SC, B; ~∧ MS(17-A), TS

120.36   Stahr.] W, SC, B; ~, MS(17-A), TS

121.2   Stahr.] W, SC, B; ~, MS(17-A), TS

121.5   repeated.] B; ~, MS(17-A), TS, SC

121.6   the company spirit] MS(17-A); The Company spirit TS; The
company spirit W, SC; The Company Spirit B

121.7   impatiently.] W, SC, B; ~, MS(17-A), TS

121.17   said.] W, SC, B; ~, MS(17-A), TS

121.18   dancer] ed; Dancer MS(17-A), TS, SC, B
121.20   saying∧] MS(17-A); ~, TS, SC, B
121.20   those] MS(17-A); these TS, SC, B
121.21   dance.' "] W, SC, B; ~.∧" MS(17-A), TS
† 121.23   Anti-Nazi] ed; anti-~ MS(17-A), TS, SC, B
121.30   farmers'] W, SC, B; ~∧ MS(17-A), TS
† 121.34   Terrace] ed; Avenue MS(17-A), TS, SC, B
121.37   walked her to the registry office] *stet* MS(17-A), TS, SC, B
           A three-day waiting period before a marriage was required in
           California. There is no registry office in Los Angeles; the office
           has always been known as the Marriage License Bureau. These
           errors have been allowed to stand.
122.8   table,] W, SC, B; ~∧ MS(17-A), TS
122.13   Stahr.] W, SC, B; ~, MS(17-A), TS
122.21   Brimmer.] W, SC, B; ~, MS(17-A), TS
122.23   Guild] W, SC, B; guild MS(17-A), TS
122.29   who] MS(17-A); that TS, SC, B
122.31   Brimmer.] W, SC, B; ~, MS(17-A), TS
122.36   Stahr.] W, SC, B; ~, MS(17-A), TS
123.6   Stahr.] W, SC, B; ~, MS(17-A), TS
123.16   and most efficient] W, SC, B; and efficient MS(17-A), TS
           MS originally read 'one of the most hard working and effi-
           cient'; Fitzgerald crossed out 'most hard working' and inserted
           'hardest working'.
123.17   West] W, SC, B; west MS(17-A), TS
123.20   said.] W, SC, B; ~, MS(17-A), TS
123.21   Brimmer.] ed; ~, MS(17-A), TS; ~: W, SC, B
123.24   Baptist] W, SC, B; baptist MS(17-A), TS
123.25   the] MS(17-A); them TS, SC, B
† 123.27   Frankensteen] SC, B; Frankenstien MS(17-A), TS; Franken-
           stein W
123.32   yes," he said] MS(17-A), SC, B; yes," said TS
123.33   Stahr.] W, SC, B; ~, MS(17-A), TS
123.35   said.] W, SC, B; ~, MS(17-A), TS
124.18–19   ping-pong] B; ping∧pong MS(17-A), TS, SC
124.20   "Little Man, You've Had a Busy Day∧"] ed; "~ ~∧ you've
           had ~ ~ ~∧" MS(17-A), TS; ∧*Little Man, You've Had a Busy
           Day,*∧ W, SC; ∧~ *Girl,* ~ ~ ~ ~ ~,∧ B
124.35   I never have been] ed; Ive never have been MS(17-A); I've never
           been TS, SC, B

125.4   Brimmer.] W, SC, B; ~, MS(17-A), TS
125.5   navy] ed; Navy MS(17-A), TS, SC, B
125.6   winked it fatuously] MS(17-A); winked fatuously TS, SC, B
† 125.8   soapbox] MS(17-A); soap-box TS, SC, B
125.13   right.∧] W, SC, B; ~." MS(17-A), TS
125.15   Brimmer.] W, SC, B; ~, MS(17-A), TS
125.18   watermark] W, SC, B; water mark MS(17-A), TS
125.23   Directors] MS(17-A); Director's TS, SC, B
125.25   smiling.] W, SC, B; ~, MS(17-A), TS
† 125.28   It was like Edward the VII's boast] *stet* RTS, SC; —it reminded
           me of Edward the VII's boast MS(17-A), TS; It was like Edward
           the Seventh's boast B
               Frances Kroll emended the carbon-copy to 'It was like Ed-
           ward VII boasting'. It is impossible to determine whether she
           was acting on Fitzgerald's instructions.
125.30   me,] W, SC, B; ~∧ RTS
               See "Fitzgerald's Revisions."
125.34   Red] ed; red MS(17-A), TS, SC, B
125.37   budging an inch. A] MS(17-A); budging. A TS, SC, B
126.5   so-and-so's] W, SC, B; ~-~-sos MS(17-A), TS
126.16   attitude.] W, SC, B; ~, MS(17-A), TS
126.16–28 I understand. . . . than
               MS(17-A) for this passage consists of a typescript fragment
           Fitzgerald revised in holograph.
126.18   pleasantly.] W, SC, B; ~, MS(17-A), TS
126.24   difficult,] W, SC, B; ~∧ MS(17-A), TS
126.29   be*longed*] MS(17-A), W, SC, B; belo*nged* TS
127.6   was a gentle] W, SC, B; was gentle MS(17-A), TS
127.8   ago.] MS(17-A); ~∧ TS; ~— W, SC, B
127.16   Brimmer.] W, SC, B; ~, MS(17-A), TS
127.18   No,] B; ~∧ MS(17-A), TS, SC
127.18   Stahr.] W, SC, B; ~, MS(17-A), TS
127.19   ping-pong] B; ~∧~ MS(17-A), TS, SC
127.22   ping-pong] B; ~∧~ MS(17-A), TS, SC
128.2   Stahr.] W, SC, B; ~, MS(17-A), TS
128.6   said.] W, SC, B; ~, MS(17-A), TS
128.13   saying,] W, SC, B; ~∧ MS(17-A), TS
128.14   *person*] MS(17-A); person TS, SC, B
128.16   held] MS(17-A), W, SC, B; had TS
128.21   right.] W, SC, B; ~, MS(17-A), TS

128.22   table.] B; ~, MS(17-A), TS; ~: W; ~; SC
128.28   again, a] W, SC, B; ~∧ ~ TS
         The comma is possibly a dash in MS(17-A).
128.30   In] MS(17-A); After TS, SC, B
         MS inserts 'In' above deleted 'After'.
129.2   ping-pong] B; ~∧~ MS(17-A), TS, SC
129.3   stars] *stet* TS, SC, B; Stahrs MS(17-A)
129.7   into the house till] *stet* TS, SC, B; into till MS(17-A)
129.10   Bacchic] W, SC, B; Bachic MS(17-A), TS
129.13   house;] W, SC, B; ~, MS(17-A), TS
129.14   verandah] MS(17-A); veranda TS, SC, B
129.16   finally I sat] W, SC, B; finally sat MS(17-A), TS
129.19   said.] W, SC, B; ~, MS(17-A), TS
129.20   it." After] W, SC, B; ~," ~ MS(17-A); ~," after TS
129.28   studio?] SC, B; ~. MS(17-A), TS
129.31   Fairbanks'] SC, B; Fairbank's MS(17-A), TS
129.32   night?∧ He asked me—∧I] MS(17-A); ~?" he ~ ~, "~ TS;
         ~?" ~ ~ ~. "~ W, SC, B

FITZGERALD'S REVISIONS,
CORRECTIONS, AND ANNOTATIONS
IN THE LATEST TYPESCRIPTS

This list includes Fitzgerald's textual alterations as well as notes to himself; his word counts have been omitted. The first reading in each entry is the typescript reading, followed by a right-pointing bracket and Fitzgerald's holograph alteration. Editorial comments are provided in angle brackets. The first parenthetic page-line reference is keyed to the Cambridge edition; it is followed by the reference for the latest typescripts as renumbered by Wilson. Approximate line numbers are provided for placement of marginal notes.

(3)1.upper left and top margin (crossed out)   *Note:* Rewrite from mood. Has become stilted with rewriting. Don't look—rewrite from mood ⟨This note also appears in Kroll's handwriting on the first page of an earlier CC (draft I–G).⟩

(3)1.top margin (crossed out)   *Note:* (Episodes 1, 2, 3)

(above 21.15)26.top margin   *Note:* Robby

(21.17–18)26.3–4   studio—as I parked my car I could see them bent over the pin-games inside. [studio—I could see them bent over the pin-games inside—as I parked my car

(21.18)26.5   ∧Old∧ ["∼"

(21.25)26.11   drop [dropping

(21.28)26.14–15   microphone. ¶ Around [microphone. Around

(21.30)26.16   in [among

(21.31)26.18   by [in front of

(22.2)26.22   earthquake—but that [earthquake. That

(22.34)28.3   to meet him; I [to; I

(23.11)28.19   Borwits' or [Borwits' pictures or

(23.29)29.9   your [our

(23.30)29.9   cord [cords

(23.30)29.9   you [us

(24.7)29.26   For the record it [The office

(24.11)30.2–3   ring. ¶ I [ring. I

(24.12)30.4   phones [phone

(24.13)30.4   dictographs [dictograph

(24.15)30.6 Three [A couple of

(24.15)30.6 've [have

(24.16)30.6 all [they're

(24.35)30.26 trouble-shooter—you know, fixed [trouble-shooter—fixed

(opposite 24.35–37)30.left margin *Note:* Only Fair

(opposite 25.10–13)31.left margin *Note:* words too long

(above 27.28)35. top margin *Note:* (Episode 7 is out)

(27.28)35.1 Episode 8 [~ 7

(27.32)35.4 grapple [graph

(29.24)37.17–19 All right. I called about Pedro Garcia—he tried to kill
       himself in front of Warner Brothers last week. Mr. Brown says
       he's going blind . . . I've ["Yes, Mr. Stahr. I've

(opposite 29.24)37.left margin *Note:* Dots don't properly separate ideas

(29.33)37.27 one [Prince

(29.34)37.28–38.5 "And that's all." Stahr was annoyed and then retrospec-
       tively amused. ¶"Is he the one who wants to learn about pictures
       from the beginning?" ¶"Yes," said Catherine, "He's very Princely.
       Very handsome". She was ["He's very handsome." She was

(29.34)38.5 pointlessly∧—[~ "—

(30.2–7)38.7–14 Tell the Prince he can come to a story conference with
       me." ¶" 'God's Convict' at noon?" ¶Yes in Bieman's office. I
       don't want that gang in here with those cigars." ¶"It's five to
       twelve now." ¶ As Stahr went out he turned. ¶ "Did [Send the
       Prince out on the sets and tell him we'll lunch at one." ¶ "And Mr.
       George Boxley—looking very angry in a Brittish way." ¶ "I'll see
       him for ten minutes." ¶ As she went out he asked. ¶ "Did

(30.19)38.27up —The [∧~

(below 30.24)39.left margin *Note:* Space here

(30.26)39.6–8 He walked with the tall Dane along the balcony, down an
       iron stair along a grey alley of projection rooms. ¶ "Oh, they
       won't mind," he said. The Dane noticed the [Stahr smiled at Mr.
       George Boxley. It was a

(30.34)39.17–28 outright. ¶ "I'll introduce them—not you," said Stahr.
       ¶ "I will be much impressed." ¶ Outside the long bungalow used
       by directors and supervisors an office boy stepped out from a
       doorway and gave Stahr a note with a surreptitious murmur. Stahr
       read it, smiled and handed it to the Dane. ¶ *The Marquands know
       about Hastings and Boles and are going to quit. I mean they know.*
       ¶ *Tod* ¶ "I don't understand," said the Dane. ¶ "We're walking in
       on a situation." ¶ "Oh." [outright. ⟨Following deleted "Oh." was

a typed page which Fitzgerald revised in holograph and inserted in MS(11-A) for Episode 11. See Textual Note on 57.31 and Illustration p. 229.⟩

(above 31.1)40.upper left margin   *Note:* re ⟨The letters 're' (possibly 'rl') appear at the head of several episodes in Fitzgerald's hand. Their significance is not known, but they may mean 'rewrite'.⟩

(above 31.1)40.1 Episode 9 [~ 8 ⟨see p. 30⟩

(31.1)40.2   The Englishman [Mr. Boxley did not smile back. He

(31.20)40.22   froth [forth

(31.36)41.10   Is [Isn't

(opposite 31.36–37)41.right margin   ⟨large question mark deleted⟩

(opposite 32.9–10)41.left margin   *Note:* slow + calm

(32.21–22)42.6   stove—but the [stove You notice that there's a stiff wind blowing in the window—but just then your

(32.22)42.7   She [The girl

(32.23)42.7–8   hello—and then listens and says into [hello—listens—and says deliberately into

(32.25)42.9–10   stove, lights the match. You [stove again, and just as she lights the match you

(32.26)42.10–11   see what you never saw before—that [see that

(32.26)42.11   office∧ [~,

(32.29)42.15   happens. [~?

(32.33)42.19   Anyhow [In any case

(33.6)42.28   ∧I ["I

(opposite 37.8)49.upper left margin   *Note:* rl but transfer last page to end of Episode 7

(37.8)49.1   Episode 9 ⟨TS deleted; restored in holograph⟩

(37.9)49.2–3   The group that met in Stahr's office at twelve were entitled to [It was noon already and the conferees were entitled to exactly

(37.20)49.14   included Rienmund [included, besides the writers, Rienmund

(37.21)49.14   best [most favored

(37.21–22)49.15–50.4   supervisors; Broaca the director and two writers Wylie White and Rose Meloney—the latter a dried up little blonde of fifty about whom one could hear the fifty assorted opinions of Hollywood—"a sentimental dope", "The best writer on construction in Hollywood", "a veteran", "that old hack," "the smartest woman on the lot", "The cleverest plagiarist in the biz", and of course in addition a nymphomaniac, a virgin, a push-over, a lesbian and a faithful wife. Without being an old maid she was like most self-made women rather old maidish. She had ulcers of the stomach and her salary was over a hundred thousand a year. A complicated treatise could be written on whether she was "worth it" or more than that or nothing at all. Her value lay in such ordinary assets as the bare fact that she was a woman and adaptable, quick and trustworthy, "knew the game" and was without egotism. She had been a great friend of Minna's and over a period of years he had managed to stifle what amounted to a sharp physical revulsion. [supervisors and John Broaca, the picture's director. ⟨The deleted material was transferred to p.36.⟩

(37.23)50.5–6   the engineer type of director—tall, broad, [an engineer—large and

(37.24)50.6   masterful [resolute

(37.30)50.12   Freudian/\ [~;

(38.6)50.21   was a good supervisor [got his pictures out in time

(38.7)50.22   Stahr, had seemed [Stahr, seemed

(opposite 38.10–12)50.left margin   *Note:* Questionable

(38.10–12)50.25–27   Then there was Wylie White, civilized and voluble, simple and acute, dazed and saturnine. In any country he would have been recognizable as an intellectual of the second order. His intense [Wylie White, of course, in any country would have been recognizable in any country as an intellectual of the second order. he was civilized and voluble, both simple and acute, half dazed half saturnine. His

(38.13)51.1   flashes/\ [~,

(38.13)51.1–2   intermingled [mingled

(44.2–3)58.29–59.1   over. ¶ "Mr. [over. *Space here* ¶ "Any messages?" ¶ "Mr.

(above 44.28)61.top margin   *Note:* Dramatize and make clear

(opposite 44.28)61.upper left margin   *Note:* rl except for the last page; transfer?

(44.28)61.1   Episode 11 [~ 10

(above 48.18)66.top margin   *Note:* (End of Episode 10)

(above 49.25)69.upper left margin   *Note:* re

(above 49.25)69.top margin   *Note:* No good——I think, <u>Out</u>

(opposite 51.23)71.left margin   *Typed note:* more

(opposite 51.33)71.left margin   *Typed note:* longer

(opposite 52.15–19)73.upper left margin   *Note:* cut first 8 pages—then continue cut from foot of 11 to end

(52.22)73.8   sat daily at [sat at

(52.22)73.9–10   and six-thirty and watched [and again at six-thirty watching

(52.23)73.11   tenseness [tensity

(50)

quick and trustworthy, "knew the game" and was without ego~~tism~~.
She had been ~~a great friend of Minna~~ and over a period of years
he had managed ~~to stifle~~ what amounted to a sharp physical
revulsion.

Broaca, on the surface, was ~~the~~ an engineer *large and* ~~type of director--~~
~~tall, broad,~~ without nerves, quietly *resolute* ~~masterful~~, popular. He was
an ignoramus, and Stahr often caught him making the same scenes
over and over--one scene about a rich young girl occurred in all
his pictures with the same action, the same business. A bunch
of large dogs entered the room and jumped around the girl. Later
the girl went to a stable and slapped a horse on the rump. The
explanation was probably not Freudian, more likely that at a drab
moment in youth he had looked through a fence and seen a beautiful girl with dogs and horses. As a trademark for glamor it was
stamped on his brain forever.

R~~ien~~mund was a handsome young opportunist, with a fairly
good education. Originally a man of some character, he was being
daily forced by his anomalous position into devious ways of
acting and thinking. He was a bad man now, as men go. At thirty
he had none of the virtues which either *gentile* ~~native~~/Americans or Jews
are taught to think admirable. But he *got his pictures out in time,* ~~was a good supervisor~~ and
by manifesting an almost homosexual fixation on Stahr, ~~had~~ seemed
to have dulled Stahr's usual acuteness. Stahr liked him--considered
him a good all=around man. *half*

half *Wylie White, of course,* ~~Then there was Wylie White,~~ *he was* civilized and voluble, *both* simple
and acute, dazed ~~and~~ saturnine. *"* ~~In~~ *any country* ~~he~~ would have been
recognizable as an intellectual of the second order. His ~~intense~~ *in any country*

See 38.10–12.

(52.24)73.11   proceedings—one [occasion—he

(52.25)73.12   months buying [months of buying

(52.27)73.14   and [or

(52.28)73.15   The [At this point the

(52.28–29)73.16   over now [staged and in suspension

(52.30)73.17–18   With Stahr in judgment sat the heads of the sound, art and [Besides Stahr there were present the representatives of all

(52.31)73.18   departments and [departments together with

(53.3)73.24   stuff [staff

(opposite 53.9)74.left margin   *Note:* Explain

(53.11)74.5   actors relaxed [actors on the screen relaxed

(53.14)74.8   "takes" [∧~∧

(53.14)74.9   ∧a "good ["a ∧~

(56.36–57.7)79.3–11   indifferent. ¶ "But the man's good," said Stahr, "Can't we use him as the old Russian Prince in Steppes." ¶ "He *is* an old Russian Prince," said the casting director, "But he's ashamed of it. He's a red. And that's one part he says he wouldn't play." ¶ "It's the only part he could play," said Stahr. "Somebody sent up a test of that girl two years ago. She must be getting around—but she isn't getting any better." [indifferent. ¶ "Somebody sent up a test of that girl two years ago. She must be getting around—but she isn't getting any better. But the man's good, "Can't we use him as the old Russian Prince in Steppes." ¶ "He *is* an old Russian Prince," said the casting director, "But he's ashamed of it. He's a Red. And that's one part he says he wouldn't play." ¶ "It's the only part he could play," said Stahr.

(57.15–16)79.20–21   without one for a century. [without a happy ending for a century and a half.

(62.6)86.1   Episode 13 [~ 12

(62.7)86.2   commissary after dinner a [commissary a

(62.19)86.15   close to him and [close and

(62.25)86.21   corner [crossing

(62.26)86.22   sky and on [sky. On

(62.26)86.23   glittering [gleaming

(66.9)91.19   Carleton [Carlton

(67.8)93.1   valet [butler

(above 67.15)94.top margin   *Note:* (End of 12)

(above 67.26)95.top margin   *Note:* Not too hot

(above 67.26)95.upper left margin   *Note:* rl

(above 78.1)110.top margin   *Typed note:* Criticism—time lapses not
    good. No drawing together.

(82.31)116.22–117.1   hand. Then a bell jangled loud out of nowhere and
    close at hand. ¶ There [hand. ¶ There

(below 82.31)116.bottom margin   *Typed Note:* (Phone scene to be in-
    vented, much slower—the hunt etc., and more significant.)

(84.26)120.11   ranpe [range

(opposite 92.17–18)131.left margin   *Typed Note:* Note: Stress the negro's
    effect on Stahr.

(94.15–17)133.26–29   all—things being as they are. My heart's in the
    grave—" He paused fractionally, wondering for the first time if
    this was quite true, "—and perhaps yours is too. But I think
    you're a fine [all. As you've probably guessed my heart's in the
    grave—" He hesitated, wondering if this was quite true, "—but
    you're the most attractive woman

(95.2)134.21–135.1   did but / but they [did but / they

(below 96.34)137.15   *Typed note in text:* (etc. whole cast)

(97.34)138.19   *Typed note in text:* (Now the idea about young and gener-
    ous)

(98.19)139.14   ∧I [(I

(below 99.19)140.bottom margin   *Typed note:* Comment: This may not
    be terse and clear enough here. Or perhaps I mean strong enough.
    It may be the place for the doctor's verdict. I would like to leave
    him on a stronger note.

⟨Wilson mis-numbered pp. 174–82⟩

(opposite 99.20)174.upper left margin   *Possible Fitzgerald note:* rl except
    if continues C's rôle in story

(100.25–26)175.14   down and he [down he

(above 102.7)178.top margin   *Note:* Not very *good*

(103.13)179.12   Evylyn [Evelyn

(opposite 105.32–33)141. upper left margin   *Note:* rl except for picture
    of Stahr at work

(opposite 118.3)157.upper left margin   *Note:* rl

(119.29–30)159.7   He seemed extremely nervous except [He was white
    and nervous and troubled—except

(120.2)159.16   smaller [shorter

(121.10)161.6   sassing me around [telling me my business

(121.12)161.8   sassed around [told his business

(123.2)164.1–4   formidable enemy of the labor movement in Holly-
    wood." ¶ This was what Stahr had come to hear. His negotiations

with the Guild which had continued over a year were approaching a dead end. He took [¶ Stahr took

(123.2)164.4   out [himself

(123.16)164.12   you were [you're

(125.27)167.18   were [used to be

(125.27–28)167.18–19   proudly—it reminded me of Edward [proudly. ¶ It was like Edward

(125.29–30)167.20   Europe—"But some of them never forgave me for [Europe. ¶ "But some of them have never forgiven me" he continued, "—for

(126.22)168.8   Hitts [Fitts

WILSON'S ALTERATIONS IN THE LATEST TYPESCRIPTS

The first reading in each entry is the reading in the latest typescripts as revised by Fitzgerald in holograph, followed by the right-pointing bracket and Wilson's holograph alteration on the TS. Editorial notes are provided in angle brackets. The reading of the Cambridge edition is provided in angle brackets when it differs significantly from the readings recorded in the collation. The page-line references are keyed to the facsimiles in *F. Scott Fitzgerald Manuscripts V*, Part 3.

The following categories of Wilson's alterations have not been recorded individually: (1) placement of punctuation with quotation marks; and (2) character name changes (see Introduction, pp. lxxxvi–vii).

1.7–8	"The Producers Daughter" [*The Producer's Daughter*	11.9	known∧ [~,
		11.11	Esquire [*Esquire*
4.13	Washington∧ [~,	11.16	said, [~.
4.28	stewardess, [~.	11.28	you!." [~!∧"
5.1	Bradogue [Brady	12.3	it∧ [~,
5.5	*Bradogue*∧ [*Brady*,	12.18	toughies∧ [~,
5.15	satelites [satellites	13.6	words∧ [~,
5.29	up, [~:	13.8	smugly, [~.
6.28	White, [~.	13.12	Eastern [eastern
7.24	oasis [oases	13.26	President [president
8.4	Premiers [premiers	14.5	anything∧ [~,
8.14	Top Hat and Cheek to Cheek∧	14.23	allignments [alignments
–15	[*Top Hat* and *Cheek to Cheek*,	14.23	elms: [~.
8.19	us∧ too∧ [~, ~,	14.26	house∧ [~,
8.20	desk∧ [~,	14.27	raven∧ [~,
8.24	see∧ [~,	15.9	surprise, [~.
8.27	anymore [any more	15.11	smiling, [~.
9.22	him, [~.	16.29	competitor∧ [~,
9.24	he∧ [~,	17.7	"Lost" [*Lost*
9.27	Wylie, [~.	17.9	"Gone" [*Gone*
10.8	fresh∧ [~,	18.2	and∧ [~,
10.11	you∧ [~,	18.8	man∧ [~,
10.11	there∧ [~,	18.10	shepard [shepherd
10.16	pictures∧ [~,	18.28	times∧ [~,
10.22	in∧ [~,	19.16	Monro [Monroe
11.3	me, [~:	19.25	said, [~.
11.5	lay [lie	19.30	Wylie, [~.

19.31 me∧ [~,
20.4 said, [~.
20.8 advice∧ [~,
20.11 Wylie, [~.
20.12 man∧ [~,
20.19 sour belly [sourbelly
20.19 Stahr, [~.
20.20 himself∧ [~,
20.24 up∧ [~,
20.29 me∧ [~,
21.4 said∧ [~,
21.4 No!." [~!' "
21.9 said. "Would [~, "—would
22.5 borwn [brown
22.12 pictures, [~—
22.13 "42nd Street" [∧*42nd Street*∧
22.13 example∧ [~,
22.20 love∧ [~,
22.21 Man∧ [~,
23.12 up∧ [~,
23.16 volunteered, "Up [~∧ "—up
23.18 name.∧ [~."
23.25 mentality∧ [~,
23.29 business∧ [~,
23.29 said∧ [~,
24.5 suddenness∧ [~,
24.7 Goodbye.∧ [~."
25.5 them∧ [~,
25.9 off∧ [~,
26.1 Episodes 4 and 5. [Chapter 2
26.7 Bell Harte [Bill Hart
26.8 him∧ [~,
26.20 singing∧ [~,
26.20 "Come∧ come∧ I love you
      only" [∧*Come, come, I love*
      you only∧
27.4 office∧ [~,
27.8 name∧ [~,
27.9 speak∧ [~,
27.11 capitalists∧ [~,
27.14 studio [studios
27.16 rooms∧ [~,
27.19 below∧ [~,
28.4 himself∧ [~,
28.9 producer∧ [~,
28.19 catastrophic∧ [~,
−20
28.25 apology, [~.

28.27 forty∧three", [~-~,"
29.2 lip∧reading∧ [~-~,
29.5 Beach∧ [~,
29.13 disappeared∧ [~,
−14
29.14 shouted∧ [~,
29.15 "I love you only" [∧*I love you*
−16 *only*∧
29.20 Jaques∧ [Jacques,
29.22 out∧ [~,
29.28 asleep∧ [~,
30.4 dictographs∧ [~;
30.9 Station∧ too∧ [~, ~,
30.10 Corner, what [~. What
30.11 passing∧ [~,
30.11 gravely, [~;
30.13 off∧ [~,
30.18 evenings∧ [~,
30.23 Dolan [Doolan
31.4 repeated, [~.
31.10 me∧ [~,
31.14 long— [~∧
31.14 —before [∧~
31.bottom margin *Note:* SPACE
32.1 Episode 6 [*deleted*
32.4 Chateaux [châteaux
32.8 that∧ [~,
32.10 arrived∧ [~,
32.12 thirty-sixth street [Thirty-Sixth
      Street
32.13 moment, [~.
32.17 Burma∧ [~,
32.25 bogs∧ [~,
33.4 Demille [De Mille
33.5 fly∧ though∧ [~, ~,
33.7 arrived∧ [~,
33.8 pretty∧ [~,
33.10 strays∧ [~,
33.12 them, [~.
33.15 idol∧ [~,
33.18 them∧ [~,
33.21 moonlight∧ [~,
33.22 forehead, [~;
−23
33.23 lingered∧ [~,
33.23 pattern, [~;
33.24 him∧ [~,
34.1 voice, [~.

34.3   truckers∧ [~,
34.7   first∧ [~,
34.7   sake∧ [~ . . .
34.8   ∧A∧ pipe∧ ['A' ~,
34.8   down, [~ . . .
34.8   plastic∧ . . . [~" . . .
34.12 slush∧ [~,
34.13 him∧ smiling∧ [~, ~,
34.13 speaking∧ [~:
34.14 ∧Hello∧ Monroe ["~, ~
34.14 Hello∧ Mr. [~, ~
34.14 night∧ [~,
34.15 Stahr.∧ [~."
34.20 upset∧ [~,
34.20 came∧ [~,
34.21 depression∧ [~,
34.22 everywhere∧ [~,
35.1   Episode 7 [Chapter 3
35.2   quake∧ [~,
35.8   shrewdness, [~∧
35.11 picture∧ [~,
35.13 Ballyhegan∧ [~,
−14
35.15 hand∧ [~,
35.16 and∧ [~,
35.17 muscle∧ [~,
35.19 Lumiere [Lumière
35.26 as how [as to how
36.7   "A Producer's Day" [*A Pro-*
      ducer's Day
36.12 time∧ [~,
37.1   thousands [hundreds
37.5   coffee∧ [~,
37.13 salvage∧ [~,
37.20 Stahr, [~.
37.22 exaggerating∧ [~,
37.22 people∧ [~,
37.26 *Toute passe—l'art seule dure a*
      l'eternite. [*Tout passe—l'art*
      seul dure à l'éternité.
38.5   pointlessly∧" — [~:" —
38.13 out∧ [~,
38.13 asked. ¶ "Did [~: "~
38.16 sound∧ [~,
38.16 from∧ [~,
38.19 else. [~?
38.21 too? [~.

38.27 dames∧ [~,
38.28 'em∧ [~,
38.29 Chevvy, [~—
39.1   sore. [~?
39.5   *Note:* SPACE
−6
39.13 kindness∧ [~—
39.14 tired∧ [~,
39.14 there∧ [~—
39.16 insult∧ [~,
40.1   Episode 8 [*deleted*
40.3   dragged∧ [~,
40.4   chair∧ [~,
40.6   invitation∧ [~,
40.15 Boxley, [~.
40.17 say∧ [~,
40.23 mildly, [~.
41.11 wells. [~?
41.14 Stahr, [~.
41.25 you∧ [~,
42.6   box∧ [~,
42.6   stove∧ [~.
42.8   phone∧ [~,
42.10 match∧ [~,
42.15 smiling, [~.
42.16 Stahr, [~.
42.19 case∧ [~,
42.24 Oh∧ [~,
42.28 demanded, [~.
43.2   Or [or
43.6   Boxley∧ [~,
43.6   said, [~.
43.7   it∧ [~,
43.8   said, [~.
43.10 said, [~.
43.13 said, [~.
43.14 Boxley, [~:
43.19 room∧ [~.
43.25 Boxley∧— [~,—
43.26 Stahr, [~:
44.1   explained, [~.
44.3   blown∧up [~-~
44.15 dictagraph∧ [dictograph,
44.17 office∧ [~,
44.26 Send——— [~——
44.26 Stahr, [~.
45.4   said, [~.

45.5	Stahr, [~.		50.21	time∧ [~,
45.5	Variety. [~?		50.24	all∧around [~-~
45.6	pictures [picture's		51.4	Stahr, [~.
45.9	want∧ [~,		51.8	thoughtfully, [~.
45.10	on∧ [~,		51.9	all∧ [~,
45.17	Stahr, [~.		51.13	said, [~.
45.24	impatiently, [~.		51.15	Rienmund, [Reinmund;
46.12	thought, [~.		51.27	Stahr, [~.
46.13	all∧ [~,		51.28	Coleman [Colman
46.14	dinner∧ [~,		52.3	desk∧ [~,
46.15	it∧ [~,		52.4	physically∧ [~,
46.18	up∧ [~,		52.5	said, [~.
46.21	in∧ [~,		52.6	somewhere∧ [~,
46.22	party∧ [~,		52.8	smiled∧ [~,
46.27	myself∧ even [~: ~		52.11	Broaca, [~.
46.28	myself∧ I'll [~, ~		52.13	sharply, [~.
47.4	Stahr. [~,		52.15	myself∧ [~,
47.6	And [and		52.15	what?'." [~?'∧"
47.8	Stahr, [~.		52.16	said, [~.
47.10	office∧ [~,		52.18	Stahr, [~.
47.12	dried∧up [~-~		52.20	regard∧ [~,
47.17	lesbian [Lesbian		52.26	sequence∧ [~,
47.18	maid∧ [~,		52.28	suddenly, [~.
47.18	was∧ [~,		52.28	see∧ Monroe∧ [~, ~,
47.18	women∧ [~,		53.5	said, [~.
47.19	stomach∧ [~,		53.12	play∧ [~,
47.28 -29	supervisor∧ [~,		53.13	Meloney∧ [~,
			53.13	Stahr∧ [~,
47.29	office∧ [~,		53.15	picture∧ [~,
47.29	director∧ [~,		53.17	Broaca∧ [~,
48.1	on∧ [~,		53.17	three∧day [~-~
48.7	said∧ [~,		53.19	Rieny [Reiny
48.9	role [rôle		53.22	limousine∧ [~,
48.13	asked, [~—		53.24	Shall [shall
48.bottom margin *Note:* SPACE			53.29	Well∧ [~,
49.1	Episode 9 [*deleted*		54.3	bluntly, [~.
49.5	more∧ [~,		54.4	time∧ [~,
49.7	Miracle [*Miracle*		54.8	unkindly, [~.
49.11	to problem∧ [~ ~,		54.10	you∧ [~,
49.12	wish∧ [~,		54.14	warningly, [~.
49.14	included∧ [~,		54.16	twenty∧five [~-~
49.14	beside [besides		54.17	to man [to a man
49.14	writers∧ [~,		54.24	back∧ [~,
49.15	supervisors∧ [~,		54.24	right∧ [~,
50.7	ignoramus∧ [~,		55.1	Wylie, [~.
50.17	character∧ [~,		55.5	up∧ [~,
50.20	native [gentile		55.9	and [And

55.10   understand∧ [∼,
55.12   swiftly∧ [∼,
55.15   play∧ [∼,
55.16   he∧ [∼,
55.18   role [rôle
55.23   was which∧ [∼ ∼,
55.23   it was∧ [∼ ∼,
55.27   sigh, [∼.
56.5   does∧ [∼,
56.11   facts∧ [∼,
56.15   them∧ [∼,
56.16   half∧closed [∼-∼
56.23   danger∧ [∼,
56.26   said. [∼,
57.1   Meloney, [∼.
57.3   Stahr, [∼.
57.25   back∧ [∼,
57.28   week∧ [∼,
58.1   caring∧ [∼,
58.6   half∧naive [∼-∼
58.8   foredoomed∧ [∼,
58.15   fauned [fawned
58.19   Wilshire∧ [∼,
58.21   Peels [Peel's
58.21   alpine [Alpine
58.22   war∧ [∼,
58.25   room∧ [∼,
58.26   desk∧ [∼,
58.bottom margin   *Note:* SPACE
59   ⟨Wilson holograph interpola-
         tion in TS (after CUP 44.2:
         'The conference was over.') cop-
         ied from Fitzgerald's Rejected
         Episode 10⟩

[Stahr was to have received
the Danish Prince Agge, who
"wanted to learn about pictures
from the beginning" and who is
mentioned in the author's cast
of characters as an "early Fascist."]

"Mr. Marcus calling from
New York," said Miss Doolan.

"What do you mean?" de-
manded Stahr. "Why I saw him
here last night."

"Well, he's on the phone—
it's a New York call and Miss
Jacobs' voice. It's his office."

Stahr laughed.

"I'm seeing him at lunch," he
said." There's no airplane fast
enough to take him there."

Miss Doolan returned to the
phone. Stahr lingered to hear
the outcome.

"It's all right," said Miss
Doolan presently. "It was a mistake. Mr. Marcus called East
this morning to tell them about
the quake and the flood on the
back lot, and it seems he asked
them to ask you about it. It was
a new secretary who didn't understand Mr. Marcus. I think
she got mixed up."

"I think she did," said Stahr
grimly.

Prince Agge did not understand either of them, but, looking for the fabulous, he felt it
was something triumphantly
American. Mr. Marcus, whose
quarters could be seen across
the way, had called his New
York office to to ask Stahr
about the flood. The Prince
imagined some intricate relationship without realizing that
the transaction had taken place
entirely within the once brilliant steel trap mind of Mr.
Marcus, which was intermit-
tently slipping.

"Any other messages?" asked
Stahr.

60.2   name∧ [∼,
60.22   regency [Regency
60.24   curiously∧ [∼,
60.bottom margin   *Note:* SPACE
61.1   Episode 10 [*deleted*
61.4   rulers∧ [∼;
61.4   guest∧ [∼,

61.5 sometimes asking questions
−6 sometimes about [sometimes asking questions about
61.8 foreign∧born [∼-∼
61.9 Englishman∧ [∼;
61.11 Leanbaum∧ [∼,
61.14 functioned, as has been said, [still managed to function
61.15 resillience [resilience
62.5 at [to
62.6 auditing∧ [∼,
62.7 themselves∧ [∼,
62.20 Brady∧ [∼,
62.21 picture∧ [∼,
62.22 early∧ [∼,
62.24 Monroe, [∼?
63.5 Hell's Angels or Ben Hur [*Hell's Angels* or *Ben Hur*
63.7 Populous [Populos
63.8 talk that reminded Prince Agge
−10 of Mike Van Dyke except that it tried to be and succeeded in being clear instead of confusing [talk① ⟨Wilson added footnote number: see below⟩
63.15 table∧ but∧ [∼, ∼,
63.15 forewarned∧ [∼,
63.21 said, [∼.
63.27 Popolous, [Populos.
63.bottom margin *Wilson footnote:* ①See notes.
64.15 amazement∧ [∼,
64.18 Oh∧ [∼,
64.21 occulist [oculist
64.21 afternoon, [∼—
64.21 Kennedy∧ [∼—
64.22 understand. [∼?
65.2 occulist [oculist
65.3 Stahr, [∼.
65.8 watched, [∼.
65.8 here∧ [∼,
65.14 now∧ [∼,
65.17 Stahr, [∼.
65.21 one∧ [∼,
65.22 up∧ [∼,
65.23 shing [shining
65.24 Hell's Angels∧ [*Hell's Angels,*

65.25 Brady said [Brady has said ⟨CUP: Brady says⟩
66.1 eyes∧ [∼,
66.2 down cast [downcast
66.3 table∧ [∼,
66.3 now∧ [∼,
66.5 room∧ [∼,
66.7 soldiers∧ [∼,
66.8 side burns [sideburns
66.8 first empire [First Empire
66.10 ago∧ [∼,
66.12 Lincoln∧ [∼,
66.14 where Moolay's Biography [when Nicolay's biography
66.15 admire∧ [∼,
66.16 instead∧ [∼,
66.17 forty∧cent [∼-∼
−18
66.20 Agge∧ [∼,
66.26 mouth∧ [∼,
67.1 Stahr∧ [∼,
67.2 him, [∼.
67.11 woman was [woman. He's sure it was
67.13 shoes∧ [∼,
67.15 moment, [∼:
67.bottom margin *Note:* SPACE
The following 9 entries refer to a typed page replacing 49.26–50.5.
68.1 *Correction for 10* [Chapter 4
68.6 that∧ [∼,
68.7 walked∧ [∼,
68.11 was delivery of effects and was the [was the
68.12 situations∧ [∼,
68.12 not   him [not out-
−13 play him
68.15 and [—with
68.15 had been as he [that he had
68.15 anticipated. His [∼: his
−16
69.1 For Episode 10 [deleted
69.2 "How are you, Monroe?" . . .
−15 "It's no good," said Rid-ingwood. [⟨deleted and re-placed with '*Correction for*

10," 68.1–17; see Emendations
and Textual Notes⟩

69.18   him, [~.
69.18   art [Art
69.21   But [but
69.23   set/\up [~-~
69.25   Stahr/\ [~,
69.27   procession/\ [~,
70.2   exema [eczema
70.3   take/\ [~,
70.3   emolument [emollient
70.5   blood/\ ~,
70.7   speak/\ [~,
70.9   director/\ [~,
70.27   range/\ [~,
71.17   said, [~.
71.26   grimly, [~.
72.4   tersely, [~.
72.6   mess/\ [~,
72.9   in [of
72.10   with Stahr/\ [~ ~,
72.11   customer/\ [~,
72.12   suddenly, [~.
72.bottom margin   *Note:* SPACE
72.bottom margin   *Note: Fitzgerald's
         Note:* What is missing in Rid-
         ingwood scene is passion and
         imagination, etc. What an extra-
         ordinary thing that it should all
         have been there for Riding–
         wood and then not there.
73.1   Episode 11 [*deleted*
73.7   before/\ [~,
73.14   fruit alike of [fruit of
73.14   or counsels [or of counsels
73.18   departments/\ [~,
73.25   quickly/\ [~,
74.4   tank/\ [~,
74.4   take/\ [~,
74.12   *de* [*du*
74.12   Coleman)/\ [Colman),
74.13   through/\ [~,
74.24   quietly, [~.
74.27   se [see
75.2   Stahr, [~.
75.5   take/\ [~,
75.6   head/\ [~,

75.8   Stahr, [~.
75.18   imperturable [imperturbable
75.22   Put [put
75.23   not/\ [~,
75.29   story/\ [~,
76.1   darkness, [~.
76.6   Flieshacker, [Fleishacker.
77.6   matter/\ [~,
77.12   row/\ [~,
77.13   said, [~.
77.21   out/\ [~,
77.24   said, [~.
77.29   man/\ [~,
78.3   has [had
78.13   it/\ [~,
78.20   picture./\ [~."
78.28   finished— [~;
78.29   chairs— [~;
79.4   good, "Can't [~. /\~
79.5   Steppes [*Steppes*
79.18   devise [device
79.19   ending/\ [~,
79.20   had before [had had before
79.24   giving/\ [~,
79.25   twenty/\five [~-~
79.26   well/\ [~,
79.27   occulist [oculist
79.28   20, [~;
80.4   sets/\ [~,
80.4   talked/\ [~,
80.8   Agge, [~.
80.9   anyone? [~!
80.11   Oh/\ [~,
80.11   them/\ [~,
80.11   here/\ [~,
80.13   Like [Such as
80.16   pairs/\ [~,
80.17   down/\ [~,
81.4   another/\ [~,
81.5   expected/\ [~,
81.6   picture/\ [~,
81.10   gone/\ [~,
81.14   wanted? [~.
81.15   of the [about ~
81.18   Minna/\ [~,
81.24   him/\ [~,
82.6   screen/\ [~,

82.9   trick. [~?
82.11   if it were [whether it might not be
82.13   desk∧ [~,
82.15   way∧ [~,
82.22   brush∧off [~-~
82.25   said, [~.
82.28   again∧ [~,
83.7   you∧ [~,
83.11   movies. [~?
83.15   you, [~?
83.19   meet∧— [~?—
83.24   then∧ [~,
84.7   year∧ [~,
84.9   states∧ [~,
84.12   picture∧ [~,
84.13   outside∧ [~,
84.14   Cornhill∧ [~,
84.19   room∧ [~,
84.21   office∧ [~,
84.22   Diocenes [Euripides ⟨CUP:
        Diogenes⟩
84.23   pictures [picture
84.23   simply, [~.
84.23   Esculpias [Aristophanes ⟨CUP:
        Asclepius⟩
84.23   Minanorus [Menander
84.28   Garcia, [Zavras.
85.3   now. [~?
85.5   did∧ [~,
85.8   the oracle [the Delphic oracle
85.8   Garcia, "The solver of
−9   Elusianian mysteries. "I [
        Zavras. "I
85.13   Pedro, [~. ⟨CUP: Pete.⟩
85.17   My [my
85.22   black∧ [~,
85.26   chair∧ [~,
85.bottom margin   *Note:* SPACE
86.1   Episode 12 [*deleted*
86.5   gate∧ [~,
86.14   studio∧ [~,
86.14   tense∧ [~,
86.15   close∧ [~,
86.16   boulevard∧ [~,
87.1   her∧ [~,
87.7   asked, [~.
87.10   polite, [~.

87.10   smile, [~.
87.15   her get [her to get
87.16   car∧ [~,
87.19   face∧ [~,
87.21   said, [~.
87.22   startled, [~.
88.4   intuition, [~.
88.12   asked, [~.
88.14   said, [~.
88.19   road∧ [~,
89.6   door∧ [~,
89.7   inquired∧ [~,
89.7   it?"∧ [~?",
89.15   benificence [beneficence
89.16   Edna∧ [~,
89.16   said, [~.
89.23   Edna, [~.
90.2   forehead, [~.
90.3   both—, [~,
90.3   —come [∧~
90.6   Davis' [Davis's
90.7   Edna∧ [~,
90.10   offensiveness∧ [~,
90.10   said∧ [~,
90.14   Stahr, [~.
90.27   said, [~.
91.12   royal— [~:
91.13   queen— [~;
91.25   laughed∧ [~,
92.2   said, [~.
92.3   come∧ [~,
92.11   and left [and it left
92.14   car; [~,
92.15   him, [~;
92.26   on∧ [~,
93.1   lonliness [loneliness
94.2   illness∧ [~,
94.3   secretive∧ [~,
94.6   something∧ [~,
94.8   profit∧sharing [~-~
94.9   lot∧ [~,
94.11   me∧ [~,
94.11   then∧ [~,
95.1   Episode 13 [Chapter 5
95.2   morning∧ [~,
95.8   suggested, [~.
95.9   second∧hand [~-~

that it must be seen to, nor so insignificant that it could be
ignored So he postponed it again and sat motionless at his desk
for a moment thinking about Russia. Not so much about Russia as
about the picture about Russia which would consume a hopeless
half hour presently. He knew there were many stories about Russia,
not to mention The Story, and he had employed a squad of writers
and research men for over a year, but all the stories involved had
the wrong feel. He felt it could be told in terms of the American
thirteen states, but it kept coming out different, in new terms that
opened unpleasant possibilities and problems. He considered he was
very fair to Russia--he had no desire to make anything but a
sympathetic picture, but it kept turning into a headache.

"Mr. Stahr--Mr. Drummon's outside, and Mr. Kirstoff
and Mrs. Cornhill, about the Russian picture."

"All right--send them in."

Afterwards from six-thirty to seven-thirty he watched
the afternoon rushes. Except for his engagement with the girl
he would ordinarily have spent the early evening in the projection
room or the dubbing room, but it had been a late night with the
earthquake and he decided to go to dinner. Coming in through
his front office, he found ~~Pedro Garcia~~ *Pete Zarras* waiting, his arm in a sling.

"You are the Aeschylus and the ~~Euripides~~ *Euripides* of the moving
picture," said ~~Garcia~~ *Zarras* simply "Also the ~~Esculpias~~ *Aristophanes* and the ~~Minanorus~~ *Menander*."
He bowed.

"Who are they?" asked Stahr smiling.

"They are my countrymen."

"I didn't know you made pictures in Greece."

"You're joking with me, Monroe," said ~~Garcia~~ *Zarras* "I want

Wilson's alterations on the latest draft. His Pedro [Pete and Garcia
[Zavras alterations are not listed on p. 263.

to say you are as dandy a fellow as they come. You have saved me
one hundred percent."

"You feel all right now?"

"My arm is nothing. It feels like someone kisses me
there. It was worth doing what I did, if this is the outcome."

"How did you happen to do it here?" Stahr asked
curiously.

"Before the oracle," said ~~Garcia~~ Zavias ~~The solver of
Elusinian mysteries.~~ "I wish I had my hands on the son-of-a-bitch
who started the story."

"You make me sorry I didn't get an education," said
Stahr.

"It isn't worth a damn," said Pedro, "I took my
baccalaureate in Salonika and look how I ended up."

"Not quite," said Stahr.

"If you want anybody's throat cut anytime day or night,"
said ~~Garcia~~ Zavias "My number is in the book."

Stahr closed his eyes and opened them again. Zavias's ~~Garcia's~~
silhouette had blurred a little against the sun. He hung on to
the table behind him and said in an ordinary voice.

"Good luck, Pete ~~Pedro~~."

The room was almost black, but he made his feet move
following a pattern into his office and waited till the door
clicked shut before he felt for the pills. The water decanter
clattered against the table; the glass clacked. He sat down in
a big chair, waiting for the benzedrine to take effect before he
went to dinner.

SPACE

95.10   book, [~.
95.11   east [East
95.17   smart∧ [~,
95.17   money∧[~,
95.20   The Thundering Beat of My Heart [*The Thundering Beat of My Heart*
95.22   round∧ [~,
95.22   touch∧ [~,
95.23   legs∧ [~,
95.24   nature∧ [~,
95.24   that. [~?
96.2   day∧ [~,
96.5   offer. [~?
96.6   said∧ [~,
96.7   money∧ [~,
96.11   "*Gone*" or "*Lost*" [∧*Gone*∧ or ∧*Lost*∧
96.13   depression∧ [~,
96.14   hot∧ [~,
96.15   "Blue Heaven" [∧*Blue Heaven*∧
96.15   "When Day Is Done" [
–16   ∧*When Day Is Done*∧
96.17   "Little Girl You've Had a
–18   Busy Day" [∧*Little Girl You've Had a Busy Day*∧
96.20   Lost and Gone [*Lost and Gone*
96.20   mood∧ [~,
96.21   Lovely to Look At∧ [*Lovely to Look At,*
96.23   mountain [Mountain
96.24   sometime [sometimes
96.27   Stahr, [~?
96.27   said, [~.
96.28   do∧ [~,
97.2   think∧ [~,
97.4   Cecelia∧ [Cecilia, ⟨CUP: Celia∧⟩
97.10   And [and
97.19   Wylie, [~.
97.23   shiver, [~.
97.28   couch∧ [~,
98.4   city∧ [~,
98.5   section∧ [~,
98.6   bungalows∧ [~,

98.8   Hampshire∧ [~,
98.12   fire∧ [~,
98.12   everything∧ [~,
–13
98.13   fifty∧fifty [~-~
98.15   in [on
98.16   ∧Hello∧ ["~"
98.17   expected. [~:
98.18   knowing∧ [~,
98.19   sure∧ [~,
98.27   than [from
98.28   down∧ [~,
98.28   telephones∧ [~,
98.29   appendage∧ [~,
98.29   him∧ [~;
99.4   married∧ [~,
99.5   Robbie [Robby
99.11   Yes. [~,
99.12   there∧ it [~, ~
99.13   unexpectedly, [~.
99.20   minute, [~.
99.25   difference, [~:
99.25   way∧ [~,
100.4   as my [as in my
100.18   was pasted [had been pasted
100.bottom margin   *Note:* SPACE
101.1   13 (continued) [*deleted*
101.4   pretty∧ [~,
101.6   everyone∧ [~,
101.11   semi-star∧ [~,
–12
101.14   party∧ [~,
101.17   Cafe [Café
101.23   self∧respect [~-~
102.2   pocket∧ [pockets,
102.5   finished∧ [~,
102.6   Heine [Henie
102.16   sneak-preview [~∧~
–17
102.17   him∧ [~,
102.18   theatre∧ [~,
102.22   her∧ [~,
102.25   him∧ [~,
103.3   close∧ [~,
103.5   real∧ [~,
103.21   laughed, [~.
103.21   curiosity? [~!

103.24 this∧ [~,
104.1 to∧ "it's [~, "It's
104.2 chink∧ [~,
104.5 dancing∧ [~,
104.7 you∧ [~,
104.12 And [and
104.16 Cafe [Café
104.17 Louden [Loudoun
104.17 County∧ [~,
104.17 Odessa∧ [~,
104.19 that Jews [that the Jews
−20
104.20 a super-symbol [a symbol
104.22 horses∧ [~,
104.28 there, [~∧
105.3 There— [~∧
105.3 —goes [∧~
105.12 picture∧ [~,
105.14 But [but
105.16 wearily, [~.
105.20 Stahr, [~.
105.21 depths [depth
106.13 retracted, [~.
106.15 little∧ [~,
106.16 is Sunday∧ [~ ~,
106.16 on Sunday∧ [~ ~,
106.19 opened∧ [~,
106.21 said, [~.
106.23 alone. [~?
107.1 said, [~.
107.1 tomorrow∧ [~,
107.3 harm∧ [~,
107.5 too∧ [~,
107.6 hall∧ [~,
107.7 police∧ [~,
107.13 alley∧ [~,
107.15 now∧ [~,
107.21 ∧What [—what
107.22 here∧ [~,
107.26 thirty-five∧ [~-~,
107.28 grimly, [~.
107.29 tomorrow∧ [~,
107.29 you. [~?
108.4 swimming∧ [~,
108.5 please∧ [~,
108.6 would out [would find out
108.10 said, [~.

108.10 here∧— [~?—
108.14 car∧ [~,
108.19 three∧ [~—
108.25 to ride [for a drive
108.25 innocently, [~.
109.1 ∧Changed [—changed
109.2 exactly∧ [~,
109.3 amplified, [~:
109.6 ∧Someone [—someone
109.10 No— [~:
109.13 "I'm on a See-saw" [∧I'm on
         a See-saw∧
109.13 now∧ [~,
109.18 nothing∧ [~,
109.18 absent∧minded [~-~
109.bottom margin Note: SPACE
110.1 Section 14 [*deleted*
110.4 veil, [~∧
110.5 him∧ [~,
110.6 strange∧ too∧ [~, ~,
110.8 when they first [the night
−9 they had first
110.10 person before— [person as
−11 before:
110.16 eyes∧ [~,
111.5 lightly, [~:
111.26 ago∧ [~,
111.28 things∧ [~:
112.5 said, [~.
112.12 said, [~.
112.13 it∧ [~,
112.16 me∧ [~,
112.18 I gave [I'd given
112.20 light∧ [~,
112.25 her∧ [~,
112.29 east [East
113.10 word∧ [~,
113.12 Monica∧ [~,
113.17 ∧Much [—much
114.1 ∧Another [—another
114.2 roof. [~?
114.5 A [a
114.7 out∧ [~,
114.8 try∧ [~,
114.13 said, [~.
114.23 out∧ [~,
115.1 Kathleen, [~.

115.5   promontary [promontory
115.5   fusilage [fuselage
115.7   wood∧ [~,
115.9   front∧ [~,
115.13   cheerfully, [~.
−14
115.17   that∧ [~,
115.19   manana [mañana
115.27   laid beyond [laid sod beyond
115.28   admitted, [~.
116.5   Oh∧ [~,
116.7   seagulls∧ [~,
116.10   ∧Not [—not
116.10   girls. [~?
116.11   plans∧ [~,
116.20   go∧ [~,
116.21   absent∧mindedly [~-~
117.1   ⟨before 'There'⟩ *Note:* No ¶
117.3   house∧ [~,
117.4   garden∧ [~,
117.16   decade— [~:
117.17   discordant∧ [~,
117.17   impressed∧ [~,
117.22   benefit∧ [~,
117.25   Kathleen, [~:
117.26   winked∧ [~,
117.27   attention∧ [~,
118.3   then∧ [~:
118.7   orangutang [orang-outang
118.11   orangutang [orang-outang
118.12   Kathleen∧ [~,
118.13   phone∧ [~,
118.19   minute, [~.
118.22   Hello∧ [~,
118.22   orangutang [orang-outang
118.23   changed∧ [~,
118.24   ∧hello∧ ['Hello'
118.26   Hello∧ [~,
118.26   orangutang [orang-outang
118.28   King Kong∧ [*King Kong,*
118.29   the Hairy Ape [*The Hairy
         Ape*
119.2   and changed [and had
         changed
119.2   manner∧ [~,
119.3   ridiculous∧ [~,
119.4   orangutang [orang-outang

119. below line 4   *Note:* SPACE
120.1   Section 14 (2nd part) [*deleted*
120.7   structure∧ [~,
120.15   malting [matting
120.21   road∧ [~,
120.22   gasoline∧ [~,
121.11   done∧ [~,
121.12   loneliness∧ [~,
121.14   sour∧ [~,
121.14   waitress∧ [~,
121.15   and∧ when [~, ~
121.22   hill∧ [~,
121.24   head lights [headlights
121.27   quickly∧ [~,
121.28   this, [~.
122.6   house∧ [~,
122.13   night∧ [~,
122.17   in∧ [~,
122.19   right∧ [~,
122.20   long∧ [~,
122.21   toughed [touched
122.22   eyes∧ [~,
122.23   tight∧clutched [~-~
122.24   sigh∧ [~,
122.24   then ∧oh∧ [~ "Oh"
122.26   faintly∧ [~,
122.26   frowning∧ too∧ [~, ~,
122.28   apart∧ [~,
122.28   still∧ [~,
123.1   moment. [~?
123.2   this∧ [~,
123.3   exultant∧ [~;
123.4   him∧ [~,
123.5   exultation∧ [~,
123.7   inside∧ [~,
123.9   ∧Not [—not
123.13   relief∧ [~,
123.16   car∧ [~,
123.17   faces∧ [~,
123.bottom margin   *Note:* SPACE
124.1   Section 14 (Part III) [*deleted*
124.2   grey∧ [~,
124.13   chink∧ [~,
124.17   her∧ [~,
124.20   landmarks∧ [~,
124.20   away∧ [~,
125.1   arms∧ [~,

125.6   this∧ [~,
125.7   desirous∧ [~,
125.12   time∧ [~,
125.13   provocatively∧ [~,
125.17   again∧ [~,
125.19   speaking∧ [~,
125.25   darkness∧ [~,
125.27   up . . . [~. . . .
125.27   room the room [room, it
126.4   seat∧ [~,
126.11   person∧ [~,
126.18   asked, [~.
126.21   brooded, [~.
126.24   ring∧ [~,
126.25   mood∧ [~,
126.26   past∧ [~,
126.29   thoughts, [~.
127.7   ENGLISH∧ [~, ⟨TS read
         'British' but Wilson accepted
         Graham's emendation to 'EN-
         GLISH' and added comma.⟩
127.11   closet∧ [~,
127.13   candles∧ [~,
127.22   time. [~,
127.22   Edna∧ [~,
127.27   her, [~.
128.1   said, [~.
128.8   slightly, [~.
128.14   chrystaline [crystalline
128.22   by second∧ [~ ~,
128.26   said, [~.
129.6   him∧ [~,
129.8   said∧ [~,
129.22   beach. [~?
130.1   me, [~—
130.2   smiling, [~.
130.10   said, [~.
130.10   university∧ [~,
130.19   Spengler∧ [~,
130.24   patiently∧ [~,
130.27   learning∧ [~,
131.4   anything∧ [~,
131.6   said∧ [~,
131.6   up, [~.
131.7   know∧ [~,
131.8   beyond∧ [~,
131.12   eyes, [~.

131.15   grunnion [grunion
131.18   door∧ [~,
131.24   turn∧ [~,
131.26   tide∧ [~,
131.28   in [on
131.28   negro [Negro
131.29   them∧ [~,
131.29   collecting quickly [collecting
         the grunion quickly
132.3   scornful∧ [~,
132.3   plague [plaque
132.4   bounder [boulder
132.5   negro [Negro
132.8   Malibu∧ [~,
132.8   it∧ [~,
132.10   receeded [receded
132.10   swiftly∧ [~,
132.16   Rosecrucian [Rosicrucian
132.17   me∧ too∧ [~, ~,
132.19   down∧ [~,
132.20   negro [Negro
132.25   him∧ [~,
132.27   spray∧ [~;
132.28   again∧ [~,
133.1   Rosecrucian [Rosicrucian
133.6   gone∧ [~,
133.6   negro's [Negro's
133.6   full∧ [~,
133.9   house∧ [~,
133.15   moment∧ [~,
133.18   deliberately, [~.
133.20   all∧ [~,
133.25   said, [~.
133.27   guessed∧ [~,
133.29   true, [~.
134.2   eyes∧ [~,
134.4   laughing, [~.
134.6   with∧ [~,
134.6   an [as
134.10   true∧ [~,
134.20   incroaching [encroaching
135.1   close∧ [~,
135.5   house∧ [~,
135.15   light∧ [~,
136.16   door, [~.
135.25   Well∧ [~,
136.1   words∧ [~,

136.1	you [You
136.3	arms∧ [~,
136.4	change∧ [~,
136.6	hill∧ [~,
136.6	inside, [~∧
136.9	presently∧ [~,
136.11	below∧ [~,
136.12	tatoo [tattoo
136.18	persistently∧ [~,
136.18	other∧ [~,
136.19	negro [Negro
136.20	fish∧ [~,
136.22	wrong∧ [~,
136.24	of pictures∧ [~ ~,
136.27	interest∧ [~,
136.28	negro [Negro
137.1	rest∧ [~,
137.2	negro [Negro
137.3	door∧ [~,
137.3	on∧ [~,
137.4	Phillipino [Philippino
137.5	library∧ [~,
137.16	Phillipino [Philippino
137.18	Stahr, [~.
137.20	No∧ [~,
137.21	esq. [Esq.
137.24	phone∧ [~,
137.33	Minna∧ [~,
138.1	died∧ [~,
138.2	surprised∧ [~,
138.4	into [in
138.11	men∧ [~,
138.12	twelve∧ probably∧ [~, ~,
138.13	see [See
138.14	sham—∧ [~—,
138.15	do∧ [~;
138.16	are∧ [~,
138.17	himself∧ [~,
138.18	forebearance∧ [forbearance,
138.19	lessons∧ [~.
138.20	Phillipino [Philippino
138.21	fruit∧ [~,
138.27	Kathleen∧ [~,
138.29	hand∧ [~,
139.2	stranger∧ [~,
139.left margin	*Note:* Roman Set same as letter in first chapter

139.24	first thought [second ~
140.2	again∧ [~,
140.6	now∧ [~,
140.8	itself∧ [~,
140.15	landing∧ [~,
140.18	room∧ [~,
140.19	out∧ [~,
140.22	hours∧ [hours'
140.bottom margin	*Note:* SPACE *(Wilson mis-numbered pp. 174–82.)*
174.1	*Section 15* (first part) [*deleted*
174.6	table∧ [~,
174.7	was∧ [~,
174.8	Also∧ [~,
174.12	Martha∧ [~,
174.18	same∧ [~,
174.20	playwrights∧ [~,
174.24	writer's [writers'
174.26	resounding the [resounding with the
175.5	typewriter∧ [~,
175.8	Rose, [~.
175.12	University∧ [~,
175.13	school∧ [~,
175.14	down∧ [~,
175.16	eyes∧ [~,
175.20	lot∧ [~,
175.23	funny∧ [~,
175.28	close∧up [~-~
176.5	him∧ . . . [~" . . .
176.7	Monroe∧ [~,
176.10	it. . . . [~ . . .
176.11	God∧ [~,
176.14	morning∧ [~,
176.15	Stahr∧ [~,
176.21	the Saturday Evening Post [*The Saturday Evening Post*
176.24	gentile [gentle
176.25	screen∧ [~,
176.27	loveable [lovable
177.2	Oh— [~,
177.2	—that [∧~
177.3	afterwards∧ [~,
177.5	said, [~.
177.6	break∧ [~,

177.12   cooperate [coöperate
177.bottom margin   *Note:* SPACE
178.1   15 (second part) [*deleted*
178.3   restaurant∧ [~,
178.4   lunch∧ [~,
178.6   eat∧ [~,
178.7   girl∧ [~,
178.9   washed∧out [~-~
178.12   ∧Thirty [—thirty
178.14   Spring [spring
178.22   high pitch∧ [~ ~,
178.22   neglect∧ [~,
178.23   acquiescence∧ [~,
178.24   Martha∧ [~,
178.28   was [had been
178.28   up to [up so as to
−179.1
179.1   oh∧ [~,
179.3   natural∧born [~-~
179.3   skivies [skivvies
179.4   throw∧overs [~-~
179.6   Florence∧ [~,
179.8   debut [début
179.10   Dodd∧ [~,
179.12   Swanson∧ [~,
179.12   cowboy∧ too∧ [~, ~,
179.12   Brent∧ [~,
179.15   all∧ [~,
179.17   office∧ [~,
179.18   down∧ [~,
179.19   and∧ [~,
179.19   easy∧ [~,
179.21   called, [~.
179.22   conference∧ [~,
179.24   another door∧ [~ ~,
179.25   day∧ [~,
179.26   hot∧ [~,
179.27   said, [~.
179.29   Dodd∧ [~,
180.5   Or [or
180.8   said, [~.
180.8   God damn [goddam
180.11   God damn [goddam
180.15   sniffed∧ [~,
180.16   said, [~.
180.20   despair∧ [~,
180.22   hours∧ [~,

180.22   sick∧ [~,
180.25   bathroom, [~.
180.27   herself∧ [~,
180.28   transfixed∧ [~,
180.29   again∧ [~,
181.1   outside∧ [~,
181.2   know∧ [~,
181.5   floor∧ [~,
181.6   clothes∧ [~,
181.8   me∧ [~,
181.11   couch, [~.
181.14   out∧ [~,
181.15   asked∧ [~,
181.15   matter∧ dear∧ [~, ~?
181.15   anything, [~:
181.20   emulsion [immersion
181.23   unlocked∧ [~,
181.25   about∧ [~,
181.27   said∧ [~:
182.3   around∧ [~,
182.4   almost∧ [~,
182.7   Martha, [~.
182.bottom margin   *Note:* SPACE
141.1   *Episode 16, First Part* [*deleted* (Wilson wrote 'Chapter 6' at the head of the page and then crossed it out.)
141.6   gettin [getting
141.13   smiling, [~.
141.17   medium∧ [~,
141.21   suggestions∧ [~,
142.4   conscriptions [inscriptions
142.5   said, [~.
142.7   Stahr, [~.
142.12   peoples' [people's
142.26   supervisor∧ [~,
142.26   stale-mate [stalemate
143.17   Kitty [kitty
143.18   Boxley∧ [~,
143.19   secretary∧ [~,
143.19   talley [tally
143.20   time∧ [~,
143.21   end∧ [~,
143.22 $5.50∧ [~,
144.1   But [but
144.3   feel∧ [~,
144.9   it∧ [~,

144.14 said, [~.
144.15 mean∧ [~,
144.16 'Put Yourself in My Place' [
 ∧*Put Yourself in My Place*∧
144.19 tomorrow∧ [~,
144.bottom margin   *Note:* SPACE
145.1 Episode 16 (Part 2) [*deleted*
145.4 waist∧ [~,
145.9 early∧ [~,
145.19 minutes∧ [~,
145.21 Stahr, [~.
145.21 good∧ [~,
145.26 looking [liking
146.1 said, [~.
146.6 around∧ [~,
146.12 differently∧ [~,
146.14 poison∧ [~,
146.17 before∧ [~,
146.21 know. [~?
146.23 own∧ [~,
146.27 closed∧ [~,
146.29 Moore. [~?
147.13 desk∧ [~,
147.21 letter∧ [~,
147.22 that∧ [~,
147.26 pompously, [~.
148.1 laughed, [~:
148.7 demanded, [~.
148.11 Oh∧ [~,
148.11 begged, [~.
148.17 himself, [~.
148.19 considered, [~.
148.20 suggested, [~.
148.26 idea "Riding [idea of "riding
148.28 them∧ [~,
149.1 beginning∧ [~,
149.5 plainly∧ [~,
149.6 down∧ [~,
149.9 summer∧ [~,
149.13 brave∧ [~,
149.13 stimulating∧ [~,
149.14 going—to any pole". [going."
149.15 brough [brought
149.17 way∧ [~,
149.18 in life [in his life
150.10 a piece∧ [apiece,
150.11 died∧ [~,

150.13 oh∧ [~,
150.16 uncle∧ [~,
150.27 tans [Tans
150.28 'Last Blessing' [∧*Last Blessing*∧
151.19 My King [~ king
151.10 of job [of a job
151.26 said, [~.
152.2 old∧fashioned [~-~
152.4 syndicalist∧ [~,
152.10 her∧ [~,
152.12 saying∧ [~,
152.20 say∧ [~,
152.25 today∧ [~,
152.25 another a week [another
 week
152.27 now∧ [~,
152.28 she [She
153.3 Oh∧ [~,
153.4 half∧way [~-~
153.8 ∧Oh∧ yes∧ ["~, ~"
153.19 Kings [kings
153.21 Pennsylvania∧ [~,
153.23 cavern∧ [~,
153.23 betrayed behind [beyond behind ⟨CUP: behind⟩
153.28 asked∧ [~,
154.13 philandering— [~:
154.14 analymous [anomalous
154.25 implicity [implicitly
154.26 smiling, [~.
154.26 open∧ [~,
154.29 And [and
155.10 said∧ "it is [~, "It *is*
155.10 life∧ [~,
155.12 And tell [And not to tell
155.13 him∧ [~,
155.15 more∧ [~,
155.15 slowly∧waving [~-~
155.18 grown [grow
155.20 know [knows
155.26 being enchanted [being an enchanted
156.4 a kin [akin
156.5 ageing [aging
156.5 time-need∧ [~-~,
−6
156.6 heart∧ [~,

156.8	say∧ [~,
156.11	power∧ [~,
156.17	o'clock∧ [~,
156.18	luncheon∧ [~,
156.20	suing [sueing
156.23	*send* [*Send*
157.1	Episode 17 [Chapter 6
157.2	Louise∧ [~,
157.14	college∧ [~,
157.18	seriously, [~.
157.23	I barged [I had barged
158.1	said, [~.
158.5	writers' guild [Writers' Guild
158.9	Films [films
158.10	Doctor Caliagarri [*Doctor Caligari*
158.10	Salvatore [Salvator
158.11	Le Chien D'Analou [*Le Chien d'Analou*
158.13	twenties∧ [~,
159.2	descendent [descendant
159.4	occasion∧ [~,
159.8	voice∧ [~,
159.18	suggested, [~.
159.20	him, [~.
159.20	crutch∧ [~,
159.24	they. [~?
159.25	years so∧ [years or so,
159.27	said, [~.
160.4	said, [~.
160.7	this∧ [~,
160.9	said, [~.
160.12	Member∧ [~,
160.12	announced∧ [~,
160.16	Tracy∧ [~,
160.20	please∧ [~,
160.23	Stahr, [~.
160.27	Stahr, [~.
161.2	Company [company
161.3	impatiently, [~.
161.10	back∧ [~,
161.13	said, [~.
161.17	dance.∧" [~.' "
161.26	farmers∧ [farmers'
162.6	morning∧ [~,
162.7	in how to [in trying to think of a way to
162.8	say∧ [~,

162.10	relief∧ [~,
162.10	along∧ [~,
162.11	other∧ [~,
162.13	table∧ [~,
162.15	room∧ [~,
162.18	Stahr, [~.
162.22	say∧ [~,
162.26	Brimmer, [~.
162.28	guild [Guild
162.29	power∧ [~,
163.4	Stahr∧ [~,
163.7	Brimmer, [~.
163.12	Stahr, [~.
164.7	Company Tec [company tec
164.8	Stahr, [~.
164.11	them∧ [~,
164.18	and efficient [and most effi-
-19	cient
164.19	west [West
164.20	you∧ [~,
164.22	said, [~.
164.23	Brimmer, [~:
164.26	baptist [Baptist
164.29	Frankenstien [Frankenstein
165.6	Oh∧ [~,
165.6	Stahr, [~.
165.8	said, [~.
165.11	yourself∧ [~,
165.11	right∧ [~,
165.17	it∧ too∧ [~, ~;
165.18	quarter, but [quarter. But
165.18	do it∧ [~ ~,
165.20	me∧ [~,
165.22	midsummer∧ [~,
165.28	pong∧ [~,
166.1	"Little Man∧ you've had a Busy Day∧" [∧*Little Man, You've Had a Busy Day,*∧
166.3	drive∧ [~,
166.8	Bernie∧ [~,
166.9	table∧ [~,
166.11	cocktails∧ [~,
166.18	them. [~:
166.22	Brimmer, [~.
166.26	navy [Navy
166.28	evening∧ [~,
166.28	faintly∧ [~,
166.29	smiling∧ [~,

167.1   tradition∧ [~,
167.2   conversation∧ [~,
167.2   right." [~.∧
169.3   succintly [succinctly
167.4   Brimmer, [~.
167.6   picture∧ [~,
167.7   water mark [watermark
167.9   forward∧ [~,
167.16   smiling, [~.
167.20   me∧ [~,
167.22   over∧ [~,
167.24   writers∧ [~,
168.4   so-and-sos [~-~-so's
168.12   virtuoso∧ [~,
168.15   said∧ [~,
168.16   attitude, [~.
168.18   pleasantly, [~.
168.25   difficult∧ [~,
168.29   —that [∧~
169.1   belo*nged* [belo*nged*
169.11   different∧ [~,
169.12   us∧ [~,
169.14   was gentle [was a gentle
169.16   ago∧ [~—
169.17   nine. [~,
169.18   college∧ [~,
169.18   twenty-five∧ [~-~,
169.25   Brimmer, [~.
169.27   Stahr, [~.
169.28   drink∧ [~,
170.2   bat∧ [~,
170.4   back∧ [~,
170.4   playing∧ [~,
170.5   Brimmer∧ [~,

170.6   arrived∧ [~,
170.13   schitzophrania [schizophre-
         nia
170.18   Stahr, [~.
170.20   forward∧ [~,
170.22   said, [~.
170.29   face∧ [~,
170.29   saying∧ [~,
171.1   half∧sick [~-~
171.4   had [held
171.4   minute∧ [~,
171.6   back∧ [~,
171.9   right, [~.
171.10   table, [~:
171.10   dollars∧ [~,
171.16   again∧ [~,
171.16   repose∧ [~,
171.18   grass∧ [~,
171.24   fool. [~?
172.1   handkerchief∧ [~,
172.3   sick∧ [~,
172.4   right∧ [~,
172.5   mouthwash∧ [~,
172.8   Bachic [Bacchic
172.9   him∧ [~,
172.10   house, [~;
172.11   veranda∧ [~,
172.13   off∧ [~,
172.13   finally sat [finally I sat
172.16   said, [~.
172.17   it," after [~." After
172.17   added, [~:
172.24   room∧— [~?—
172.29   me, [~.

VARIANTS IN THE SCRIBNERS SETTING COPY AND THE FIRST PRINTING

The right-pointing brackets indicate the sequence of variation after the latest typescripts as revised by Fitzgerald and altered by Wilson. The reading in the Cambridge edition (CUP) is provided in angle brackets when it differs significantly from the variants recorded in the collation. Editorial notes are provided in angle brackets.

WTS latest typescripts as revised by Fitzgerald and altered by Wilson (i.e., the text Wilson delivered to Scribners)
SC   Scribners setting copy (retyped from WTS)
CSC holograph correction in an unidentifiable hand on the Scribners setting copy
WSC Wilson holograph correction on the Scribners setting copy
B   book (the 1941 Scribners first printing of the first edition)

3.5–6	"*The Producer's Daughter*", WTS, SC [∧~ ~ ~∧, B	6.3	Brady WTS [*Brady* SC [*Brady* B
3.14	Smith WTS, SC [Bennington B	6.4	him, WTS, SC [~. B
3.20	her∧ WTS, SC [~, B	6.4	*thought* WTS [*thought* SC, B
3.21	it∧but WTS, SC [~, ~ B		
3.21	class∧ WTS, SC [~, B	6.6	Wylie!" WTS [~?. " SC [~!", B
4.1	Junior WTS, SC [junior B	6.6	brushed WTS [burshed SC [brushed B
4.1	alone∧ WTS, SC [~, B		
4.11	me∧ WTS, SC [~, B	6.8	defiantly. WTS, SC [~: B
4.13	it, WTS, SC [~: B	6.19	∧I WTS ["I SC, B
4.14	Jew∧ WTS, SC [~, B	6.29	*night?* WTS [*night?* SC, B
4.21	to, WTS, SC [~— B	7.1	Schwartz", WTS [~," SC, B
4.24–25	hurricane, WTS, SC [~. B	7.2	father's∧ WTS, SC [~, B
4.33	nice— WTS, SC [~, B	7.4	saying, WTS, SC [~: B
4.33–34	approvingly "—if WTS, SC [~, "~ B	7.11	Schwartz, WTS [~∧ SC, B
		7.20	unmistakeably WTS [unmistakably SC, B
5.5	West WTS [west SC [West B		
5.6	depression∧ WTS, SC [~, B	8.17	Northampton WTS, SC [Bennington B
5.11	stewardess, WTS, SC [~. B	8.21	then.) WTS [~." SC [~.) B
5.19	father WTS, SC [Father B	8.36	White, WTS, SC [~. B
5.28	father WTS, SC [Father B	9.7	*he's* WTS, SC [*he's* B

9.12   kneecap WTS, SC [knee-cap B
9.32   flanks/\ WTS, SC [~, B
10.7   grey WTS, SC [gray B
10.12   farm house WTS, SC [
        farmhouse B
10.17   Memphis, WTS, SC [~/\ B
10.18   Cecilia/\ WTS, SC [~, B
10.20   enough/\ WTS, SC [~, B
10.22   Smith WTS, SC [Bennington B
10.24   *jun*ior WTS, SC [*junior* B
10.25   Juniors WTS, SC [juniors B
10.29   time WTS, SC [times B
10.35   Cecilia, WTS, SC [~: B
11.2   you!/\" WTS, SC [~!' " B
11.4   narcissus/\ WTS, SC [~, B
12.21   said, WTS, SC [~. B
13.11   lonely, WTS, SC [~/\ B
13.11   still, WTS, SC [~/\ B
13.12   car—only WTS, SC [~. Only
        B
13.26   ghetto WTS, SC [Ghetto B
13.32   nourishment— WTS, SC [~: B
13.33   on WTS [one SC, B
14.4   hotel/\ WTS, SC [~, B
14.8   Frenchy WTS [French SC, B
14.18   Smith WTS, SC [Bennington B
−19
14.20   crash— WTS, SC [~, B
14.20   said, "—if WTS, SC [~, "/\~
        B
14.21   Bradogue WTS, SC [Brady B
14.22   father's WTS, SC [Father's B
14.25   father WTS, SC [Father B
15.1   awful/\looking WTS, SC [~-~
        B
15.1   discernably WTS, SC [discern-
        ibly B
15.6   time/\ WTS, SC [~, B
15.19   ho WTS [how SC, B
15.22   shepherd, WTS, SC [~/\ B
15.23   sleepless/\ WTS, SC [~, B
15.26   father's WTS, SC [Father's B
16.11   hearing/\ WTS, SC [~, B
16.11   question, WTS, SC [~: B
16.17   taxi/\ WTS, SC [~, B
16.18   /\Dear WTS, SC ["~ CSC, B
16.22   /\Your WTS, SC ["~ B

16.23   MANNY/\/\ WTS, SC [
        MANNY." B
16.26   done, WTS, SC [~— B
17.34   "—would WTS ["/\~ SC,
        B
18.24   course, WTS, SC [~/\ B
19.3   said, WTS, SC [~. B
19.3   new, WTS, SC [~?— B
19.5   interest, WTS, SC [~: B
19.22   volunteered/\ "—up WTS [~.
        "—Up SC [~, "/\up B
19.24   name." WTS, SC [~—" B
20.26   one, WTS, SC [~; B
20.28   wings/\ WTS, SC [~, B
21.3   home/\ WTS, SC [~, B
21.9   him/\ WTS, SC [~, B
21.15   Chapter 2 WTS [CHAPTER 2
        SC [~ II B ⟨CUP: Episodes 4
        and 5.⟩
21.18   car/\ WTS [~. SC, B
21.19   clothes/\ WTS, SC [~, B
21.33   goodnight WTS, SC [good
        night B
22.5   floor/\ WTS, SC [~, B
22.7   Stahr/\ WTS, SC [~, B
22.10   father's WTS, SC [Father's B
22.12   Glenola WTS, SC [Birdy B
22.14   Dean WTS, SC [dean B
22.16   father's WTS, SC [Father's B
22.17   Glenola WTS, SC [Birdy B
22.18   week/\ WTS, SC [~, B
22.22   windows/\ WTS, SC [~, B
22.26   father's WTS, SC [Father's B
22.23   father WTS, SC [Father B
22.36   father WTS, SC [Father B
23.1   Borwitz/\ WTS, SC [~, B
23.8   oh, WTS, SC [~/\ CSC, B
23.11   father WTS, SC [Father B
23.14   hand/\ WTS, SC [~, B
23.15   father, "all WTS, SC [Father.
        "All B
23.19   father WTS, SC [Father B
23.21   sometime WTS, SC [some time
        B
23.25   out/\ WTS, SC [~, B
23.31   wall/\ WTS, SC [~, B
23.34   father WTS, SC [Father B

24.2	ante-room WTS, SC [	29.8	Beach/\ WTS, SC [~, CSC, B
	anteroom B	29.17	father's WTS, SC [Father's B
24.4	then/\ WTS, SC [~, B	29.25	Hello/\ WTS, SC [~, B
24.5	impulse/\ WTS, SC [~, B	29.31	/*Tout passe—l'art seul dure à*
24.7	was big/\ WTS, SC [~ ~, B	−32	*l'éternité.*/\ WTS, SC ["*Tout*
24.7	father's WTS, SC [Father's B		*passe.—L'art robuste / Seul a*
24.15	father WTS, SC [Father B		*l'éternité.*" B
24.17	father WTS, SC [Father B	29.32	*l'éternité.*/\ space break ¶ "And
24.20	gravely; WTS [~: SC, B	−33	WTS, SC [*l'éternité.*" no break
24.21	father WTS, SC [Father B		¶ "And B
24.30	Before WTS [before SC, B	29.34	pointlessly: WTS [~, SC, B
24.34	father WTS, SC [Father B	30.4	Brittish WTS, SC [British CSC,
25.8	said, WTS, SC [~. B		B
25.14	long/\ WTS [~, SC, B	30.10	night. WTS, SC [~? B
25.18	red head WTS, SC [redhead B	30.14	that/\ WTS, SC [~, B
25.27	châteaux WTS [Chateaux SC [	30.24	that/\ WTS, SC [~, B
	châteaux B	30.31	was, WTS, SC [~: B
25.30	attic/\ WTS, SC [~, B	31.12	equal/\ WTS, SC [~, B
26.10	Robby, WTS, SC [~. B	31.15	decent/\ WTS, SC [~, B
26.13	women/\ WTS, SC [~, B	31.18	yourself, WTS, SC [~? B
26.16	De Mille WTS [DeMille SC, B	31.26	dueling WTS, SC [duelling B
27.11	plastic" . . . WTS, SC [~. . . ."	31.33	"Movie WTS, SC [/\~ B
	B	31.33	Boxley/\ WTS, SC [~, B
27.16	Hello Monroe . . WTS, SC	31.36	dueling WTS, SC [duelling B
−17	[~~. . . . B	32.15	table— WTS, SC [~——— B
27.20	looking/\ I suppose/\ WTS, SC	32.20	box, WTS, SC [~/\ B
	[~, ~ ~, B	32.22	window—but WTS [~-~
27.20	old guard WTS, SC [Old		SC [~——— B
	Guard B	32.27	makes— WTS, SC [~——— B
27.21	heroes/\ WTS, SC [~, B	32.33	Stahr, WTS, SC [~. B
27.25	now/\ WTS, SC [~, B	33.2	laughed, WTS, SC [~. B
27.25	everywhere, WTS, SC [~; B	33.12	it, WTS [~/\ SC [~, B
27.28	Chapter 3 WTS [CHAPTER 3	33.19	Boxley: WTS [~; SC [~: B
	SC [~ III B ⟨CUP: Episode 7⟩	33.24	about— WTS, SC [~——— B
27.31	About father WTS, SC [~ Fa-	33.25	lots WTS, SC [lot B
	ther B	33.27	Katie WTS, SC [Katy B
27.31	loved father WTS, SC [~ Fa-	33.28	Boxley,—"back WTS, SC [~,
	ther B		"—~ CSC, B
28.3	course/\ WTS, SC [~, B	33.32	Katie WTS, SC [Katy B
28.4	father WTS, SC [Father B	33.34	Katie WTS, SC [Katy B
	nor have WTS, SC [nor did he	34.2	bird— WTS, SC [~——— B
	have B	34.4	—And WTS, SC [—and B
28.14	age/\ WTS, SC [~, B	34.4	ran— WTS, SC [~/\ B
28.20	general— WTS, SC [~, B	34.19	Send——— WTS [~——————— SC
28.29	eye witness WTS, SC [		[Send Mr. Roderiguez B
	eyewitness B	34.21	in/\ WTS, SC [~, B
29.1	said, WTS, SC [~. CSC, B	34.25	Variety WTS, SC [*Variety* B

34.31	anymore WTS, SC [any more B	40.24	fresh. WTS, SC [~? B
		40.26	Rose WTS, SC [Jane B
35.4	separating. WTS [~? SC, B	40.33	for one/\third WTS, SC [~ ~-~ CSC, B
35.24	Rainy Day WTS, SC [*Rainy Day* B	40.34	she's one/\third WTS, SC [~ ~-~ CSC, B
35.25	25,000 WTS, SC [twenty-five thousand B	40.35	Rose WTS, SC [Jane B
35.26	27,000 WTS, SC [twenty-seven thousand B	41.1	Hayes WTS, SC [Hays B
		41.3	*however*— WTS, SC [~——B
35.31	him. WTS, SC [~? B	41.6	to— WTS, SC [~—— B
35.33	28,000 WTS, SC [twenty-seven thousand B	41.13	And WTS [and SC [And B
36.11	Rose WTS, SC [Jane B	41.14	up— WTS, SC [~—— B
36.16	biz," WTS, SC [~"; B	41.21	rôle WTS [role SC, B
36.16	and/\ of course/\ WTS, SC [~, ~ ~, B	41.32	Stahr, WTS, SC [~. B
36.16	addition a WTS, SC [addition she was variously described as a B	42.9	Rose WTS, SC [Jane B
		42.11	gag/\men WTS, SC [~-~ B
		42.14	wide/\awake WTS, SC [~-~ B
36.24	Minna's/\ WTS, SC [~, B	42.23	Rose WTS, SC [Jane B
36.25	he WTS, SC [Stahr B	42.27	wide/\awake WTS, SC [~-~ B
37.1	No/\ WTS, SC [~, B	43.7	asked WTS [saked SC [asked B
37.1	rôle WTS [role SC, B		
37.4	Rose WTS, SC [Jane B	43.8	Rose WTS, SC [Jane B
37.23	an WTS [all SC, B	43.17	half-naive WTS, SC [~-naïve B
38.1	fairly WTS [fiarly SC [fairly B	43.21	Rose WTS, SC [Jane B
38.11	he WTS [He SC, B	43.27	up—not yet. He WTS, SC [up. He B
38.12	dazed half WTS [dazed and half SC, B	43.29	a cheap English shoe he bought WTS, SC [a pair of cheap English shoes he had bought B
38.25	Reinmund; WTS [~: SC, B		
38.27	it/\ WTS, SC [~, B		
38.32	Rose WTS, SC [Jane B		
38.37	it— WTS, SC [~—— B		
39.3	if were/\ WTS [if it were/\ SC [~ ~ ~, B		

The following 5 entries record variants between Wilson's holograph interpolation and the book (43.29–44.17); this material is not in the Cambridge edition.

39.5	wouldn't WTS [Wouldn't SC [wouldn't B		
39.12	end/\ WTS, SC [~, B	1.	had WTS [has SC [had CSC, B
39.15	on— WTS, SC [~—— B	2.	office to to ask WTS [office to ask SC, B
39.31	boss/\ WTS, SC [~, B		
39.33	way/\ WTS, SC [~, B	3.	steel/\trap WTS [~-~ SC, B
40.1	Rose WTS, SC [Jane B	4.	slipping. ¶ "Any WTS [slippery. ¶ "Any SC [slipping. ¶
40.8–9, 14–15	Carrol and McMurray WTS, SC [Corliss and McKelway B		
40.12	around, "/\shall WTS, SC [~. "—~ B		

"I think she was a very new secretary," repeated Stahr. "Any WSC, B ⟨Wilson salvaged '¶ "I think . . . Stahr.' from Fitzgerald's Rejected Episode 10.⟩

5. messages?" asked Stahr. ¶ "Mr. WTS, SC [messages?" ¶ "Mr. CSC B

44.15 sick— WTS, SC [~—— B

44.16 eye∧trouble WTS, SC [~-~ B

44.20 luncheon∧ WTS [~, SC, B

45.1 children, WTS [~∧ SC [~, CSC, B

45.12 gray WTS, SC [grey B

45.14 it—nature WTS, SC [it. Nature B

45.30 Fleishhacker WTS, SC [Fleishacker CSC, B

45.33 foreign legion WTS, SC [Foreign Legion B

46.8 pair WTS, SC [pairs B

46.16 Populos WTS, SC [Populos B

46.25 signaled WTS, SC [signalled B

46.30 genius WTS, SC [genuis B

47.17 hello∧ WTS, SC [~, B

47.18 Garcia WTS [Zavras SC, B

47.18 it . . . WTS, SC [~. . . . B

47.19 Good . . . Good WTS, SC [~. . . . good B

47.19 do∧ WTS, SC [~, CSC [~: B

47.20 afternoon— WTS [~∧ SC [~— CSC, B

47.20 Kennedy— WTS [~∧ SC [~— CSC, B

47.23 Pedro Garcia WTS [Pete Zavras SC, B

47.30 much∧ WTS, SC [~, CSC, B

47.36 fast∧ WTS, SC [~, CSC, B

48.6 senses— WTS, SC [~—— B

48.15 public∧ WTS, SC [~, B

48.17 quickly∧ WTS, SC [~, B

49.2 This∧ then∧ WTS, SC [~, ~, B

49.4 —This∧ WTS, SC [∧~, B

49.25 Chapter 4 WTS [CHAPTER 4 SC [~ IV B ⟨CUP: For Episode 11⟩

49.34 Ridinghood WTS [Rid-
−50.1 ingwood SC,B

50.5 Ridingwood, WTS [~. SC, B

50.6 it— WTS, SC [~—— B

50.11 sorry∧ WTS, SC [~, B

50.26 radiunt . . . radiunt WTS [radiant . . . radiant SC [radiunt . . . radiunt B

51.6 said, WTS, SC [~. B

51.6 She's WTS [she's SC [She's B

51.10 said, WTS [~. SC, B

51.12 performance— WTS, SC [~—— B

51.26 if WTS [it SC, B

51.32 take, WTS [~? SC, B

51.33 Stahr, WTS, SC [~∧ B

51.34 hell— WTS, SC [~—— B

51.37 Monroe— WTS, SC [~—— B

52.9 always ∧ right WTS, SC [~— ~ B

52.30 Stahr∧ WTS, SC [~, B

52.33 done— WTS, SC [~, B

53.5 chair∧ WTS, SC [~, B

53.24 for— WTS, SC [~—— B

53.28 beautifully∧ WTS, SC [~, B

54.8 —Pedro Garcia WTS [—Pete Zavras SC [∧~~ B

54.22 it . . . WTS, SC [~. . . . B

54.22 Brown . . . WTS, SC [~. . . . B

54.23 who— WTS, SC [~—— B

54.28 lollypops WTS, SC [lollipops B

54.29 Mort WTS, SC [Lee B

54.30 Mort Fleishacker, WTS, SC [
−31 Lee Kapper. B

54.31 stage six WTS, SC [Stage 6 B

55.8 said, WTS [~. SC, B

55.13 Kapper— WTS, SC [~—— B

55.30 Mort WTS, SC [Lee B

56.8 so∧ WTS, SC [~, B

56.12 They did it wrong. Again they
−13 met, they started, they went on. WTS [omitted SC, B

56.21 long." WTS [~.∧ SC [~." B

56.33 finished;∧ WTS [~;- SC [~;∧ CSC, B

56.36 girl— WTS, SC [~; B

57.3 *Steppes.* WTS [~? SC, B

57.4   But WTS [but SC, B
57.18   subject— WTS, SC [~: B
57.24   Pedro Garcia WTS [Pete
        Zavras SC, B
57.24   20, WTS, SC [~: B
57.25   Garcia WTS [Zavras SC, B
57.29   Marquand WTS, SC [Tarleton
        B
57.31   Agge. "And WTS, SC [~, "and
        B
57.33   Why∧ WTS, SC [~, B
58.8   Marquands WTS, SC [
        Tarletons B
58.9   east WTS, SC [East B
58.15   Marquands WTS, SC [
        Tarletons B
58.16   Marquand WTS, SC [Tarleton
        B
58.20   credit∧ WTS, SC [~, B
58.25   Stahr∧ WTS, SC [~, B
58.26   in to WTS [into SC, B
59.3   said, WTS, SC [~. B
59.5   Oh∧ WTS, SC [~, B
59.13   Oh∧ WTS, SC [~, B
59.17   touched it, WTS, SC [~ ~— B
59.27   skin∧deep WTS, SC [~-~ B
−28
59.30   that— WTS, SC [~—— B
59.34   know," WTS [~, ∧ SC [~,"
        B
60.13   restaurant. WTS, SC [~? B
−14
60.19   right∧ WTS, SC [~, B
60.19   here. WTS [~? SC, B
60.20   drugstore WTS, SC [drug-store
        B
60.20   Wilshire— WTS, SC [~—— B
60.24   ignored∧ WTS [~. SC, B
60.25   moment∧ WTS, SC [~, B
61.5   girl∧ WTS, SC [~, CSC, B
61.7   earthquake∧ WTS, SC [~,
        CSC, B
61.11   Aristophanes WTS [
        Aristophany SC [Aristophanes
        WSC, B ⟨CUP: Asclepius⟩
61.23   Zavras. "I WTS, SC [Zavras.
−24   "The Oedipus who solved the

riddle. I B ⟨CUP: Zavras. "The
solver of Eleusinian mysteries.
I⟩
61.27   Pedro WTS [Pete SC, B
61.32   Zavra's WTS, SC [Zavras' B
62.1   move∧ WTS, SC [~, B
62.2   pattern∧ WTS, SC [~, B
62.7   commissary∧ WTS, SC [~, B
62.32   hello∧ WTS [~, SC, B
63.4   polite. WTS [~, SC [~. B
64.9   I'm— WTS, SC [~—— B
64.13   goodnight WTS, SC [good
−14   night B
64.19   it?", WTS [~?"∧ SC, B
64.27   Oh∧ WTS, SC [~, B
64.32   closer WTS [slower SC, B
64.34   thought— WTS, SC [~—— B
65.5   Stahr WTS [stahr SC [Stahr B
65.18   —Now WTS, SC [∧~ B
65.29   here∧ WTS, SC [~, B
65.37   threshhold WTS, SC [threshold
        B
66.6   pictures. WTS, SC [~? B
66.9   test∧ WTS, SC [~, B
66.27   nowhere∧ WTS, SC [~, B
66.35   lip∧ WTS, SC [~, B
67.14   sorry. *no space break* ¶ That
−15   WTS, SC [~. *space break* ¶ ~
        WSC, B
67.26   Chapter 5 WTS [CHAPTER 5
        SC [~ V B ⟨CUP: Episode 13⟩
67.28   me∧ WTS, SC [~, B
67.32   car, WTS, SC [~? B
68.15   that?∧ WTS [~?" SC [~?∧ B
68.18   four. WTS [~? SC, B
68.28   Southhampton WTS, SC
        [Southampton B
68.32   twenties∧ WTS, SC [~, B
68.35   father WTS, SC [Father B
68.35   *Girl*∧ WTS, SC [~, B
69.6   "Lovely to look at—de—
        lightful to know—w," WTS,
        SC [*"Lovely to look at—de-
        lightful to know-w,"* B
69.9   said, WTS [~. SC, B
69.16   child— WTS, SC [~—— B
69.21   kiss. WTS, SC [~? B

69.28 says— WTS, SC [~—— B
70.5 "They asked me how I
–6 knew," ... "—my true love
was true." WTS, SC [*"They
asked me how I knew," ...
"—my true love was true."* B
70.17 tonight, WTS, SC [~? B
70.20 Oh∧ WTS, SC [~, B
70.20 considered, WTS, SC [~. B
70.22 you've WTS, SC [you'd B
71.4 Oh∧ WTS, SC [~, CSC, B
71.5 time— WTS, SC [~—— B
71.6 It'd be like marrying a doctor.
WTS, SC [*omitted* B
71.15 day-dream∧ WTS, SC [
~-~, B
71.24 ageing WTS, SC [aging B
71.29 White∧ WTS, SC [~, B
72.11 table∧ WTS, SC [~, B
72.11 Café WTS [Cafe SC [Café
CSC, B
72.15 it∧ WTS, SC [~, B
72.18 way∧ WTS, SC [~, B
72.31 table— WTS, SC [~—— B
74.10 Café WTS [Cafe SC [Café
CSC, B
74.10 Loudoun WTS, SC [Loudon B
74.12 fast∧ WTS, SC [~, CSC, B
74.25 There∧ WTS [~, SC, B
74.25 ∧Wylie WTS ["~ SC [∧~ B
74.27 lobby∧ WTS, SC [~, B
75.16 me— WTS, SC [~—— B
75.19 "∧you WTS, SC ["—~ B
76.13 drugstore WTS, SC [drug-store
B
76.15 did∧ WTS, SC [~, B
76.16 said, WTS, SC [~. B
77.13 secret, WTS [~∧ SC [~, B
77.17 Oh∧ WTS, SC [~, CSC, B
77.19 amplified; WTS, SC [~: B
77.29 *See-saw* WTS, SC [*See-Saw* B
77.32 ball-room WTS, SC [
ballroom B
78.11 brow—the coco-colored WTS [
~—the coca-~ SC [brown, the
cool-~ B
78.30 lightly; WTS, SC [~: B

78.32 away∧ WTS, SC [~, CSC, B
79.36 on∧ WTS, SC [~, B
80.14 nice". WTS, SC [~." B
80.26 so WTS [too SC, B
81.28 mixers WTS, SC [mixer B
81.29 sea-scape WTS, SC [
seascape B
81.34 said, WTS, SC [~∧ B
82.1 minute, WTS, SC [~. B
82.2 can't you. WTS [~ ~? SC, B
82.4 mañana WTS [manana SC [
mañana CSC [*mañana* B
82.10 a ping∧pong WTS, SC [~ ~-
~ B
82.11 another ping∧pong WTS, SC [
~ ~-~ B
82.19 who WTS, SC [which B
83.1 ring. WTS [~? SC, B
83.5 Mr. WTS, SC [Mr∧ B
83.19 said∧ WTS, SC [~, B
83.21 Who? .... WTS, SC [~? ... B
83.25 Kathleen. WTS, SC [~: B
83.36 hand— WTS, SC [~—— B
84.2 year ... WTS, SC [~. ... B
84.6 Hello'." WTS [~.' " SC, B
84.9 his name ... WTS, SC [
~~. ... B
84.11 *Ape* ... WTS, SC [~. ... B
85.10 drugstore WTS, SC [drug-store
B
85.14 drugstores WTS, SC [drug-
stores B
85.36 I WTS [It SC, B
86.16 again∧ WTS, SC [~, B
86.28 "—not WTS ["∧~ SC, B
86.30 Oh∧ WTS [~, SC, B
86.33 one WTS, SC [it B
87.12 side∧ WTS, SC [~, B
88.4 discovered WTS [siscovered SC
[discovered WSC, B
88.16 bright, WTS, SC [~∧ B
88.17 up. ... WTS [~∧ ... SC
[~. ... B
88.19 said, WTS, SC [~. B
89.2 needn't∧ WTS, SC [~, B
89.3 happening WTS [happeneing
SC [happening B

89.7   said∧ WTS, SC [~, B
89.25   Also∧ WTS, SC [~, B
89.28   time, WTS, SC [~— B
89.32   said, WTS, SC [~. B
89.33   not, WTS, SC [~. B
90.9   up∧ WTS, SC [~, B
90.17   intently∧ WTS, SC [~, B
90.20   with meagre WTS, SC [with
-21   the meagre B
90.33   hair." WTS [~.∧ SC, B
92.3   forget it," WTS, SC [forget,"
        B
92.3   Stahr∧ WTS, SC [~, B
92.4   schules WTS, SC [*schules* B
92.17   Oh∧ WTS, SC [~, CSC, B
92.19   up WTS, SC [~, B
92.33   Negro WTS, SC [negro B
92.34   quickly∧ WTS, SC [~, B
92.34   twigs∧ WTS, SC [~, B
93.3   Negro WTS, SC [negro B
93.17   Negro WTS, SC [negro B
93.31   Negro's WTS, SC [negro's B
94.12   up∧ WTS, SC [~, B
94.20   world— WTS, SC [~—— B
94.24   girl— WTS, SC [~—— B
94.26   here— WTS, SC [~—— B
94.32   go", WTS [~," SC, B
95.2   car∧ and she did∧ WTS, SC [
        ~, ~ ~ ~, B.
95.30   words, WTS, SC [~: B
95.31   arms, WTS, SC [~∧ B
96.2   auto-horns WTS, SC [~∧~ B
96.10   Negro WTS, SC [negro B
96.19   Negro WTS, SC [negro B
96.22   Negro WTS, SC [negro B
96.25   calls. WTS, SC [~: B
96.26   ∧La WTS, SC ["~ B
96.34   Fleishacker ¶ The WTS, SC [
-35   Fleishacker," *etc.* ¶ The B
97.18   foward WTS [forward SC, B ⟨
        CUP: toward her⟩
97.29   here— WTS, SC [~: B
97.31   son∧of∧a∧bitch WTS, SC [
        ~-~-~-~ B
98.12   ∧Dear WTS, SC ["~ B
98.13   ∧In WTS, SC ["~ B
98.16   ∧I WTS, SC ["I B

98.20   night∧ WTS, SC [~, B
98.24   ∧I WTS, SC ["I B
98.24   women∧ WTS, SC [~— B
98.27   ∧With WTS, SC ["~ B
98.28   ∧Kathleen Moore.∧ WTS, SC
        ["Kᴀᴛʜʟᴇᴇɴ Mᴏᴏʀᴇ." B
99.17   remembered, WTS, SC [~: B
99.25   Dodd's: to WTS, SC [~. To B
99.30   name. WTS, SC [~! B
99.33   Rose WTS, SC [Jane B
99.34   Rose WTS, SC [Jane B
100.1   writer∧ but WTS, SC [~, ~
        B
100.7   did∧ they WTS, SC [~, ~ B
100.8   Rose's WTS, SC [Jane's B
100.8   building". WTS, SC [~." B
100.17 Rose WTS, SC [Jane B
100.28 Rose WTS, SC [Jane B
100.36 rang∧ WTS, SC [~, B
100.36 conversation. WTS [~∧ SC,
        B
101.8   him" . . . WTS [~." . . SC
        [~." . . . B
101.15 do. . . . WTS, SC [~ . . . B
101.16 Crisp. . . . WTS, SC [~ . . . B
101.17 pages. . . . WTS, SC [~ . . . B
101.21 Rose's WTS, SC [Jane's B
101.21 coca-cola WTS, SC [Coca-
-22   Cola B
101.22 Rose WTS, SC [Jane B
101.26 it∧ WTS, SC [~, B
101.35 Oh,∧ WTS [~,— SC [~∧—
        B
101.35 Rose WTS, SC [Jane B
101.36 name∧ WTS, SC [~, B
102.5   Rose WTS, SC [Jane B
102.6   coöperate WTS [cooperate
        SC [coöperate WSC, B
102.16 a long WTS [along SC [a
-17   long WSC, B
102.21 father WTS, SC [Father B
102.26 Rose WTS, SC [Jane B
102.29 father WTS, SC [Father B
102.31 eeked WTS, SC [eked B
102.33 father WTS, SC [Father B
103.2   God∧ WTS, SC [~, CSC, B
103.4   sex, WTS, SC [~∧ B

103.5   father WTS, SC [Father B
103.9   début WTS [debut SC [début
         CSC, B
103.12   office/\ WTS, SC [~, B
103.23   to— WTS, SC [~—— B
103.25   father WTS, SC [Father B
103.25   shirt sleeves WTS, SC
         [shirtsleeves B
103.30   he could WTS [could he SC,
         B
103.31   employment. WTS, SC [~? B
104.2   Oh/\ WTS, SC [~, B
104.7   along. WTS, SC [~? B
104.9   a long/\ WTS [along/\ SC [
         along, B
104.23   father WTS, SC [Father B
104.25   opened it/\ WTS, SC [~ ~, B
104.26   father's WTS, SC [Father's B
104.29   father WTS, SC [Father B
104.34   *up*! WTS [*up*! [*up*! B
104.37   asked, WTS, SC [~: B
105.11   Also/\ WTS, SC [~, B
105.12   table/\ WTS, SC [~, B
105.32   ¶ "If you were in a drug
-106.1   store," said Stahr, "—having
         a prescription filled—" ¶
         "You mean a chemist?"
         Boxley asked. WTS [*omitted*
         SC [¶ "If you were in a drug
         store," said Stahr, "—having
         a prescription filled"— ¶
         "You mean a chemist's?"
         Boxley asked. WSC [¶ "~ ~
         ~ ~ ~ drug-store," ~ ~, "—
         ~ ~ ~ ~ ~——" ¶ "~ ~ ~
         ~?" ~ ~. B
106.4   sick— WTS, SC [~—— B
106.10   Stahr/\ WTS, SC [~, B
106.12   see./\" WTS, SC [~.' " B
106.20   way— WTS, SC [~—— B
106.22   go— WTS, SC [~—— B
106.27   quarry/\ WTS, SC [~— B
106.27   newly/\cut WTS, SC [~-~ B
106.28   half/\obliterated WTS, SC [
         ~-~ B
107.11   Borwitz's WTS [Borwitz' SC,
         B

107.14   stalemate/\ WTS, SC [~, B
107.22   dollar/\ WTS, SC [~, B
107.32   coins/\ also/\ WTS, SC [~,
         ~, B
108.5   tuhkey WTS, SC [turkey B
108.10   "but WTS [/\~ SC ["~ B
108.25   *Place*." WTS [*Place*." SC [
         Place." B
109.12   ones/\ WTS, SC [~, B
110.32   sat down/\ WTS, SC [~ ~, B
111.7   Oh/\ WTS, SC [~, CSC, B
111.13   anything— WTS, SC
         [~—— B
111.22   either/\ WTS, SC [~, B
111.33   wait WTS, SC [Wait B
112.1   It WTS [He SC, B
112.21   awhile WTS, SC [a while B
-22
112.34   step-mother WTS, SC [
         stepmother B
112.36   step-mother watched WTS,
         SC [stepmother ~ B
113.1   step-mother died WTS, SC [
         stepmother ~ B
113.7   twenty/\two WTS [~-~ SC,
         B
113.33   see/\ WTS, SC [~, B
113.34   see/\ WTS, SC [~, B
114.11   ¶ "They were the standard ar-
         ticle," he said. WTS, SC [
         omitted B
114.19   airports/\ WTS, SC [~, B
114.22   Oh/\ WTS, SC [~, B
114.29   Oh/\ WTS, SC [~, CSC, B
114.34   Then/\ WTS, SC [~, B
114.36   all/\WTS, SC [~, B
115.9   Oh/\ WTS, SC [~, CSC, B
115.37   afraid— WTS, SC [~—— B
116.1   laughed, WTS [~. SC, B
116.6   —or he WTS, SC [—he B
116.9   Palace WTS, SC [palace B
116.28   said, WTS, SC [~. B
116.29   tomorrow/\ WTS, SC [~, B
117.6   it/\ WTS, SC [~, B
117.12   enchanted WTS [enchanged
         SC [enchanted B
117.12   limousine— WTS, SC [~, B

117.18   was WTS, SC [were B
117.21   him∧ WTS, SC [~, B
117.35   sueing WTS, SC [suing B
118.3   Chapter 6 WTS [CHAPTER
          6 SC [~ VI B ⟨CUP: Episode
          17⟩
118.20   Oh∧ WTS, SC [~, CSC, B
118.23   blonde, WTS, SC [~∧ B
118.25   father WTS, SC [Father B
118.28   He was like a brazier out of
–29   doors on a cool night. WTS,
          SC [omitted B
119.6   d'Analou WTS, SC [Analou B
119.9   two∧page WTS, SC [~-~ B
–10
119.10   Communist Manifesto WTS,
          SC [Communist Manifesto B
119.19   room— WTS, SC [~: B
121.5   repeated, WTS, SC [~. B
121.6   company spirit WTS, SC [
          Company Spirit B
121.33   Later∧ WTS, SC [~, B
122.2   in trying to think of a way
–3   WTS, SC [about how B
          ⟨CUP: in how⟩
122.4   Listen∧ WTS, SC [~, B
122.31   Oh∧ WTS, SC [~, B
123.20   crazy∧ WTS, SC [~, B
123.22   Oh∧ WTS, SC [~, B
123.27   Frankenstein WTS, SC [
          Frankensteen WSC, B
123.32   Oh∧ yes," said WTS [Oh∧
          yes," he said SC [~, ~," ~ ~
          CSC, B

124.18   ping∧pong WTS, SC [~-~ B
–19
124.19   father WTS, SC [Father B
124.20   Man WTS, SC [Girl B
124.21   off∧ WTS, SC [~, B
125.28   VII's WTS, SC [Seventh's B
125.30   continued, "—for WTS, SC [
          ~, "∧~ B
126.7   father WTS, SC [Father B
126.10   him∧ WTS, SC [~, B
126.11   that∧ WTS, SC [~, B
127.2   was∧ WTS, SC [~, B
127.12   so, WTS [~∧ SC [~, CSC, B
127.13   conflict∧ WTS, SC [~, B
127.15   drive∧ WTS, SC [~, B
127.17   No∧ WTS, SC [~, B
127.19   ping∧pong WTS, SC [~-~ B
127.22   ping∧pong WTS, SC [~-~ B
128.15   close WTS [alose SC [close B
128.19   table∧ WTS, SC [~, B
128.22   table: WTS [~; SC [~. B
128.26   help— WTS, SC [~—— B
129.2   ping∧pong WTS, SC [~-~ B
129.10   freshmen∧ WTS, SC [~, B
129.13   father WTS, SC [Father B
129.19   Oh∧ WTS, SC [~, CSC, B
129.23   happened∧ WTS, SC [~,
          CSC, B
129.26   Oh∧ WTS [~, SC, B
129.27   who WTS [Who SC [who B
129.28   studio. WTS [~? SC, B
129.31   Fairbank's WTS [Fairbanks'
          SC, B

WORD DIVISION

1. END-OF-THE-LINE HYPHENATION IN THE CAMBRIDGE TEXT

The following hyphenated compounds at line endings in the Cambridge critical edition are to be retained.

22.21–22	one-/way
31.12–13	two-/edged
57.20–21	twenty-/five
59.27–28	skin-/deep
101.21–22	Coca-/Cola

2. END-OF-THE-LINE HYPHENATION IN THE BASE-TEXTS

The following compounds, or possible compounds, are hyphenated at the end of the line in the base-texts. The form given in the list that follows is the form printed in the Cambridge critical edition.

9.25	countryside
14.3	Sleepy-eyed
40.33	one-third
43.23	one-fifteen
72.6	semi-star
72.10	semi-star
87.7	grandfather
113.17	twenty-two

EXPLANATORY NOTES

Space restrictions make it impossible to annotate every factual detail in the novel. With the advice of the editor at Cambridge University Press, it was decided to annotate this edition for an attentive American or British undergraduate. Information readily available in standard reference works has not been glossed unless editorial comment is required. Actual places in and near Los Angeles are located on the map. Fictional movie productions and fictional figures have not been identified as such. These notes demonstrate the need for fully annotated editions of widely taught and generally read works of modern fiction.

title: TYCOON

The title by which the shogun of Japan was described to foreigners; the earliest *Oxford English Dictionary* citation is 1857. The *OED Supplement* (1986) adds: "An important or dominant person, especially in business or politics; a magnate," noting that "tycoon" was applied to Abraham Lincoln. Its appearances in *Time*, beginning in 1926, gave it currency in America.

3.2 Rudolph Valentino

1895–1926; romantic lead in silent movies, he began his movie career in 1918 and achieved stardom in *The Four Horsemen of the Apocalypse* (Paramount, 1921).

3.8 Lolly Parsons

Louella Parsons (1880–1972), writer of an influential movie gossip column for the Hearst newspapers (see also 129.34).

3.14 Bennington

Women's college in Bennington, Vermont, which opened in 1932 to provide progressive education for students interested in the arts and social sciences; it became coeducational in 1969. Fitzgerald originally had Cecelia attending Smith (founded 1875), a women's college that offered traditional programs of study (see Textual Note).

4.1 when I was a junior

Cecelia's emotional distance from her sister's death suggests that it occurred during the third year of her preparatory (or convent) school. She is now a college junior.

4.5 Depression

The period of financial and social distress in America that began with the stock-market crash in October 1929 and lasted through the Thirties.

4.10–11, 22 turn in . . . berth

In a canceled MS passage Fitzgerald identifies the plane as a Douglas Mainliner; the Douglas Sleeper Transport had seats and berths.

In 1936 the American Airlines Mercury Flight left Newark, New Jersey, at 6:10 P.M. for Los Angeles with stops at Memphis, Tennessee; Dallas, Texas; and Tucson, Arizona. The trip took seventeen hours and forty-one minutes. By August 1937 the schedule was changed to substitute a Nashville, Tennessee, stop for Memphis.

4.25 Nembutal

A short-acting barbituate, recently introduced.

4.36 car

Fitzgerald, an experienced air traveler, evokes the similarity of sensation between air and railroad travel.

5.5–6 the very lowest time of the Depression

The synopsis that Fitzgerald prepared for Kenneth Littauer in 1939 stipulates: "The Story occurs during four or five months in the year 1935"; and "I have set it safely in a period of five years ago to obtain detachment . . ." (see Introduction, p. xxiv). Sheilah Graham informed Perkins in 1941 that "the time of the book's setting was most important to Scott. . . . he wanted it to be as of five years ago. He places the period with the songs of 1934– 5 . . ." (see Introduction, p. lxviii). Yet the chronological details in the draft episodes range from 1933 to 1938, possibly because Fitzgerald began planning the novel and assembling material in 1938 and wrote the episodes during late 1939 and 1940—so that the time of the novel changed during the course of composition.

The first time signal appears on p. 5 where "the very lowest time of the Depression" (which began after the October 1929 stock-market crash) is placed "two years before" the present time of the novel—that is, any year from 1933 to 1935. On p. 8 Cecelia refers to the 1935 songs "Top Hat" and "Cheek to Cheek" as having been popular when she was a freshman; since she is a junior at the time of the novel (although it is not clear whether she has completed her junior year or is a rising junior), the year would be 1937 or 1938. On p. 27 there is a reference to "the three years of Depression"—which places the action in 1932 or 1933. Other songs— "Lost" and "Gone"—were published in 1936. The reference to Wallis Warfield Simpson on p. 116 establishes the time as later; Edward VIII abdicated in 1936 and as the Duke of Windsor married Mrs. Simpson in June 1937. The lastest datable detail in the novel is the reference to Superman on p. 124. This cartoon character was introduced in *Action Comics* in spring 1938, and the first *Superman* comic book appeared in 1939.

The year in which the events of the novel transpire cannot be established. Disregarding the references to Superman and to Mrs. Simpson, *The Love of the Last Tycoon* can be conveniently thought of as taking place during the summer of 1936. On p. 12 Cecelia states that she is reporting events that occurred "five years ago"; since Fitzgerald expected to publish his novel in 1941, the year 1936 fits the interior time scheme.

5.9 revolution

During the early Thirties there was concern that the economic depression might lead to a Soviet-style revolution in America.

5.11 Yellowstone

National park of some 3,500 square miles in northwest Wyoming, famous for its amiable wild bears; in Yellowstone it would be possible to evade discovery and revolutionary unrest.

5.15 Tory

Colonists loyal to the King of England during the American Revolution were known as Tories; they assisted loyalist refugees as well as British soldiers.

5.20–21 bonus army . . . Sacramento River

In 1932 thousands of World War I veterans came to Washington, D.C., and demanded early payment of their veterans' bonuses; they were dispersed by troops. The Sacramento River is in California.

5.27 prop department

Property Department, where furnishings for movie sets were made or stored; Fitzgerald probably meant the Wardrobe Department.

5.28 Disappear into the Crowd

The capital letters indicate the director's reliance on a familiar movie-script stage direction.

6.6 another man

It seems odd that Cecelia does not recognize the voice and figure of the man she has idealized for two years; but Fitzgerald wanted to delay the introduction of his hero.

7.21 Alice in the rabbit hole

A long, slow fall at the beginning of *Alice's Adventures in Wonderland* (1865) by Lewis Carroll.

7.33 stage-stops

Places for changing horses along the routes of stagecoach lines.

8.13 made a dead set for me

Showed sexual interest by allowable attention and manner.

8.18 Guy Lombardo

1902–77; leader of the Royal Canadians orchestra that played "the sweetest music this side of heaven."

8.19 "Top Hat" and "Cheek to Cheek"

Songs written by Irving Berlin for the movie *Top Hat* (RKO, 1935).

10.2 Laemmle studio

Carl Laemmle (1867–1939) founded Universal Pictures in 1912.

10.7 Cortez or Balboa

A reference to the error in John Keats's sonnet "On First Looking into Chapman's Homer" (1816) in which Cortez is incorrectly identified as the first European to sight the Pacific—instead of Balboa.

10.24 'Esquire'

Monthly magazine for which Fitzgerald wrote in the Thirties; aimed primarily at a male readership, it was regarded as a sophisticated publication.

11.13 First National? Paramount? United Artists?

First National was a Hollywood studio that operated between 1917 and 1929; it was taken over by Warner Brothers. Paramount Pictures merged with Famous Players in 1914. United Artists was founded in 1919.

11.20 lotus land

A place of luxury and voluptuous idleness; eating the lotus induced forgetfulness of home in *The Odyssey*.

12.17–19 Old Hickory . . . New Orleans . . . National Bank . . . Spoils System

Andrew Jackson (1767–1845), popularly known as Old Hickory, defeated the British at the Battle of New Orleans (1815); during his presidency (1828–36) the Bank of the United States was terminated, and his political supporters were rewarded with government jobs.

14.4 iron maidens

Coffin-shaped torture instruments that drove spikes through the victims.

14.31 "Lost"

1936 song; music and lyrics by Phil Ohman, Johnny Mercer, and Macy O. Teetor.

14.32 "Gone"

1936 song; music by Franz Waxman, lyrics by Gus Kahn.

16.4 the Bronx

The Bronx at the time of Stahr's boyhood, before World War I, was largely populated by lower-middle-class families—including many Jews who had left Manhattan's Lower East Side. A passage on p. 115 indicates that Stahr's early boyhood was spent in Erie, Pennsylvania.

17.9 Charles Francis Adams

1835–1915; railroad expert, civic leader, and historian, Adams was a grandson of President John Quincy Adams and a great-grandson of President John Adams. His actual observation was: "I have known, and known tolerably well, a good many 'successful' men—'big' financially—men famous during the last half-century; and a less interesting crowd I do not care to encounter. Not one that I have ever known would I care to meet again, either in this world or the next; nor is one of them associated in my mind with the idea of humor, thought or refinement" (*Charles Francis Adams 1835–1915: An Autobiography* [Boston & New York: Houghton Mifflin, 1916], p. 190).

17.11 Gould, Vanderbilt, Carnegie, Astor

Jay Gould (1836–92), Cornelius Vanderbilt (1843–99), Andrew Carnegie (1835–1919), and John Jacob Astor (1763–1848)—American tycoons who were regarded as "robber barons."

18.5–6 Frozen Saw

The Sawtooth mountain range in Idaho; but the plane is on the southern route over Texas and Arizona.

18.26 "42nd Street"

1933 Warner Brothers musical, a popular backstage romance.

20.29–30 all the kingdoms

Echo of Luke 4:15: "And the devil, taking him up into an high mountain, shewed unto him all the kingdoms of the world in a moment of time" (King James Version).

21.10 "long shot"

Movie footage shot from a distance.

21.18 pin-games

Pin-ball machines.

21.18 Johnny Swanson

Based on cowboy actor Harry Carey (1878–1947), a star of the silent movies who became a character actor in sound movies (see Introduction, p. liv).

21.20–1 Tom Mix or Bill Hart

Mix (1880–1940) and William S. Hart (1870–1946) were cowboy stars in silent movies.

21.34 Come! Come! I love you only

Lyric by Stanislaus Stange for "My Hero" from the Oscar Straus operetta *The Chocolate Soldier (Der tapfere Soldat, 1908)*.

22.2 the earthquake

Probably based on the March 1933 California earthquake in which Long Beach was hardest hit; the newspapers reported 65 to 100 dead: "BUILD-INGS TOTTER AS FIRES LIGHT SKY Solid Walls Crumble Into Thronged Streets of Cities in Two California Counties."

22.25 Will Rogers

1879–1935; humorist and movie actor who portrayed rural sages as an extension of himself; a greatly respected figure of saintlike goodwill, he characterized himself with the statement, "I never met a man I didn't like."

24.13 Dictograph

An intercom device—not to be confused with the dictaphone, a dictating machine.

25.11 "a good property"

Hollywood expression referring to a potentially valuable script or per-former.

26.3 god Siva

The third person in the Hindu triad, with Brahma and Vishnu. Siva repre-sents the principle of destruction and reconstruction; he is also the god of the arts. Fitzgerald's drafts refer to Siva as a goddess (see Textual Note).

26.16 De Mille

Cecil B. De Mille (1881–1959), director of spectacular historical movies.

27.20 Emperor . . . Old Guard

The most honored regiment of Napoleon's Imperial Guard, formed between 1800 and 1806 and made up of veterans; Fitzgerald may be referring to Horace Vernet's painting, "Napoleon's Farewell at Fontainebleau."

28.5 dubbing . . . cutting

Dubbing is editing sound on film; cutting is editing film footage to prepare the final version of the movie.

28.6 bar boy in Ballyhegan

As a boy in Ireland, Brady worked in a pub. There is no town named Ballyhegan, but there is a Ballyheige in County Kerry.

28.7 drummer's sense of story

Drummers—traveling salesmen—were identified with vulgar anecdotes of seduction.

28.12–13 Edison and Lumière and Griffith and Chaplin

Thomas A. Edison (1847–1931), inventor of early motion-picture cameras and projectors as well as the electric light bulb; Louis Lumière (1864–1948), French cinematographer; D. W. Griffith (1874–1948), greatest of the early movie directors, whose credits included *The Birth of a Nation;* Charlie Chaplin (1889–1977), greatest of movie comedians.

29.1 gone to pot

Undergone a process of deterioration; the use of *pot* as slang for marijuana was not yet current.

29.16 for the prints

Thus in manuscript and typescript; the sense is that the newspapers ("the prints") would be told that the supervisor—an executive—was a writer, presumably because it would not damage the studio's reputation for a writer to commit an act of violence.

29.26 Morgan's

Probably movie actor Frank Morgan (1890–1949), who played eccentric or kindly characters.

29.31–32 *Tout passe.—L'art robuste / Seul a l'éternité.*

From Théophile Gautier's poem "L'Art" (1858): "Everything perishes. Only strong art endures."

33.16 rushes

Unedited film footage.

33.20–21 double wing, clutch, kick and scram

Slapstick comedy routine that Van Dyke demonstrates at pp. 33–34.

33.28 Keystone

Hollywood studio that produced slapstick silent comedies, often featuring the Keystone Kops.

33.30 Georgie Jessel

1898–1981; an entertainer and later a movie producer.

34.25 'Variety'

Show-business newspaper.

34.26 Roxy's

The Roxy, a movie palace in New York built by Samuel Rothafel, who was known as Roxy.

35.15 Claris

Presumably the name of a brothel or a madame.

37.13 Reinhardt's "Miracle."

Religious stage spectacle produced by Max Reinhardt (1873–1943) in London in 1911 and revived in New York in 1924; based on Maurice Maeterlinck's play *Sister Beatrice* (1899).

38.36 Margaret Sullavan

1911–60; actress who played romantic parts; she starred in *Three Comrades,* a 1938 M-G-M movie for which Fitzgerald received his only screenwriting credit.

38.37 Colman

Ronald Colman (1891–1958), English actor who starred in American movies, often in the role of an English gentleman.

39.36 Eugene O'Neill

1888–1953; American playwright whose tragedies portrayed introverted, brooding figures.

40.8–9 Carroll and MacMurray

Madeleine Carroll (1906–87) was an English actress who portrayed elegant women; Fred MacMurray (1907–91) was an actor who usually portrayed likeable characters in melodramas or comedies. On p. 38 Stahr referred to Margaret Sullavan and Ronald Colman as the stars intended for this script. The first edition alters the names here to Corliss and McKelway; but these names were not mentioned in the Biggs-Wilson-Ober-Perkins correspondence about possible libel problems (see Introduction, pp. lxxiii–iv).

41.1 Hays office

Will H. Hays (1879–1954), president 1922–45 of the Motion Picture Producers and Distributors of America, the industry's self-censorship office; he compiled its 1930 Production Code.

41.1 scarlet letter

In the seventeenth century the American Puritans punished adulteresses by compelling them to wear a scarlet "A." Nathaniel Hawthorne's *The Scarlet Letter* (1850) was made as a silent movie in 1926 and as a talkie in 1934; Stahr's remark "paint a scarlet letter on her back" may refer also to the numbers on athletes' uniforms.

41.5 Oscar

The Academy Awards statuettes known as Oscars were first presented in 1928 (see note on Academy, 48.15).

43.3 Joe Breen

Joseph Breen (1890–1965) was associated with Will Hays at the Motion Picture Producers and Distributors of America.

43.30 Beverly Wilshire

Luxurious hotel on Wilshire Boulevard in Beverly Hills.

43.31 Peal's

British firm of custom bootmakers.

43.32 alpine hat

This detail indicates Rienmund's bad taste; he is a flashy dresser.

44.29 Prince Agge

Prince Aage of Denmark (d. 1940) was the cousin of King Christian and the nephew of Queen Alexandra of England; he renounced his rights to the throne of Denmark in 1914. Prince Aage wrote *A Royal Adventurer in the Foreign Legion* (Garden City, N.Y.: Doubleday, Page, 1927) and *Fire by Day and Flame by Night* (London: Sampson Low, Marston, 1937). During 1934–38 Count Sigvard Bernadotte of Sweden was an assistant director at M-G-M. As Fitzgerald's reference to the House of Bernadotte (see note 46.2) suggests, he probably conflated Prince Aage with Count Bernadotte of Sweden (see Fitzgerald's Working Note on Prince Aage, p. 162; see also Gabrielle Winkel, "Fitzgerald's Agge of Denmark," *Fitzgerald/Hemingway Annual 1975*, pp. 131–2).

46.2 Bernadotte

The royal house of Sweden is Bernadotte, from Jean-Baptiste-Jules Bernadotte (1763–1844), one of Napoleon's marshals who took the throne in 1818. The royal house of Denmark is Schleswig-Holstein-Sonderburg-Glucksburg (see note on Prince Agge, 44.29).

46.14 'Hell's Angels' or 'Ben-Hur'

Hell's Angels was a 1930 movie epic produced and directed by Howard Hughes; *Ben-Hur* was a 1925 M-G-M movie epic produced by Irving Thalberg. Both went over budget but made profits.

47.2 road-show

Budd Schulberg provided the editor with this explanation: "a term that was used back in the Thirties to differentiate special films sometimes shown only twice a day, at considerably higher prices than the run-of-the-mill programmers."

47.37–48.1 veins . . . N.Y.U.

Flieshacker is making a labored display of his New York University education.

48.15 Academy

The American Academy of Motion Picture Arts and Sciences, founded in 1927 for the purposes of advancing technology, arbitrating labor problems, and enforcing self-censorship of movie content.

48.25 First Empire

France in the time of Napoleon, 1804–14.

48.31 Nicolay's biography

John G. Nicolay and John Hay, *Abraham Lincoln: A History* (New York: Century, 1890), an admiring biography by men who knew Lincoln.

49.34 Goldwyn

Samuel Goldwyn (1882–1974), head of the Goldwyn Studio, who was known for his forceful and arbitrary conduct.

50.8 Art

The studio Art Department, responsible for designing sets.

50.16–17 Knights of Columbus

Roman Catholic fraternal order founded in 1882; Fitzgerald's choice of this group emphasizes the religiosity of the Hollywood tourist and names the primal hero of the New World.

51.11 Miss Foodstuffs

A phrase used by Stahr to indicate the blandness of the actress's filmed performance.

53.17 Claudette Colbert

Actress (1905–) who often starred in romantic comedies.

53.17 *coureur du bois*

A French fur trader in Canada.

54.33 Cary

Actor Cary Grant (1904–86).

55.9 Sidney Howard

1891–1939; dramatist and screenwriter who won the Pulitzer Prize for his play *They Knew What They Wanted* (1924) and received screen credit for *Gone With the Wind* (1939).

56.1 Tracy

Actor Spencer Tracy (1900–67).

57.14 "Manon"

Histoire du chevalier des Grieux et de Manon Lescaut (1731), romance by the abbé Prévost; it was the source for two operas, Jules Massenet's *Manon* (1884) and Giacomo Puccini's *Manon Lescaut* (1893), but it was not made into a Hollywood movie.

60.26–27 picture about Russia

One of Irving Thalberg's unrealized projects was a movie about the Russian Revolution.

61.10–11 Diogenes . . . Asclepius . . . Menander

See Textual Notes.

61.23–24 Eleusinian mysteries

Forms of worship celebrated in ancient Greece at Eleusis in Attica in honor of Demeter, Persephone, and Dionysius. Zavras's ironic hyperbole identifies the studio administration with gods.

62.4–5 benzedrine

A stimulant in common use in the 1930s.

66.9 Carlton

An expensive hotel in London.

66.15 reefer

British term for a close-fitting jacket of heavy cloth.

68.11 "The Thundering Beat of My Heart"

"The Beat of My Heart" (1934); music by Harold Spince, lyrics by Johnny Burke.

68.12–13 skin they seemed to love to touch

Reference to the slogan for Woodbury Facial Soap: "For the skin you love to touch."

68.27 last man tapped for Bones

Skull and Bones is a senior society or "secret society" at Yale University that elects fifteen undergraduates each year at a ritual known as Tap Day. Election to Bones was regarded as the highest social distinction at Yale, and it was a particular honor to be the fifteenth man tapped.

68.28 Southampton

Affluent community on the South Shore of Long Island, New York.

68.32 Benny Goodman

1909–86; bandleader known as "The King of Swing"; his big band was at the Palomar Ballroom in Los Angeles during the Summer of 1937.

68.33 "Blue Heaven"

"My Blue Heaven," popular song introduced in 1924; music by Walter Donaldson, lyrics by George Whiting.

68.33 Paul Whiteman

1892–1968; bandleader known as "The Jazz King."

68.33 "When Day Is Done"

Originally a Viennese song ("Madonna") with music by Robert Katscher, it became popular in America when B. G. DeSylva provided English lyrics in 1926.

68.35–6 "Little Girl, You've Had a Busy Day"

Brady has modified the 1934 song "Little Man, You've Had a Busy Day"; music by Mabel Wayne, lyrics by Maurice Sigler and Al Hoffman.

69.1 "Lovely To Look At"

1935 song introduced in the movie production of *Roberta;* music by Jerome Kern, lyrics by Dorothy Fields and Jimmy McHugh.

69.3 Sunset Mountain

Unidentified, but Fitzgerald may have been referring to Lookout Mountain, which overlooks Sunset Boulevard.

69.32 casting couch

This reference to Hollywood executives' reputed practice of sexually auditioning aspiring actresses indicates Wylie's vulgarity, not Stahr's conduct.

70.5–6 "They asked me how I knew . . ."

From "Smoke Gets in Your Eyes" (1933) in the stage production of *Roberta;* music by Jerome Kern; lyrics by Otto Harbach. The phrases "heart was fire" and "smoke was in my eyes" echo the lyrics of this song.

70.19 Ambassador

The Ambassador Hotel on Wilshire Boulevard, Los Angeles.

70.21 sneak preview

An unannounced movie preview, intended to test audience reaction.

71.27 Coronado to Del Monte

Coronado is a southern California town near San Diego; Del Monte is a resort on the Monterey peninsula, 300 miles north of Los Angeles.

72.3 Raphael's corner angels

Some of the large religious paintings of Raffaello Sanzio (1483–1520) were peripherally decorated with luminously rosy cherubs.

72.7 getting a bit

The actress hopes to be offered a small part.

72.11 Cafe Society

People who frequented expensive nightclubs; hence an ostentatiously affluent class.

72.17 to be Hemingway characters

To behave stoically and not to reveal anxiety.

72.25–6 Hollywood Bowl

Amphitheatre for outdoor events.

72.26 Sonja Henie

1910–69; Norwegian Olympic ice-skating champion who became a Hollywood star.

74.10 Grand Street

Street in the Lower East Side of Manhattan and at that time a poor Jewish neighborhood.

74.10–11 Loudoun County

Horsey locale in rural northern Virginia, near the Maryland line; these settings indicate the variety of backgrounds of the movie people.

74.31 dancing with the Prince of Wales

When Edward VIII (1894–1972) was the bachelor Prince of Wales (1911–36), dancing with him was a coveted experience and inspired the 1928 song "I've Danced With a Man, Who Danced With a Girl, Who Danced With the Prince of Wales"—music by Herbert Farjeon, lyrics by Harold Scott.

76.16–17 John Barrymore

1882–1942; actor in silent and sound movies known as "the great profile"; member of a notable theatrical family.

76.17 Pola Negri

1897–1987; Polish-born actress, a star of the American silent movies who performed *femme fatale* roles.

76.17–18 Connie Talmadge

1898–1973; Constance Talmadge, silent screen comedienne.

77.28 Glenn Miller

1904–44; leader of a popular swing orchestra.

77.29 "I'm on a See-Saw"

Song published in England in 1934; music by Vivian Ellis, lyrics by Desmond Carter.

79.34 Randolph Hearst

Newspaper magnate and publisher William Randolph Hearst (1863–1951), who became one of the most powerful men in America.

80.16–17 Coney Island

Amusement park in Brooklyn, New York; it became a generic term for crowded resorts catering to the masses.

81.24 cheaters

Slang for sunglasses.

83.35 McKinley

William McKinley (1843–1901) was the twenty-fifth President of the United States. He was not ape-like; there is no particular reason for Fitzgerald's selection of this figure to extend the presidential theme.

84.2 John Gilbert

1895–1936; romantic star of the silent movies who was unable to make the transition to sound.

84.10 'King Kong'

This celebrated movie about a giant gorilla was produced and directed by Merian C. Cooper in 1933.

84.11 'The Hairy Ape'

1922 play by Eugene O'Neill; the title refers to a ship's stoker.

84.25 Malibu

In the 1930s this beach community northwest of Los Angeles had not yet become expensive and enviable (see map).

89.13 call-houses

Establishments that dispatch prostitutes in response to telephone calls.

91.13 Venus on the half shell

The painting "The Birth of Venus" by Italian artist Sandro Botticelli (1445–1510) depicts Venus on a large scallop shell, and it is jocularly referred to as "Venus on the half shell" echoing menu terminology.

91.27 Sorbonne

University in Paris.

91.31 Spengler

Oswald Spengler (1880–1936), author of *The Decline of the West* (translated into English 1926–28), an erudite work of history and philosophy that influenced Fitzgerald.

92.4 shuls

Yiddish word that means schools and synagogues.

92.20 grunion

Leuresthes tenuis, small Pacific fish that spawns on particular nights by burying fertilized eggs in the sand at high tide.

93.1 Sir Francis Drake

The English explorer Drake (1540?–96) nailed a brass plate to a stake in 1579 at what is now Point San Quentin, California; the authenticity of the plate discovered in 1936 has been challenged.

93.10–11 Emerson

Ralph Waldo Emerson (1803–82), key figure in American Transcendentalism.

93.13 Rosicrucian

The Rosicrucians are a religious group claiming esoteric wisdom from ancient times.

95.19 Bel-Air

Exclusive residential section of Los Angeles northwest of Beverly Hills (see map).

96.26–34 Harlow . . . Fairbanks . . . Skouras

Jean Harlow (1911–37), actress who played wisecracking sexy characters; Douglas Fairbanks (1883–1939), star of swashbuckling silent movies; Skouras, one of the three brothers who controlled Twentieth Century-Fox.

100.27–8 In disgrace with fortune and men's eyes

From Shakespeare's Sonnet 29.

101.3 Griffith invented the close-up

This is incorrect. The first close-up shot is believed to be that of actor Fred Ott sneezing in an untitled 1900 movie made by Thomas A. Edison.

101.14 Buddy Ebsen

Actor-dancer (1908–   ) in the movies who later became a star of television series.

101.15–16 Harry Davenport . . . Donald Crisp

Davenport (1886–1949) and Crisp (1880–1974) were character actors
who played benevolent older men (see Emendations List).

101.25 "The Saturday Evening Post"

Mass-circulation magazine in which Fitzgerald's work frequently appeared
during the Twenties and early Thirties.

102.8 Bev Brown Derby

Restaurant across from the Beverly Wilshire Hotel; one of three Brown
Derby restaurants in the area, it was favored by celebrities and would-be
celebrities.

103.4 skivies and biddies

Skivies (skivvies) are scullery maids; biddies are chambermaids.

103.4–5 Sex, Fifth Avenue

Pun on the upscale Manhattan department store, Saks Fifth Avenue.

104.2 Vine Street

Hollywood Boulevard and Vine was one of the main intersections in
Hollywood.

106.34 Gary Cooper

1901–61; movie actor best known for portraying cowboys and other
strong, silent types.

107.3 Troc

The Trocadero nightclub was on Sunset Boulevard in Hollywood.

107.4 Lord Charnwood

Godfrey Rathbone Benson, Lord Charnwood (1864–1945), author of *Abraham Lincoln* (London: Constable, 1916).

107.8 "A productions"

High-budget movies, as differentiated from cheaper B productions.

108.27 hepcats

Jazz musicians engaged in collective improvisation.

113.17 Black and Tans

Special constables recruited in England in 1920 to suppress the Irish rebellion; their uniforms were khaki trousers and black tunics, or vice versa. They became notorious for their reprisals against the Irish Republican Army.

114.14 Syndicalist

Member of radical movement that seeks to gain worker control over production.

115.16 suicide bridge

A high wire fence was erected to deter would-be suicides from utilizing this Pasadena bridge.

115.22 White Way

A downtown area with bright lights; New York's Broadway was known as "The Great White Way."

115.28 Beautiful Doll

Reference to the 1911 song "Oh, You Beautiful Doll"; music by Matt D. Ayer, lyrics by A. Seymour Brown.

116.11 Mrs. Simpson

See note on the time scheme, 5.5–6.

117.8 Albuquerque

City in New Mexico on the Southern Pacific transcontinental railroad route.

117.35 Jews were dead miserably

Victims of the violent anti-Semitism that accompanied Hitler's appointment as Chancellor of Germany in 1933 and escalated thereafter, being legitimized by the anti-Jewish "Nuremberg Laws" adopted in September 1935. Fitzgerald is not referring to the "Final Solution"; he had been dead seven months when in July 1941 the extermination of the Jews became official Nazi policy.

118.4 Lake Louise

Resort in Alberta, Canada.

118.15 Harry Bridges

Australian-born American labor leader (1901–90), head of the West-coast International Longshoremen's Association and later of the International Longshoremen's and Warehousemen's Union; he denied Communist Party membership but supported its positions.

118.17–18 "The New Masses"

Radical magazine (1926–48) that followed the Communist Party line.

118.22 "I AM" cult

An occult faith founded in California in 1929; the term "I AM" designates the Primal Light or the energy of God, the basis for all manifested form.

118.31 Bulgarian musician

Radicals were depicted in cartoons as strangely dressed bearded figures, as were classical ("long-hair") musicians.

119.1 Writers Guild

The first Screen Writers Guild was established in 1920; it was reorganized in 1933 as an organization that would give writers more control over story material. The leftist contingent in the Screen Writers Guild pushed for amalgamation with other writers' unions—the Authors' League, the Dramatists' Guild, the Newspaper Guild, and the Radio Writers Guild. Irving Thalberg opposed the Screen Writers Guild (see Introduction, pp. xix, xxii).

119.6 "Doctor Caligari"

The Cabinet of Dr. Caligari (1919), an experimental German movie.

119.6 "Un Chien Andalou,"

Surrealist movie written and directed by Luis Buñuel (1900–83) and Salvador Dali (1904–89) in 1928.

119.9–10 a two-page "treatment"

Producers were accustomed to reading digests or "treatments" prepared by professional readers.

119.17 Sloane's

Manhattan department store that sold furniture and provided interior decorators.

120.11 Fanny Brice

1891–1951; comedy star of Broadway and the movies. She also portrayed Baby Snooks on radio.

121.17 Balanchine

George Balanchine (1904–83), Russian-born ballet dancer and choreographer, who worked in Hollywood on *The Goldwyn Follies* (Goldwyn, 1938), *On Your Toes* (Warner Brothers, 1939), and *I Was an Adventuress* (Twentieth Century-Fox, 1940).

121.18 Ritz Brothers

Three brothers (Al, Jim, and Harry) who formed a comedy act popular in the Thirties and Forties.

121.20 Warner Brothers

Four brothers (Jack, Harry, Albert, Samuel) who founded the Warner Brothers studio in 1923 and made the first sound movie in 1927.

121.23 Anti-Nazi League

Incorporated in June 1936 as the Hollywood League Against Nazi-ism; it became the Hollywood Anti-Nazi League in September. It was organized by screenwriter Dorothy Parker and lyricist Oscar Hammerstein II; screenwriter Donald Ogden Stewart was chairman.

121.34 Goldwyn Terrace

Goldwyn Terrace intersects Washington Boulevard near the M-G-M studio in Culver City; it is named for producer Samuel Goldwyn.

123.5 Company Tec

Private detective or policeman on the company payroll.

123.27 Frankensteen

Richard Frankensteen (1907–) and Walter Reuther, United Auto Workers union officials, were beaten by Ford strikebreakers in the May 1937 Detroit "Battle of the Overpass." Although described in the novel as "this big Jew," Frankensteen is an Episcopalian.

124.16 Superman

See note on the time scheme, 5.7–8.

125.8 soapbox

Public orators—usually of a radical persuasion—often stood on the wooden crates made for shipping soap.

125.19 Legion of Decency

Roman Catholic board organized in 1934 to combat immorality in movies; the organization prepared lists of movies unfit for Catholics.

125.28 Edward the VII's boast

1841–1910; Queen Victoria's son who became King of England in 1901; he was a leader of fashionable and sporting life in Great Britain and was described as "The First Gentleman of Europe." His comment about his place in society was not intended as irony.

126.1 Carole Lombard

1908–42; movie star of Thirties "screwball comedies."

126.22 Fitts

Buron Fitts, District Attorney for Los Angeles County in the Thirties, was allegedly in the pay of the studios.

APPENDIX 1: THE SANITARIUM FRAME

The fifth draft (8½" × 11" yellow paper; ribbon TS revised in pencil). See "Inventory of Drafts"—Sanitarium Frame E.

5.

— 1 —

(W)
~~The~~ two ~~of us listening~~ were fascinated by that young

ago
face. A few months ~~before~~, we had made a short trip to the canyons

of the Colorado, as if for a last gape at life; ~~and~~ now back ~~here~~

at the hospital, this girl's face ~~seemed~~ in the sunset, and with

Arizona
the fever, to share some of the primordial rose tints of ~~these~~ *that*

"natural wonder⅓".

"Go on tell us," we said. "We don't know about such

things."

She started to cough, changed her mind--as one can.

"I don't mind telling you. But why should our friends,

the asthmas, have to hear?"

"They're going," we assured her.

(cant
We three waited, our heads ~~leaned~~ back on our chairs,

would
while a nurse marshalled a flustered little group that ~~could not~~

heard the
have ~~helped hearing her~~ remark--and edged them toward the sanitarium.

The nurse cast a reproachful glance back at Cecelia, as if she

return
wanted to ~~come back~~ and slap her--but the glance changed its mind, and

the nurse hurried in after her flock.

"~~You see?~~ They're gone. Now tell us."

-2-   5.

Cecilia stared up at the
~~The slate-pink cheeks remained tilted up toward the~~
brilliant
bright Arizona sky. ~~If there was Heaven beyond, she showed~~ neither
     She regarded it — the

~~a hope of breaking through, nor any regret that she~~ had missed the
                              looked
~~plane. She was of her time, looking at~~ the blue air which to us
      once   not with regret but rather with the aversure
had stood for hope in the morning ~~with that tense rationalized~~
      of those   the depression caught in mid-adolescence Now she
confusion ~~peculiar to her generation.~~ She was twenty-five.
                                       ^

"Anything you want to know," she promised. "I don't

owe <u>them</u> any loyalty. Oh, they fly over and see me sometimes, but

what do I care--I'm ruined."

"We're all ruined," I said mildly.

She sat up~~right~~, the Aztec figures of her dress emerging

from the Navajo pattern of her blanket. The dress was thin--gone

native for the sun country--and I remembered the round shining
                                                          but
knobs of another girl's shoulders at another time and place ~~But~~

here we must all stay in the shadow.

"You shouldn't talk like that", she assured me, "I'm

~~plen~~ty ruined, but you're just two good guys who happened to get

a bug."

"You don't grant us any history," we objected with
                                allowed
senescent irony, "Nobody over forty is ~~considered to have~~ a history."

-3-   5.

"I didn't mean that. I mean you'll get well."

"In case we don't, tell us the story. You still hear
this stuff about him. ~~What was he--'Christ in industry?'~~ *What was he: Christ in Industry?* I know

boys who worked on the coast and hated his guts. Were you crazy

about him? Loosen up, ~~Cecil~~ *Cecelia* Something for a jaded palette! Think

of the hospital dinner ~~we've got to eat~~ *well face* in an hour." *half*

    Cecelia's glance suspected, then rejected our existance,

not our right to live but our rights to any important feelings of

loss or passion or hope or high excitement. She started to talk,

waited for a tickle to subside in her throat.

    "He never looked at me," she said ~~with scorn~~ *in desperately*, "And I

won't talk about him when you're in this mood."

    She threw off the blanket and stood up, her center-

parted hair falling ~~over~~ *from* her wan temples, ~~like~~ ripples from a brown

dam. She was high-breasted and emaciated, still perfectly the

young woman of her time, ~~the middle 1930's.~~ ~~Indignation and~~ Super-

iority was implicit in her heel taps as she walked through the

open door into the corridor of the building--~~which was~~ our only

road to wonderland. ~~Though~~ *A*pparently Cecelia believed in nothing

~~much~~ at present *but it* ~~it~~ seemed she had once known another road--~~though~~

-4-   5

~~she'd~~ passed by it a long time ago. //~~But~~ We were sure, nevertheless,

that she would tell us about it ~~some time~~--and so she did. What

follows is our imperfect version of her ~~imperfect~~ story.

APPENDIX 2: SPECIMEN WORKING DRAFTS

These facsimiles provide examples of instructive stages of Fitzgerald's work in progress on the novel.

Early draft of the opening pages (5 pages; 8¼″ × 11″ yellow paper; pencil). See "Inventory of Drafts," I-A.

②

anything so ambitious. It's just
as well — it would have been
as dull as an old column by
~~Lolly~~ Parsons. My father was in the
picture ~~business~~ as another man might
be in cotton or steel so I ~~accepted~~ took
it ~~with tranquility~~. To put it *in another way*
I accepted Hollywood ~~move~~ as a ghost
might accept his assignment
to a haunted house, ~~rather~~ than with
the nervous tension of ~~the~~ a
family moving in.
   This is ~~to~~ easy to say, hard to
make people understand. When I
was ~~at~~ Smith some of the *eugan* teachers
who pretended indifference to
Hollywood or its products really
<u>hated</u> it. Hated it way down deep

③

as a threat to their existence. Even
before that when I was in a
convent a ^sweet little nun ~~I was fond of~~
asked me to get her a ~~scenario~~ ^screenplay
so she could "teach her class movie
writing." I got it for her and I
suppose she puzzled over it and
puzzled over it but it was never
mentioned in class and she
gave it back to me without a
single comment but with an air
of offended surprise. That's what I
half expect to happen to this story.
You can take Hollywood for granted
like I did, or you can ~~hate it~~ ^destroy it with contempt ~~but~~
~~only a very few have ever been able to~~
~~understand it~~ we reserve for what we

[left margin, vertical:] On who had taught them about the essay and this first story

④

don't understand. It can be understood
too, but dimly and in flashes, much
as one ~~gets~~ grows to feel how Early
French ~~came~~ came out of Latin. ~~or~~ Not
~~that a two page equation is~~
~~hanging at~~ half a dozen men
have ever been able to keep the
whole equation of pictures in their heads. And
~~the closest a mere woman~~ could ~~can come~~
~~of a mere woman~~ — well as ~~only one~~
~~to it is to try~~ and understand one
~~of those men~~ that I've tried, imperfectly
~~of those men. I~~ seem to be falling in love
with that word — to understand, to
stand under, to understand.

<u>Space Here</u>

The world from an aeroplane I
knew. ~~for~~ Father always had us travel

(5)

back and forth that way from school
and college. After my sister died
when I was a Junior ~~at the~~ and
I travelled to and fro alone, the
~~plea~~ journey always made me
think of her, made me a little solemn
and subdued. Sometimes there were
picture people I knew on board, and
occasionally a college boy, but not
often ~~that I~~ during the depression
I seldom went to sleep what with
the thought of Eleanor and ~~there~~
sense of that sharp up between
coast and coast until we had
left those lonely little airports —
Knotville? Nashville? in Tennessee.

2 of 3 carbons

CHAPTER I

Though I haven't ever been on the screen I was brought
up in pictures. Rudolph Valentino came to my fifth birthday
party--or so I was told. I put this down only to indicate that
even before the age of reason, and whether *willingly or unwillingly*,
I was in a position to watch the wheels go round.

I was going to write my memoirs once, "The Producers
Daughter", but at eighteen you never quite get around to anything
so ambitious. It's just as well--it would have been as dull as
an old column of Lolly Parsons'. My father was in the picture
business as another man might be in cotton or steel, so I took
it with tranquility. To put it in another way I accepted
Hollywood *more* as a ghost might accept his assignment to a
haunted house, than with the nervous tension of a family moving in.

This is easy to say, but harder to make people understand. When I was at Smith some of the English teachers who
pretended an indifference to Hollywood or its products, really
hated it. Hated it way down deep as a threat to their existence.
Even before that, when I was in a convent, a sweet little nun
asked me to get her a script of a screen play so she could "teach
her class about movie writing" as she had taught them about the
essay and the short story. I got the script for her and I suppose she puzzled over it and puzzled over it but it was never
mentioned in class and she gave it back to me without a single
comment but with an air of offended surprise. That's what I
half expect to happen to this ~~believe-it-or-not~~ story.

Intermediate draft for opening (5 pages; 8¼" × 11" white paper; ribbon TS
revised in pencil). See "Inventory of Drafts," I-D.

-2-

You can take Hollywood for granted like I did, or you
can dismiss it with the contempt we reserved for what we don't
understand. It can be understood too, but dimly and in flashes.
Not half a dozen men have ever been able to keep the whole equation of pictures in their heads. And the closest a mere woman
can come to it is to try and understand certain one of those
men. I seem to be falling in love with that word--to understand.

The world from an aeroplane I knew. Father always had
us travel back and forth that way from school and college. After
my sister died when I was a Junior, I travelled to and fro alone
and the journey always made me think of her, made me somewhat
solemn and subdued. Sometimes there were picture people I knew
on board the plane, and occasionally there was an attractive
college boy--not often during the depression. I seldom really
fell asleep during the trip, what with the thoughts of Eleanor
and the sense of that sharp rip between coast and coast--at
least not till we had left those lonely little airports in Tennessee.

This trip it was so rough that the passengers divided
early into those who turned in right away and those who didn't
want to turn in at all. There were two of these latter right
across from me and I was pretty sure from their fragmentary conversation that they were from Hollywood--one of them because he
looked like it, a middle-aged Jew who alternately spoke with
nervous excitement or lingered in a fiery, harrowing silence;
the other a pale, stocky every day looking man of thirty, whom
I was sure I had seen before. He had been to the house or somewhere. Also I thought his name began with W. But it might have

-3- 2.

been a long time ago when I was a little girl, and I wasn't
offended that he didn't recognize me.

The stewardess--she was tall, handsome and flashing
dark, a type they seemed to run to, asked me if she could make up
my berth.

"--and, dear, do you want an aspirin?" She perched
on the side of the seat and rocked precariously back and forth
with the June hurricane, "--or a nembutal?"

"No."

"I've been so busy with everyone else that I've had
no time to ask you." She sat down quickly beside me and buckled
us both in. "Do you want some gum?"

This reminded me to get rid of the piece that had been
boring me for hours. I wrapped it in a piece of magazine and
put it into the automatic ash-holder.

"I can always tell people are nice--" the stewardess
said approvingly, "--if they wrap their gum in paper before they
put it in there."

We sat for awhile in the half light of the swaying car.
It was vaguely like a swanky restaurant at that twilight time
between meals. We were all lingering against our wills. Even
the stewardess I think--had to keep reminding herself why she
was there. Definitely We were waiting.
She and I talked about a young actress I knew, whom she had
flown West with two years before. It was in the very lowest
plunge time of the depression and the young actress kept staring out
the window in such an intent way that the Stewardess was afraid
she was contemplating a leap. It appeared though that she was
not afraid of poverty, but only of revolution.

-4-   2.

"I know what mother and I are going to do," she confided

to the stewardess, "We're coming out to the Yellowstone and we're

just going to live simply ~~these~~ till it all blows over. Then

we'll come back. They don't kill artists--you know?"

The ~~odd~~ proposition pleased me. It conjured up a pretty

picture of the actress and her mother being fed by kind Tory

bears who brought them honey, and by gentle fawns ~~who made~~ pillows

who brought them extra milk from

for their heads at night. In turn I told the stewardess about

the director and the lawyer who told their plans to father one

night in those ~~brave~~ *courageous* days. If the bonus army conquered Washington

the lawyer had a boat hidden in the Sacramento River, and he was

going to row up stream for a few months and then come back "because

they always needed lawyers after a revolution to straighten out

the legal side."

The director ~~tended~~ *had* more toward ~~despair~~. *defeatism.* He had an old

suit, ~~an old~~ shirt and ~~old~~ shoes in waiting--he never did say

whether they were his own or whether he got them from the prop

department--and he was going to **D**isappear into the Crowd. I

remember father saying: "But they'll look at your hands, man!

They'll know you haven't done manual work for years. And they'll

ask for your union card." And I remember how the director's face

fell, and how gloomy he was ~~for awhile and~~ *while he ate his desert,* how funny they ~~all~~ *and puny*

~~sounded~~ *looked* to me.

"Is your father an actor, Miss Bradogue?" asked the

stewardess, "I've certainly heard the name ~~I've heard the name~~."

At the name ~~Bradogue~~ both the men across the aisle *no period here.*

looked up. Sidewise--that Hollywood look, that always seems thrown

over one shoulder. Then the young, *pale,* stocky, ~~every-day-looking~~

one unbuttoned his safety strap and stood in the aisle beside us.

-5-   2.

"Are you Cecelia Bradogue?" he demanded accusingly, as
if I'd been holding out on him, "I thought I recognized you.
I'm Wylie White."

He could have omitted this--for at the same moment a
new voice said, "Watch your step, Wylie!" ~~and~~ another man
brushed by him in the aisle and went forward in the direction
of the cockpit. Wylie White ~~started, turned~~ started and a little too
late called after him:

"I take ~~my~~ orders only from the pilot."

I say too late, because I know the kind of joke that
goes on between the powers in Hollywood and their satelites. It's
~~suppose it's~~ the same everywhere. Behind ~~some of~~ half these pleasant-
ries: "That's wonderful. That's ~~funny~~ rich! That's great." I can ~~hear~~
hear: "My God, I didn't know that ~~word~~ was still around."

~~"I take my orders from the pilot", was what~~ Wylie White's
voice had been ~~said so~~ brave and defiant. But the

~~It was the~~ stewardess ~~who~~ corrected him:

"Not so loud, ~~some of the~~ passengers
please— some are asleep."

~~And~~ I saw now that the other man across the aisle, the
middle-aged Jew, was on his feet also, staring ~~with intensity~~ intensely
after the man who had just gone by. Or rather at the back of the
man, who now gestured sideways with his hand and went out of my
sight. ¶ I asked the stewardess: "Is he the assistant pilot?"

She was unbuckling our belt, ~~prepared~~ about to abandon me to
Wylie White.

"No. That's Mr. Smith. He has the private compartment. The
"bridal suite" — only he has it alone. The
~~The~~ assistant pilot is always in uniform." She stood up, "I want
to find out if the plane's going to be grounded in Nashville."

with a shameless comme
lethery

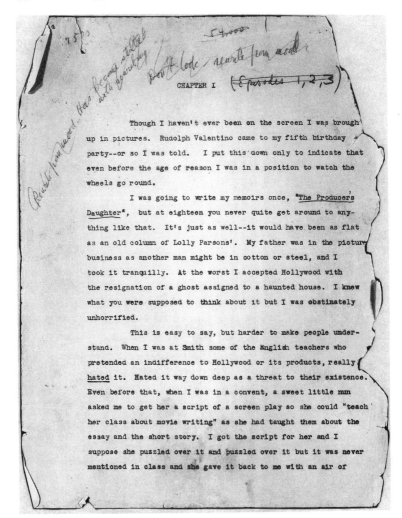

CHAPTER I

Though I haven't ever been on the screen I was brought up in pictures. Rudolph Valentino came to my fifth birthday party--or so I was told. I put this down only to indicate that even before the age of reason I was in a position to watch the wheels go round.

I was going to write my memoirs once, "The Producer's Daughter", but at eighteen you never quite get around to anything like that. It's just as well--it would have been as flat as an old column of Lolly Parsons'. My father was in the picture business as another man might be in cotton or steel, and I took it tranquilly. At the worst I accepted Hollywood with the resignation of a ghost assigned to a haunted house. I knew what you were supposed to think about it but I was obstinately unhorrified.

This is easy to say, but harder to make people understand. When I was at Smith some of the English teachers who pretended an indifference to Hollywood or its products, really hated it. Hated it way down deep as a threat to their existence. Even before that, when I was in a convent, a sweet little nun asked me to get her a script of a screen play so she could "teach her class about movie writing" as she had taught them about the essay and the short story. I got the script for her and I suppose she puzzled over it and puzzled over it but it was never mentioned in class and she gave it back to me with an air of

Latest revised draft of the opening (8¼″ × 11″ ribbon TS; revised in pencil). See "Inventory of Drafts," I-I. The editing in lines 7–8 is Wilson's.

Draft for various opening (4 pages; 8¼″ × 11″ yellow paper; pencil). See "Inventory of Drafts," I-J.

⑤ Douglas Mainliner

Mainliner to fly back home, to the coast.
Father had written that everything was
better and better and enclosed me a check for
— but I wont make you hate me by
saying how much. I had bought a regular trousseau
for myself and gifts for everybody — I I had except stocks.

plane left Navark airport at
4.30 and by five we had all
stuffed our chewing gum
particuly into the little ash
holders — and then there was
nothing much except getting used
to the motors and to the usual qualms
and finding out of you
who was on board. Id
seen the list in the airport
Les Spurgeon, Stones, Mortimer,
Flesh Fleshhacker, Grallacel — but

(6)

these ought to be phoney names
for people I knew. ~~I just sat~~
~~for awhile a couple of hours, I~~
~~for awhile — hours I guess — and wondered~~
~~if anybody was truthe to come into my life on this trip. I'd~~
never seen in
pictures but was very much of
them, and I had an actresses
psychology about staring
staring straight ahead ~~fairly~~
~~used tell I ka~~ many new
situation — until I found
where I was.

My father James Bradogue was a
self made man, half Irish and half
Pennsylvania ~~Minnesota~~ ~~Dutch. He was a~~ ~~on the map but~~
~~publicity man and then an agent and~~
~~and it stabbed into me when I was a~~
then an executive and then a
capitalist like now.

. I was born
about when the ~~Birth of~~ a nation
was previewed, I guess, I know
Rudolph Valentino came to my
fifth birthday party. I can
remember when there wasn't any Garbo
or Shearer and Crawford and I'm
one of the few people who killed
Desmond Taylor but you'll never find out
about that from me. We were in the
picture business just like other families
are in the grain business or the furniture
business and I just accepted it I
guess, the way angels accept heaven
or a ghost accepts his haunted house.
But except for a few odd stray moments
and most of them
I'm going to tell you about — it never
had any magic or romance or glamor for me

Chapter II

~~It was~~ ~~early~~ ~~writing~~ ~~hot and~~ A camera crew was
throwing a cone of white light against a
storehouse wall as I went by, and in ~~in~~ front
of the wall a man in rubber boots was
hosing ~~off a car.~~ a car. ~~Stepping~~ ~~gingerly~~
~~washing off an automobile. Picking my~~
~~way across the tangle of cables I went~~
over ~~the~~ tangle of cables I went, on ~~up~~ ~~the~~
~~street toward father's office~~ ~~on the~~ studio street ~~through~~
the warm night toward father's office in
the old Administration Building. There is
never a time when a studio is deserted. ~~I~~
~~nothing~~ no company ~~starting~~ working there is always maintained the night shift of watchmen,
outfits ~~and demand or big producers~~ ~~and~~ extra-astwating producers
trying to catch up with themselves in the dubbing
rooms. Or something. The commissary never closes
and ~~you always have to look out for the padded~~
every once in awhile ~~a~~ the padded hush of
to keep
~~keeping~~ the endless belt rolling, and the

and lets conferences

she'd reach the high notes "caught can efface you something would go wrong and the cadence would transpose about it...

~~husk of trees in the narrow alleys~~
tires creeps by you in the narrow
alleys. It is more friendly at ~~night, without~~
~~the California glass beating down~~ after dark,
more polite and civilized in some way. If you
passed somebody you knew, it was like
passing someone on the campus back
at college.
only and everything Tonight a soprano was singing over and over Come Come I love you
~~When~~ the earthquake came I ~~was~~ had ~~standing~~ reached
at the head of the stairs wishing the
~~stairs door would open~~ door of Stairs
suite would open down the corridor.
We didn't get the full shock ~~at~~ like they did at Long
Beach, where hotels broke in two right down
the middle, but for a minute and a half
the whole area jerked back and forth and
sank underfoot ~~so that~~ until your bowels seemed to
be one with the bowels of the earth, as if ~~the there some~~
~~justly there was~~ was some nightmare attempt
to tie your naval cord again and drag
you back into the womb of creation.

My instinct was to get away from the
stairs which I thought had given
in, and then ~~to bang~~ after an
instant of utter terror when I ~~saw~~ realized that
~~that there might be a for the good~~
that there ~~might be a time~~ time
~~when there was and~~ this was a time
and place when there was nothing
to hang on to — or rather when I
realized that there _were_ such times —
I went weak in the knees and said
Holy Mary mother of god.

There were cries everywhere and
over it, I swear, "Come — come —
naught can efface you!" Though
I have since figured it out that maybe
they were playing it back to the
singer on the phonograph.

That was one of the points where I might, just

might, have had a chance of Stahr, you see. If he had appeared at that exact moment, ~~bring~~ me into his offices and perhaps looked at me. He was a ~~woman~~ in a mood to see a woman as she was ~~Certes~~, my gallant gentleman, ~~for~~ and the proof of the pudding is. It was ~~that~~ not an hour later that he found his Thalia. That was the night he found that wretched trollop — be fair, be fair my heart — like a puppy, a tailless tyke ~~washed~~ into his backyard by a flood.

For there was an actual flood (all this next is from what Thalia told me ~~before~~ on the one afternoon I could stand ~~seeing~~ her) and of course Stahr, who had a finger in every ~~pie~~ mudpie on the lot, had to go to it. A watermain burst ~~and poured~~ ~~a deluge not~~ — This turned out to be the ~~only~~ serious damage, ~~soon~~ — and flowed not ~~only~~ on to the lot but to the back areas where the big exteriors are taken. ~~All studios have different names~~ Some times these are near the studios — sometimes far away but ~~it was~~ our studio was rich so ~~our~~ "ranch" was ~~in our~~ the back yard.

P I saw Stahr ~~somewhere~~ ~~in the company of those~~ ~~neither miniatures nor~~ grey with fatigue, knife-like ~~reflecting all the everything~~ ~~that would~~ ~~around~~ but ~~he~~ his glossy brown eyes seemed immediately to reflect everything that ~~would hab~~ happened, that could happen, ~~that that~~ ~~was~~ ~~part of he~~ ~~out about~~ ~~so that hit of~~ was a sort of ~~tabernacle~~, ~~himself a sort of~~ an arc of the covenant — I had forgotten he was a Jew; ~~but now~~ it seems odd to apply ~~all those old~~ that Jewish ~~symbol~~ to him — ~~he created~~ creating a ~~space feeling~~ zone of quiet around himself wherever he moved. I think I was lying ~~I was~~ on a couch in father's office when I saw him and I ~~think~~ ~~suppose~~ he said to father:

"I wont ~~argue~~ talk to Warburg any
more. ~~He~~ ~~~~ Why not take
care of him yourself. As far as I'm
concerned he looks like nothing and
he acts like nothing and he —"

He took off his ring, ~~and~~ exactly
like the one he gave me, ~~and~~ threw
it up behind his back with one hand
and caught it in front with the
other, ~~saying~~ making a click with ~~the~~ his tongue against
side of his ~~tongue~~ cheek.

"— and if you add him to
anything he decreases it."

With ~~that~~ ~~their que~~ pronouncement, he went away from
where ever we were to see ~~a~~ ~~us~~ about
everything, and meet ~~~~ ~~~~ what he
met.

That night, after the earthquake, the moon
was up rosy gold with a haze around. Over
on the backlot it shone upon ~~~~ ~~~~

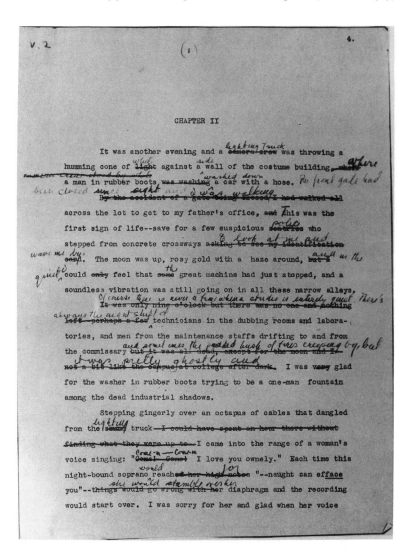

Intermediate draft for start of Chapter II (6 pages; 8¼″ × 11″ yellow and white paper; ribbon TS revised in pencil). See "Inventory of Drafts," II-M.

-2-   v.l. n.c.

grew faint from her mysterious oubliette.

When the earthquake came I was half way up the

stairs to father's office. We didn't get the full shock

like they did at Long Beach, where hotels broke in two right

down the middle and drifted out to sea--but for a minute and

a half the whole area jerked back and forth, and seemed to sink

like a cosmic elevator
underfoot until your bowels were one with the bowels of the

earth, as if there was some nightmare attempt to attach your

naval cord again, and drag you back into the womb of creation.

My instinct was to get away from the stairs, which

I thought had given in. Then after a moment of utter terror *as* *with*

the realization
~~I realized~~ that ~~this was a time and place whe~~n there was nothing

to hang on to, I went weak in the knees and said "Holy Mary,

Mother of God." There were outcries everywhere, and over them,

I swear: "Come-mm--Come-mm--naught can erface you!" Though

I have since thought that maybe they were playing it back to

the singer on the phonograph.

First I wanted to run downstairs and outside but

in a moment the building stood still, just shimmying a little

and I pulled myself up by the bannister and tottered into

-3-   V.16 n.0.

father's suite. He was in the inner orrice with Stahr. They

were both hanging on to desks and frowning and looking into

space, ~~completely off guard--and of course that made me laugh~~

~~and in a minute Stahr laughed too.~~ Then the phones began to

ring.

        It should have happened differently. I ought to

have been hurt on the stairs and Stahr, coming along, ~~should~~ *might*

have carried me chivalrously into his office. ~~Later~~ that *I was in his office later*

that night ~~I was in his office~~ but something had happened by then--

he had found his Thalia--found her like a puppy, a nameless

t yke washed into his backyard by a flood. Be fair, be fair

my heart.

        For, as the telephones soon informed us, there

was a flood and of course Stahr had to go to it. The quake

, its only serious damage,

had burst three water mains and they flowed ~~in toto~~ out to the   *with a vengeance*

" *lot* "

" back ~~areas~~ where the big exteriors are filmed. Sometimes

back   *from from*

these lots are ~~near~~ the studios--~~sometimes far away--~~but our

happened to be practically

ranch ~~was~~ in the backyard.

        Stahr was grey with fatigue, knife like--~~too much~~ *too*

worn down

~~so~~ for a man of his age--but as ~~the catastrophe developed~~ his

he got reports over the phone

-4-

V.l. n.c.

shiny eyes seemed to reflect every aspect of ~~it.~~ ^which had happened — that cn^ He ordered

a car and went out, taking with him a zone of quiet that had

gathered ~~quickly~~ about him--as if he were ^a sort of^ ~~the~~ Arc of the

Covenant.

Outside, ~~so Thalia told me later,~~ he was ^joined^ ~~met~~ by

Joe Robinson, ~~Joe was~~ a hard-jawed ~~technician and trouble~~ ^technical man supposed to be^

~~shooter. One~~ of the best cutter~~s~~ in the business ^He was^ ~~he had often~~

~~been asked to direct pictures. But he didn't want to be at~~ ^part of taking one of the headman aets in Stahrs^

^gang. Taken^ ~~the head of anything because he had despised his officers in~~

~~the war. He had no faith in anyone except himself and Stahr.~~

There was a car waiting and the two men drove

quickly past stages and storehouses and new building construc-

tion, and across a street through a gate into the back lot.

This was a gigantic curiosity shop under the moon which, coming

up rosy gold with a haze around it, shone upon the great per-

manent sets--upon French Chateaux and Southern mansions, upon

a professional jungle and a railway station which had done

duty for the meetings and partings of lovers from Vladivostok

to Kalamazoo. It shone upon a medieval gateway and into the

little caves of the Kasbah, upon a once bombarded village

-27- 6-

who had a finger in most of the mudpies on the lot, had to go to it.
The earthquake burst three water mains, its only serious damage,
and they flowed with a vengeance out to the "back lot" where the
big exteriors are filmed. Sometimes these back lots are far from
the studios--ours might be said to have been in the backyard. So
I saw Stahr bound for there sometime in the confusion of those
next few minutes. He was grey with fatigue, knife-like, but his
shiny brown eyes seemed immediately to reflect everything that had
happened, that could happen--so that he was sort of an arc of the
covenant--I was a Catholic and I forgot he was a Jew, and it seems
odd to apply that religious symbol to him. But he created a zone
of quiet around himself wherever he moved. I was lying on a couch
in father's office and I remember him saying:

"No, I've got to go but I won't talk to Wharton any more.
Why don't you take care of him yourself. As far as I'm concerned
he looks like nothing and he acts like nothing and he--"

He took off his ring, exactly like the one he gave me,
played with it.

"--and if you add him to anything he decreases it."

So much for Wharton. Stahr departed, joined outside
by Jack Robinson, a hard-jawed technical man supposed to be the
best cutter in Hollywood and attached to Stahr in a very special
way.

"Hey, Munroe, did it rock you?"

They went on toward the commissary where a car was to
meet them. Robby Robinson was Stahr's gang. Father had often
tried to get him to direct a picture, but from the time Robby was
called from his job on the tops of telephone posts in Michigan
thunderstorms, and sent to France--from then on he didn't want

-20-   - 5 -   4.

to direct anything. He was content to repair other peoples'
mistakes. There was more than that but it can be told later.

Getting in the car they drove quickly past stages and
storehouses and through new building construction and then up to
a wire fence and across a street to the back lot. Here the moon
shop was open to the moon —
then French Chateaux and Southern mansions, upon a professional
jungle and a great railway station which had seen the meetings and
partings of lovers from Vladivostok to Kalamazoo. It shone into
There were
the little cubbyholes of the Kasbah, upon a once bombarded village
and
now miraculously restored; on a lake you could throw a stone
across that housed one side of a troop ship and half a schooner,
on a medieval gateway and the fading towers of a mosque that were
to have played a part in a story of the Russian Revolution. They were
perennially afraid to wake.
My Star leaned out, looked into the rushing gutters that
Presently the
the broken water main had made, and whistled. The car could go
no further and they got out and walked. Already there were groups
spotted around and pumps working; as far as the eye could see
clusters of improvised lights already picked out the danger spots
in the flood. Along the traces of what had been a walk an hour
before they headed toward the largest blur of light, dragging
through   when they reached it Joe
their legs up from great bogs. The night superintendent was in
Robinson took charge, nipping like a sheep-dog, at a confused
charge and Robby who was ahead did not wait for Stahr before lay-
superintendant   on the confusion.
"Stop yelling, for christ's sake," he said. "There's
for them and   they
some big pumps by the tanks on Stage Four. Telephone Phone
how when the pumps get here--look! We'll run it all out
thirty-ninth
into the swamp down on 36th Street. It's city property but this
is an act of God, isn't it?" He saw the man was in a hopelessly
manager   and put
muddled, spotted a second unit director who happened to be on the
in charge.
lot and pressed him into service. Stahr coming up could hear him
"It's not so bad," he assured Stahr. "but that